Sports Finance and Management

Real Estate, Entertainment,
and the Remaking of the Business

Sports Finance and Management

Real Estate, Entertainment, and the Remaking of the Business

Jason A. Winfree and Mark S. Rosentraub

CRC Press
Taylor & Francis Group
Boca Raton London New York

CRC Press is an imprint of the
Taylor & Francis Group, an **informa** business

CRC Press
Taylor & Francis Group
6000 Broken Sound Parkway NW, Suite 300
Boca Raton, FL 33487-2742

Printed in the United States of America on acid-free paper
Version Date: 20110804

International Standard Book Number: 978-1-4398-4471-7 (Hardback)

Library of Congress Cataloging-in-Publication Data

Winfree, Jason (Jason A.)
Sports finance and management : real estate, entertainment, and the remaking of the business / Jason Winfree and Mark S. Rosentraub.
p. cm.
Includes bibliographical references and index.
ISBN 978-1-4398-4471-7
1. Sports--United States--Finance. 2. Sports--United States--Management. 3. Sports--Economic aspects--United States. I. Rosentraub, Mark S., 1950- II. Title.

GV716.W558 2012
338.43796--dc22   2011013749

Visit the Taylor & Francis Web site at
http://www.taylorandfrancis.com

and the CRC Press Web site at
http://www.crcpress.com

Dedication

To my family, Nikki, Max, and Grace, without whose support I would not have had the motivation or incentive to co-author this book. Also to my parents, who have always been there for me for all my endeavors.

JAW

For my children's husbands and wife, the people Karen and I entrust our real treasures to for safekeeping, for well-being, and for love and peace. Jennie (David), Jason (Natalie), John (Alexa), and Danny (Sabrina), thank you for keeping our children in your hearts and as part of your souls.

MSR

Contents

Preface

This book grew from conversations we had with our colleagues and sport industry leaders who serve on the University of Michigan's Sports Management program's advisory board. These discussions, occurring across more than two years, had become dominated by one theme—the business of sports has been dramatically changed. These alterations involved the new ways in which teams and facilities had become integral parts of the business of real estate development, real estate management, entertainment, and the media. Students still need to understand the core financial and management issues of the sports industry. But, they also need a greater appreciation of financial and management issues that link teams to real estate development and management, the entertainment industry, and the dynamic forces that now make it possible to listen to or watch games at home, on the road, or anywhere a fan happens to be.

In developing a book that meets the needs of teachers and their students, we did not use sports examples to help teach general financial and management concepts. Rather, we used basic financial and management concepts to illustrate the differences and uniqueness of the sports industry. In this way, this volume should meet the needs of those tackling finance issues for the first time; the applications to sports will allow those more expert in financial issues to apply their skills and knowledge to the unique dimensions of the sport industry.

Chapter 1 explains the four changes in the sports industry that create a need for this book. First, sports teams are becoming part of bigger companies. The reason this changes the financial landscape is because integrated companies can and do leverage teams to advance related enterprises. If a team has an impact on real estate, entertainment, or media businesses, then the value or financial returns generated by players change. Similarly, the value of a sports facility's location and its design also can be dramatically different based on the related business interests of an owner. These interconnecting financial issues are an integral part of this book.

Second, the revenues teams earn from media sources have skyrocketed. While this is not necessarily a new trend, it is certainly escalating as some teams and leagues have formed their own networks. National Football League (NFL) franchises derive most of their revenue from television contracts and that income has propelled franchise values. In the other team sports, the networks created by individual franchises are, in some instances, more valuable than the team itself. Students need to understand the financial issues associated with this dramatic change in the sports business especially as teams and leagues expand their Internet footprint. All of these changes have altered the local nature of fan loyalty and the possible business opportunities to capture income from the loyal members of the Red Sox Nation, the Cleveland Indians Nation, or the numerous alumni associations linked to college sports.

Third, the design of sports facilities has dramatically changed, creating numerous new revenue streams. Gone are the multipurpose stadiums that served as home to both baseball and football teams. While those facilities were cost effective in the sense that two teams played there at different times of the year, far more revenue is generated with the improved sight lines that exist in football-only and baseball-only venues. Those improved sight lines and myriad other amenities translate into higher revenues for teams. Luxury seating, an unknown concept in the 1970s and 1980s, is now not only a staple but increasingly valuable to individual team owners as those revenues are frequently not shared with other teams.

Fourth, league policies, such as revenue sharing, luxury taxes, and salary caps, are becoming much more prevalent, which again changes the financial landscape for teams. For example, teams will sign players for less money if they have to share a percentage of revenues generated from those players with other teams. The collective finances of teams in the National Hockey League (NHL) led them to decide that the only viable option was a salary cap. Given the market structure of the sports industry, these policies often decide how revenues will be split between owners and players.

This is not an exhaustive list of the changes that suggested the need for a new book on sports finance and management. This volume also looks at the effects of public financing, unique pricing structures, and the effect of roster depreciation allowances. A detailed treatment of the measurement of risk is also included, especially given that second-place finishes in sport are sometimes worth far less than a championship. That could mean there is more value in strategic risk taking for a team owner than for an owner of any other business. Lastly, team owners only have a fixed number of roster slots and, hence, their investment horizon is far different than that which exists for any other business owner.

With *Sports Finance and Management: Real Estate, Entertainment, and the Remaking of the Business*, we hope to shed light on these and other issues that are unique to the sports business. Given that teams are constantly making multimillion dollar decisions, it is imperative that students interested in becoming the people who are making these decisions understand finance and management as well as the idiosyncrasies of the sports industry.

Acknowledgments

Those considering this book for their own courses should know that we owe a large debt of gratitude to our students who suffered through preliminary drafts of chapters and countless lectures based on the ideas that became the chapters that follow. The comments and reactions received from our students helped to improve every part of this book. We also benefitted from countless conversations with friends and colleagues, and a special debt of gratitude is owed to Professor Rodney Fort who, too often, was forced to listen to our arguments, points, and perspectives. Individually or together, we also benefitted from ideas and discussions that took place in Ann Arbor and elsewhere with Jeff Wilpon, Paul Dolan, John Moores, Janet Marie Smith, James Irsay, Richard Browne, Dan Gilbert, and Alan Ostfield. These people have graciously given of their time to help us and our students understand the "real" business world of today's sports industry.

They and Rod Fort, as well as our students and other colleagues and friends, tried to alert us to the many mistakes we had made in our thinking and in earlier drafts of individual chapters. We were not so foolhardy as to ignore the collected wisdom and advice that was given to us. But, where our arrogance convinced us not to follow the learned suggestions made, and for all of the errors that remain, we accept full responsibility.

This book could not have been written without the intellectual resources afforded to us by the University of Michigan and its School of Kinesiology. Mark S. Rosentraub is especially grateful to Bruce and Joan Bickner for their generosity that allowed the creation of the Bruce and Joan Bickner Endowed Chair in Sports Management. That chair made this book possible, and both of us hope what has been produced is a source of pride for the Bickners, the University of Michigan, our colleagues and friends, and, most of all, our students.

We also thank Greg Kinney and the Bentley Historical Library at the University of Michigan for allowing us to use his article on financing stadiums.

About the Authors

Jason A. Winfree, Ph.D., is an associate professor of sports management at the University of Michigan. He is a sports economist, whose primary research focuses on professional sports. This research encompasses fields of economics such as Industrial Organization, Labor Economics, and Public Economics. His research involves analyzing issues such as consumer demand for sports, league policies and player pay. Specifically, much of his research focuses on how fans substitute between teams
and what this means for teams' market power and profitability. He has written or co-authored 21 articles in peer-reviewed journals. These journals include *Economic Inquiry*, *Applied Economics*, the *Review of Industrial Organization*, the *Journal of Sports Economics*, the *International Journal of Sport Finance* and the *Journal of Sport Management*.

After receiving his Ph.D. in Economics and M.S. in Statistics, Dr. Winfree joined the Sport Management faculty at the University of Michigan in 2003. Since then he has taught Sports Economics, Financial Management of the Sports Industry (to both undergraduate and master's degree students) and The Economics of Sports League Policy in the Sport Management program. He has also taught The Economics of Sport Public Policy in the Ford School of Public Policy at the University of Michigan. He has also worked with teams such as the Detroit Pistons.

Mark S. Rosentraub, Ph.D., is the Bruce and Joan Bickner Endowed Professor of Sport Management at the University of Michigan. He has been studying and writing about the business of sports and the linkage between sports, amenities, and urban development for more than 30 years. He has written or co-authored four different books and more than 30 academic articles and book chapters on different aspects of sports, tourism, amenities, and local economic development. *Major League*

Winners: Using Sports and Culture for Economic Development (2010) explores the theoretical framework behind and the efforts of several communities to use sports in the competition to attract and retain human capital for economic development. *Major League Losers: The Real Cost of Sports and Who's Paying For It* appeared in 1997, and *The Economics of Sports: An International Perspective* with two other colleagues was published in 2004.

Dr. Rosentraub has also helped numerous cities across North America and governments in the Balkans frame redevelopment strategies involving sports, culture, and real estate. He worked with the San Diego Padres in designing the Ballpark District plan that resulted in more than $2 billion in real estate development. He has also advised two different mayors of Indianapolis on downtown redevelopment strategies. He has or is working with the Detroit Pistons, Indianapolis Colts, New York Mets, San Francisco Giants and the city of Edmonton (in their efforts to build a new arena with the Edmonton Oilers and redesign their downtown area). In the 1990s Professor Rosentraub helped the Mayor's office in Los Angeles with work involving the Staples Center and the building of *L.A. LIVE*. In 2003 the Cuyahoga County Commissioners appointed Dr. Rosentraub to the board of the Gateway Economic Redevelopment Corporation. "Gateway" is the public agency responsible for Progressive Field, home to the Cleveland Indians, and Quicken Loans Arena, home to the Cleveland Cavaliers. Dr. Rosentraub helped rewrite the leases for both teams that avoided substantial financial problems for Cleveland and Cuyahoga County saving taxpayers more than $4 million each year.

Chapter 1

The Redefinition of the Sports Business

Introduction

The sports business has been dramatically changed across the past two decades. A series of "this changes everything" innovations and events involving labor relations, facility development, media, and revenue generation have occurred. These changes require students to have a very different knowledge base and perspective as they seek jobs with the horizontally and vertically organized teams that today are real estate corporations, entertainment businesses, and, in some instances, media corporations. At the heart of each of these conglomerates is a team. But, how each owner operates his or her franchise and plans for its financial success depends on how the corporation's managers maximize revenue streams related to team operations, the media, real estate in and around facilities, and entertainment options at facilities. Each of these revenue streams grows when fans enjoy enhanced experiences. Those teams, with managers who understand how best to provide those experiences, maximize revenues. Those managers who lack the necessary skills will find fewer and fewer employment opportunities. This book is organized to provide you with the base of knowledge the twenty-first century manager needs to maximize revenues and succeed in what has become the very dynamic world of sports management and finance.

The changes taking place in the sports world are not unique. Every business is challenged to keep pace with increasingly dynamic and rapidly shifting market environments to remain profitable. While examples abound of how rapidly corporations must adapt or face dramatically declining revenues and levels of profitability, the news and information business provides stark evidence of how quickly the marketplace can change. While many people had grown accustomed to living in metropolitan areas with only one major daily newspaper, few envisioned a time when even one daily newspaper would be an economically obsolete concept. The ability to access news and information through the Internet has made the newspaper obsolete for generations either raised on computers or accustomed to accessing information and news through smartphones, iPads, and tablet computers. To remain viable, some newspapers have dramatically increased their web presence. That is but one example of how every business must adopt and adapt to emerging technologies. Every enterprise must strive to ensure that its service or product satisfies the changing preferences of consumers and while remaining attractive and unique. While this has always been a factor for every business and for every product produced, what has made the pressure more intense is the current ability of customers to more easily select services and products from a wide-ranging set of producers located almost anywhere. The Internet makes the cost of accessing an unlimited number of substitutes for almost every product practically zero. This level of competition to manufacture, package, and deliver products with appropriate pricing to serve rapidly changing markets is nothing new for any enterprise. What is new, however, is the rate of change and how quickly businesses and their managers must (1) adapt their financing and management skills to meet consumers' expectations; (2) identify new revenue streams and profitable opportunities; (3) carefully evaluate the profitable potential of new revenue streams, products, and methods of delivery; (4) project and evaluate the revenue potential and profitability from different mixes of labor; and (5) respond to the expanding range of choices made available by the Internet and reduced shipping costs. Those businesses and managers that are unable to innovate and adapt to the "real-time" age of the Internet, hundreds of television channels, and demands of consumers for enhanced "experiences" as opposed to merely new products, falter.

Some might think the sports business is insulated from these dynamic pressures, but this industry has undergone seismic shifts in the past few decades that future managers must understand and then master. These changes have completely altered the business management and financial practices that now define the difference between profit and loss and the ability to afford the payrolls still associated with winning championships. This book was written to help today's students interested in a career in sports management understand these changes and their effect on the sports business. Simply put, those clubs and leagues that capitalize more quickly and more extensively on each of the changes will have more revenues than those that fail to understand the changes and opportunities created. Those students who are not trained in what has become "the sports business in real time" will not meet the needs of their employers. Four major changes have irrevocably changed sports finance.

Change Number 1: Ownership Structure, Entertainment Complexes, and Real Estate Development

Teams are certainly not the "mom and pop" operations of the past. While some teams are still owned by families, more and more are owned by conglomerates. Teams today are (or have been) owned by sole proprietors, partnerships, corporations, and local governments. Some teams sell shares and are publicly traded. College sports represent another unique form of ownership. Regardless of the ownership type, however, all teams are now looking to enhance the experience enjoyed by fans that attracts them to venues. Every team, league, and college conference is exploring ways to expand and exhance the experiences available through television and the Internet. Differences in ownership structures also create opportunities. Certain structures may make it easier to create different or new revenues streams or access different tax benefits. One only needs to note the number of teams owned by media, real estate, or concession companies to recognize how quickly the sports business has been changed. In Major League Baseball (MLB), some teams prefer to own their minor league franchises, while others do not. Understanding all these changes is critical for today's new sports managers.

Three North American sports teams underscore the scale of the changes underway and the different management structures in place. The Dallas Mavericks are owned by a sole proprietor, Mark Cuban, who claims to own the team because of his love for sports and the Mavericks. As a result, the Mavericks' business model would be classified as "traditional" with a focus only on the team and the classical revenue streams: tickets, the leasing of rights to broadcasters, and in-facility advertisements. The Atlanta Braves, on the other hand, have had a very different ownership history. When Ted Turner was promoting his new cable channel, TBS, he also owned the Braves. Turner used the Braves as a programming backbone for his cable station and that helped attract millions of viewers. The team, as part of a cable television station that became a regional and then a national presence, substantially extended the Braves' fan base and built a sort of "Braves Nation" across the United States. The Braves helped build the Turner broadcasting empire and that empire, in turn, helped to build the Braves' national image and brand. TBS gave baseball fans, in markets without a team, a team they could root for consistently. This increase in the number of Braves' fans still helps the franchise today. As scores of cable subscribers began demanding Turner's station so they could follow the Braves. The team gave TBS the viewership and revenues they needed to become the basis of a media empire.

The Green Bay Packers have a completely different model. The Packers are community-owned in the sense that a board is linked to a community-based organization in Green Bay, the Sullivan Post of the American Legion. If the team is ever sold, the proceeds go to the Sullivan Post to build a memorial for soldiers from the area. This was done to ensure that the team would never leave Green Bay and, if it was sold or did move, there would be no financial benefit for shareholders. The

Packers use this ownership to their advantage, emphasizing their link to the community to secure tax-supported investments for Lambeau Field and public support for extensive real estate development around the stadium to enhance the team's fiscal strength (Walter, 2010). A committee initially established in the 1920s manages the team and can appoint new members. This ensures a level of continuity, but also restricts the "public ownership and management" to an elite group that, in turn, appoints the professional managers. The important lesson from Green Bay's experience is that, even though the team's management structure is far different than the one that existed for the Atlanta Braves under Ted Turner, the Braves became part of a media corporation and the Green Bay Packers are now becoming a real estate development firm. Mark Cuban's fortune provides an option to maintain a basketball team as only a sports franchise, but that model of ownership is on the decline. As will be illustrated in Chapter 2, regardless of ownership form, today's teams are increasingly real estate, media, or entertainment corporations. Indeed, it will be argued that all teams have become real estate businesses, even if the team limits that activity to their arena, ballpark, or stadium. Most others, such as the Green Bay Packers, are now full-fledged development corporations.

An urban legend of sort asserts that when Walt Disney saw all of the hotels and other tourism-related businesses spreading out from his Anaheim, California Disneyland, he vowed that when he built another complex it would include all of these amenities. Walt Disney World Resort (Orange and Osceola Counties, Florida) was the fulfillment of that vision or business plan and the concept of including all or most of the infrastructure to support consumption activities associated with a visit to an attraction became known as *Disneyfication*. Walt Disney World Resort included hotels, restaurants, convention and meeting room space, a series of other parks that built off the reputational advantage or attraction of a Disney-themed park, and destinations for evening (and late evening) entertainment. In later years, a cruise ship line was even added to the mix.

The idea of ensuring that there are ample venues to capture the activities related to attending a professional sports game (retail centers, restaurants, pubs, and entertainment activities including games for children and adults and museums dealing with the history of the individual clubs) spread slowly in the sports world. As a consequence, even those facilities built in the 1960s, 1970s, and 1980s—long after Walt Disney learned his lesson—were not designed to incorporate these sorts of activities into a fan's game-day experience. Then, once ownership realized the value of teams and their games as attractions and how much ancillary revenue could be earned from a Disneyfication business plan and facility design, a literal race to build new facilities with extraordinary physical "footprints" was initiated. The penultimate conclusion to this race was Yankee Stadium and the Cowboys' Stadium that opened in 2009 followed by the Giants/Jets Stadium in 2010. Each of these facilities included an ample supply of luxury seating (suites and club seats, field, dugout, or floor-level seats with remote and secluded dining and entertainment facilities) with an appropriate complement of dining, meeting, and entertainment spaces for customers in every seating class (nonluxury, club seats, suites, etc.). Explicit in each design was a large (and increasing) number of amenities and attractions designed to be sure that teams could capture more of the anticipated pre- and postgame spending that their business-oriented customers and fans would plan when entertaining clients and guests at an event. As newer facilities opened, newer innovations were incorporated (e.g., "all one can eat" sections, party sections, etc.) bringing a clamor to redesign facilities that lacked the latest twist on *Disneyfication*.

Expanding retail outlets, food and beverage locations, and providing other forms of entertainment (batting cages, speed throwing areas, etc.) were designed to both cater to and expand the pre- and postgame spending by fans seated in nonluxury seating. The inclusion of larger and larger sets of amenities that grew to include brand-name restaurants and pubs and outdoor barbecue areas, substantially expanded the footprint of facilities. Without any changes at all in the playing surfaces (and, in some cases, to increase the number of home runs playing fields were actually smaller), the size of sports facilities dramatically increased. For example, Yankee Stadium that opened in 2009 had 3,000 *fewer* seats and the exact same field dimensions of the facility it replaced (the old Yankee Stadium was built in 1924, but when it was renovated in the 1970s, the dimensions of the playing field were dramatically different from what existed in the original design). Yet, the modern Yankee Stadium has a footprint that is 1.63 times the size of the legendary ballpark it replaced translating into 523,000 additional square feet. The Cowboys' new stadium can accommodate far more fans than could be seated at their older facility in Irving, Texas, and, with a 30-acre footprint, the Arlington-based facility is so big that the Cowboys' previous home or the new domed stadium home of the Indianapolis Colts (Lucas Oil Stadium) could each fit within the new Arlington stadium. The size of Cowboys' Stadium, the new Yankee Stadium, and the New Meadowlands Stadium facility built by the New York Giants and New York Jets, is no small change for sports finance and management. Lucas Oil Stadium, with a seating capacity of 63,000, sits on 13 acres making it 185 percent larger than the RCA Dome it replaced. Clearly the sports business has changed.

The first phase of the Disneyfication of sports, then, involved the expansion of facilities to capture pre- and postgame spending and this change has important implications for the seating capacity that a facility can sustain (a point that will be analyzed and discussed in Chapter 4), but it was only a matter of time before some entrepreneurs, developers, and team owners began to realize that there may well be other Disneyfication elements created by sports facilities that could be captured. An initial glimpse into this possibility was generated by Oriole Park at Camden Yards, but far larger windows into this possibility were provided by political events in San Diego and the economic opportunities created by the existence of large tracts of land in downtown Los Angeles. Those will be detailed in subsequent chapters, but a few points are essential.

Oriole Park at Camden Yards in Baltimore was built in close proximity to the Inner Harbor entertainment and cultural center. Depicted in Figure 1.1, the

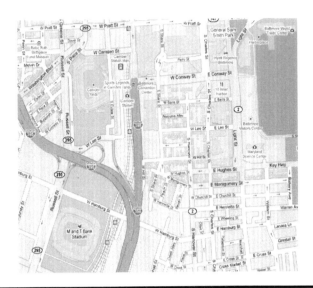

Figure 1.1 Oriole Park at Camden Yards, M&T Bank Stadium, and Baltimore's Inner Harbor: A glimpse of the Disneyfication of sports and real estate development. (From Google Maps.)

ballpark (labeled Camden Yards though its official name is Oriole Park at Camden Yards) and the football stadium (home to the Baltimore Ravens, M & T Bank Stadium) are in close proximity to Harborplace and 10 Inner Harbor, but not quite adjacent to these entertainment and dining complexes. Surrounding both of these retail and entertainment facilities are numerous apartment and condominium complexes as well as townhouse developments. The Harborplace complex produced a demand for new residences that emanated from the nightlife and ambience created by the water and the extensive entertainment, dining, and cultural amenities developed around the waterfront (Figure 1.2). Developers and team owners quickly realized that sports facilities can create a similar ambience and that the crowds attending events at these facilities can sustain complementary amenities that allow new urban neighborhoods to be built complete with hundreds, if not thousands, of residential units. Those residential units, as well as the complementary amenities, created new revenue and profit opportunities. For decades, the neighborhood surrounding Wrigley Field in Chicago had been a favorite of fans and others for the excitement and amenities that surround that facility. The crowds attending events at Oriole Park and at the Inner Harbor suggested to many that a carefully planned, multiuse neighborhood anchored by a sports facility could create profitable development options, allowing a team owner or investors to capitalize on the crowds attracted to games.

The impetus for first testing this perspective and its application rested in the political environment for a new ballpark in San Diego. Years of conflicts between

Figure 1.2 The Inner Harbor: Entertainment, residential, and commercial properties create a new urban neighborhood for Baltimore. (Photo courtesy of Mark S. Rosentraub.)

the city and the San Diego Chargers meant that any taxpayer support for a new ballpark would have to be tied to innovative approaches and an entirely new paradigm regarding the use of public money for a sports facility. To secure electoral support for the City of San Diego's investment in a new ballpark for the Padres, the team's owner, John Moores, had to guarantee more than $450 million in new real estate development across two phases. Initiated in the 1990s, before the end of the agreed to first phase, more than $2 billion of new development had taken place (Newman, 2006; Rosentraub, 2010). The profits from this development vividly illustrated that sports facilities as part of new urban neighborhoods, if anchored by the right mix of other retail and commercial facilities, could create new revenue streams in an expanded vision of Disneyfication.

From an integrated real estate development perspective, the Inner Harbor showed how sports or other cultural and entertainment venues could anchor the building of a new urban neighborhood. The incremental or anchoring effects of the sports teams were somewhat muted by their separation from the Inner Harbor. That separation was a function of the building of the sports facilities years after the development of the Inner Harbor had been initiated. What was apparent, however, was that the crowds attracted to sports events could be the anchor for new urban neighborhoods just as other entertainment and cultural amenities were the cornerstones of the Inner Harbor's success.

The Inner Harbor, the Sports Facilities, and Baltimore

In noting that the Inner Harbor has been a success relative to the attraction of visitors and tourists and the anchoring of a new urban neighborhood, the challenges confronting Baltimore's overall development and the pervasiveness of decline in numerous other parts of the city are not minimized. Marc Levine has written extensively on the dichotomy of worlds that exists between the Inner Harbor and the other parts of Baltimore. His work also attempted to assess the effects of Oriole Park at Camden Yards as a tool for moving economic activity and observed that "Camden Yards cannot be considered a successful urban redevelopment catalyst. Despite hopes to the contrary, public investment in the Camden Yards sports complex did not catalyze a 'dramatic transformation' of the western edge of downtown. While it expanded the tourist bubble to the west, little development spilled into nearby areas desperate for an influx of investment and consumer spending. While bringing even larger crowds to the Inner Harbor area, the sports facilities "have done little in terms of catalyzing development in those areas most in need of it; the Howard Street corridor still sags, Pigtown and other western-edge neighborhoods remain economically and socially separated from the thriving downtown, and Sharp-Leadenhall still teeters at the precipice of gentrification and decline." Levine (2000) noted that Baltimore's challenges were less severe than those facing Detroit and some other former industrial capitals of North America. He notes, though, the creation of a "Fantasy City" image and environment (Harrigan, 1998) in the Inner Harbor has not led to a successful attack on any of the "city's core difficulties . . . with people, jobs, and businesses continuing to desert the city . . . By the end of the 1990s, after three decades of 'fantasy city' redevelopment strategies, city policy makers seem to have run out of answers short of 'slum clearance' or 'planned shrinkage' to the problems of ghetto poverty and neighborhood decay" (Levine, 2000).

For students and practitioners of sports finance and management, Baltimore's experience with the two facilities at Camden Yards and the Inner Harbor provided several lessons. *First,* the facilities generated substantial visitor traffic that enhanced attendance at the amenities adjacent to the water. *Second,* the physical separation or distance between the amenities and the sports facilities, further constrained by road traffic and the presence of an interstate highway, reduced the seamless integration and also might have minimized the effect of the teams' presence on the other amenities. *Third,* the Inner Harbor was extremely well planned and, in recent years, agreements with different community groups ensured that diverse and lower income households also benefitted from the development. Relative to the highly appropriate criticisms raised by Levine (2000) and Chapin (2004), there are political and social reasons for teams to maintain the profitability of their real estate ventures while also (1) extending the effect of the facilities and (2) documenting what is indeed accomplished for a city from the presence of teams and a fully integrated development plan. These lessons would be addressed in the efforts put forth by Los Angeles and their deal with the Los Angeles Lakers and Kings, in San Diego where the owner of the Padres would agree to develop the Ballpark District as a new downtown neighborhood replete with a new ballpark that was subsidized and, in Columbus, where Nationwide Insurance and an expansion NHL franchise committed to the building of an arena in a mixed-use downtown neighborhood.

In Los Angeles, in exchange for the rights to build advertising towers along two major freeways and the ability to purchase sufficient land assembled by the public sector, the Anshutz Entertainment Group (AEG) and its partner, together with the Lakers and Kings, invested approximately $2.8 billion across 13 years and helped to transform a section of downtown Los Angeles. The integrated plan and its scale led to the building of thousands of residential units together with a specified set of community benefits for nearby neighborhoods and new tax revenues for the City of Los Angeles (that substantially exceeded the public sector's investment). San Diego's new downtown neighborhood includes the demanded 1,000 new hotel rooms and more than three times the amount of real estate development guaranteed by the then owner of the Padres. In Columbus, too, the public sector's liabilities were guaranteed by Nationwide Insurance, although subsequent issues with another new arena built by The Ohio State University threatened to undermine some of the positive tax outcomes from that arrangement (Rosentraub, 2010). Examples of the effects of these carefully planned real estate developments are depicted in Figure 1.3, Figure 1.4, and Figure 1.5.

These redevelopment efforts underscore the substantial economic benefits for team owners from leveraging the activity produced by the attraction of large crowds to venues and their simultaneous ability to produce benefits for community groups and respond to the criticisms that facilities, entertainment, and tourist centers do

Figure 1.3 New downtown housing across from Los Angeles's STAPLES Center and L.A. LIVE. (Photo courtesy of Mark S. Rosentraub.)

Figure 1.4   The ballpark district surrounding PETCO Park in San Diego and the building of new downtown neighborhood anchored by a ballpark. (Photo courtesy of Mark S. Rosentraub.)

Figure 1.5   Columbus's Arena District, Nationwide Arena, and the building of another new neighborhood anchored by a sports facility. (Photo courtesy of Mark S. Rosentraub.)

not improve the economic and fiscal conditions in a host city. To maximize the economic and social returns from teams, sports management now requires a far greater understanding of the many real estate development opportunities. Teams that do not consider myriad real estate development options that exist lose the opportunity to enhance revenue streams and create benefits for their home cities.

Change Number 2: A New Media World

It seems almost implausible, but in the earliest era of the growth of television's popularity and its ubiquitous presence in every home, restaurant, and sports bar, some wondered if the telecasting of games would have a negative effect on attendance at games. That fear initially convinced team owners in the NFL to "black out" the telecast of home games in their local markets. The justification for blackouts was anchored in a fear of an overexposure of games on television that could lead to declining attendance levels if fans could simply watch from the comfort of their own homes or favorite restaurants and pubs.* The blackout rule used by the NFL even applied to championship games, meaning that the legendary 1958 game between the Baltimore Colts and New York Giants was not seen in the New York metropolitan area. The earliest Super Bowls also were not available on television in the host market.

With fan resentment at a fever pitch over blacked-out games (even when games were sold out weeks and even months in advance), no fewer than 20 different pieces of legislation were introduced in the early 1970s to force the NFL to televise games that had been sold out. Some were quite threatening to the NFL's control and hinted at taking away the right to package all games into a single bundle or set of bundles to be broadcast by several networks. With broadcast revenue growing at extraordinary rates, team owners wanted to be sure their control was not limited by antitrust laws or a possible Federal Sports Commission that was proposed by some members of Congress (Hochburg, 1973). The NFL avoided the possibility of more controlling or strident Congressional action by implementing its own antiblackout policy. As introduced and sustained since 1973, any game that is sold out 72 hours in advance of kick-off is televised in the local market. In addition, a team can petition to have the 72-hour guideline reduced to 48 or 24 hours. That has been done numerous times and in many markets few if any games have been blacked out since 1973. Teams also are allowed to give away a certain number of tickets to community organizations and those tickets can count toward the definition of a "sell out" that permits a game to be televised. In most markets, NFL teams routinely sell all of their tickets. The recent economic recession, however, brought the return of blackouts in selected markets including Jacksonville and Detroit. In other markets, there have been times when local businesses bought unsold tickets to distribute to community organizations, permitting games to be telecast in the team's home market.

---

* In a similar vein, many predicted that movie audiences would dwindle when home VCRs became common. After all, why would somebody go to the movies when they could watch the movie at home? Even though fans of sports and movies can watch their favorite entertainment at home, people still want to go out and see sports and movies in public. There could be many reasons for this, but it appears that various types of consumption are a good thing for both consumers and producers.

Fears of declining attendance if local games were telecast or of over exposure if too many games were broadcast in particular markets have been shown to be grossly unwarranted. Indeed, what has dramatically changed across the past two decades has been an extraordinary expansion in the broadcasting of sporting events and with it an unprecedented rise in revenues. The 1990s witnessed the advent of dozens of new sports networks including the family of stations operating as part of Fox Sports Net, the creation of networks by collegiate conferences (e.g., The Big Ten Network or the SEC Digital Network), and individual teams operating their own networks or networks in partnership with other teams. Examples of these networks and their ownership include the New York Yankees (Yankee Entertainment and Sports), the Boston Red Sox and Boston Bruins (New England Sports Network), the New York Mets (Sports New York), the Cleveland Indians (Sports Time Ohio), and the Baltimore Orioles and Washington Nationals (Mid Atlantic Sports Network).

Fox Sports Net (or Fox Sports, FSN) was born from the buyout of the Prime Network and the eventual addition of other networks. Today there are 19 individual regional networks that form FSN together with five affiliated or co-owned companies. In total, then, the FSN umbrella includes 24 networks serving numerous regions across the United States. ESPN (Entertainment and Sports Programming Network), the pioneer in the creation of media devoted to sports, comprises 20 different networks serving 150 countries, providing programming in 15 different languages. The ESPN family of networks broadcasts the games of numerous professional leagues in North America, Europe, and Asia.

The importance of these networks for sports business and finance is most easily understood by looking at outcomes from the Big 10 Network after only a few years of operations. In 2009, the network was able to provide each of its member schools with returns of $6.3 million (approximate profit was $70 million in its second year of operations). The Big 10 Network provides television programming of a full complement of sports competitions to cable and satellite television networks serving more than 70 million homes (Hyland, 2009). The network's reach and delivery of programming covers more than the borders of its members' states: Pennsylvania, Ohio, Indiana, Michigan, Illinois, Minnesota, Iowa, and Wisconsin. The Big 10 Network now reaches 19 of the 20 largest markets in the United States. Even in the recessionary period, the Big 10 Network discussed the possibility of profits doubling to more than $12 million per school in short order. The network's profitability will increase in later years after the investment by the Fox Network is repaid (Walker, 2009). The profitability of the venture after just two years (and in the midst of a severe recession) underscores the direct financial impact of more extensive media distribution systems for teams and universities. Not to be left behind, the NFL and MLB each created their own networks and MLB launched a baseball scores and news nightly report to compete with ESPN's show, *Baseball Tonight*. Comcast joined the "create your own network mania" to capitalize on its vast cable delivery systems. Comcast bought the Outdoor Life Network and signed agreements to telecast individual college football games, NHL games, and other sporting events

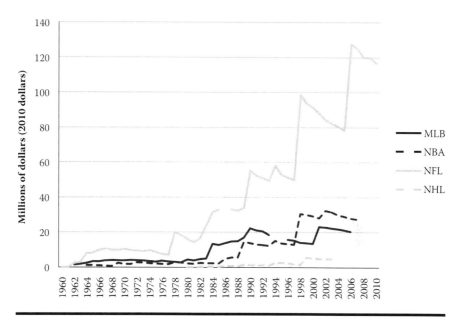

Figure 1.6 Annual revenue for each team from national television contracts by league: 1960–2010 (in constant or 2010 dollars).

not covered by other networks. Comcast acquired NBC in 2011, adding new level of sports programming to its inventory.

Revenue from national and local television contracts skyrocketed in the past 40 years. Revenues increased more for some leagues than others. Figure 1.6 shows league revenues per team from national contracts adjusted for inflation (2010 dollars).

This graph shows that the NFL has always done well in terms of television revenue, but it is dramatically increasing and far and away surpasses the revenue earned by any other league. On the other end of the spectrum, the revenue that NHL teams receive is rather minimal although recent contract numbers are unknown. It is not just league-wide revenue from national contracts that have become an integral part of team revenues. As previously stated, teams' local contracts (or their own network) have dramatically risen as well. Figure 1.7 shows local television revenues for Major League Baseball adjusted for inflation.

Unfortunately, teams do not release a great deal of information regarding the revenue they earn from the telecast of games in their local markets. Figure 1.7 does illustrate that local television revenues dramatically increased in the 1980s. More recently, *Forbes* magazine has reported that the Yankees earn more than $184 million each year from the YES network (the Steinbrenner family owns 34 percent of the YES network).* There are estimates that the YES network may be

---

* http://www.forbes.com/lists/2010/33/baseball-valuations-10_New-York-Yankees_334613.html

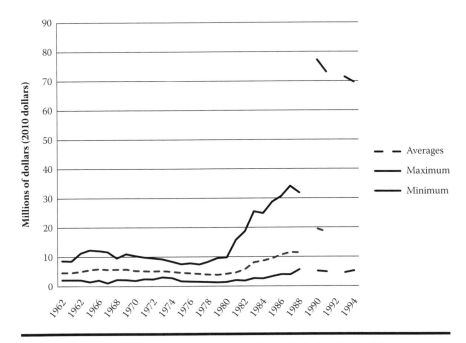

Figure 1.7 Annual revenue for MLB teams from their local television contracts by team: Selected years (in constant or 2010 dollars).

worth as much as $3 billion.* Other MLB teams like the Boston Red Sox and Cleveland Indians also have created independent networks.

This brief history of the explosion of media outlets—leaving aside for the moment MLB.Com, ESPN360.Com, ESPN3.Com and a number of other Internet broadcast and transmission options—has dramatically changed the financial and management world of professional and collegiate sports. Understanding the sports business in real time requires an appreciation for how quickly the dynamics of the relationship between sports and television and sports and the Internet has changed. In turn, these changes have had and will continue to have profound economic, revenue, and financing consequences for teams and universities while also creating many new opportunities. It is important as well to identify a set of issues that surrounds future media and Internet broadcast issues and how each has the potential to further alter the financial environment for teams and universities.

Change Number 3: The Real Estate Management Issues within New Sports Facilities and Luxury Seating

Sports facilities today are dramatically different from those built 25 or 30 years ago. Possibly the biggest difference is that teams are returning to single-purpose facilities.

---

* www.nytimes.com/2007/08/03/sports/baseball/03yes.html (accessed May 17, 2011).

Stadium construction through the early 1970s was dominated by the building of facilities that would serve as the home for two different sports teams. For much of the twentieth century, community leaders and team owners were content with baseball and football teams playing their home games in the same stadium; basketball and hockey teams also shared arenas. The 1960s and 1970s was dominated by the building of new facilities to serve a region's baseball and football teams with one notable exception. Before focusing on that notable exception (separate facilities were built for the Kansas City Chiefs and the Kansas City Royals), it is important to recognize that the building mania in the 1960s and 1970s was dominated by the design and building of facilities to host baseball and football teams and arenas where hockey and basketball teams would play.

New York's Shea Stadium opened in 1964 as the most innovative of the dual sport stadiums as it incorporated moveable sections of the lower deck to enhance sight lines for both baseball and football. The movable seats were positioned behind home plate and near the first- and third-base lines for baseball. For the football season, these seats moved along a track that permitted their placement between the 30-yard lines on both sides of the football field. This technological innovation was not included in multiuse facilities that were built in Cincinnati, Houston, Minneapolis, Philadelphia, Pittsburgh, or St. Louis. In many other cities, football or baseball teams moved into facilities that were primarily built for one sport and the other team just "made do" with the fact that some of the best seats for baseball were located behind the end zone for football. Upper deck outfield seats for baseball sometimes provided the best views of a football game, but were located a considerable distance from the sidelines.

The exception to the pattern of building single-use facilities took place in Kansas City. In 1967—in the face of demands for a new ballpark from Charles Finley who would move his Athletics to Oakland, California—voters throughout Jackson County supported a tax increase to pay for a bond of more than $102 million ($671.8 in 2010 dollars) to build two facilities covered by a roof that would move from one facility to the other when needed. The public support for this bond package was successful in securing a new baseball franchise for the region after the Athletics moved to Oakland, and the Royals began play in Kansas City in 1969. The movable roof was never built; as plans emerged, the movable roof would prove too expensive. Instead, the community's leaders approved the building of separate facilities for the teams. Arrowhead Stadium, the home of the Kansas City Chiefs opened in 1972, and Kaufmann Stadium, the home of the Royals, opened in 1973. Instantly, team owners from both MLB and the NFL could see the value of separate facilities resulting from improved sight lines for fans. With a wave of new stadiums having just been built, the widespread acceptance of the need for and desirability of separate facilities would not emerge until events contributed to Baltimore having to build a baseball-only facility to ensure that the Orioles would not follow their beloved Colts to a new city that offered a new stadium.

Before focusing on the game-changing characteristics of Oriole Park at Camden Yards, it is important to understand how dramatic a change in sports management and finance for franchises and fans it was to move from the concept of shared to separate facilities. From 1921 through 2010, baseball and football teams in 25 different metropolitan areas shared facilities for varying lengths of time (Table 1.1). By 2010, in all but two major metropolitan areas, baseball and football teams were playing in separate facilities. In Oakland, California, the Athletics are seeking approval to relocate to a new ballpark in San Jose. In Toronto, the Canadian Football League franchise, the Argonauts, continues to play in the Rogers Centre (formerly known as the Skydome) with the Blue Jays. In addition, the Buffalo Bills are planning to play some of their home games at the Rogers Centre to enhance their financial position. In some cities, there was never any sharing of facilities by baseball and football teams as smaller regions were not serious candidates to be the home to both an MLB and NFL team (e.g., Charlotte, Indianapolis, and Jacksonville). More importantly, when cities have been awarded new franchises, or were able to attract a team to move into a community, a single-purpose facility has been the "currency of the realm." No new franchises were created nor did any team move unless a separate facility was provided. Why is it economically beneficial to have a single-use facility and what makes it impractical for baseball and football teams to share stadiums? Why do both baseball and football teams earn more money playing in facilities designed for their sport?

The action in baseball and football is concentrated in two very different physical spaces. Football's action takes place within a $120 \times 53\frac{1}{3}$-yard rectangle. While there is a degree of concentration of the action near the end zones, on a regular basis plays occur across the entire expanse. The substantial level of play across such a large area means higher-level seats can offer panoramic views of the action. In addition, with play occurring within a 120-yard rectangle, seats located along the entire length or certainly between the 20-yard lines (a 60-yard expanse) provide excellent views of play. As a result, the design that produces the largest number of seats with excellent sight lines involves two crescent-shaped seating areas from goal line to goal line with somewhat shorter seating areas built behind each end zone.

Baseball's action is concentrated in a 30×30-square yard diamond and the best views for fans result when the vast majority of seats are concentrated along the baselines and behind home plate. Even when balls are hit to the outfield, the action that results as runners and the batter try to advance from base to base occurs in the 900-square yard diamond infield. To provide the largest number of seats with the best views of the action in baseball and football, two very different physical designs are needed. One stadium can accommodate teams from both sports, but only at the cost of offering to fans of either team fewer seats with excellent sight lines. Larger numbers of seats with excellent sight lines produce more revenues as fans are willing to pay higher prices for the enhanced views of the playing field.

Camden Yards at Oriole Park—a baseball-only facility—opened on April 6, 1992, and was an immediate "game changer" on several levels. The new ballpark for the Baltimore Orioles enjoyed strong political support as the community had lived through the loss of its storied football franchise, the Colts. Robert Irsay moved the Colts to Indianapolis because that city had just built a football-only domed stadium as part of an expanded convention center. Indianapolis had no illusions about its ability to host a MLB team and site design constraints (railroad tracks) made it impossible to build a dome that would be even remotely capable of hosting baseball and football games similar to Seattle's Kingdome. After the Colts left Baltimore, and with no NFL team in town (the Browns did not relocate from Cleveland to Baltimore to become the Ravens until three years after Oriole Park opened), the Orioles had the luxury of insisting upon and being supported in their quest for a baseball-only facility in a community where voters and elected officials were aligned in an effort to avoid the possibility of the loss of another professional team (Miller, 1990; Rosentraub, 1999). From the vantage point of local politics, the issue of building a facility that could serve both a baseball and football team was not relevant. The region had lost their football team. In addition, the Washington Redskins played their homes games in suburban Maryland, a mere 18 miles from the site where Oriole Park at Camden Yards would be built. While a number of people might have dreamed of hosting another NFL franchise, the reality was that the NFL's expansion was taking place in southern states and any thought about a possible NFL team would require a team's relocation. As such, the dream of an NFL team was part of an unpredictable future.

These factors created an opportunity for the Orioles to come forward with an entirely new vision for their baseball park. That vision would benefit from the lessons learned from the Royals' Kaufmann Stadium and would have a profound, immediate, and dramatic effect on sports management and finance, and cities across America. Camden Yards combined a design that paid homage to the ballparks of the early twentieth century with the improved sight lines offered by Kaufmann Stadium, but added into the design a unique retail space and luxury seating that would provide substantial new revenue streams for the team. These innovations underscored for every MLB owner that there were substantial revenue enhancements possible from building ballparks that incorporated improved sight lines, nostalgic if not "retro" designs, and vast expanses for enhanced retail activities. These new designs created an entire new area of management as the "real estate" inside of ballparks and then stadiums and arenas was dramatically increased to support new revenue streams. Camden Yards was the result of the work of several designers and its "retro" image not only provided more seats closer to the action, but evoked in fans a feeling for baseball's glorified past and the importance of that history for current teams and the game today. The Orioles addition of a unique area for the sale of food and beverages—Eutaw Street—and the inclusion of other retail outlets in an adjacent railway facility created an immediate tourist attraction. Overnight the Orioles had a park with excellent sight lines and a retail area that reconstructed an image of Baltimore in the early part of the twentieth century. The team's ownership had hired its own urban planner, Janet Marie Smith, and after rejecting the initial designs provided

Table 1.1 The era of shared facilities and its demise into economic obsolescence

Teams	Years of Dual Use	Year New Facility Built (Date Old Facility Built)	
		Ballpark	Stadium
Baltimore Orioles/Colts	1954–1983	1992 (1953)	1998 (1953)
Boston Red Sox/Patriots	1963–1968	1912	1971, 2002 (1912)
Chicago Cubs/Bears	1921–1970	1916 (1893)	1971, 2003 (1916)
Cleveland Indians/Browns	1946–1995	1932,1994 (1910)	1999 (1932)
Detroit Tigers/Lions	1938–1974	2000 (1912)	1975, 2002 (1912)
Kansas City Royals/Chiefs	1969–1972	1973 (1923)	1972 (1923)
Los Angeles Angels/Rams	1961–1997	1966 (1925)	1995 (1966)
Minnesota Twins/Vikings	1961–2009	1982 (1961)	1982 (1961)
New York Yankees/Giants	1956–1973	2009 (1923)	1976, 2010 (1883, 1923)
Oakland Athletics/Raiders	1968–1981, 1995–2010	1968	1966 (1922)
Seattle Mariners/Seahawks	1976–1994, 1995–1999	1999 (1976)	2002 (1976)
Toronto Blue Jays/Argonauts	1959–1989, 1989–2010	1989 (1959)	1989 (1959)[1]
Atlanta Braves/Falcons	1966–1991	1997 (1965)	1992 (1965)
Cincinnati Reds/Bengals	1970–1999	1970, 2002 (1912)	2000 (1970)
Colorado Rockies/Denver Broncos	1993–1994	1995	2001 (1948)
Florida Marlins/Miami Dolphins	1993–2010	1993	1987 (1937)

Houston Astros/Oilers[2]	1968–1996	2000 (1965)	2002 (1965)
Los Angeles Dodgers[3]/Rams[4]	1958–1961	1962 (1913, 1923)	1966, 1995 (1923)
New York Mets/Jets	1964–1983	2009, 1964 (1891, 1911)	2010, 1964 (1911)
Philadelphia Phillies/Eagles	1940, 1942, 1944–1957, 1971–2002	2004, 1971, 1938 (1895)	2003, 1971 (1938, 1895)[5]
Pittsburgh Pirates/Steelers	1933–1963[6], 1970–2000	2001, 1970 (1909, 1891)	2001, 1970 (1909)
St. Louis Cardinals/Cardinals	1960–1987	2006, 1966 (1920, 1892)	2006 (1966, 1958)[7]
San Diego Padres/Chargers	1969–2003	2004 (1967)	1967 (1915)
San Francisco Giants/49ers	1971–2000	2000, 1960 (1891)	1971 (1922)
Washington Redskins[9]	1930–1997		1997 (1961, 1921)[10]

Notes:

1 The Argonauts and Blue Jays have shared two facilities.

2 The Oilers moved to Tennessee when a new facility was not built.

3 The Dodgers initially played games at the LA Coliseum before Dodger Stadium was built.

4 The Rams moved from the LA Coliseum to Anaheim Stadium, which they shared with the Angels before moving to St. Louis.

5 During some periods the Eagles played home games at the University of Pennsylvania's stadium while also sharing facilities with the Phillies in other years.

6 The Steelers also moved to collegiate facilities in some years while in others shared facilities with the Pirates.

7 The football Cardinals moved from Chicago to St. Louis and then to Phoenix. They shared facilities in Chicago and St. Louis with baseball teams.

8 The Washington Nationals initially played in Montreal where there was an older facility and then a newer domed facility.

9 The Washington Redskins shared facilities with the Washington Senators who moved to Minnesota. The second Washington Senators franchise became the Texas Rangers leaving the Redskins as the major tenant in RFK Stadium.

10 The Redskins played initially in facilities built for both baseball and football teams. Those facilities were built in 1921 and 1961.

by architects, what emerged resembled the smaller facilities of the nineteenth and early twentieth centuries that placed fans closer to the infield diamond. The much-improved sight lines (from those available in Memorial Stadium where the Orioles had played since 1953) commanded higher ticket prices that fans were only too eager to pay. Janet Marie Smith and Oriole team president Larry Lucchino worked together to revolutionize sports management and finance.

The Orioles' success sent a message to every team owner. Nostalgia sells, unique retail settings generate more revenue, and good sight lines sustain elevated ticket prices while also drawing more fans to the ballpark. How successful was this complex concept? Table 1.2 summarizes attendance at Orioles' games before and after the opening of Camden Yards. The opening of the new ballpark produced a 42 percent increase in attendance compared to the next to the last season played by the Orioles at Memorial Stadium. In Camden Yards' second season, attendance increased by more than 50 percent. To be sure, there were years when attendance levels were less robust, but even when the team finished no higher than third in its division, attendance levels were often far larger than they had been at Memorial Stadium. The message was clear. Build a new ballpark with improved sight lines and other revenue generating outlets (restaurants, for example) and attendance will increase (as well as revenues). In a relatively short period of time, every team tried and most succeeded in having new facilities built. When the new home of the Florida Marlins opens in 2012, 23 of MLB's 30 teams will be playing in post-Camden Yard facilities (Table 1.3).

The new real estate management in a sports facility included luxury seating. Just as Oriole Park at Camden Yards was not the first baseball-only facility, it also was not the first to offer luxury seating. What it did do is illustrate fans' interest in paying for more luxury and the resulting revenue growth that would exist if a facility had suites, clubs seats, and other assets that consumers wanted. Luxury and even a degree of lavishness began to dominate facility designs in the aftermath of Oriole Park's success. The popularity of luxury seating—suites with private entertainment areas and other private amenities and club seats with their excellent sight lines and shared (by all club seat holders) entertainment areas adjacent to the special seating—substantially bolstered revenues.

The presence of luxury seating dramatically changed the way teams sold tickets. The building of luxury seating now meant that teams were marketing different "seating products" to multiple markets. The improved seats in nonluxury areas (usually referred to as *the deck*) were the seats upon which most of the business management literature had been focused. That work looked at sports fans and the revenue they could generated through perhaps lower ticket prices that ensured higher levels of consumption of food and beverages and longer-term tendencies to buy tickets when team performance lagged. Luxury seating is focused on the corporate markets where pricing is more complex and related to the creation of environments for entertainment, negotiations, and advertising for the firms involved. It may well

Table 1.2   Attendance at Baltimore Orioles games, 1954–2009. (Ticket price and revenue data available only from 1991.)

Season	Finish	Wins	Losses	Attendance	Average Ticket Price[1]	Ticket Revenue
1954	7th AL	54	100	1,060,910		
1955	7th AL	57	97	852,039		
1956	6th AL	69	85	901,201		
1957	5th AL	76	76	1,029,581		
1958	6th AL	74	79	829,991		
1959	6th AL	74	80	891,926		
1960	2nd AL	89	65	1,187,849		
1961	3rd AL	95	67	951,089		
1962	7th AL	77	85	790,254		
1963	4th AL	86	76	774,254		
1964	3rd AL	97	65	1,116,215		
1965	3rd AL	94	68	781,649		
1966	1st AL	97	63	1,203,366		
1967	6th AL	76	85	955,053		
1968	2nd AL	91	71	943,977		
1969	1st AL East	109	53	1,062,094		
1970	1st AL East	108	54	1,057,069		
1971	1st AL East	101	57	1,023,037		
1972	3rd AL East	80	74	899,950		
1973	1st AL East	97	65	958,667		
1974	1st AL East	91	71	962,572		
1975	2nd AL East	90	69	1,002,157		
1976	2nd AL East	88	74	1,058,609		
1977	2nd AL East	97	64	1,195,769		

(continued)

Table 1.2 (continued)   Attendance at Baltimore Orioles games, 1954–2009. (Ticket price and revenue data available only from 1991.)

Season	Finish	Wins	Losses	Attendance	Average Ticket Price	Ticket Revenue
1978	4th AL East	90	71	1,051,724		
1979	1st AL East	102	57	1,681,009		
1980	2nd AL East	100	62	1,797,438		
1981	Split[2]	59	46	1,024,247		
1982	2nd AL East	94	68	1,613,031		
1983	1st AL East	98	64	2,042,071		
1984	5th AL East	85	77	2,045,784		
1985	4th AL East	83	78	2,132,387		
1986	7th AL East	73	89	1,973,176		
1987	6th AL East	67	95	1,835,692		
1988	7th AL East	54	107	1,660,738		
1989	2nd AL East	87	75	2,353,208		
1990	5th AL East	76	85	2,415,189		
1991	6th AL East	67	95	2,552,753	$8.04	$20,524,134
Oriole Park at Camden Yards Opens for the 1992 Season						
1992	3rd AL East	89	73	3,567,819	$9.55	$34,072,671
1993	3rd AL East	85	77	3,644,965	$11.12	$40,532,011
1994	2nd AL East	63	49	2,535,359	$11.17	$28,319,960
1995	3rd AL East	71	73	3,098,475	$13.14	$40,713,962
1996	2nd AL East	88	74	3,646,950	$13.14	$47,920,923
1997	1st AL East	98	64	3,612,764	$17.02	$61,489,243
1998	4th AL East	79	83	3,684,650	$19.77	$72,845,531
1999	4th AL East	78	84	3,432,099	$19.82	$68,024,202
2000	4th AL East	74	88	3,295,128	$19.78	$65,177,632
2001	4th AL East	63	98	3,094,841	$18.23	$56,418,951

Table 1.2 (continued) Attendance at Baltimore Orioles games, 1954–2009. (Ticket price and revenue data available only from 1991.)

Season	Finish	Wins	Losses	Attendance	Average Ticket Price[1]	Ticket Revenue
2002	4th AL East	67	95	2,655,559	$18.23	$48,410,841
2003	4th AL East	71	91	2,454,523	$20.15	$49,458,639
2004	3rd AL East	78	84	2,744,018	$22.53	$61,822,726
2005[3]	4th AL East	74	88	2,624,740	$22.53	$59,135,392
2006	4th AL East	70	92	2,153,250	$22.53	$48,512,723
2007	4th AL East	69	93	2,164,822	$22.45	$48,600,254
2008[4]	5th AL East	68	93	1,950,075	$23.85	$46,509,289
2009	5th AL East	64	98	1,907,163	$23.42	$44,665,758
2010	6th AL East	66	96	1,733,018	$23.42	$40,587,282
Memorial Stadium Average		84	74	1,307,045		
Camden Yards Average		74	83.8	2,842,117	$18.52	$50,695,684

Notes:
[1] Consistent ticket price data are not available prior to 1991. However, 1991 does represent the last year of Memorial Stadium.
[2] Split—Refers to MLB's only split season format used after a labor dispute that led to the cancellation of numerous games.
[3] Washington Nationals begin play at RFK Stadium in downtown Washington, D.C.
[4] Washington Senators open their new ballpark.

be that the factors that affect the pricing of luxury seating are different than those involved in the selling of seats in the deck to individual sports fans.

In the new facilities, for both luxury and nonluxury seating, team owners were able to capitalize on fans' desire for wider seats, aisles, and concourses, and for the ability to enjoy games surrounded by amenities that were an increasingly common part of their homes and offices. Carpeted entertainment areas that included appropriate furnishings and televisions were the keys to enhanced revenues as fans were more than willing to pay premium prices for the ability to entertain clients, friends, and family members in luxurious settings. The sports fan market always included people willing to pay premium prices for luxury and the ability to see games. In the 1990s, every team wanted to provide their fans who wanted these amenities with

Table 1.3 Year new ballparks opened and the year old parks were built

Teams	Year of New Ballpark (Year Old Park Built)
Arizona Diamondbacks	1998
Atlanta Braves	1997 (1965)
Baltimore Orioles	1992 (1953)
Chicago White Sox	1991 (1910)
Cincinnati Reds	2002 (1970)
Cleveland Indians	1994 (1932)
Colorado Rockies	1995
Detroit Tigers	2000 (1912)
Florida Marlins	2012 (1987)
Houston Astros	2000 (1965)
Milwaukee Brewers	2001 (1953)
Minnesota Twins	2010 (1982)
New York Mets	2009 (1964)
New York Yankees	2009 (1923)
Philadelphia Phillies	2004 (1971)
Pittsburgh Pirates	2001 (1970)
Seattle Mariners	1999 (1976)
St. Louis Cardinals	2006 (1966)
San Diego Padres	2004 (1967)
San Francisco Giants	2000 (1960)
Texas Rangers	1994 (1965)
Washington Nationals	2008 (1977)

suites and club seats. For those fans who were purchasing seats in the deck, they, too, were quite willing to pay higher prices for improved sight lines and easier access to food, beverages, and souvenirs. More and varied food and beverages were offered at every new facility and team stores made it easier to buy souvenirs.

Almost overnight, teams that played in facilities without luxury seating found themselves at a substantial revenue disadvantage. Suites routinely included private bathrooms for the added convenience of families and others and closets to hang coats to provide even greater comfort. Indoor and outdoor heating was provided to improve comfort and the suite area was also air conditioned. These suites were leased for several years and each had its own package of tickets. Oriole Park at Camden Yards provided 72 suites, each with excellent sight lines and, since 1992, no ballpark, stadium, or arena has been built for a major sports team that did not include a substantial number of suites (Table 1.4). How many suites? The number depended on the team owners' assessment of the demand for this luxury product in the local market.

Luxury seating was actually built into some facilities in the 1970s and the 1980s. Oriole Park at Camden Yards included suites and club seats into the basic design or cornerstone of the facility. The success with the concept illustrated fan demand for this product and just as air conditioning had become a necessity for new homes and cars, luxury seating became a staple for the financial success of a sports team. Those teams that played in facilities with well-designed and appointed luxury seating were able to realize far more revenue than teams that played in older venues lacking this amenity. The Cowboys' new stadium in Arlington, with 300 luxury suites on four different levels and more than 15,000 club seats, and the new stadium for the Jets and Giants are but the endpoints on a feature that became a requirement after the opening of Oriole Park. The sale and marketing of this amenity brought a new issue and set of financing options in the world of sports finance and management. What Oriole Park documented was that sports fans in every market, like many other consumers of other goods, will pay premium prices for luxuries that improve their experiences. Just like some people prefer leather seating in their cars or seat warmers (not to mention higher end sound systems and other amenities), some fans want to have wider seats, a greater selection of food and beverages served in a living room setting, and other benefits while they are at a ballpark or stadium. These fans or consumers were and remain very willing to pay premium prices for their seats. Luxury seating inexorably changed sports finance and management, and in the post-Oriole Park era, every team wanted a new "retro look," single-use facility with ample luxury seating options.

Change Number 4: League Policies

While the explosion of income from media and new facilities have changed team finances, just as critical has been the way the different leagues handle these revenues. The way league revenue is distributed between players and teams has changed drastically in the last half-century. Fifty years ago, leagues had reserve clauses. This meant that each team had virtually unlimited control of players' rights, eliminating the ability of athletes to change teams or engage in having teams bid for their services. After decades of challenges, courts eventually supported the players' rights to control the ability to offer their services to more than one team. Today, all major sports leagues have some version of free agency and player drafts, negotiated as

Table 1.4   Luxury seating at select facilities in North America

Team	Facility	Year Opened/ Renovation	Number of...	
			Suites	Club Seats
NFL Franchises				
Arizona Cardinals	University of Phoenix Stadium	2006	88	7,400
Atlanta Falcons	Georgia Dome	1992	203	5,600
Baltimore Ravens	M&T Bank Stadium	1998	108	7,904
Buffalo Bills	Ralph Wilson Stadium	1973/1999	164	6,878
Carolina Panthers	Bank of America Stadium	1994	159	11,358
Chicago Bears	Soldier Field	2003	133	8,600
Cincinnati Bengals	Paul Brown Stadium	2000	114	7,620
Cleveland Browns	Browns Stadium	1999	145	8,754
Dallas Cowboys	Cowboys Stadium	2009	300	15,000
Denver Broncos	Invesco Field at Mile High	2001	106	8,500
Detroit Lions	Ford Field	2002	120	7,000
Green Bay Packers	Lambeau Field	2003	167	6,260
Houston Texans	Reliant Stadium	2002	187	8,200
Indianapolis Colts	Lucas Oil Stadium	2008	137	7,100
Jacksonville Jaguars	Alltel Stadium	1995	75	11,000

Kansas City Chiefs	Arrowhead Stadium	2001/2010	80	10,199
Miami Dolphins	Sun Life Stadium	1987	195	10,209
Minnesota Vikings	Mall of America Field at the Humphrey Metrodome	1982	113	0
New England Patriots	Gillette Stadium	2002	87	6,600
New Orleans Saints	Louisiana Superdome	1975/2008/2012	137	14,077
New York Giants	Giants/Jets Stadium	2010	217	9,300
New York Jets	Giants/Jets Stadium	2010	217	9,300
Oakland Raiders	McAfee Stadium	1966		
Philadelphia Eagles	Lincoln Financial Field	2003	172	10,828
Pittsburgh Steelers	Heinz Field	2001	129	7,300
Saint Louis Rams	Edward Jones Stadium	1995	124	6,500
San Francisco 49ers	Monster Park/Candlestick	1972/1995	93	0
Seattle Seahawks	Century Link Field	2000	111	7,000
Tampa Bay Buccaneers	Raymond James Stadium	1998	195	12,232
Tennessee Titans	LP Field	1999	175	11,800
Washington Redskins	Fed Ex Field	1997	280	15,044

(continued)

Table 1.4 (continued) Luxury seating at select facilities in North America

| | | | Number of… | |
Team	Facility	Year Opened/ Renovation	Suites	Club Seats
MLB Franchises				
Arizona Diamondbacks	Chase Field	1998	69	4,400
Atlanta Braves	Turner Field	1996	64	5,372
Baltimore Orioles	Oriole Park at Camden Yards	1992	72	4,631
Boston Red Sox	Fenway Park	1912/2008	80	1,871
Chicago Cubs	Wrigley Field	1914	67	None
Chicago White Sox	US Cellular Field	1991	84	N/A
Cincinnati Reds	Great American Ball Park	2003	57	2,276
Cleveland Indians	Progressive Field	1994	122	2,064
Colorado Rockies	Coors Field	1995	52	4,400
Detroit Tigers	Comerica Park	2000	108	2,000
Florida/Miami Marlins	Marlins Stadium[1]	2012	50	3,000
Houston Astros	Minute Maid Park	2000	62	5,000
Kansas City Royals	Kauffman Stadium	1973	19	2,487
Los Angeles Angels	Angel Stadium of Anaheim	1966	74	5,000

[1] Naming rights deal expected in 2011.

Los Angeles Dodgers	Dodger Stadium	1962	33	565
Milwaukee Brewers	Miller Park	2001	70	3,500
Minnesota Twins	Target Field	2010	60	3,400
New York Mets	Citi Field	2009	54	7,800
New York Yankees	Yankee Stadium	2009	47	4,374
Oakland Athletics	McAfee Stadium	1966	143	9,000
Philadelphia Phillies	Citizens Bank Park	2004	72	6,600
Pittsburgh Pirates	PNC Park	2001	65	3,374
St. Louis Cardinals	Busch Stadium	2006	63	3,600
San Diego Padres	PETCO Park	2004	58	5,000
San Francisco Giants	AT&T Park	2000	67	5,300
Seattle Mariners	SAFECO Field	1999	82	7,000
Tampa Bay Rays	Tropicana Field	1990	63	3,600
Texas Rangers	Rangers Ballpark in Arlington	1994	122	5,699
Toronto Blue Jays	Rogers Centre	1989	120	5,700
Washington Nationals	Nationals Park	2008	66	2,500

part of a more inclusive collective bargaining agreement (CBA), along with some combination of revenue sharing, luxury taxes on owner spending for players, salary caps, and salary floors. These policies play an integral part in determining player pay, small-market team profits, large-market team profits, and competitive balance. Therefore these issues are often very contentious and pit players against owners or even small-market owners versus large-market owners. Often one can tell the winners and losers of a policy by simply seeing who is for and against the policy. For example, the 2004–2005 NHL season was lost because the players did not want a salary cap and the owners did. In the end, the owners got their way. It is easy to understand why players' associations are typically against salary caps; few people would support a ceiling on how much they can earn. Salary cap policies are somewhat complicated as they not only divide the financial pie between owners and players, but they can grow or shrink total league revenues as well. Managers need to understand why and how a salary cap could lead to lower revenues for both owners and players. There are always short- and long-term implications to changes in the distribution of funds between players and owners. In the chapters that follow, we explain that it is possible that various policies can elevate revenues for both players and owners and agreements to "cap" players' salaries can lead to higher or lower league-wide revenues. In the case of the NHL, for example, it is possible the salary cap might help the players in the long run if it increases demand for the league by creating more parity. Even if this did happen, however, it might be a different group of players that benefit, and some players could actually be worse off.

There are interesting questions regarding all league policies. For example, how can a league devise a player draft so that teams do not want to lose games so they get high draft picks? Even though revenue sharing gives money to small-market teams, does the policy really help competitive balance? If a luxury tax does help competitive balance, is that necessarily good for the league? Under what conditions would owners be against a salary cap? The effects of the policies are not always as obvious as they may seem. For example, economic incentives given by revenue sharing are very different than what most fans believe. While revenue sharing might help the bottom line of small-market teams, that does not mean these teams will spend that money on players. Any financial manager of a team must fully understand the effects of all of these policies.

Managers and analysts have to think about the choices that teams and leagues make about their investment in talent, which, in turn, affects team quality or a team's winning percentage. Certainly shrewd front office leadership plays an important role as well as luck, but a team's payroll is certainly an important component. Like any good financial manager in any industry, teams will make an investment if it generates a positive return. Therefore, investments in players depend on demand for the product. If talent investment leads to winning and winning leads to more ticket and merchandise sales, then teams will invest heavily in talent. This same principle or expectation will be used to give you an overview of each policy and explain how the policies change the amount of revenue that teams and players receive.

Once it is understood how teams will respond to these policies, a league needs to decide what its goals are. For example, there seems to be a difference in philosophy between the NFL and MLB. In the NFL, most revenues are shared and there is a fairly strict or hard salary cap. This seems to imply that NFL owners believe the league will be best off if all teams are relatively similar, both on and off the field. The NFL does not want certain teams to dominate even though some have been more successful than others (e.g., New England Patriots, Dallas Cowboys, Indianapolis Colts, etc.) even with a salary cap. While MLB has some revenue sharing and luxury taxes, there is much more variance in team revenues. This implies that MLB owners believe team equality is not critical to league success. It might be in MLB's best interest to see some of their large-market teams win most of the time. As is often the case, it is difficult to know which philosophy is right. Many fans have a knee jerk reaction to say that more balance is needed. The NFL might be better off if larger-market teams won more often. There is also evidence that the NFL might be doing what is in their best interest while MLB is doing what is right for them. These are two different leagues with inherent differences. Ultimately the "optimal" league policies depend on things like fan reaction to different balance levels, market structures, and possibly the league's vision of fairness.

All major professional sports leagues have a player draft. The teams that finish with the fewest wins are the first to choose players. It would seem that this would help the smaller-market teams or the teams that typically finish poorly. That expectation is dependent on several assumptions. For example, does team quality completely depend on demand from fans? A team's quality does ultimately come from fan demand if teams are efficiently maximizing profits. If that is in fact the case, then the draft has very little effect on competitive balance. The draft will not help bad teams get better if owners in some markets are convinced they should not pay higher salaries to better players as their customers will not spend any more money for tickets if the team wins more games. If teams in the largest markets will ultimately attract and retain the best players, then a draft accomplishes little. A player draft, however, does decrease the pay of players in the short run. Why? A team that drafts a player has the rights to that player for a specific amount of time, eliminating the ability of the athlete to auction his/her services among competing franchises. The lack of an auction lowers salaries.

Teams and leagues also claim that revenue sharing increases balance, but that is not clear either. Revenue sharing means that teams share their income with other teams who cannot or do not earn as much. This means that on net, money will be going from larger-market teams to franchises in smaller markets where there is less wealth and less spending by fans on sports. This is why large-market owners rarely like revenue-sharing policies. Players often do not oppose revenue-sharing plans. Economic models, however, illustrate that it is the players who lose the most income when revenues are shared. Why? Since teams must give away part of their revenue, this reduces the incentive to earn more. That, in turn, reduces the incentive to invest in talent and leads to a disincentive for all teams to invest in players. Therefore, all teams will reduce their payrolls and possibly their investment in their stadium, depending on which revenue is shared. If all teams invest less in players, it is not clear that balance will improve. Again, it does seem clear that this will reduce player salaries since teams are investing less. The Pittsburgh Pirates are a perfect illustration of these deductions. In 2010, their financial documents were leaked to the public. Some fans and pundits were outraged because even though the Pirates were spending a minimal amount of money on player salaries, they were making a profit. Furthermore, they were making a profit because of MLB's revenue-sharing plan. It is easy for fans to ask, why aren't they spending that money on talent? The answer is simple. Spending the money from revenue sharing on player talent would probably cost the team more than they would earn in return through an increase in revenues. These and other issues are addressed in the chapters that follow to make you a knowledgeable manager.

Sports Finance and Management in Real Time

The extraordinary scale of these changes establishes the need for a book that unites the basic tool kit of skills required to understand sports finance with a far more exhaustive assessment of the management issues that can enhance the profitability of franchises or college sports (to assist in the funding of a college or university's complete athletic program). Along the way, various management "myths" need to be exposed as you acquire the understandings and skills needed to be a modern sports manager. This book seeks to accomplish these goals by providing you with the professionals skills needed to realize the economic and social benchmarks that define success and profitability. The changing face of sports finance and the management of its business affairs is probably best illustrated by the Boston Red Sox having a senior vice president for economic development, and the Baltimore Orioles having their own urban planner. The Mets have experts in real estate management throughout their organization, and media managers are now part of the operations of numerous teams that own part or all of their own networks. Two decades ago, expertise in these areas was unnecessary for the modern sports manager. Today those skills define success and profitability, and people with the needed skills are as integral to success as an eighth inning set-up man.

This book is designed to help you understand various aspects of the dynamic world of sports finance and management. Traditional topics, such as ticket pricing and player valuation, are covered, as are the tax implications of player depreciation. Added to the array of materials usually found in sports financing books are sections dealing with the complex web of team ownership arrangements, real estate development, entertainment, the media, and the Internet. Revenue-sharing models also are analyzed together with a complete analysis of the cross pressures created by the very different prices owners pay for their franchises and the revenue possibilities that exist in different market areas.

As each topic is explored and analyzed, the data are presented in the context of pricing or revenue-enhancement activities entered into by specific teams. In this manner, financing and management is joined together providing practical applications of theoretical arguments. For example, in looking at ticket pricing issues, the policies and practices of specific teams are considered to provide insight into the choices made with regard to maximizing revenue from a single source (ticket prices) or multiple sources that might result if attendance was maximized (lower ticket prices leading to higher attendance levels and more sales of food, beverages, and souvenirs, and, perhaps, higher viewership of televised games that yields more advertising dollars). Economists also have debated these issues and illustrated the tradeoffs through graphic representations. This volume looks at and analyzes management decisions made by different teams. The same strategy is employed to assess the outcomes from different decisions made regarding player payrolls and revenue levels.

References

Chapin, T. 2004. Sports facilities as urban redevelopment catalysts: Baltimore's Camden Yards and Cleveland's Gateway. *Journal of the American Planning Association* 70 (2): 193–209.

Hannigan, J. 1998. *Fantasy city: pleasure and profit in the postmodern metropolis.* New York: Routledge Press.

Hochberg, P. R. 1973. Second and goal to go: The legislative attack in the 92 nd Congress on sports broadcasting practices. *New York Law Forum* (180) 841–896.

Hyland, T. 2009. The big ten network: It's here to stay. *About.com Guide to College Football,* March 12 on-line edition, http://collegefootball.about.com/b/2009/03/12/the-big-ten-network-its-here-to-stay.htm (accessed September 23, 2009).

Levine, M. V. 2000. A third world city in the first world: Social exclusion, racial inequality, and sustainable development in Baltimore, Maryland. In *The social sustainability of cities: Diversity and the management of change,* eds. M. Polese and R. Stren, 123–156. Toronto: University of Toronto Press.

Newman, M. 2006. The neighborhood that the ballpark built. *The New York Times,* April 26 online edition, http://www/nytimes.com/2006/04/26/business/26ballpark.html (accessed April 17, 2011).

Rosentraub, M. S. 1999. *Major league losers: The real cost of sports and who's paying for it.* New York: Basic Books.

Rosentraub, M. S. 2010. *Major league winners: Using sports and cultural centers as tools for economic development.* Boca Raton, FL: CRC Press/Taylor and Francis.

Walker, D. 2009. The big ten network is alive and well. *Milwaukee Journal Sentinel,* September 23, on-line edition, http://www.jsonline.com/blogs/sports/40560627.html (accessed September 23, 2009).

Walter, T. 2010. Green Bay Packers have big plans for real estate surrounding Lambeau Field. *Green Bay Press Gazette,* July 25 on-line edition, http://www.greenbaypressgazette.com/article/20100725/GPG0101/100722122/Green-Bay-Packers-have-big-plans-for-real-estate-surrounding-Lambeau-Field (accessed January 23, 2011).

Chapter 2

The Structures of Ownership

Introduction

A central theme of this book is that three sets of business opportunities have dramatically changed the sports business. First of all, new, large-scale, and mixed-use real estate development projects have been anchored by sports facilities. Sports facilities attract large crowds. Their presence and, of course, the spending of money by fans creates development opportunities if facilities can be built adjacent to land that can be used for residential, retail, and commercial enterprises. In some areas, new urban neighborhoods have been built; in others, new entertainment zones have been created. Some of these real estate projects have involved several billion dollars in new construction. Even in the midst of the severe recession of the past few years, new real estate projects anchored by sports facilities were or are being contemplated in the New York City area (two projects in different parts of the region are being considered), Los Angeles, Northern California, Edmonton (Alberta), and in the province of Ontario.

Second, while the income that teams received from the telecasts of their games exploded in the 1960s and grew robustly for some leagues through the 1990s, the first years of the twenty-first century saw the birth of team and league-owned networks (e.g., YES [Yankee Entertainment and Sports Network], the Big 10 Network, the PAC 12 Network, etc.) and even more revenue opportunities. Just when some sports business leaders were worried that income from televising games had peaked, new summits were established even for teams in smaller markets (e.g., the Cleveland Indians and Sports Time Ohio). The continuing growth in the number of entertainment outlets (cable television stations and through the Internet) divided audience sizes. The only events, however, that continued to draw large audiences were sports-related, such as the World Cup, the Super Bowl, selected NCAA events, some World Series and NBA Finals games, and even some hockey contests. Annually these events set ratings records for larger and larger audiences. The advent of high definition (HD) and three-dimensional telecasts created huge markets as the enhanced imagery made games easier to follow and enjoy. The improved images attracted even more fans.

Third, in every market and in the building or remodeling of every venue, team owners sought to enhance and expand the game-day experience offered to fans. Through the inclusion of museums, halls of fame, children's play areas, games of skill (batting cages, football passing and baseball pitching machines, etc.), and other attractions, the time people spent at facilities increased, as did their in-house spending for these activities, souvenirs, food, and beverages. In addition, venues were being used for more and more events—sports and nonsports. This was hardly unique. The original Yankee Stadium, for example, had hosted boxing matches, college football games, and religious events for decades. The difference, then, was one of scale or the number events that could be held at sporting facilities. As a result, there was now an increased emphasis on facility designs with excellent views of the action for the primary team and the flexibility to ensure that myriad events, concerts, and meetings could be hosted. Owners did not want the saucer-like designs of the 1970s that failed to offer fans of baseball or football an excellent view of the action. Team owners wanted facilities like the one built by the Dallas Cowboys or the new stadium in the Meadowlands of New Jersey (home to the New York Giants and New York Jets). These billion-dollar structures permitted the team owners to offer fans an unprecedented view of games while also aggressively seeking a wide range of other sports and entertainment events. Some facilities are large enough that with temporary walls it becomes possible to host as many as four events with space for 20,000 attendees at each activity. The new Meadowlands facility hosted a number of concerts and sporting events before either the Giants or Jets had their first games in the 82,566-seat stadium.

These multipurpose ballparks and stadiums are fundamentally altering the landscape of the sports and entertainment business in their home regions. The Yankee ownership has renewed its interest in hosting college football games at the new stadium. The Cowboys host myriad events including what may become a season-ticket mix of college football games involving different teams in a set of four or five games each year. The Mets' new home, Citi Field, has also hosted concerts with the anticipation of attracting college football, college hockey, and professional hockey games to the new venue.

Teams, too, have been linked or merged into entertainment divisions of larger corporations. Palace Sports and Entertainment is one example. The anchor franchise or entertainment property of Palace Sports and Entertainment (PSE) is the

Detroit Pistons. The team's owner paid for the Palace at Auburn Hills ,
privately owned venue, the team owner alone pays for all maintenance). The a┌
hosts all types of entertainment and sporting events. PSE also owns an outdoor
concert venue. The list of teams that are anchors in large entertainment corporations includes the Detroit Red Wings and Detroit Tigers (Olympia Entertainment
(OE)), the New York Knicks and New York Rangers (Madison Square Garden
(MSG) Corporation), and the Los Angeles Kings and Los Angeles Lakers (whose
owners built LA LIVE, a multibillion-dollar entertainment complex across from
the teams' home, the STAPLES Center, which is an integral part of the new entertainment, commercial, and residential district.

These new business opportunities for team owners led to changes in the organizational and management structure of their corporations that included their sports
franchises. Teams now routinely had managers (or several vice presidents) responsible for real estate development and management, media and network operations,
Internet and web-based applications (linked to their individual leagues), and entertainment (attracting and managing other events). These divisions were in addition
to the usual mix of media and marketing specialists and the staff responsible for
player development and the team itself. If a team's ownership was not involved in
real estate, media, and entertainment, those critical revenue streams were lost. In
some instances, the team was one of several different entertainment divisions within
a larger holding company, such as PSE, OE, MSG, or the Anshutz Entertainment
Group (AEG) that owns LA LIVE. Those franchise owners with interests in all of
these different entertainment and real estate activities quickly saw the value of their
teams escalate. Before providing an in-depth exploration of the resulting ownership patterns created by these opportunities, it is necessary to look at the history of
ownership to appreciate its evolution and changes.

The Emergence of Team Sports and Profitable Markets

A market for spectator sports began in the decades after the Civil War and then
dramatically expanded in the first years of the twentieth century. Three factors
helped to drive the demand. First, the increasing number of large cities created
viable market sizes to support speculative investments in new emerging businesses,
such as entertainment or spectator sports. Second, the increasing wealth of industrial workers produced a level of "discretionary" income that could be spent on
pastimes like entertainment, which soon included team sports. Third, coinciding
with rising levels of wealth was an increase in free or available time for workers to
enjoy their slowly increasing wages. The industrial workweek began to shrink to six
days, and then five and a half days, and finally to the more standard five days that
many enjoy today. The emergence of days or time off, holidays, and weekends created hours that could be filled with entertainment.

The demand for sports and other forms of entertainment attracted the interest of investors and some of these entrepreneurs became the first owners of professional sports teams. Professional sports were similar to many of the entertainment businesses starting at this time (e.g., amusement parks, theaters for live entertainment, etc.) and were fraught with risk. Many failed as investors experimented with different ownership models and business practices. As with any emerging industry, successes followed failure until sustainable business models emerged (a league structure with defined market areas for each franchise would become the model for success in professional team sports). The franchises created by each league would eventually settle into the largest and fastest-growing cities and, once those "shake outs" concluded, sustained profitability and stability resulted. In the course of this evolution, some cities that dreamed of hosting major league teams had market sizes that could not generate sufficient revenues to ensure profitability. As a result, relocations from smaller to larger markets were relatively common, especially when team owners decided to initially launch their enterprises outside of the largest cities. For example, Fort Wayne, Indiana was the location for one of the teams in the initial years of the NBA. In the 1950s, the team's owner, Fred Zollner, decided to move the Zollner Pistons to Detroit. Syracuse, another early home to an NBA team, was abandoned for Philadelphia (Warriors). In several instances where competitive leagues formed and then merged, two teams existed in the same market. Over time, the number of markets with more than one team in the same sport would decline as franchise owners would decide that a smaller city or regional market without a team was a better home than a larger market with two teams. The Boston Braves would leave the Red Sox as the only baseball team in New England. That franchise moved to Milwaukee before relocating to Atlanta. The Chicago Cardinals of the NFL left the Chicago market to the Bears and for decades called St. Louis home. When the Cardinals' owner could not find a stadium deal to his liking, he relocated the team to the Phoenix metropolitan area. In the early days of the American Football League (AFL), the Los Angeles Chargers moved south to San Diego (leaving the Rams in Los Angeles until they too relocated). The Dallas Texans relocated to Kansas City (as the Chiefs) ceding the Dallas/Fort Worth area to the NFL's Cowboys.

While entrepreneurs experimented with different ways to organize the business of professional team sports, it is important to keep in mind the social changes taking place in the country during this period (1870–1920). It was these changes that created a market (with fans as ticket-buying consumers, professional athletes as paid labor, and entrepreneurs as team owners) for what was essentially a new *commercial* product for North America and Western Europe—team sports. Spectator sports, of course, have existed for centuries. Most of the games or athletic events that preceded the late nineteenth century involved individuals competing against each other. The original Olympics featured individual athletic events and not team sports. The gladiatorial games that were held across the Roman Empire also were dominated by events involving individuals fighting against each other. Chariot racing was popular for centuries, but while there were teams of horses, there was but a single driver. There is some evidence that team sports were part of the life of North, Central, and South American native populations, but it is not clear if those forms of athletic competitions involved spectators as paying customers. Team sports, as they are practiced today, are a product of the nineteenth century and the changes wrought by industrialization and urbanization (Mandelbaum, 2004).

What drove an interest or focus on the development of team sports?

First, many tie the invention, development, or codification of team sports in the nineteenth century to the need to train people and focus society on the importance and success from coordinated activities among groups of people. Prior to the industrial age, economic activity largely involved individuals working alone (agriculture) or small-scale activities with just a few workers. The industrial revolution created the factory and the need for coordinated activities among large groups of workers. Team sports mirrored the need for coordinated activity and the success (or profitability) that only occurs when each individual coordinates his or her actions and activities with others. Successful economic development was a function of teams of workers united in pursuit of high-quality products that were efficiently manufactured. Winning team efforts in baseball, basketball, cricket, football, hockey, and soccer required groups of individuals performing their roles and executing their work in a timely (clutch) manner. Throughout the twentieth and twenty-first centuries, sports metaphors became integral parts of workday life and normal conversations (hit a home run, cross the goal line, a "Hail Mary" pass, It's the ninth inning, etc.). Through language and the accomplishments of teams organized for sports or business, there was soon an inexorable link between the world of work and athletic competitions on the court, field, pitch, or rink.

Second, the nineteenth and twentieth centuries also saw a rapid growth in the number of cities with large population bases. This meant there were now a sufficient number of people capable of supporting amusement and entertainment businesses. Finding large enough markets to support sports and entertainment in rural areas where population densities were far lower was a daunting task. As is to be expected, in these larger and denser population centers, there were sufficient numbers of people living in close proximity to places where venues could be built. As these larger population groups acquired sufficient discretionary income to afford some form of entertainment, entrepreneurs rushed different products to the emerging marketplaces. Large population densities (as compared to rural areas) also reduce the costs for spectators to get to the locations where games are played. Facilities were sometimes within walking distance of places of work and residential communities (e.g., Fenway Park, Wrigley Field, etc.) or at the nexus of transportation lines.

The expanding number of population centers provided markets of scale, and team owners had confidence that within these larger population centers there were sufficient numbers of people interested in spectator sports. For example, at the outbreak of the Civil War, only New York had more than a million residents (when Brooklyn, an independent city at the time, is included in the count). Philadelphia with 565,529 residents was the second largest city and Chicago was a rather small community of less than 113,000 residents, but still the country's ninth largest city. In 1890, there were 19 different urban areas of 100,000 or more residents, and, by 1910, New York had more than 4 million residents. In that same year, three other urban centers had more than 1.6 million residents. A total of 50 urban regions had more than 100,000 residents and, by 1920, a dozen urban areas had more than half a million residents. America had become an urbanizing society with large markets that had the potential to support several different forms of entertainment.

Third, the wealth of these new urban residents was steadily increasing and, by the advent of the twentieth century there was a sufficient population base with a robust enough level of income to afford a modest amount of discretionary spending for entertainment. It is difficult to find accurate data on household income prior to the 1930s and surveys of consumer spending were not undertaken until the post-World War II decades. To be sure, workers' salaries at the turn of the twentieth century were quite modest by today's standards. In addition, most of the money earned by families had to be spent for the necessities of life (housing, food, healthcare, and education). There are data, however, that indicate that more and more wealth was being produced, increasing the likelihood of some funds being available for discretionary spending. In 1860, before the Civil War began, U.S. businesses exported $333.6 million in goods (as tabulated by the U.S. Department of Commerce). In 1880, the figure was $835.6 million and by 1900 more than $1.3 billion in exports was produced by U.S. businesses. To be sure, entrepreneurs retained more of the profits than did workers, but these data, combined with the growing number of people attracted to cities, illustrate there was a growing base of wealth. The emergence of a middle class with some level of discretionary income was beginning and factory workers who likely earned even less also began to have a small amount of money available for leisure-time entertainment. The growth in the number of teams, leagues, and other entertainment options during this time period also attest to the increasing levels of discretionary spending in America's growing urban centers (Hannigan, 1998).

The increasing prosperity of the country, the growth of cities across the continent, and a wave of invention and manufacturing techniques that led to the creation and availability of new products (e.g., light bulbs, kitchen appliances, automobiles, airplanes, etc.) created a sense of optimism and a feeling that the future would be even brighter. That optimism contributed to a growing economy. As illustrated in Figure 2.1, personal consumption would soar into the trillions in the 1970s and continued to grow through 2009.

Sports were not the only form of entertainment attracting the interest of entrepreneurs. At the same time that professional teams and leagues were emerging, burlesque was attracting crowds to small theaters in America's cities and the "nickelodeon" was offering movies for a small price (one penny and up to a nickel). The growing popularity of nickelodeons and then theaters that showed movies attracted the interest of a commercial artist in Kansas City. That artist, Walt Disney, began his journey that led to the redefining of both the entertainment and sports industries (Hannigan, 1998; Gottdiener, 2001; Gabler, 2007). All of these new forms

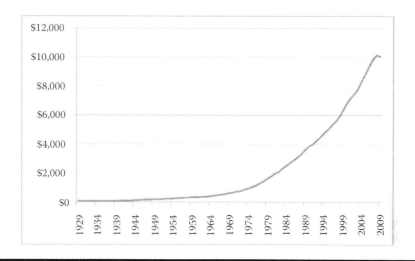

Figure 2.1   Personal consumption expenditures by year, 1929–2009 (in billions of dollars). (From author's calculations using U.S. Department of Commerce data.)

of entertainment competed with each other for consumers' attention and dollars. In latter years, there would be an interesting merging of sports and entertainment into single, larger business syndicates. The competition with other forms of entertainment, however, would be a persistent issue especially in the latter parts of the twentieth century as many smaller metropolitan areas sought to add some level of professional sports to their regional list of amenities. An oversupply of event days and forms of entertainment (including college-level sports) would lead to financial problems for teams in Columbus (Ohio), Indianapolis, Jacksonville, Miami, metropolitan Phoenix, and Tampa/St. Petersburg.

Fourth, there was growing support for sports as it began to assume a large and vital role as a socializing institution promoting stability. How did or does sport fulfill a role as a socializing institution promoting stability? This is accomplished in several ways. With its emphasis on performance and skill, sport creates an environment that demonstrates that success has an egalitarian dimension. Anyone can be successful if they have the right sets of skills regardless of class or status. This underscores an element vital to the long-term acceptance of the organization of a capitalist society. To be sure, for long periods of time, discriminatory practices reduced this democratic function, but across the decades these have been overcome and sports has been an avenue for economic success for many members of different ethnic and racial groups. For too many years, the democratic function of sport was reserved only for white males, but that continues to dissipate and certainly in the current time period many different minorities have achieved levels of success underscoring the democratic nature of the capitalist aspect of sport and Western civilization.

Sports also underscore the importance and need for rules to govern affairs, and through the behavior of players and the role played by umpires or referees, an adherence to rules and a demonstration of respect for authority is shown. In the nine-teenth century, government and community leaders looked to the rules established by leagues as a tool to reduce violence (what behavior or contact between players is acceptable and what is not) and an illustration of how games (and life) are to be played. The growing popularity of soccer in Europe, for example, was at first subject to disdain from governments as the game was quite brutal and played without ref-erees or structured rules. Rules and officials were seen as unnecessary to regulate a game played by "gentlemen." Gentlemen recognized infractions and would admit to their occurrence and allow the other team to offset any disadvantage resulting from a foul. When the game became popular among the working class, violence was rife and the establishment of rules and penalties not only made the game more civilized, but provided lessons on the extent of physical confrontation that would be tolerated and behaviors that would result in penalties. These lessons and the value of team-work fit well into the emerging factory life that also required adherence to rules and cooperation with others to reach the desired goal. The umpire and referee in America provided vivid examples and underscored the need and value of rules.

In both North America and Western Europe there also was interest in creating fac-tory and community teams as diversions from the dreariness of manufacturing jobs. In the absence of these diversions, it was feared political or social protest could result or workers could become less productive (McIntosh, 1971; Riess, 1980; Thompson, 1981). These many positive outcomes from sports meant that community leaders were eager to sustain team operations even when public support and subsidies were required.

The role of sports in maintaining and advancing social control and stability meant that governments were often eager to ensure that teams enjoyed a special status or were treated differently than other forms of business. In the United States, there was a critical U.S. Supreme Court decision that allowed MLB to function for decades as monopoly-protected from market forces. At the collegiate level, the National Collegiate Athletic Association (NCAA) was established in response to President Theodore Roosevelt's threat to intervene if violence and injuries in foot-ball were not reduced. While the U.S. Supreme Court decision did not specifically deal with or mention social control, the majority opinion underscored that base-ball had a special societal role that exempted it from antitrust laws. For decades Congress never saw fit to change that status.

Ownership and Expansion: From Individual Entrepreneurs to Large-Scale Entertainment, Real Estate, and Media Firms

An excellent history of the ownership of professional sports teams in North America is contained in an appendix to Quirk and Fort's *Pay Dirt: The Business of Professional Team Sports* (1992). There are several key points to understand or take away from a reading of the entertaining history of the humble beginnings of what became the mega-billion-dollar sports leagues of the twenty-first century. First, sports teams in the United States were created in the decades after the Civil War (the post-reconstruction period) and the decades before and after the advent of the twentieth century. The initial owners were usually individual entrepreneurs or partnerships that often merged into syndicates (or groups of individuals who owned the teams). This strategy, still emulated in many instances today, spread the risks of ownership across many people while ensuring there were many "deep pockets" to reach into if cash-flow problems emerged. As teams became successful, they were sometimes sold from one group to another as some investors wanted to capitalize on the possible returns. For example, a Baltimore baseball franchise was sold in the 1890s for $40,000 (or more than $998,000 in today's dollars). In 1909, the Phillies were sold for $350,000 or about $8.7 million today. The value of sports franchises was rapidly escalating in the nation's largest markets. What must have appeared as a princely sum for a baseball team was shattered by the $500,000 paid in 1915 for the Cubs. Then in 1919, the Boston Braves were sold for $400,000 (more than $8.8 million in constant dollars). Most revealing in terms of the value of sports franchises in the early part of the twentieth century was the $1,092,000 sale price of the New York Giants in 1919 ($14 million in today's dollars). Buying and selling teams is not a phenomenon of the late twentieth or early twenty-first century. Ownership groups have been capitalizing on the rising popularity of sports and the value or desirability of ownership for at least 120 years.

The sales of teams among and between groups of partners, syndicates, and individuals frequently involved people focused on making money from sports, and the games themselves were the principal business activity. In this regard, the teams or the business of sports was not integrated into other enterprises. Augie Busch changed that a bit when he joined the St. Louis Cardinals to his brewing company. To be sure food and beverages were sold at games, but the principle business activity was sports. Beer companies advertised at different ballparks and stadiums, and those individuals who were involved in the distribution of beer or other staples sold at sporting events may well have been part of any number of the partnerships that formed to acquire a team.

During the early years, valuable lessons also were learned that formed the policies still used by the leagues today. In the early years, some individuals owned more than one team in the same league. When this occurred, players were moved to maximize revenue gains and the best players were placed in the larger markets. Some might argue that this continues to occur today through free agency and trades. Limiting individuals to ownership of one team in a particular sport, however, created the impression (or cynics would argue the illusion) that each owner tries as best as he/she can to win as many games as possible or to build a competitive team. The owners in each league looking at the possibility of one individual owning more than one team concluded that ownership would be restricted to one team. Later in this chapter, we will look at the collective ownership models. In that organizational structure, all of the teams are owned jointly through the sale of shares in the league. That is a model that was rejected by those owning teams in MLB, the NFL, the NBA, and the NHL. In part, of course, those who own teams in the largest markets would be reluctant to trade a share of their ownership to those with teams in smaller markets.

Every franchise owner had to agree to respect the territorial market of every other team. In practical terms, this has meant that each owner agrees not to relocate their team into the metropolitan region where other teams play. In formalistic terms, the exclusive market area has been defined as a 35- to 75-mile radius from each team's home facility (distances vary by league). Al Davis and the Los Angeles County Commission challenged this agreement as being in violation of U.S. antitrust laws and were successful in their effort to move the Oakland Raiders to Los Angeles after the Rams had moved from downtown Los Angeles to suburban Anaheim (Orange County, adjacent to Los Angeles County). Their success is a case of the exception proving the rule. No other owner has ever tried to move into an area with another team without the concurrence of fellow owners. (Another exception is the potential building of a new ballpark for the Oakland Athletics in San Jose. The San Francisco Giants may likely oppose that move as they considered San Jose to be within the market area granted to them by MLB when they considered a move to the city from San Francisco.) Other moves into market areas considered to be part of another team's territory have been adjudicated by the leagues' commissioners.

Next, to reduce the threat of competition from start-up leagues, franchise holders agreed that their teams would only play games against league members. Each league has been challenged by competitors and, in several instances, the more successful "upstarts" merged with the existing league, or some teams were absorbed and the other owners in the newer leagues agreed to compensation to fold their franchises. The National League and American League merged to form MLB; the National Football League (NFL) merged with the American Football League (AFL) in the 1960s; the NBA also absorbed some American Basketball Association teams, and the NHL admitted some teams from the World Hockey League. Some American Basketball Association and World Hockey League franchises folded and their players were dispersed among the existing teams through drafts.

Expansion has been pursued very, very slowly by established leagues. In some instances the unwillingness to move quickly to place new franchises in growing regions created openings for competitors. The American League was able to establish a secure foothold with teams in Chicago (National League had a team in this city), Cleveland, Detroit, and New York City (even when the National League had two teams in that city) that eventually forced the more established league to merge or face spiraling costs for players. The merger of the NFL with the American Football League in 1966 was a direct result of the new league's ability to sign premier players and the fear among owners in both leagues that rising playing costs would lead to diminished profits. The fear of rising playing costs prompted the NBA to admit a few more teams to its league in exchange for the dissolution of the American Basketball Association. The Denver Nuggets,

Indiana Pacers, New Jersey Nets, and San Antonio Spurs joined the NBA and compensation was provided to the owners of other franchises. The NHL absorbed the Edmonton Oilers, Hartford Whalers, Quebec Nordiques, and Winnipeg Jets from the World Hockey Association (WHA); other franchises in that league were terminated and their owners also received compensation. The Quebec franchise is now the Colorado Avalanche, the Winnipeg Jets are the Phoenix Coyotes, and the Hartford Whalers are the Carolina Hurricanes. Ironically, the financial problems confronting several NHL teams in southern U.S. cities has made it far more likely that NHL franchises will return to one or two of the Canadian cities that lost teams when the WHA terminated operations or when teams in the NHL moved. The financial problems could well stem from the inability of the sport to build a sufficiently large fan base in warmer areas.

The reluctance to expand is rooted in the very small additional fiscal returns to existing owners when a new team is added. Why? Adding a new team means that existing owners' portion of shared revenues declines. Suppose a league has 30 members and earns $100 million dollars from its national media contract. Prior to adding a 31st team, each franchise, received $3,333,333. The existence of a 31st team reduces that share to $3,225,806. To offset this loss of more than $100,000, the existing team owners will charge a franchise fee that, in essence, represents their assessment of the present value of the future shared revenues the new team owner will receive. That fee has to be larger than the present value of the foregone revenues. Even if a new market generates sufficient returns to attract investors who can pay the franchise fee, that fee has to be very large for each existing owner to realize revenues substantially larger than what would be received if the expansion did not take place. Indeed, it might be that expansion is only desirable if (1) competition for players is reduced as when another league ceases operations or (2) the creation of a new team thwarts a legal or political challenge to a league's ability to control the supply of franchises. That threat was sufficient when Ohio's Congressional delegation sponsored legislation seeking to ensure that the NFL grant Cleveland a new franchise after Art Modell decided to relocate his franchise to Baltimore. That legislation, if it ever became law, could have resulted in the reestablishment of a new American Football League as a separate entity to ensure that there was competition for new markets.

The loss of shared revenues is rarely offset by new income for other owners from the mere presence of another team. Each league already has teams in the largest and most viable markets. Through national media contracts, games are already delivered to every market area and revenue from the media partners already takes into account the viewership in every market area. Some have argued that if the NFL places a team (or two) in Los Angeles viewership could increase. And given the size of the Los Angeles market, added viewers would be substantial. The NFL's media partners, however, deliver each week a set of competitive games in the Los Angeles market and whether or not new fans will be created is an unresolved research issue. As a result, a new team could produce very little, and in some instances, no new revenue for existing franchises. Without the threat of a competitive league forming because of an underserved market or markets, there really is no incentive for owners to add additional teams. Further, those teams in smaller markets who are trying to secure favorable investments from the public sector in new arenas do not want expansion teams to exist. Having a few markets without a team gives those owners a viable relocation option to use in their negotiations for local governments to invest tax money in new facilities.

The absence of a franchise in Los Angeles has been an important asset for some NFL owners. The lack of a franchise in this large market provides owners of teams in other market areas with an attractive bargaining chip when trying to secure financial and political support for a new stadium. Currently four teams are seeking new facilities, and three of them are in California: the Oakland Raiders, the San Diego Chargers, and the San Francisco 49ers; the fourth team is the Minnesota Vikings. While the legal and political issues associated with relocation makes it difficult for teams to move, it is not impossible as demonstrated by Al Davis and the Oakland Raiders and several other teams (Houston Oilers, Los Angeles Rams, etc.) Given that new stadiums have still not been built for the Raiders or Chargers (as this book was being prepared, new facilities for the Vikings and 49ers appeared likely) there is some usefulness to having the Los Angeles "card" in play. There is also one NFL team, the Jacksonville Jaguars, that has struggled with attendance especially as the economy in Florida has floundered in the aftermath of the recent severe recession. The remote possibility that the team could or would relocate has convinced leadership in several North Florida communities to convince fans to support the team.

NFL owners likely remain skeptical that a Los Angeles franchise would add revenues. The league's broadcast partners televise two to three games in the Los Angeles market each Sunday. All national broadcasts (Monday, Thursday, and Sunday evenings) are also available. Would a local team increase viewership and, therefore, persuade the league's broadcast partners to pay more for television rights? To secure that potential gain, the owners would have to expand the number of teams sharing in pooled revenues by one. As a result, the lack of clarity that additional revenues would be generated has been at the forefront of the lack of urgency to expand into the Los Angeles market. The wealth in the region, however, will make the team profitable and that is why a hefty expansion fee will be asked for by the league and paid by some investors.

The NFL's last expansion was in 2002 when the Houston Texans began play. The NFL returned to Cleveland in 1999 and the Jacksonville Jaguars and Charlotte Panthers began play in 1995. The Tampa Bay Devil Rays and the Arizona Diamondbacks, the last teams added by MLB, began play in 1998. Five years earlier, the Colorado Rockies and the Florida Marlins joined the league. The Washington Nationals relocated from Montreal (Expos) in 2005. The NBA last added teams in 1995 (the Toronto Raptors and Vancouver Grizzlies). The Vancouver franchise relocated to Memphis and then, in 2009, the Seattle Supersonics moved to Oklahoma City. The NHL went through a period of rapid expansion in the 1990s and then added the Columbus Blue Jackets and Minnesota Wild for the 2000 season. The gregarious expansion may have been too aggressive. In 2009, the Phoenix Coyotes (a former World Hockey League team that had relocated from Winnipeg (nee Jets)) declared bankruptcy. The franchises in Atlanta, Columbus, South Florida, Nashville, and North Carolina were each reportedly losing money or facing severe financial challenges that threatened their long-term operations in their current markets. There are now 30 teams in MLB, the NBA, and the NHL. There are 32 NFL franchises and there appears to be little substantial interest from any of the leagues in expanding within the United States. The only exception may well be the NFL that continues to look at the opportunity in the Los Angeles region. MLB floated the idea of contracting or eliminating one or two franchises in years past, but that threat or proposal was never widely supported. The NHL, however, may well have to consider relocation of some of the franchises encountering financial stress if local fan support in several southern markets does not increase. Ironically, LeBron James' decision to play for the Miami Heat could reduce fan interest in the NHL's Florida Panthers and weaken their already deteriorating financial position. It is likely another team that anchored the NHL's southern strategy will join Atlanta's Thrashers that are now the Winnipeg Jets.

Ownership Patterns Today

To help explore the structure and changing patterns of ownership, Table 2.1 identifies the majority owners of each franchise from the four major sports leagues and their principal business (source of wealth generated to acquire the team or the related businesses developed with the team as the anchor). In only a few instances is the principal business interest "sports," which means the team itself and its direct operations alone are the central business of the owner. There are a few teams that were initially purchased to be the main or sole business interest and some of these owners have expanded into the real estate, media, or entertainment businesses. For example, George Steinbrenner essentially focused almost entirely on the Yankees and, with his passing, his sons now operate the team. The family, as noted, owns 34 percent of the highly successful YES television network. The Yankees, therefore, are focused on sports and media. The Rooney family founded the Pittsburgh Steelers, and descendants still retain control; this ownership family has not created a television network. The far more common outcome is for owners who have accumulated wealth from other enterprises to add a team to their holdings. The shift to teams as part of real estate development efforts, entertainment corporations, or media corporations is vividly illustrated in Table 2.1. It is easier to understand or appreciate this shift against a backdrop of the types of ownership structures that existed prior to the changes in the sports business. We turn to those next before refocusing on the role of teams in real estate development, entertainment, and the media in subsequent chapters.

Table 2.1   Team owners and related business interests

League/Franchise	Majority Owner	Related Business Interest/ Source of Wealth
Major League Baseball		
AZ Diamondbacks	Ken Kendrick	Software, education, banking
Atlanta Braves	Liberty Media	Media
Baltimore Orioles	Peter Angelos	Law
Boston Red Sox	John Henry	Sports, entertainment
Chicago Cubs	Ricketts family	Financial services
Chicago White Sox	Jerry Reinsdorf	Real estate and sports franchises
Cincinnati Reds	Robert Castellini	Food services
Cleveland Indians	Lawrence Dolan	Cable television
Colorado Rockies	C. & R. Monfort	Food services
Detroit Tigers	Michael Ilitch	Sports, entertainment, food services
Florida Marlins	Jeffrey Loria	Sports, new real estate project
Houston Astros	R. D. McLane Jr.	Retail
Kansas City Royals	David Glass	Retail
Los Angeles Angels	Arturo Moreno	Billboards, real estate
Los Angeles Dodgers	Frank McCourt[1]	Real estate
Milwaukee Brewers	Mark Attansio	Financial services
Minnesota Twins	James Pohlad	Mixed business conglomerate
New York Mets	Wilpon family	Real estate
New York Yankees	Steinbrenner family	Sports, media
Oakland Athletics	L. Wolff and J. Fisher	Retail
Philadelphia Phillies	D. Montgomery	Sports, syndicate
Pittsburgh Pirates	Robert Nutting	Media and resorts
San Diego Padres	Jeff Moorad	Sports
San Francisco Giants	William Neukom	Law

[1] Filed for bankruptcy in June 2011.

Table 2.1 (continued)   Team owners and related business interests

League/Franchise	Majority Owner	Related Business Interest/ Source of Wealth
Seattle Mariners	Hiroshi Yamauchi	Nintendo
St. Louis Cardinals	William DeWitt Jr.	Sports, real estate
Tampa Bay Rays	Stuart Sternberg	Financial services
Texas Rangers	Nolan Ryan	Sports
Toronto Blue Jays	Rogers Communication	Media
Washington Nationals	Theodore Lerner	Real estate, entertainment, media
National Football League		
Arizona Cardinals	William Bidwell	Sports
Atlanta Falcons	Arthur Blank	Retail, sports
Baltimore Ravens	Stephen Bisciotti	Business services
Buffalo Bills	Ralph Wilson Jr.	Sports, syndicate
Carolina Panthers	Jerry Richardson	Food services
Chicago Bears	McCaskey family	Sports
Cincinnati Bengals	Michael Brown	Sports
Cleveland Browns	Randolph Lerner	Financial services
Dallas Cowboys	Jerral Jones	Oil, sports, entertainment
Denver Broncos	Patrick Bowlen	Oil, sports
Detroit Lions	William Clay Ford	Automobile
Green Bay Packers	Shareholder owned	Public with vested control
Houston Texas	Robert McNair	Energy
Indianapolis Colts	James Irsay	Sports
Jacksonville Jaguars	Wayne Weaver	Retail
Kansas City Chiefs	Lamar Hunt family	Oil, sports
Miami Dolphins	Stephen Ross	Real estate

(continued)

Table 2.1 (continued)   Team owners and related business interests

League/Franchise	Majority Owner	Related Business Interest/ Source of Wealth
Minnesota Vikings	Zygmunt Wilf	Real estate
New England Patriots	Robert Kraft	Business conglomerate
New Orleans Saints	Thomas Benson	Financial services
New York Giants	J. Mara and S. Tisch	Entertainment
New York Jets	R. W. Johnson	Pharmaceuticals
Oakland Raiders	Al Davis	Sports
Philadelphia Eagles	Jeffery Lurie	Entertainment
Pittsburgh Steelers	Art Rooney	Sports
San Diego Chargers	Alexander Spanos	Real estate
San Francisco 49ers	D. DeBartolo York	Retail/shopping malls
Seattle Seahawks	Paul Allen	Computer software
St. Louis Rams	S. Rosenbloom and S. Kroenke	Sports, real estate, business syndicate
Tampa Bay Buccaneers	Malcolm Glazer	Business syndicate
Tennessee Titans	Kenneth Adams Jr.	Energy, ranching, real estate
Washington Redskins	Daniel Snyder	Advertising
National Basketball Association		
Atlanta Hawks	Atlanta Spirit	Sports
Boston Celtics	Wycliffe Grousbeck	Financial services, medical information
Charlotte Bobcats	Michael Jordan	Sports
Chicago Bulls	Jerry Reinsdorf	Real estate and sports franchises
Cleveland Cavaliers	Dan Gilbert	Financial services
Dallas Mavericks	Mark Cuban	Information technology
Denver Nuggets	Stanley Kroenke	Real estate, business syndicate, media
Detroit Pistons	Karen Davidson	Manufacturing
Golden State Warriors	Chris Cohan	Cable television

Table 2.1 (continued)   Team owners and related business interests

League/Franchise	Majority Owner	Related Business Interest/ Source of Wealth
Indiana Pacers	Herbert Simon	Shopping malls, real estate
Houston Rockets	Leslie Alexander	Financial services
Los Angeles Clippers	Donald Sterling	Law, real estate
Los Angeles Lakers	J. Buss and P. Anschutz	Sports, real estate, media, entertainment
Memphis Grizzlies	Michael Heisley	Business syndicate
Miami Heat	Micky Arison	Tourism
Milwaukee Bucks	Herbert Kohl	Retail
Minnesota Timberwolves	Glen Taylor	Manufacturing
New Jersey Nets	Mikhail Prokhorov	Oil & gas
New Orleans Hornets	Sale to new owner in process	
New York Knicks	Dolan Family	Cable television
Oklahoma City Thunder	Clayton Bennet	Oil, financial services
Orlando Magic	Richard Devos	Retail sales
Philadelphia 76ers	Comcast Spectacor[1]	Media
Phoenix Suns	Robert Sarver	Banking, real estate
Portland Trailblazers	Paul Allen	Software
Sacramento Kings	Gavin and Joseph Maloof	Sports, gaming
San Antonio Spurs	Peter Holt	Manufacturing
Toronto Raptors	Pension Plan	Financial services
Utah Jazz	Miller family	Auto dealerships, media
Washington Wizards	Ted Leonsis	Software
National Hockey League		
Anaheim Ducks	H. & S. Samueli	Communication equipment

[1] Comcast/Spectacor has agreed to sell the team to a consortium led by financier Joshua Harris

(continued)

Table 2.1 (continued)   Team owners and related business interests

League/Franchise	Majority Owner	Related Business Interest/ Source of Wealth
Atlanta Thrashers	Atlanta Spirit (9 partners)	Various
Boston Bruins	Jeremy Jacobs	Sports, entertainment
Buffalo Sabres	Thomas Golisano	Computer services
Calgary Flames	Calgary Flames LP	Sports
Carolina Hurricanes	Peter Karmanos Jr.	Software, computer sales
Chicago Blackhawks	William Wirtz	Food services, real estate, banking
Colorado Avalanche	Stan Kroenke	Real estate, sports, media
Columbus Blue Jackets	John P. McConnell	Manufacturing
Dallas Stars	Thomas Hicks[1]	Financial services
Detroit Red Wings	M. & M. Illitch	Food services, entertainment
Edmonton Oilers	Daryl Katz	Pharmaceutical sales, real estate
Florida Panthers	Alan Cohen	Pharmaceuticals
Los Angeles Kings	Phil Anschutz/AEG	Entertainment, real estate
Minnesota Wild	C. Leipold and P. Falcone	Financial services
Montreal Canadiens	Geoff Molson	Food services
Nashville Predators	David Freeman	Medical services
New Jersey Devils	Jeffrey Vanderbeek	Financial services
New York Islanders	Charles Wang	Computer services
New York Rangers	James Dolan/MSC L.P.	Media, entertainment
Ottawa Senators	Eugene Melnyk	Pharmaceuticals
Philadelphia Flyers	Comcast Spectacor	Media
Phoenix Coyotes	League owned[2]	In bankruptcy

[1] Sale in process.
[2] League seeking a buyer.

Table 2.1 (continued)   Team owners and related business interests

League/Franchise	Majority Owner	Related Business Interest/ Source of Wealth
Pittsburgh Penguins	M. Lemieux and R. Burkle	Retail, manufacturing, sports
San Jose Sharks	K. Vompton and G. Jamison	Sports
St. Louis Blues	David Checketts	Media, sports, entertainment
Tampa Bay Lightning	Jeff Vinik	Financial services
Toronto Maple Leafs	Ontario Teachers' Pension Plan[1]/ Larry Tanenbaum	Pension fund
Vancouver Canucks	Francesco Aquillini	Real estate development
Washington Capitals	Theodore Leonsis	Computing services

[1] In May 2011, it was disclosed that the Ontario Teachers' Pension Plan was in discussions to sell its ownership to TD Capital.

Ownership Structures

The three most common forms of business ownership structures are sole proprietorships, partnerships, or corporations. While the sports industry has many examples of these three types, sport is somewhat unique in that it also has other types of structures. Because of sports' public nature, communities also own sports teams, but this is limited to the minor leagues. The Green Bay Packers have a unique structure, but there is no public ownership in the sense that a city owns that team. There also have been instances where shares have been sold in some teams, but when that has happened in North America, shareholders have not had substantial voting roles in team operations. Furthermore, numerous universities "own" teams whose gross revenues rival those of professional franchises, and college sports have emerged with their own unique ownership structure that also needs discussion. The sports industry has become an impressive laboratory in which to study different and unique business ownership structures.

Sole Proprietorship

A sole proprietorship is simply when one individual owns a team. There are many individuals who own teams and, thus, are sole proprietors. Far more common, however, are arrangements when a dominant majority partner functions like a sole proprietor, but actually has rather silent minority owners who have made important financial investments in the team. There are many advantages to a sole proprietorship including low organizational costs, easy decision making, secrecy, and independence. Sole proprietors rarely have to answer to anybody. This can be crucial in sports because, as noted, sports are becoming part of more complicated entertainment empires. Therefore, a single owner has the opportunity to utilize the team as he or she envisions and can fit the team into a long-term strategic plan. While the rewards can be high with a sole proprietorship, so can the risk. A sole proprietor has unlimited liability, meaning the owner's total wealth is at risk to pay off creditors.

Divorce American Style: Sole Proprietors and Community Property States

Sole proprietorship does not exempt ownership from the community property laws that guide divorce settlements in numerous states. The complications that can arise when an individual who owns a team seeks a divorce from his/her spouse have been vividly illustrated when John Moores (San Diego Padres) and Frank McCourt (Los Angeles Dodgers) and their wives separated. There were also complications or special circumstances created when Robert Irsay (Indianapolis Colts) died regarding the inheritance of the team by his son from his first marriage. These are each instances of sole proprietors not having the singular control many usually expect when one person owns a team.

The NFL has very strict ownership rules and while partnerships are permitted, it does require that somebody own at least 10 percent of the team.* The NFL sees some value in having one person in charge of the team; however, given the increasing value of NFL teams, it is getting harder to own a large percentage of the team. Large ownership shares can create problems for families that must deal with estate planning issues. These have been concerns for at least two families where patriarchs had been the sole owners (Pittsburgh Steelers and Buffalo Bills). Given the 2010 valuation of all NFL franchises, if the league still required one individual to own at least 30 percent of the team, it would mean that an investment of $218 million would be needed to acquire the least valuable team. For half of the teams in the NFL, a 30-percent ownership stake would mean an investment worth more than $300 million. In 2010, *Forbes* estimated that the Jacksonville Jaguars were worth $725 million while the Cowboys topped the chart with a projected value of $1.8 billion.That level of wealth of ownership can be hard to sustain from generation to generation when a family seeks to retain control of a team.

---

* This is down from 20 percent in 2009, which was down from 30 percent before 2004.

Partnerships and the Single-Entity Ownership Model

A partnership is a business owned by two or more people. The most obvious drawback to having a team owned by two or more people is that there might be disagreements among the owners. The benefit, however, compared to a sole proprietorship is that there is less financial risk for each owner. If a team must raise cash, each partner can contribute and the inclusion of partners also means people with different ideas regarding revenue generation could be incorporated into the management of the franchise.

One unique type of partnership that is sometimes seen in sports is a single entity league. A syndicate or group of individuals owns all of the teams that comprise Major League Soccer (MLS). Individuals do not own particular teams. Instead, they own a percentage of the entire league. In the MLS's initial years, some owners operated multiple teams. While owners might run a particular team, all of the profits are divided among the different owners and all business decisions about teams and the league are made by the entire partnership. Player contracts are negotiated through the league and not with an individual owner. This would mean that the players who would attract fans willing to pay the highest prices (generally, these fans are in the largest markets) would produce the most profits if they were assigned to teams in the largest markets. This does not mean that the best players will always be on the teams in the largest markets, but the best use of all available resources would suggest that is the best business practice. Popularity, visibility, and "best" are usually related, but an older player whose productivity has declined might still be more valuable in a larger market then a better skilled but less known athlete. In single-entity ownership models, player assignment could be based on collective agreements regarding which market will generate the most revenue by the assignment of a player to a particular market.

Corporation Ownership

Corporations are legal entities with all of the rights of citizenship except for the right to vote. They, in essence, are considered "artificial beings" created by law and given all of the legal rights in business that individuals enjoy. Approximately 15 percent of the businesses in the United States are incorporated (and, therefore, classified as corporations), but corporations produce 80 percent of the net profits made by private firms (Gitman, 2003). A board of directors oversees the work of corporations. Shareholders (those who own stock in the corporations) own the corporation and those shares could be held by a small group of family members or unrelated individuals, or by many people. The shares themselves could be publicly traded on one of the stock exchanges, or the shares and the company may elect not to be listed on any of the stock exchanges. If a company is not listed on a stock exchange, then the shares cannot be publicly traded (as when you buy shares of Apple® or Microsoft®), but they could be privately traded among individuals. Stockholders benefit by receiving profits in the form of dividends from the corporation. While a corporation might retain some current profits to increase investments and future profits, the goal of most corporations is to maximize the value of depreciated dividends. The board of directors, elected by shareholders, makes the general policies for the firm and addresses the issue of the use of profits. Also, corporations typically have a treasurer in charge of financial activities and a controller in charge of accounting activities. The benefit of a corporation over another ownership structure is that it limits owner liability. Investors can lose their investment, but they are not legally liable for any fiscal losses and cannot be held financially responsible in any lawsuits against the franchise. There are also many types of corporations, such as an S corporation. These different definitions of a corporation provide variations on the issue of liability for financial responsibilities in the event of a failure.

Some teams are owned by corporations, but there is far less use of this ownership model than one might expect. The NFL does not allow corporate ownership as the league's preference is for each team to be controlled by one person (although other investors are allowed). That individual is expected to be the person from the ownership group whose attention is completely focused on the NFL, the team, and the game of football. In addition, and, more importantly, if a sports league permitted corporate ownership, some of its decisions and deliberations could be made public if a shareholder demanded to know or learn about decisions or policies enacted by the league. In the absence of corporate ownership, league meetings can be as secretive as the owners desire. As noted, some corporations are publicly traded and some are not. While it is not common in North America, a few sports teams have been publicly traded. Recently, the Boston Celtics and Cleveland Indians sold shares of stock. The Indians, however, were taken private in 2000 and the Celtics were taken private in 2002 when the team was sold to a new owner. It is more common for English soccer teams to be publicly traded companies. Many sports-related firms, like Nike, are publicly traded companies.

Corporate ownership is more common in some foreign leagues, although in those settings, the team is typically part of a larger conglomerate and, in some instances, known by their corporate sponsor. Many Japanese teams are not known by the city, region, or province in which they play (the typical naming pattern in North America), but by the corporation that owns them. For example, Nippon Ham, a food processing company, owns the Nippon Ham Fighters baseball team.

Community Ownership

While community ownership is not common in professional sports, it does exist. Community ownership does not imply that a team is a publicly traded company. Rather, community ownership means that a local organization or government owns the team in one manner or another. It also could mean that local residents own some form of stock. When this exists, there is usually some local board that controls the team and it is operated through the city, county, another public entity, or a community organization.

The most famous example or the most cited involves the Green Bay Packers. The Packers are in a sense owned by the community of Green Bay through a very unique structure created at a time when the NFL was in its infancy and was seeking to preserve the existence of teams. The Packers do have more than 100,000 "stockholders" with rights to vote on some issues. The shareholders, however, receive no dividends. Shareholders may only own a limited number of shares and, if they elect to sell their shares, they can only be purchased by the team. There is no market for the shares. While there is a real financial benefit to being a shareholder, individuals who own shares do so out of a sense of pride in the team and its presence in the same small city (where the team was created).

The key element that ensures that the team will not move is the requirement established in the 1920s that the proceeds from the sale of the franchise would accrue to the local American Legion post and not to the shareholders or the governing board and its members. In theory, the management could decide to relocate the team without a sale, but there would be no financial benefit. And, again, if sold, the proceeds accrue to the American Legion post. This ownership structure and articles of incorporation with the stipulation regarding where the proceeds from a sale must go ensures that the team will stay in Green Bay. The NFL no longer allows this type of community ownership. This could be because they do not like financial statements being made public (like the Packers are), but it also could be because the best interests of the team or league are not always the same as the best interest of the community.

In 1984, Joan Kroc tried to donate the San Diego Padres to the city of San Diego, but MLB would not allow her to do so under their authority to approve new owners when anyone sells a franchise. If San Diego owned the team, all of the franchise's financial statements would be subject to public scrutiny and it also could mean that meetings where the city was present (with other owners) would fall under open records laws requiring MLB to divulge the contents of its discussions. Public ownership of this type would eliminate any bargaining with the city as well. For example, it is conceivable that San Diego would not have built PETCO Park if the city already owned the Padres.

The situation is quite different for minor league teams. As Table 2.2 shows, there have been quite a few minor league teams that have been community owned in one way or another. The exact ownership structure is not the same for these teams, but all of them are or have been controlled by a local government, usually a city or county. Interestingly, community-owned teams do not perform very well in terms of attendance, but it is not clear if this is because public agencies operate the teams poorly or if local governments purchase teams where demand is low to be sure the franchise does not leave.

Fan Ownership

There is an example of a club that is actually owned by its fans. Ebbsfleet United is an English football (soccer) team that has tried this unique form of ownership that allows fans to make key decisions about the

Table 2.2 Minor league baseball teams, community owned or previously community owned

Team	Classification	League
Columbus Clippers	AAA	International League
Rochester Red Wings	AAA	International League
Syracuse Skychiefs	AAA	International League
Toledo Mud Hens	AAA	International League
Memphis Redbirds	AAA	Pacific Coast League
Harrisburg Senators	AA	Eastern League
Beloit Snappers	A	Midwest League
Burlington Bees	A	Midwest League
Wisconsin Timber Rattlers	A	Midwest League
Auburn Doubledays	Short-Season A	New York-Penn League

club's operations. Since 2008, a "web community," My Football Club, manages the club. Fans pay a fee to join the group that then controls the team. Members of this community are then allowed to make proposals and vote on various policies. Although Bill Veeck tinkered with the idea of letting fans vote on critical game decisions for one of his MLB teams, the structure in place for Ebbsfleet United allows fans to set team policy and select personnel through their participation in the group. Since this concept was implemented, other teams across the globe have experimented with similar ideas. Soccer fans around the world who, through the Internet and their "global ownership group," can now claim to have a role and a small part in "running a team." They can even claim to be a part owner of Ebbsfleet United. Perhaps this is a form of fan participation and ownership that will become a new type of Fantasy Sports with entrepreneurs forming teams in a league that allows fans to actually trade players and establish starting lineups.

College Sports

Another unique ownership structure is college sports. College sports teams are part of athletic departments that are themselves part of college or universities. Nonetheless, somebody must run the team from a financial standpoint even though the college or university is ultimately responsible for the team. That task usually falls to the university's athletic director. This means that "ownership" is vested in the Board of Trustees or Board of Regents for the particular college or university, but the athletic director is a sort of chief executive officer or president of every team. At some public institutions, the state's governor appoints all board members; in other states, university alumni elect the board members. Private institutions have their own rules regarding board members and their appointments. Directors appointed by the president and approved by the board are in charge of all athletic programs and teams. The form of board selection does not affect outcomes, nor does it change the authority vested in the athletic director. If a college football team was a profit-maximizing corporation not associated with the university, would they sell discounted tickets to students or permit free admission? Colleges and universities know that they often need to make the college attractive to students, so they may offer attendance at sporting events for free or at a reduced rate. The University of Southern California did not want luxury seating at the Los Angeles Memorial Coliseum because one of the presidents did not want to reduce overall capacity for fear that some students who wanted tickets would not be able to purchase them. Building luxury seating would have required the removal of some seats leading to a reduction in overall capacity.

While the goals for athletic programs might differ from those of a business, the school still wants athletic programs to operate as efficiently as possible relative to the goals established for it by the school. While it might not seem so at times, colleges and universities use sports to advance their goals. These goals might include support from alumni and other donors or using the popularity of sports to attract students. While there is often some tension between the athletic department and the academic side of a university regarding the admission of athletes, schools use athletics as a means to advance the university and its academic goals. Some faculty members at universities belittle the emphasis or use of sports for those goals and, to be sure, mistakes are made that lead to adverse publicity for the university. Some have suggested that academic institutions have sacrificed their principles to keep athletic programs operating and popular. If athletics does help a school attract more students, faculty, and philanthropic contributions, these contributions can have a profound and positive effect on a college or university. Of course, the question always comes down to what is the optimal amount of focus the institution should put on athletics.

Horizontal and Vertical Integration

One of the major reasons ownership structures are becoming more complex in the sports industry is because teams are becoming more integrated, both horizontally and vertically. Horizontal integration implies that firms are buying their competition. Vertical integration means a firm owns various parts of its supply chain or owns other firms related to the business.

Horizontal Integration

We have already noted that most major sports leagues prevent individuals from owning multiple teams within a league, so perfect horizontal integration is not really possible. Teams, however, do compete for fans with other franchises in their area. If an individual owns more than one sports team that serves the same market but different leagues, there is a level of horizontal integration. Spectator sports are also a form of entertainment. Horizontal integration in the entertainment business exists when a franchise owner incorporates the team into a set of other amusement options. As described earlier, PSE, OE, and MSG are each examples of horizontal integration. Cross-ownership of teams from different sports is not a new phenomenon. As early as 1946, the MSG Corporation owned the New York Rangers and Knicks. Today, there are approximately a dozen owners or ownership groups with multiple teams and or multiple forms of entertainment.

There are several reasons for owners to pursue horizontal integration strategies. The classic reason is to eliminate competition in the sports and entertainment businesses. If the same individual or partnerships owns many or all of the teams and numerous entertainment venues in an area, profits can be increased by raising ticket prices without fear that competitors will reduce their fees. Another reason for owning multiple sports teams is that there may be some efficiency gains. For example, when buying a second team a firm is more knowledgeable about the product and might be able to use many of the same resources. It might be possible to use the same sales staff for two or more teams and it becomes easy to advertise in other stadiums that the owner owns. A third reason for owning multiple sports teams might be to minimize risk. Some fans will decide to go watch whatever team in town is playing the best. If the same people own all the teams, then they do not care which team that is. We will talk about this as a case of negatively correlated assets later in the book.

Horizontal Ownership and the NFL

As we have pointed out, the NFL has very strict ownership rules. The principal owner must own 10 percent of the company and the NFL does not allow corporate or community ownership. It also does not allow ownership across sports, at least in the same market. So, while an NFL owner can own other major sports teams, those other sports teams may not be in NFL markets. Even though cross-ownership has been on the rise the last couple of decades, it has not among NFL owners. There are, however, exceptions. Paul Allen owns the Seattle Seahawks and the NBA's Portland Trailblazers, which is a different market. He is able to do this because there is no NFL team in Portland. On the other hand, the NFL seems to have made an exception for Stan Kroenke, owner of the Denver Nuggets and Colorado Avalanche (the same market as the

NFL's Denver Broncos). In an effort to sell the St. Louis Rams, they have allowed Kroenke to purchase a majority stake in the team while he yielded control of his other franchises to his children.

One more restriction is that NFL owners may only borrow $150 million using the team as security for the loan. This means that although NFL teams are clearly worth more than $150 million, that is all they can use as collateral. The NFL does this so, if an owner goes bankrupt, a creditor does not assume control of the team. This policy is in place to ensure the other ownership rules, such as no corporate ownership, remain intact.

Vertical Integration

There are many ways sports teams can vertically integrate implying that there is common ownership within the supply chain. Many food and beverage companies own teams. Not only does this ensure that teams will exclusively sell those products at the venue, but it is also a great marketing tool. For example, part of the justification for naming Toronto's MLB team the Blue Jays resulted from their initial ownership by the Labatt Blue brewing company. The Blue Jays were the equivalent of an advertisement for the company. While Anheuser-Busch beers are sold at St. Louis Cardinal games, their stadium is also named after the company. Beer companies sponsor stadiums as well, such as Miller Park in Milwaukee and Coors Field in Colorado.

Another crucial change has been the relationship between teams and media outlets. Because media revenue is rapidly increasing in its importance, it might be better to have the same company operate both the sports team and the media outlet and, as a result, more leagues and teams are creating their own television networks. The NFL, MLB, and the Big 10 Conference—to name a just a few—each has its own network and is quite successful. While the main showcases of the Big 10 Network are football and basketball games not broadcast as part of NCAA contracts, it also televises other sports and shows produced by Big 10 universities. The Boston Red Sox, Cleveland Indians, New York Mets, and the New York Yankees have each created their own networks and those, too, are quite successful. While there is a trend of teams creating networks, already existing media outlets also have purchased teams. The Disney Company, which owns ESPN, owned the Anaheim Ducks for a brief time, and the Fox Entertainment Group purchased and then sold the Los Angeles Dodgers. It appears that Disney and Fox Entertainment have decided to focus on delivery of games instead of the ownership of teams. The Dolan family used its fortune from Cablevision Systems in New York City to purchase the New York Rangers and Knicks and then to merge all of their assets into the MSG Corporation.

The question of whether a team or league should have the same ownership as a media outlet can be a complicated one. While some might think that it obviously makes sense to be integrated, there are reasons not to. The most common explanation is that it is sometimes more efficient to have separate owners. Sports companies might be more effective than media companies at operating teams and vice versa. Sometimes it might be better to have a contractual relationship. For example, the Southeastern Conference (SEC) created its own network, but unlike the Big 10 network, the SEC network is owned and operated by ESPN. The SEC's member universities decided it was in their best interest not to run the network. There are examples as well where integration has not worked. In 1964, CBS bought 80 percent of the New York Yankees for $11.2 million (and later bought the remaining 20 percent). In 1973, George Steinbrenner purchased the Yankees for a reported $8.8 million. The ownership of the Yankees by CBS did not work out well financially or on the field. An example that *did* work well involved Ted Turner and his purchase of Superstation WTBS and the Atlanta Braves. During Turner's ownership, the value of the Braves dramatically increased. Integration worked well for both the team and the media outlet. When Turner bought the team, cable television was in its infancy. Putting an MLB team on the network legitimized the network. Furthermore, putting the Braves on television allowed baseball fans without a local team a team to root for and become involved in. Vertical integration works best when it is beneficial for both sides.

One other way teams can vertically integrate is by owning their minor league teams. Because the NFL does not have a minor league system, this is not applicable, but MLB and the NHL have extensive minor league systems and the NBA has a development league with 16 teams. It may surprise some to know that most minor league baseball teams are not owned by their major league affiliate. Most minor league teams have what is called a player development contract with a major league team. This means that the major league team is in charge of everything that happens on the field or ice, but the minor league owner is in charge of the facility and promoting the game.

Sometimes there are cross-marketing benefits if a major league team owns its minor league affiliate. This can be done by strategically deciding where the minor league affiliates are placed. For example, some MLB teams try to have minor league affiliates throughout the country to have a national fan base. Other teams pursue an exact opposite strategy and instead have affiliates nearby to bolster their local fan base and to allow local fans to see future major league stars. Either way, the actual development of players is not affected.

Strange Bedfellows in Minor League Baseball

Some minor league teams are owned by their major league affiliate and some are not, but an interesting thing happened with the minor league team in Vero Beach, Florida. From 1980 to 2006, the Los Angeles Dodgers owned and operated the Vero Beach Dodgers in the single A, Florida State League. In fact, Vero Beach had been the home of the

Dodgers' spring training facility and was part of the Dodgertown complex. But, in 2006, the team became an affiliate of the Tampa Bay Rays, who took over operations of the team on the field and renamed the team the Vero Beach Rays. The Rays, however, did not buy the team. Apparently, nobody else wanted to buy the team either. As a result, for a couple of years the Rays were in charge of a team on the field with the Dodgers in charge of off-the-field activities. The Dodgers also received the revenues from the team.* It is difficult to know if the Dodgers were rooting for or against the Vero Beach Rays (Shelley, 2006).

The Integration of Real Estate Development, the Media, Entertainment, and Team Ownership

More than half of the owners (or ownership groups) of North America's professional teams have business interests that originated in or are now focused on entertainment, media, and/or real estate development. This includes some owners who have formed new corporations centered on the team. How has this changed across the years? In any year and decade, there were team owners who derived their wealth solely from the team. There are still some owners whose principal business activity is the team they own. For example, James Irsay owns the Colts and, while he may have other business interests, the team is not at the center of an entertainment, media, or a real estate company. The Steinbrenner family, on the other hand, while having the Yankees as its principal business, has positioned the team at the center of the YES television network, but still relied on external financing to build the infrastructure required for the network. As a result, YES is an independent company, owned by the Steinbrenners and others, with the baseball team as its anchor. Jerry Jones has tethered the Dallas Cowboys to his new stadium, but the new facility in Arlington is essentially the largest (by seating capacity), multipurpose entertainment complex in the United States hosting a variety of sports and other entertainment events. Its financial success is dependent on the hosting of a large number of entertainment events to complement the 10 games played by the Cowboys. While no one knows for sure how many other events must take place at this facility to ensure its financial success, what is clear is that 10 Dallas Cowboys games are not sufficient to ensure that the needed funds are available to support Jones's investment. In that regard, then, the new stadium is a venue for numerous events including Dallas Cowboys football.

It is the positioning of teams at the center of entertainment, media, and real estate development that we argue has changed the sports business and the relationships between teams and cities. Separate chapters will focus on each of these

---

* More details can be found at http://dodgers.scout.com/2/586774.html

business opportunities and what they have produced and meant. Detailed in the next sections of this chapter are brief examples of the ways in which teams are now anchors for extensive investment strategies. In the past, when shopping malls were designed, developers initially approached large department stores. These anchor tenants were seen as the first steps in building a popular mall because the larger crowds attracted to these stores would then encourage smaller retailers or owners of boutique stores to sign leases. Malls that incorporate outdoor pedestrian areas (Lifestyle Centers) have extended this concept to include popular restaurants (e.g., The Cheesecake Factory, Maggiano's, P. F. Chang's China Bistro, etc.) and very popular retailers that seek unique locations (e.g., Apple Computer Stores, The North Face, etc.). Movie theaters also have frequently assumed critical roles as anchor tenants for traditional closed malls as well as the more in-vogue life-style centers. In each of these settings, the anchor tenant ensures a level of customer traffic that convinces other retailers to locate at the site because their store will benefit from the additional traffic generated by a successful anchor. Sports teams, because of the predictably large crowds they attract, have emerged as anchor tenants as well. The anchor tenant ensures that there is sufficient traffic or paying customers to help finance the building. That gives a team owner the opportunity to ask, "If a facility exists that predictably attracts between 800,000 (football) and 4 million (baseball) visits, what other forms of development and entertainment, or other business opportunities, exist?"

There are, of course, a number of answers depending on markets and the availability of land, but there are other factors to keep in mind for the reason this question is now posed with increasing regularity. First, through recessions and expansions of the economy, attendance at sporting events has remained relatively robust. This does not mean that some teams in selected markets, hard hit by the recession or when a team's performance declines, have not seen sharp declines in attendance. The Indiana Pacers and Cleveland Indians have both seen their ticket sales plummet, but during the same time period, the Indianapolis Colts and Cleveland Cavaliers (prior to LeBron James' departure) retained their popularity even through a severe recession. In Miami, with the arrival of LeBron James and Chris Bosh (joining Dwayne Wade), the Heat are poised to dramatically increase their ticket sales even while the region is still in the midst of a recession and home values continue to decline. Even during that decline, however, interest in the Dolphins remained robust. The popularity of sports then assures the presence of large crowds and creates an opportunity for owners to figure out how best to leverage that attendance into other revenue streams. Declining ticket sales for games played by the Tampa Bay Rays and Florida Marlins have been attributed to the economic contraction in Florida and the depressed real estate prices. Yet, overall, in 2009, MLB teams sold more than 115 million tickets, and that total was exceeded only four other times in history. More than two-thirds of all NFL teams sold at least 90 percent of their tickets in that same year. The continual attraction of customers during recessions underscores the value of a sports team as an anchor tenant.

Second, in many instances the revenues generated from entertainment or real estate are neither shared with other teams (not part of sports-related income) nor the players (defined gross revenues that has guided the team payroll levels in football). Revenue that Jerry Jones earns from hosting the NBA All Star Game or college football games at the Cowboys' Stadium is not classified as football-related income. Similarly, the real estate developments surrounding PETCO Park in San Diego and the entertainment facilities adjacent to the STAPLES Center in Los Angeles (LA LIVE) are not part of any calculation of sports-related income. The situation confronting the New York Yankees and the YES network, or any of the other networks owned by baseball teams is different. While teams retain that income, it is included in the calculation of income earned for the revenue-sharing program. Nevertheless, the Yankees, as well as several other teams, are earning substantial profits from their related activities even though they do transfer money to other team owners.

Sports Teams at the Center of Media and Entertainment Corporations: Two Examples

Every ownership group is different, but a few are briefly described to highlight the role teams are playing at the center of media, entertainment, and real estate development syndicates. The Detroit Tigers and Detroit Red Wings, for example, are part of Olympia Entertainment (OE) and the holdings of the Ilitch family. The Tigers play their home games at Comerica Park, one of six downtown entertainment venues managed by OE. The Red Wings play in another downtown facility, Joe Louis Arena, and OE also manages Cobo Arena (large convention center venue), the Fox Theatre (renovated large, live entertainment showplace), the Masonic Temple Theatre (home to 4,300- and 1,600-seat theaters), and the City Theatre (430-seat venue for concerts, theatrical plays, and comedy shows). Illitch Holdings includes all of these entertainment venues, the two teams, and the Motor City Casino Hotel (downtown Detroit), Little Caesar's Pizza, Blue Line Foodservice Distribution, Champion Foods, and a real estate development corporation. The Tigers and Red Wings are part of a large entertainment and food services corporation providing patrons with sports, concerts, gambling, plays, and other forms of live entertainment in downtown Detroit.

Another example of the integration of sports into an entertainment corporation involves the New York Knicks and Rangers and Cablevision. James L. Dolan launched Cablevision and used the ensuing financial success to acquire the Knicks and Rangers and Madison Square Garden. The WNBA team, the New York Liberty, is also part of MSG. The Garden itself includes an 18,200-seat main arena and a 5,600-seat Forum for smaller live performances. The television empire has grown to include MSG, MSG Plus, MSG 2, MSG 2 Plus, and the Fuse Networks. MSG also operates the Radio City Musical Hall annually producing the Christmas spectacular and many other shows. The Rangers and Knicks, together with Madison Square Garden, are the anchors of a large media and entertainment corporation with annual revenues of almost $1 billion. This is another example of the integration of sports teams into a media and entertainment corporation.

References

Gabler, N. 2007. *Walt Disney: The triumph of the American imagination,* 2nd ed. New York: Alfred A. Knopf.

Gitman, L. J. 2003. *Principals of managerial finance.* New York: Addison Wesley.

Gottdiener, M. 2001. *The theming of America: American dreams, media fantasies, and themed environments,* 2nd ed. Boulder, CO: Westview Press.

Hannigan, J. 1998. *Fantasy city: Pleasure and profit in the postmodern metropolis.* London: Routledge.

Mandelbaum, M. 2004. *The meaning of sports: Why Americans watch baseball, football, and basketball and what they see when they do.* Cambridge, MA: Perseus Books Group, Public Affairs.

McIntosh, M. 1971. Changes in the organization of thieving. In *Images of deviance,* ed. S. Cohen. Harmondsworth, U.K.: Penguin.

Quirk, J. P., and Fort, R. D. 1992. *Pay dirt: The business of professional team sports.* Princeton, NJ: Princeton University Press.

Riess, S. A. 1980. Sport and the American dream: A review essay. *Journal of Social History* 14: 295–303.

Shelley, B. 2006. No more Vero Dodgers? Not entirely! Message posted November 4 http:// dodgers.scout.com/2/586774.html (accessed May 10, 2011).

Thompson, E. P. 1981. *Protest and survive.* London: Monthly Review Press.

Chapter 3

Financial Statements, Revenues, and Costs

Financial Statements

This chapter examines the financial statements and sources of revenues and costs for different types of sports teams and businesses. As Chapter 2 made clear, because of the various ownership structures, sports teams often indirectly affect various revenue streams of a larger entertainment company. This implies that the full value of a team may not be found on a team's financial statements. Nonetheless, this chapter focuses more on direct revenues and costs of sports teams. Financial statements provide the raw data that is vital to understanding the financial health and growth of a firm. Sometimes financial data in sports can be difficult to obtain. Publicly traded companies, like those on the New York Stock Exchange or the NASDAQ, are required to periodically file with public agencies four different financial statements: balance sheets, income statements, a statement of cash flows, and a statement of retained earnings. Although most professional sports teams do give those financial statements to their league, these documents do not have to be filed with any regulatory agencies by privately held sports teams. While academicians do not have access to the financial statements for most professional sports teams, these documents are available for many sports-related businesses, such as Nike or Callaway Golf. Also, some financial documents of professional sports teams are occasionally made available to the public. In addition, since the Green Bay Packers franchise is owned by a community institution, much of their financial data are disclosed. Furthermore, many college athletic departments are part of state universities and data from their operations are therefore available to the public.

Financial statements should be used to examine the health of the company, identify financial shortcomings, and focus the attention of leaders on remedial steps. The financial statements of publicly traded companies are typically used to ensure that stock prices are appropriate. The financial statements give investors the knowledge to discover the value of the company. In professional sports, however, statements are sometimes divulged legally or illegally, but few are able to determine the strength of the team's finances. Documents that are released are often part of a negotiation either between the players and owners trying to set parameters for payrolls or between an owner and local governments being asked to provide a subsidy for a new facility. Because of these circumstances, and the sports industry's elevated public profile, the financial statements that are released are often done to sway voters, fans, or the media. In the weeks and months leading up to the end of the agreement between the players and owners in the NFL, NBA, and NHL, numerous owners made statements regarding the lack of viable business plans given the salaries being paid to athletes. Their message was clear: The players need to accept lower salaries.

In the case of college sports, the athletic departments of public universities must disclose their financial documents. This permits insight into the magnitude of various revenues and costs for different universities and even for different sports. Athletic departments, however, are part of a university and the total contribution of sports to the university, or the contribution the university may make to the athletic program, is not easy to detect. The financial statements from the athletic department do offer insight into where college teams get a majority of their revenue.

Financial statements rarely tell the whole story of a firm. Knowledge of the industry and firm is always useful. For example, financial statements of a team do not describe its impact on other holdings of the company. Also, it is very easy to transfer profits within a conglomerate. For instance, if a team is owned by a food or beverage company, the team could simply "overpay" for the concession rights. This is not a common practice, but it shows the ease with which the financial statements can be manipulated. Furthermore, sometimes owners will pay themselves or family members a salary. That salary item appears as an expense and lowers the reported profits. There are various ways teams can change the profit levels described to fans. As Paul Beeston, former vice president of baseball operations for the Toronto Blue Jays, once said, "Anyone who quotes profits of a baseball club is missing the point. Under generally accepted accounting principles, I can turn a $4 million profit into a $2 million loss, and I can get every national accounting firm to agree with me."

Casual observers might wonder why teams would have an incentive to manipulate financial statements. One reason might be taxes. If there are different tax rates for various holdings of a company, owners will want to move profits to where the tax rate is the lowest. Another reason to obscure profits is to present as strong a case as possible for government support for arenas, ballparks, and stadiums, or for lower salary demands. Remember, these documents are often made public during a negotiation. Therefore, an owner may have an incentive to report lower profits or even operating losses. Even if the documents are not made public during some type of negotiation, there is still some incentive to deflate profit levels. For example, financial statements of some MLB teams were made public in 2010. Some fans were frustrated after reviewing the documents because some small-market teams were making profits as a result of revenue sharing after years of claiming team operations were producing losses. While it may not have been in the best interest of those teams to use profits or revenue-sharing funds for player development, fans of those teams wanted a more competitive franchise. So, even though there is some financial data available for some teams, it is easy to manipulate some of these figures to advance political positions. Nonetheless, in this chapter, we examine some of the available statements. Even if the financial statements might not tell the whole story, they do provide useful data in terms of revenue sources and other key aspects of the sports industry. It also is important that all future sports managers have the skill to interpret and understand these documents.

Balance Sheets

Balance sheets illustrate a firm's assets and liabilities. A firm's assets are essentially anything the firm owns, including payments owed. Liabilities are the firm's debt (anything the firm owes directly) or the equity financing (the investment made by the owners). If a firm has more assets than liabilities, the difference is stockholder's (or owner's) equity. Another way of looking at it is if the firm or team ceased operations, the value to the owners would equal its assets minus its liabilities.

$$\text{Stockholder equity} = \text{Assets} - \text{Liabilities}$$

It is important to note that the balance sheet is a snapshot in time. It essentially shows the current wealth of a firm, team, or department. Because the Green Bay Packers are "publicly" owned, their balance sheets are available. Table 3.1 shows their balance sheet from 2002 to 2009.

Balance sheets generally divide assets and liabilities into groups relative to liquidity. In other words, there are short-term assets known as *current assets* and short-term liabilities known as *current liabilities*. Usually something is considered a current asset if it can be converted into cash within one year and it is a current liability if it needs to be paid in one year. As the Green Bay Packer's balance sheet illustrates, current assets are cash, inventory, and accounts receivable (money owed to the company). Current liabilities are accounts payable, notes payable, and accruals. Fixed assets are long-term assets and usually things like automobiles or buildings. Long-term liabilities are things that do not need to be paid within one year.

Table 3.1 Green Bay Packers balance sheet, 2002–2009 (in $)

Assets	2002	2003	2004	2005	2006	2007	2008	2009
Current Assets								
Cash	3,915,022	1,749,258	2,604,925	798,279	1,942,543	2,817,452	0	3,632,166
Inventories	600,050	1,218,043	1,490,616	1,700,336	2,538,131	2,959,210	1,666,631	4,164,838
Unamortized signing bonuses	15,202,471	14,135,097	15,772,995	13,242,340	13,860,975	16,904,185	15,530,776	14,943,628
Accounts receivable	3,155,496	4,724,737	10,850,844	6,368,378	6,936,608	19,973,195	7,191,971	9,710,475
Deferred income taxes	900,000	1,000,000	2,700,000	2,300,000	6,400,000	3,900,000	7,449,867	7,425,157
Other current assets	122,819	398,618	595,154	2,689,047	1,030,075	1,623,912	2,055,972	3,974,229
Total current assets	23,895,858	24,914,616	34,014,534	27,098,380	32,708,332	48,177,954	33,895,217	43,850,493
Investments	66,839,668	99,583,050	129,483,362	167,845,584	208,542,135	228,918,872	216,324,253	166,035,479
Property and Equipment (net)	24,470,906	34,365,389	37,084,881	34,958,227	32,267,337	27,622,839	48,871,670	50,731,444
Other Assets								
Unamortized signing bonuses	40,143,400	37,212,235	41,958,112	34,949,591	36,693,335	39,559,639	27,613,660	15,266,649
Deferred income taxes	7,211,506	4,233,617	0	0	0	0	0	0

Other noncurrent assets	22,447,772	10,912,760	10,785,943	6,972,529	4,633,173	3,194,604	1,764,720	134,919
Total other assets	37,714,421	38,526,420	50,345,582	43,665,864	39,582,764	45,152,716	43,210,572	47,489,825
Total assets	298,331,837	337,617,560	355,065,247	317,183,668	269,484,955	245,735,493	202,073,627	162,696,257
Liabilities and Stockholder Equity								
Current Liabilities								
Current maturities of long-term liabilities (Deferred Compensation)	4,948,206	4,240,425	14,161,270	13,621,532	8,534,400	16,020,916	9,918,291	8,977,177
Notes payable	1,001,169	13,768,155	866,667	866,667	866,667	866,667	866,667	0
Accounts payable	2,784,481	3,609,180	2,223,394	2,688,523	2,811,921	2,677,289	2,459,457	1,088,212
Accrued expenses	12,317,625	24,114,093	27,794,581	15,831,362	9,097,580	5,251,837	5,753,973	4,347,168
Accrued income taxes	0	0	20,802,280	8,966,020	4,506,491	4,646,000	0	0
Deferred revenues	10,099,549	3,137,558	11,066,705	8,938,536	13,408,163	13,846,524	10,759,559	6,447,079
Total current liabilities	31,151,030	48,869,411	76,914,897	50,912,640	39,225,222	43,309,233	29,757,947	20,859,636
Long-Term Liabilities								
Note payable	8,466,997	8,100,000	8,666,667	9,533,333	10,399,999	11,266,666	12,133,333	0

(continued)

Table 3.1 (continued)   Green Bay Packers balance sheet, 2002–2009 (in $)

Assets	2002	2003	2004	2005	2006	2007	2008	2009
Deferred compensation	15,740,848	16,127,769	1,523,245	15,621,465	22,356,600	14,454,885	13,133,884	11,346,314
Other	4,503,950	6,618,407	8,046,778	9,538,152	15,066,279	12,725,108	12,947,511	14,243,022
Total long-term liabilities	20,244,798	34,879,509	34,545,939	35,559,616	46,956,212	35,846,660	34,181,395	34,056,333
Stockholders' Equity								
Common stock and additional paid in capital	22,332,911	22,333,111	22,335,511	22,335,711	22,335,711	22,335,711	22,335,711	22,335,711
Retained earnings	97,793,500	11,665,039	139,564,226	165,004,469	183,035,481	205,031,918	228,396,734	232,418,674
Accumulated other comprehensive income	1,465,412	−1,547,079	5,980,584	7,359,937	13,943,624	14,936,061	3,834,309	−21,629,911
Total stockholders' equity	121,591,823	137,436,171	167,880,321	194,700,117	219,314,816	242,303,690	254,566,754	233,124,474
Total liabilities and stockholders' equity	162,696,257	202,073,627	245,735,493	269,484,955	317,183,668	355,065,247	337,617,560	298,331,837

Source: http://joe.bowman.net/Balance.htm

It is easy to get a basic idea of the financial health of a team from its balance sheets. We will look at financial ratios later in the chapter, but one can tell that the Packers are, financially, quite secure. Most of their assets are in investments that more than doubled in value from 2002 to 2009. Also, total stockholder equity is $233 million and, financially, nearly doubled in value across this time period. Furthermore, the $233 million represents 78 percent of the total liabilities and stockholder equity, which is quite high. In other words, if the team paid off all of its liabilities, the team would still have 78 percent of its assets. This implies that there is little chance of the Packers going bankrupt any time soon, not that anyone was or should be worried.

Table 3.2 shows the balance sheet for Nike Inc. Since Nike is a publicly traded company, this is a slightly more traditional balance sheet. In addition to assets and liabilities, it includes some information regarding preferred and common stock. Notice that for each year the total assets must equal total liabilities and shareholder equity. As with the Packers, Nike's total assets far outweigh their total liabilities and the firm's equity seems to be increasing at a robust rate.

Table 3.2 Nike's balance sheet, 2006–2010 ($millions)

	2006	2007	2008	2009	2010
Period End Date	5/31/2006	5/31/2007	5/31/2008	5/31/2009	5/31/2010
Assets					
Cash and Short-Term Investments	2,303.0	2,847.0	2,776.1	3,455.1	5,145.9
Total Receivables, Net	2,382.9	2,494.7	2,795.3	2,883.9	2,649.8
Total Inventory	2,076.7	2,121.9	2,438.4	2,357.0	2,040.8
Prepaid Expenses	380.1	393.2	602.3	765.6	873.9
Other Current Assets, Total	203.3	219.7	227.2	272.4	248.8
Total Current Assets	7,346.0	8,076.5	8,839.3	9,734.0	10,959.2
Property/Plant/Equipment, Total—Net	1,657.7	1,678.3	1,891.1	1,957.7	1,931.9
Goodwill, Net	130.8	130.8	448.8	193.5	187.6
Intangibles, Net	405.5	409.9	743.1	467.4	467
Long-Term Investments	0	0	0	0	0

(continued)

Table 3.2 (continued)   Nike's balance sheet, 2006–2010 ($millions)

	2006	2007	2008	2009	2010
Note Receivable—Long Term	0	0	0	0	0
Other Long-Term Assets, Total	329.6	392.8	520.4	897	873.6
Other Assets, Total	0	0	0	0	0
Total Assets	9,869.6	10,688.3	12,442.7	13,249.6	14,419.3
Liabilities and Shareholders' Equity					
Accounts Payable	952.2	1,040.3	1,287.6	1,031.9	1,254.5
Payable/Accrued	0	0	0	0	0
Accrued Expenses	853.7	743.5	941.7	1,035.6	1,904.4
Notes Payable/Short-Term Debt	43.4	100.8	177.7	342.9	138.6
Current Port. of LT Debt/Capital Leases	255.3	30.5	6.3	32	7.4
Other Current Liabilities, Total	507.8	668.9	908.2	834.6	59.3
Total Current Liabilities	2,612.4	2,584.0	3,321.5	3,277.0	3,364.2
Total Long-Term Debt	410.7	409.9	441.1	437.2	445.8
Deferred Income Tax	561	668.7	854.5	842	855.3
Minority Interest	0	0	0	0	0
Other Liabilities, Total	0	0	0	0	0
Total Liabilities	3,584	3,663	4,617	4,556	4,665
Redeemable Preferred Stock	0.3	0.3	0.3	0.3	0.3
Preferred Stock—Nonredeemable, Net	0	0	0	0	0
Common Stock	2.8	2.8	2.8	2.8	0

Table 3.2 (continued)   Nike's balance sheet, 2006–2010 ($millions)

	2006	2007	2008	2009	2010
Additional Paid-In Capital	1,447.3	1,960.0	2,497.8	2,871.4	0
Retained Earnings (Accumulated Deficit)	4,713.4	4,885.2	5,073.3	5,451.4	0
Other Equity, Total	121.7	177.4	251.4	367.5	9,753.7
Total Equity	6,285.5	7,025.7	7,825.6	8,693.4	9,754.0
Total Liabilities & Shareholders' Equity	9,869.6	10,688.3	12,442.7	13,249.6	14,419.3
Total Common Shares Outstanding	512	501.7	491.1	485.5	485.7
Total Preferred Shares Outstanding	0	0	0	0	0

Income Statements

An income statement provides a financial summary of a firm across a period of time, typically a year or quarter. The income statement lists the firm's revenues, costs, and profits. Some detail regarding the firm's taxes and any earnings or dividends per share if the firm is publicly traded is also included. Fortunately, many more income statements are available for sports teams than balance sheets. The income statement for the Green Bay Packers is presented in Table 3.3.

In 2010, only 18 percent of the team's revenue came from ticket sales (both home and road games) while 37 percent of income was from media contracts. Nearly 18 percent of the team's revenue is from income from NFL properties (sale of memorabilia) and nearly 17 percent comes from their pro shop. On the cost side, salaries account for roughly 65 percent of operating expenses. Most of the rest comes from general administrative and marketing costs. The Packers' income statement seems to give less optimism than their balance sheet. The most important number on the income statement, the profit, has decreased. Even though revenues have dramatically increased from 2003 to 2010, expenses have increased as well. The income statement shows that player costs represent about two-thirds of overall costs and have increased more rapidly in percentage terms than total revenues. While this may be a concern to a casual financial observer, people close to the organization may have a good sense of whether profits will increase or decrease in the future.

Income statements are available for other major sports teams as well, but we turn next to the income statement for Nike. Table 3.4 shows revenues and expenses

Table 3.3 Green Bay Packer's income statement, 2003–2010 ($millions)

Operating Income	2003	2004	2005	2006	2007	2008	2009	2010
Ticket and Media Income								
Home games (net)	20.5	26.5	26.6	28.5	29.0	30.9	31.1	31.1
Road games	10.8	11.4	12.0	12.9	14.1	15.1	16.2	16.0
Television and radio	77.1	81.2	84.2	87.3	84.7	87.6	94.5	95.8
Total ticket and media income	108.4	119.1	122.9	128.7	127.8	133.6	141.8	142.9
Other Operating Income								
Private box income	10.5	10.5	11.0	11.3	11.8	12.1	12.8	12.9
NFL properties income (Other NFL revenue)	4.7	7.3	14.5	15.1	26.1	32.9	36.5	45.8
Expansion\revenue sharing income	*							
Marketing\pro shop (net)	21.7	29.5	35.1	36.8	40.7	50.3	43.7	43.0
Atrium revenue (Added 2004)		3.1	5.9	4.7	†			
Other—Local media, concessions and parking (net)	7.8	9.6	11.0	11.9	11.7	12.6	13.2	13.3
Total other operating income	44.7	60.0	77.4	79.7	90.3	107.7	106.2	115.1
Total operating income	153.1	179.1	200.0	208.4	218.1	241.3	247.9	258.0
Operating Expenses								
Player costs	77.6	96.1	97.9	102.9	110.7	124.7	138.7	160.1
Game expenses (Operations/Maintenance (net))†	3.0	3.6	5.4	6.3	7.2	7.6	7.7	7.4
General and administrative	47.2	15.3	20.9	23.3	27.5	35.3	31.7	32.3

Team expenses			21.2	33.7	17.7	26.5	26.4	25.6
Sales and marketing expenses			4.0	4.45	20.7	26.0	23.3	22.0
Pro shop expenses			12.0	12.9	†			
Atrium expenses			4.6	4.2	†			
Lambeau redevelopment costs	2.1	0.5	0.3					
Total operating expenses	129.9	150.0	166.3	187.5	183.8	219.9	227.8	248.2
Profit (Loss) from operations	23.2	29.2	33.7	20.9	34.2	21.4	20.1	9.8
Other Income (Expense)								
Interest expense	-0.5	-0.5	-0.6	-0.8	†			
Interest and dividend income	2.2	2.5	4.2	5.8	†			
Gain on sale of investments and other assets (net)	-1.6	1.2	2.2	3.1	†			
Other Income (Expense)					6.2	14.4	-11.2	-2.1
Income before * Expansion revenue and provision for income taxes	23.3	32.3	39.6	29.0	40.4	35.8	8.9	7.7
Provision for income taxes	7.7	11.5	14.1	11.0	18.4	12.4	4.9	2.5
NET INCOME before expansion revenue	15.5	20.8	25.4	18.0	22.0	23.4	4.0	5.2

* In fiscal 2003 and 2004, the Club received an expansion fee payment from Houston of $3,333,333 and $5,000,000 respectively, or approximately $2,143,333 and $3,337,000, respectively, net of income taxes.

† In fiscal 2007, Atrium revenue has been added to Marketing/Pro Shop (Sales) revenue. "Other Income (Expense)" has replaced "Interest Expense, dividend income and gain on sale of investments and other assets (net)."

Source: http://joe.bowman.net/Statement.htm

Table 3.4 Income statement for Nike ($millions)

	2006	2007	2008	2009	2010
Period End Date	5/31/2006	5/31/2007	5/31/2008	5/31/2009	5/31/2010
Revenue	14,954.90	16,325.90	18,627.00	19,176.10	19,014.00
Total revenue	14,954.90	16,325.90	18,627.00	19,176.10	19,014.00
Cost of revenue, total	8,367.90	9,165.40	10,239.60	10,571.70	10,213.60
Gross profit	6,587.00	7,160.50	8,387.40	8,604.40	8,800.40
Selling/general/administrative expenses, total	4,477.80	5,028.70	5,953.70	6,149.60	6,326.40
Research and development	0	0	0	0	0
Depreciation/amortization	0	0	0	0	0
Interest expense (income), net operating	0	0	0	0	6.3
Unusual expense (income)	0	0	0	596.3	0
Other operating expenses, total	54.9	48.8	46.6	-48.3	-49.2
Operating income	2,141.60	2,199.90	2,502.90	1,956.50	2,516.90
Interest income (expense), net nonoperating	0	0	0	0	0
Gain (loss) on sale of assets	0	0	0	0	0
Other, net	0	0	0	0	0

Income before tax	2,141.6	2,199.9	2,502.9	1,956.5	2,516.9
Income tax—Total	749.6	708.4	619.5	469.8	610.2
Income after tax	1,392.0	1,491.5	1,883.4	1,486.7	1,906.7
Minority interest	0	0	0	0	0
Equity in affiliates	0	0	0	0	0
U.S. GAAP adjustment	0	0	0	0	0
Net income before extraordinary items	1,392.0	1,491.5	1,883.4	1,486.7	1,906.7
Total extraordinary items	0	0	0	0	0
Net income	1,392.0	1,491.5	1,883.4	1,486.7	1,906.7
Total adjustments to net income	0	0	0	0	0
Basic weighted average shares	518	503.8	495.6	484.9	485.5
Basic EPS excluding extraordinary items	2.7	3.0	3.8	3.1	3.9
Basic EPS including extraordinary items	2.7	3.0	3.8	3.1	3.9
Diluted weighted average shares	527.6	509.9	504.1	490.7	493.9
Diluted EPS excluding extraordinary items	2.6	2.9	3.7	3.0	3.9
Diluted EPS including extraordinary items	2.6	2.9	3.7	3.0	3.9
Dividends per share—Common stock primary issue	0.6	0.7	0.9	1.0	1.1

(continued)

Table 3.4 (continued)   Income statement for Nike ($millions)

	2006	2007	2008	2009	2010
Dividends per share—Common stock issue 2	0.6	0.7	0.9	1.0	1.1
Gross dividends—Common stock	304.9	357.2	432.8	475.2	0
Depreciation, supplemental	282	269.7	303.6	335	0
Normalized EBITDA	2,346.1	2,362.6	2,699.9	2,850.0	2,523.2
Normalized EBIT	2,054.3	2,083.0	2,387.1	2,503.1	2,523.2
Normalized income before tax	2,141.6	2,199.9	2,502.9	2,552.8	2,516.9
Normalized income after taxes	1,392.0	1,491.5	1,883.4	1,939.8	1,906.7
Normalized income available to common	1,392.0	1,491.5	1,883.4	1,939.8	1,906.7
Basic normalized EPS	2.7	3.0	3.8	4.0	3.9
Diluted normalized EPS	2.6	2.9	3.7	4.0	4.0
Amortization of intangibles	9.8	9.9	9.2	11.9	0

for Nike, but does not go into any detail. Instead, it provides details regarding financing and taxes. While Nike did not always make interest payments, it should be noted that interest payments are deducted from profits before taxes. After the taxes are taken out, the earnings are shown per share (EPS). As this shows, income statements from publicly traded companies might not provide detail on various revenue streams, but they typically do go into great detail regarding financial data.

Table 3.5 illustrates the revenues and expenses of the athletic departments for the Big 10 universities. These data are also available for specific teams, such as football, men's basketball, and women's basketball. This table illustrates a high degree of heterogeneity among Big 10 universities. While some of the athletic departments lose money, others make quite a bit. Notice, however, that a majority of schools either make or lose less than $1 million. While $1 million is a lot of money, it is not a large percentage of total revenues. The reason that revenues and costs are similar is because athletic departments often spend any surpluses or are subsidized for any losses.

Statement of Retained Earnings

Statements of retained earnings report profits a firm keeps as opposed to making a distribution to shareholders in the form of dividends. The statement typically reconciles how much of the profits go to preferred stock holders,* common stock holders, and how much the company retains against future losses or for future investments. This statement can give some useful information to investors or analysts. Some may think that if a company is not offering the highest possible dividends to shareholders, then it is not being successful. If the statement of retained earnings shows that the company is retaining profits, however, it could be a sign that the firm's leadership places a high value on quick access to funds for future investments or to protect against future losses. Retained earnings could be a sign that a firm's leadership anticipates the emergence of valuable future investment opportunities and is setting aside money to take advantage of those possibilities. For Nike, the statement of retained earnings is essentially a subset of the income statement. For example, we know from the income statement that their (diluted) earnings per share in 2010 were $3.86 and their dividend was $1.06. This implies that they retained $2.80 per share or 72.5 percent of earnings.

Statement of Cash Flows

As the name would suggest, this document reports cash flows across different time periods. The statement reports cash flows from operating, investment, and

---

* Preferred stock holders get paid a fixed periodic dividend before any profits are given to common stock holders.

Table 3.5 Revenues and expenses for Big 10 teams for 2004–05* (in nominal dollars)

Category	University									
	Illinois	Indiana	Iowa	Michigan	Michigan State	Minnesota	Nebraska†	Ohio State	Purdue	Wisconsin
Revenues										
Ticket Sales	12,917,578	8,392,688	18,971,349	31,432,123	18,530,242	18,846,753	21,578,588	34,073,089	14,806,753	21,072,976
Student Fees	2,749,207	1,015,823	1,505,016	0	0	0	0	0	0	0
Guarantees	54,700	788,050	200,000	563,003	4,145,025	280,800	158,500	768,710	456,950	260,000
Contributions	9,639,510	8,129,276	10,357,165	16,342,620	13,271,677	4,297,235	11,390,228	19,829,556	13,724,374	20,269,398
Third Party Support	0	400,000	83,000	0	0	0	0	0	1,716,428	0
Government Support	0	0	0	0	0	0	0	0	16,923	46,861
Direct Institutional Support	1,959,500	0	2,127,182	0	296,419	7,484,172	0	5,429	0	3,975,001
Indirect Institutional Support	0	684,637	0	0	2,857,869	1,555,825	0	0	660,170	1,432,156
NCAA/Conference Distributions	4,489,002	13,991,692	15,861,342	10,661,790	11,646,060	10,843,022	7,845,931	11,448,925	15,194,995	12,094,240
Individual School Media Rights	6,218,109	0	1,325,000	1,655,000	751,432	1,615,900	3,897,089	1,893,878	0	3,079,319
Concessions, Programs, Parking	1,361,936	1,509,853	1,279,956	1,705,028	927,093	1,564,703	3,635,042	5,360,393	1,119,346	6,615,739

Advertisements and Sponsorship	4,380,549	2,700,304	4,285,689	9,711,940	3,527,166	2,828,687	6,059,567	7,234,438	2,241,648	1,745,883
Sports Camps	1,899,180	0	1,526,512	178,351	2,663,120	0	0	3,041,511	98,094	1,864,703
Endowments/Investments	646,984	0	1,295,224	2,915,254	2,671,174	1,498,601	110,071	1,748,479	1,069,135	1,002,782
Other	2,080,508	356,589	2,858,822	3,259,077	882,870	2,461,145	1,201,318	4,296,571	220,630	2,355,494
Subtotal	48,396,763	37,968,912	61,676,257	78,424,186	62,170,147	53,276,843	55,876,334	89,700,979	51,325,446	75,814,552
Expenses										
Student Aid	6,297,587	7,061,633	5,954,008	11,366,586	7,605,217	7,835,288	6,408,173	10,542,719	5,989,644	7,867,347
Guarantees	1,176,350	2,456,625	5,114,298	1,267,917	4,463,868	1,005,000	1,367,707	1,071,791	3,869,747	1,080,597
Salaries	6,444,680	7,098,552	8,698,656	9,305,176	9,664,088	9,067,938	8,001,490	13,768,894	5,016,117	9,363,248
Other Coaches' Comp.	0	501,280	83,000	0	0	0	0	0	1,552,643	0
Support Staff Salaries	8,743,003	7,683,942	9,087,996	12,309,415	8,354,476	7,680,195	10,186,979	10,799,986	7,904,427	14,261,845
Other Support Staff Comp	0	27,960	0	0	0	0	0	0	163,785	0
Severance Payments	476,838	349,020	0	0	158,793	71,747	0	0	0	0
Recruiting	1,014,215	703,774	762,172	892,192	955,460	863,462	1,084,860	979,671	727,809	614,424
Team Travel	2,821,395	2,403,853	4,995,263	3,584,272	3,792,933	3,396,692	2,727,081	5,362,737	3,500,555	6,331,960

(continued)

Table 3.5 (continued) Revenues and expenses for Big 10 teams for 2004–05 (in $)

Category	Illinois	Indiana	Iowa	Michigan	Michigan State	Minnesota	Nebraska	Ohio State	Purdue	Wisconsin
						University				
Equipment	2,918,352	1,127,441	732,362	2,193,111	839,427	981,896	586,290	778,817	588,257	1,315,709
Game Expenses	1,966,915	1,209,812	1,827,057	1,538,974	2,627,714	1,398,840	2,925,258	3,303,249	1,680,246	4,759,131
Promotion	1,635,990	808,541	1,288,181	1,624,041	1,333,900	1,082,271	437,168	1,684,925	2,897,275	2,349,004
Sports Camp	1,021,993	0	1,222,666	0	1,756,556	0	0	1,760,019	51,292	1,841,201
Facilities, Maintenance	8,728,621	1,854,863	7,053,120	11,343,081	8,122,491	10,521,063	12,101,097	26,092,018	10,834,255	16,947,419
Spirit Groups	191,285	183,303	260,673	159,887	203,743	354,787	426,680	304,281	182,705	114,360
Indirect Institutional Support	0	684,637	0	0	2,857,869	1,555,825	0	0	660,170	1,432,156
Medical	369,965	1,203,505	1,163,501	267,079	813,044	509,604	704,734	2,331,356	589,909	1,279,097
Memberships	107,801	122,429	26,232	96,058	108,006	121,673	45,894	276,296	100,868	30,523
Other Operating	4,000,550	3,324,062	6,713,473	5,439,355	4,683,269	7,425,810	8,796,074	10,523,546	5,190,405	6,131,021
Total Operating	47,915,540	38,805,232	54,982,658	61,387,144	58,340,854	53,872,091	55,799,485	89,580,305	51,500,109	75,719,042
Expense to Revenue Difference	481,223	(836,320)	6,693,599	17,037,042	3,829,293	(595,248)	76,849	120,674	(174,663)	95,510

* These data are from indystar.com, but information from Pennsylvania State University and Northwestern University was not available. While more current data are available at (http://ope.ed.gov/athletics/), there is not as much detail.
† Nebraska joined the Big 10 effective with the 2011 football season.

financing activities. Operating cash flows need to be positive; if negative, a business may not be viable. The cash flow report identifies operating profits after payment of all taxes and allowances for capital depreciation and changes in inventories and accounts receivable or payable. Investment cash flows deal with buying and selling various investments, such as assets and business interests. Financing cash flows are any cash flows that deal with either debt or equity financing. An example of a cash flow statement appears in Table 3.6.

Table 3.6   Nike's statement of cash flows for selected years ($millions)

Category	2006	2007	2008	2009
Period End Date	5/31/2006	5/31/2007	5/31/2008	5/31/2009
Net Income/Starting Line	1,392	1,491	1,883	1,489
Depreciation/Depletion	282	269.7	303.6	335
Amortization	8.9	0.5	17.9	48.3
Deferred Taxes	−26	34.1	−300.6	−294.1
Noncash Items	54.2	147.7	80.4	571.9
Changes in Working Capital	−43.2	−64.8	−48.4	−411.7
Cash from Operating Activities	1,668	1,879	1,936	1,736
Capital Expenditures	−333.7	−313.5	−449.2	−455.7
Other Investing Cash Flow Items, Total	−942.9	406.4	−40.6	−342.4
Cash from Investing Activities	−1,277	92.9	−489.8	−798.1
Financing Cash Flow Items	0	55.8	63	25.1
Total Cash Dividends Paid	−290.9	−343.7	−412.9	−466.7
Issuance (Retirement) of Stock, Net	−535.8	−662.3	−904.7	−462.6
Issuance (Retirement) of Debt, Net	−24.2	−161.3	28.5	170.3
Cash from Financing Activities	−850.9	−1,111.5	−1,226.1	−733.9
Foreign Exchange Effects	25.7	42.4	56.8	−46.9
Net Change in Cash	−433.9	902.5	277.2	157.2

Notice from the income statement that net income in 2009 was $1.49 billion, which carries over to the statement of cash flows. There are, however, other things, such as deferred taxes, that are included from operating activities. In 2009, Nike's investing cash flows were negative, but this is from investments for capital items. Their cash from financing activities is also negative, but much of that includes dividends given to shareholders. Overall the company's cash flows were positive, but it is not always clear that net cash flow should be too positive. After all, the goal of a company is to give shareholders their dividends, which decreases the cash available to the company. Nike's management apparently believed that by increasing cash flow slightly in 2009 they would be able to maximize future dividends.

Table 3.7 is the statement of cash flows for the Texas Rangers. Prior to their sale, the team had been placed into bankruptcy to facilitate the transaction. Without addressing the legal issues and benefits from the bankruptcy filing to expedite the sale, the data illustrate that the previous owner, Tom Hicks, had implemented policies and practices that led to extremely poor financial performance. For the calendar years ending in 2008 and 2009, losses in excess of $10 and $11 million were reported. To operate the team, the owner had to invest $36 million in 2008 (capital contributions). By 2009, the team had more than $7.4 million in cash on hand. For an organization as large as a Major League Baseball team, however, that is a meager amount.

Table 3.7 Statement of cash flows for the Texas Rangers for 2008 and 2009 ($thousands)

	December 31, 2009	December 31, 2008
Cash Flows from Operating Activities:		
Net income	$(11,981)	$(10,435)
Adjustments to reconcile net loss to net cash used in operating activities:		
Depreciation and amortization	5,822	11,574
Amortization of player contracts	13,268	12,071
Earnings from investments in unconsolidated entities	(5,179)	(410)
Return on investments in unconsolidated entities	2,000	(1,165)
Noncash interest, net	(149)	153
Provision for bad debt expense	(581)	145
Loss from player transactions, net	207	110
Deferred tax benefit	—	(90)

Table 3.7 (continued)   Statement of cash flows for the Texas Rangers for 2008 and 2009 ($thousands)

	December 31, 2009	December 31, 2008
Changes in other assets and liabilities:		
Accounts receivable	(3,490)	7,796
Merchandise inventories	(398)	(98)
Prepaid expenses, other assets, and deposits	23,307	(19,616)
Restricted cash	(588)	638
Deferred compensation and signing bonuses	(8,128)	(26,943)
Unearned revenue	1,473	(1,727)
Accounts payable and accrued expenses	388	4,443
Other liabilities	(823)	(197)
Net cash used in operating activities	15,146	(23,751)
Cash flows from investing activities:		
Additions to facilities, property, and equipment, net	(7,450)	(8,259)
Net cash provided by investing activities	(7,450)	(8,259)
Cash flows from financing activities:		
Proceeds from the issuance of debt	765	—
Capital lease payments	1,620	(639)
Repayments of debt	(2,344)	(3,364)
Net borrowing on lines of credit, net	17,300	-
Capital contributions/distributions	(17,599)	36,000
Net cash provided by financing activities	(258)	31,997
	7,439	(13)
Cash and cash equivalents, beginning of year	3	16
Cash and cash equivalents, end of year	$7,441	$3
Supplemental disclosure of cash flow information:		
Cash paid for interest	$4,381	$3,735

Analyzing Financial Statements

There are many different ways to use and analyze financial statements. When trying to identify the health of a company, an analyst can compare it with other firms or analyze the data across years or quarters. Cross-sectional analysis involves comparing a firm with others for the same years or quarters and a time-series analysis is looking at trends over time. Table 3.5 offers a cross-sectional view of Big 10 teams while Table 3.3 and Table 3.4 are a time series assessment of the Packers and Nike.

Various analytical techniques can be used for a cross-sectional analysis and when comparing firms from the same industry. Many different statistical techniques exist to better understand if a firm is using appropriate practices and policies. Benchmarking is a popular technique where similar firms are compared with each other. A shortcoming, however, is that there are often very few firms that are similar to each other and that can limit the available comparisons. For example, suppose you were charged with analyzing the financial affairs of the Chicago Blackhawks. You could compare their profit or cash flow with all Fortune 500 companies, but this would seem rather useless since there is no reason to believe the profit of the Blackhawks should be comparable to a Fortune 500 company. A more reasonable approach would be to compare their data with other major professional sports teams. You could choose to compare the Blackhawks' financial practices with teams that have the most in common with them, which might be other NHL teams, but some of those play in much smaller markets. Or, you could decide to compare the Blackhawks to other teams in Chicago. While a thorough analysis might involve several different comparisons, it is not obvious which one would be most valid and produce the best insights. If regional concerns are the most important, then the Blackhawks should be compared with other teams in Chicago. If, however, profits are usually league dependent, it might make more sense to compare the Blackhawks to other NHL teams. This is actually done for the Big 10 universities in Table 3.5. The data are arrayed to facilitate comparisons between such rivals as Ohio State and Michigan, or between universities from the same state.

Time-series analysis is useful for identifying trends. Basic time-series analysis might entail calculating growth rates to try to predict future outcomes. For example, if the Blackhawks' profits are consistently increasing 7 percent a year, there might be reason to believe that will continue if nothing dramatically changed. Some data, however, tend to oscillate. If a firm has a large growth in revenue one year, it is possible that the firm should expect growth to slow the next year. If many years of data are available, this type of change in the data can be tested.

The most helpful analytical technique might well be panel data analysis. Using panel data means that the analyst is looking at multiple firms across numerous time periods. This framework gives the analyst the advantages of more observations and the assessment is less likely to be flawed because it is not dependent on any one firm or a year in which a single event could have impacted numerous firms. When using cross-sectional analysis, there could be an anomaly during any one year. There also could be something unique about one particular firm when using time-series analysis. If one wants to find a trend for a particular firm, the uniqueness of the firm might be lost in a large cross section of data. An analyst has to weigh the extent to which any observation can be generalized to the performance of the firm in future years.

Ratio Analysis

Having examined some financial statements, several basic analyses can be performed and financial ratios calculated. Financial ratios are basic statistics that can be calculated from the financial statements. Financial statements actually have much in common with player statistics. It is virtually impossible to settle a debate about which player is best by using one statistic. Even though *sabermetricians* are getting better at providing one statistic that is an overall metric of a player's ability, there are still disagreements and methodological problems. First, when it comes to players, it is always a challenge to calculate the most appropriate measure of performance or quality. Is a higher batting average the most important, or is a player's on base percentage the most accurate measure of quality? Second, there will always be intangible qualities that are impossible to quantify. How does one measure leadership or the value of a player to his teammates? Financial ratios are similar. Although some measures such as profit margin or even profits are crucial to a firm, there is always more information required to provide an accurate picture of a firm's performance. Regardless, financial ratios can be very useful in understanding growth rates or in diagnosing a current or emerging problem. Ratios can answer important questions, such as: Is the firm's efficiency increasing or decreasing? or Does the firm have enough cash for its short-term needs?"

One important ratio is the *current ratio*. The current ratio gives an indication of how able the firm is to meet its obligations.

Current Ratio = Current Assets/Current Liabilities

If the current ratio is high, it implies that the firm can easily pay off short-term debts. It is possible, however, that a firm does not want this ratio too high if they would rather make long-term investments as opposed to having a large amount of current assets. The *quick ratio*, or the acid test, is similar to the current ratio, but it does not include inventory in the current assets as a firm's inventory is not always a liquid asset. Some types of firms can hold inventory for a long time. As a result, they may not want to include inventories when determining if they can meet their short-term financial obligations. The quick ratio is given by:

Quick Ratio = (Current Assets − Inventory)/Current Liabilities

The current ratio and quick ratio are considered measures of a firm's liquidity.

Debt ratios can be very important to sports teams. Debt ratios give an indication of how much a firm is using other people's money for its operations. One of the more common debt ratios, the aptly named *debt ratio,* simply calculates the ratio of total liabilities and total assets:

$$\text{Debt Ratio} = \text{Total Liabilities/Total Assets}$$

Another common debt ratio is the *times interest earned ratio,* which is the ratio of earnings before interest and income taxes and interest:

$$\text{Times Interest Earned Ratio} = \text{Earnings before Interest and Taxes/Interest}$$

Some financial analysts suggest that this ratio should be at least 3, otherwise the firm might have difficulty making interest payments if profits decrease. Profitability ratios are also clearly important. The *gross profit margin* calculates what percentage of sales are gross profits. Note that gross profit <u>only</u> includes the costs of the goods sold. The ratio is calculated by:

$$\text{Gross Profit Margin} = (\text{Sales} - \text{Costs of Goods Sold})/\text{Sales}$$

The *operating profit margin* is similar except that it uses operating profits instead of gross profits, which means operating expenses, such as administrative, selling, marketing, and depreciation expenses are subtracted from the gross profit figure. The formula for operating profit margin is

$$\text{Operating Profit Margin} = \text{Operating Profits/Sales}$$

The *net profit margin* again is similar, but it includes interest payments, taxes, and any other expenses in the costs. That equation is

$$\text{Net Profit Margin} = \text{Earnings/Sales}$$

It is useful to analyze gross profit margin, operating profit margin, and net profit margin together. That way, if there is a large jump in the percentages, an analyst can tell if the change is a result of the costs of goods sold, changes in operating costs, or other financial cost alterations. If a firm is publicly traded, earnings per share is also a very common profitability ratio. Another group of ratios are *activity ratios* that measure how fast things like inventory, accounts receivables, and sales turnover are changing across a specified time period. While this might be important for some sports-related businesses, this is not usually crucial for sports teams. Teams sell entertainment (through games played), so inventory is not as vital. Also, there are market ratios, such as the price/earnings ratio, but again those are used for publicly traded companies, so they are rarely available for sports teams.

Table 3.8 Basic financial ratios for the Green Bay Packers and Nike from balance sheets

Ratio	Year								
	2002	*2003*	*2004*	*2005*	*2006*	*2007*	*2008*	*2009*	*2010*
Green Bay Packers									
Current	1.15	0.84	0.79	0.69	0.64	0.63	0.69	1.41	
Quick	1.12	0.80	0.75	0.65	0.59	0.59	0.66	1.27	
Debt	0.25	0.32	0.32	0.28	0.31	0.32	0.25	0.22	
Nike									
Current					2.81	3.13	2.66	2.97	3.26
Quick					2.02	2.30	1.93	2.25	2.65
Debt					0.36	0.34	0.37	0.34	0.32

Table 3.8 illustrates some ratios from the balance sheets for the Packers and Nike. Comparing the current and quick ratios, Nike's is far more robust implying that the company can more easily sustain their short-term debts. Most firms have a current ratio greater than 1. While a value under 1 for the current ratio can sometimes be a concern, it does depend on the time constraint on both the current assets and liabilities. As one might expect, the difference between the current ratio and quick ratio is larger for Nike than for the Packers. This is because professional sports teams do not have too much in the way of inventory because they are selling entertainment. Nike on the other hand sells a more tangible product and, thus, is expected to have large inventories to meet consumers' preferences (for a large selection of different styles and Nike must also have different size shoes for each style). The debt ratio for both firms is somewhat low and that implies that their assets are quite a bit bigger than their liabilities.

Table 3.9 examines some ratios from the income statements. The Packers have a times interest earned ratio of at least 39 for each year available. This is quite high and means there is very little chance of the club defaulting on interest payments. But, notice that starting in 2007, interest payments were grouped with dividend income and gains from investments and that obscures the magnitude of the interest payments. Nike didn't have any interest payments until 2010, and after that the obligations were still small.

It is only possible to calculate the gross profit margin for Nike since sports teams do not sell a tangible asset. As a result, production costs are quite different. The highest costs for most professional sports teams involve the players' contracts, which are operating costs. Nike's gross profit margin is approximately 45 percent. This means that when someone buys a Nike product, 55 percent of the price supports the actual

Table 3.9 Ratios from the income statements of the Green Bay Packers and Nike

Ratio/Margin	Year							
	2003	2004	2005	2006	2007	2008	2009	2010
Green Bay Packers								
Times interest earned	44.7	65.3	70.0	39.2	NA	NA	NA	NA
Operating profit margin	0.15	0.16	0.17	0.10	0.16	0.09	0.08	0.04
Net profit margin	0.10	0.12	0.13	0.09	0.10	0.10	0.02	0.02
Nike								
Times interest earned				NP	NP	NP	NP	400.5
Gross profit margin				0.44	0.44	0.45	0.45	0.46
Operating profit margin				0.14	0.13	0.13	0.10	0.13
Net profit margin				0.09	0.09	0.10	0.08	0.10

Note: NA = Not available; NP = No interest payment

costs of producing the goods. Nike's costs include marketing, which is similar to those faced by teams, but also includes research and development, costs that are typically not part of a team's business operations. The operating profit margin can be found for the Packers, Nike, and the Big 10.* The Packers' operating profit does vary over the time period from 4 to 17 percent. Nike's operating profit, on the other hand, is more consistent, ranging only from 10 to 14 percent. The Packers' net profit margin ranges from 2 to 13 percent, and there is one interesting anomaly. In 2008, the net profit margin was actually higher than the operating profit margin. Normally, the net profit margin will always be smaller than the operating profit margin because the net profit margin includes all costs, such as interest payments, taxes, and any preferred stock dividends. The Packers are unique in that they include some nonoperating revenues. They include interest, revenues from dividends, and the sale of investments as nonoperating revenue. In 2008, these revenues were more than the taxes paid. This is not simple semantics (do all revenues count as operating revenues?); analysts must be precise with what is calculated and what is included. Nike is more traditional in that it includes all revenues as operating revenues. Their net profit margin ranges from 8

---

* Although the Big 10 is not shown in Table 3.9.

to 10 percent. Big 10 athletic departments do not have a net profit margin (at least not apart from their operating profit margin) for a couple of reasons. First, they are part of a university and, as a result, interest payments or taxes would involve the department's relationship to and tax rules governing universities. Second, many universities are public institutions that do not pay any preferred stock dividends or taxes, thus their net profit margin would not be any different from their operating profit margin.

More sophisticated financial analyses will be done later in the book. This chapter provides some essential financial concepts that need to be fully understood. While financial statements can sometimes be misleading, they do give some indication of wealth from the balance sheet and income from income statements. A firm or team's wealth and income gives an indication of its location and a trajectory of its financial well-being. Furthermore, financial statements tell a story about what the company keeps and what exactly shareholders or owners are taking out of the company. The financial statements also might allow comparisons across firms or provide a sense of the firm's recent history.

Revenues and Costs

We now turn attention to the changes in team revenues and costs. Managers need to understand how these basic building blocks of financial statements have been changing for teams across the years. For example, it was noted in Chapter 1 that revenues from media sales had dramatically increased for the NFL and many teams. Facility-generated income has also increased. On the cost side, player salaries have increased as the athletes have tried to gain a share of the rising revenue streams.

Between 2008 and 2009, the Texas Rangers enjoyed a 9.9 percent increase in income from the broadcast of the team's games, from $62.6 million to $68.6 million, but as a percentage of team revenue, media-related income accounted for about the same proportion, 41.9 percent (Table 3.10). Then, in 2010, the franchise announced a new contract with Fox Sports and will receive $80 million a year for each of the next 20 baseball seasons. The dramatic increase in income from media affords numerous options for the franchise's leadership. On the other hand, NHL teams earn far less as illustrated in Table 3.11. In addition, the NHL franchises had a combined loss of more than $270 million for the 2002–03 season.

Stadium Revenue

Although stadium revenues have not grown at the same rate as those from the transmission of games, they are core components of the income for most teams, and they, too, are growing as a result of luxury seating, improved sight lines, and enhanced retail operations. One reason these funds are so important is that each team is required to share far less with other clubs. For example, in the NFL, stadium revenue is shared, but

Table 3.10   Texas Rangers' income statement for 2008 and 2009

Texas Rangers Baseball Partners and Subsidiaries		
Consolidated Statements of Operations (Unaudited) for the 12 months ended December 31, 2009 and 2008 ($thousands)		
	December 31, 2009	*December 31, 2008*
Revenue:		
Net ticket sales	$46,875	$39,978
Television and radio	68,797	62,583
Concessions	10,523	8,627
Stadium suite rentals	5,629	4,766
Parking	4,253	3,497
Advertising	13,261	14,074
Merchandise sales	7,807	5,817
Other, net	10,224	10,120
Total revenue	167,368	149,462
Operating expenses:		
Player salaries	75,948	70,671
Trade settlement costs	—	—
Other direct team costs	18,095	18,465
Player development	11,211	10,814
Scouting	7,736	7,026
Ballpark operations	13,102	11,374
Ticket Office	2,384	1,852
General and administrative	10,481	7,793
Marketing	16,016	16,752
Merchandise cost of sales	4,319	3,184
Parking	1,726	1,192
Revenue sharing, net	(5,495)	(23,129)

Table 3.10 (continued) Texas Rangers' income statement for 2008 and 2009

	December 31, 2009	December 31, 2008
Amortization of player contracts	13,268	12,071
Loss from player transactions, net	207	110
Loss on impairment of intangible assets	—	6,638
Depreciation and amortization nonplayer	5,822	5,005
Total operating expenses	174,818	149,818
Operating income (loss)	(7,450)	(356)
Other income (expense):		
Income from unconsolidated entities, net	5,179	410
Gain/(loss) on sale of net assets	—	—
Interest expense	(9,795)	(9,545)
Interest Income	21	24
Income tax benefit	63	(968)
Net income	$(11,982)	(10,435)

Source: Deadspin.com

teams keep a higher percentage, while all revenue from the league's media contracts are divided into equal shares. The importance of these agreements for managers is that an individual team can do very little to increase their share of the media revenue, but there is a lot they can do to increase their stadium revenue. As a result, team managers are keenly focused on enhancing income from in-facility operations.

While ticket sales are an important part of stadium revenue, as discussed in Chapter 1, many new revenue sources have emerged. Anyone entering a new facility is immediately greeted with myriad choices and ways can spend money. For one thing, concession sales and parking revenue can be very substantial. Also, stadium sponsorship and naming rights deals have become extremely common. For some teams, a stadium sponsorship deal can generate $10 million per year in revenue, but this value does vary widely. Other things like advertisements inside the facility can be quite large as well. The New York Mets, for example, sold the naming rights to their new ballpark, Citi Field, for $400 million. The 20-year deal began in 2009.

Furthermore, sports facilities are used to hosting many other entertainment events. While indoor facilities have a clear advantage relative to generating income from nonsports events, increasingly ballparks and stadiums also are used to host concerts, shows, and games involving sports and teams from other sports. For

Table 3.11 Summary of operations, combined league-wide tabulations for the 2002–2003 season ($millions) for all NHL franchises

Revenues	Season	Playoffs	Total
Gate receipts	886	111	997
Preseason and special games	50		50
Broadcasting and new media revenues	432	17	449
In-arena revenues	401	14	415
Other hockey revenues	82	3	85
Total revenues	1,851	145	1,996
Player costs			
Salaries and bonuses	1,415	14	1,429
Benefits	64	1	65
Total player costs	1,479	15	1,494
Other operating costs			
Other player costs	28		28
Team operating costs	259	23	282
Team development costs	69	2	71
Arena and building costs	138	7	145
General and administration	116	1	117
Advertising, marketing, public relations, and tickets	126	6	132
Total operating costs	736	39	775
Total costs	2,215	54	2,269
Operating loss (excluding depreciation, amortization, interest, and taxes)	–364	91	–273

Note: From elsewhere in the document, 19 teams lost money; combined loss = $342.4 million; 11 teams had a combined profit of $69.8 million. The net is the same as here, namely, a loss of $272.6 million (rounds to $273 million)

Source: Levitt Report, Appendix I, 2004.

example, the new stadium built by Jerry Jones is home to the Dallas Cowboys, but has already hosted numerous college football games, the NBA All-Star Game, and many concerts. Citi Field hosted a U2 concert, and the new Yankee Stadium has become home to the annual Pinstripe Bowl between two college football teams each December. Table 3.12 shows some of the top venues for the first quarter of 2010 relative to the number of entertainment events held. Madison Square Garden remains a leading venue and that is to be expected given the size of the New York City market. It is interesting, however, how well the Palace at Auburn Hills north of the city of Detroit has done. The Palace is also the home court of the Detroit Pistons. Table 3.12 uses data from Pollstar, an event tracking information website, to project the number of annual events at arenas across North America. Those with 86 major sports dates are home to both an NBA and NHL franchise. While franchise owners do not disclose the income earned from the hosting of other entertainment events, the scale of the income is substantial. Those events that are efficiently managed can and do produce substantial increments to a franchise owner who also controls all arena revenues. This highlights the opportunities for sports managers and illustrates why team owners focus on other events to enhance the value of owning a team.

Table 3.12   Event days at North American arenas, 2010

Arena	City	Concert Tickets Sold	Estimated Annual Concert Event Dates	Estimated Annual Major Sports Dates	Base Number of Event Days
Bell Centre	Montreal	461,622	41	43	84
Madison Square Garden	New York	402,164	36	86	122
Philips Arena	Atlanta	380,373	34	86	120
Sprint Center	Kansas City	376,398	33		33
Allstate Arena	Rosemont	335,310	30		30
St. Petersburg Times	Tampa	321,584	29	43	72
Toyota Center	Houston	314,353	28	43	71
Air Canada Centre	Toronto	305,702	27	86	113
Rexall Place	Edmonton	305,429	27	43	70
Staples Center	Los Angeles	265,473	24	129	153

(continued)

Table 3.12 (continued)   Event days at North American arenas, 2010

Arena	City	Concert Tickets Sold	Estimated Annual Concert Event Dates	Estimated Annual Major Sports Dates	Base Number of Event Days
American Airlines Center	Dallas	239,511	21	86	107
Target Center	Minneapolis	232,667	21	43	64
Verizon Center	Washington, D.C.	205,582	18	86	104
Palace of Auburn Hills	Auburn Hills, MI	194,932	17	43	60
Pepsi Center	Denver	154,556	14	86	100
Jobing.Com	Glendale	159,347	14	43	57
Xcel Energy	St. Paul	147,481	13	43	56
Scottrade Center	St. Louis	139,560	12	43	55
United Center	Chicago	137,171	12	86	98
Nationwide Arena	Columbus	118,538	11	43	54
Quicken Loans	Cleveland	116,325	10	43	53
Freedom Hall	Louisville	104,027	9	30	39
US Airways Center	Phoenix	101,510	9	43	52
Schottenstein Center	Columbus	97,750	9	30	39

NFL In-Stadium Revenue

It is useful to look at variances of in-stadium revenue for the NFL. The NFL divides more revenue among all its member teams than any other league. Each team owner, however, can retain most in-stadium revenue. As a result, there is a management focus on maximizing income from that source and there is a surprisingly high degree of variation. This not only surprises many, but again highlights for future sports managers why the design of facilities is so important.

Because NFL clubs do not distribute information on their earned revenues, three different estimates were developed. First, *Forbes* magazine does an annual estimate of team revenues from their facilities and this was included. Second, a fan cost index is developed by other organizations reflecting the average amount of money people spend at games and that figure was multiplied by the total number of tickets sold to provide a second estimate of in-stadium revenue. Third, the total number of tickets sold was multiplied by the average price to provide the most conservative measure of in-stadium revenues, as it does not include spending for food and beverages. As illustrated in Figure 3.1, regardless of which estimate is used, the

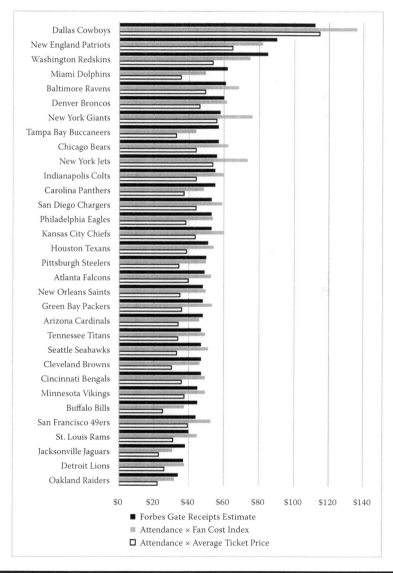

Figure 3.1   Estimates of in-stadium revenue for NFL teams in 2009.

Dallas Cowboys earn far more money and there is indeed substantial variance in the amounts each team earns. There is a clear "bunching" of high revenue teams and lower revenue earners. What is key is that there is far more variability then many would expect, illustrating the management opportunity to enhance a team's bottom line by expanding fans' spending.

NBA In-Facility Revenue

Facility-generated revenue is far more critical to NBA teams because the income from national television contracts is far less than what exists for NFL franchises. While those NFL teams with less in-stadium income have lower profits than some of their counterparts, the size of the national media contract is sufficient to ensure that each team makes money. NBA teams must realize substantial local revenues or they will have a far greater challenge to be profitable. The variation in earnings among these clubs is illustrated in Figure 3.2. The Los Angeles Lakers can generate revenue of roughly $100 million per season, while teams like the Memphis Grizzlies earn about one-fourth of that. Notice that the New Orleans Hornets are also at the lower edge and, in 2011, there was substantial fear they would need to relocate. The fiscal plight of the Indiana Pacers has forced that club to ask the City of Indianapolis for financial support in the form of an improved lease for use of the Conseco Fieldhouse.

Naming Rights

Another valuable and variable source of income for teams is the naming rights to the facilities. Table 3.13 shows most of the existing deals for facilities across North America. The New York Mets earn the most income, $20 million each year. The advertising value of Citi Field is underscored by the facility's location (visible from a major highway) and the value of the New York market. The extreme variability is often related to visibility and market size, but some anomalies underscore the need for sophisticated analyses and auctions to ensure that full value is received. Future managers are reminded of the substantial advertising value that comes from a naming rights deal and to avoid errors that allowed the Coors Brewing Company to pay just $15 million to secure the rights to the ballpark used by the Colorado Rockies. The company will enjoy those naming rights for as long as the facility exists.

Media Revenue

The growth of media and its importance will be discussed in Chapter 7. In terms of a chapter on revenue and costs, however, it is necessary to introduce its importance.

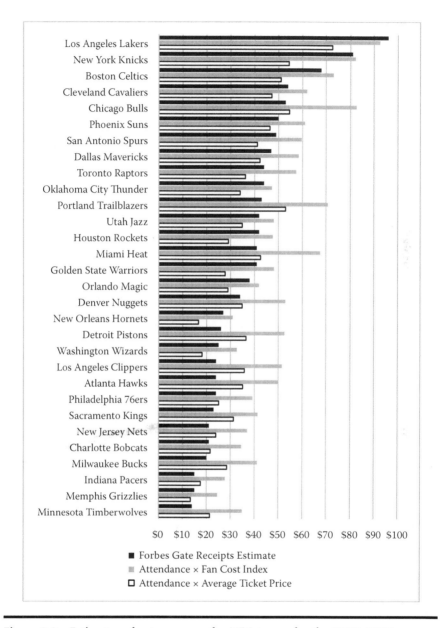

Figure 3.2   Estimates of gate revenue for NBA teams for the 2009–2010 season.

But before looking at the income earned by the four major sports leagues, some other points should be underscored. First, there are two different types of contracts, national contracts negotiated by the leagues for all franchise owners and local contracts entered into individually by each team. Revenue from the national contracts

Table 3.13 Selected naming rights deals and North American sport facilities

Facility	Sponsor	Team(s)	Annual Fee	Expiration Date
Air Canada Centre	Air Canada	Toronto Maple Leafs, Raptors	$2 million	2019
Alltel Stadium	Alltel Corporation	Jacksonville Jaguars	$620,000	2007
American Airlines Arena	American Airlines	Miami Heat	$2.1 million	2019
American Airlines Center	American Airlines	Dallas Mavericks, Stars	$6.5 million	2031
Ameriquest Field	Ameriquest Capital Corp.	Texas Rangers	$2.5 million	2007[1]
Amway Center	Amway Corporation	Orlando Magic	$4 million	2019
Arco Arena	Atlantic Richfield	Sacramento Kings, Monarchs	$750,000	2007
AT&T Center	AT&T	San Antonio Spurs	$2.1 million	2022
AT&T Park	AT&T	San Francisco Giants	$2.1 million	2024
BankAtlantic Center	BankAtlantic	Florida Panthers	$1.4 million	2015
Bank of America Stadium	Bank of America	Carolina Panthers	$7 million	2024
Bell Centre	Bell Canada	Montreal Canadiens	$3.2 million	2023
Chase Field	JP Morgan Chase	Arizona Diamondbacks	$2.2 million	2028
Cinergy Field	Cinergy	Cincinnati Reds	$1 million	2002
Citizens Bank Park	Citizens Bank	Philadelphia Phillies	$2.3 million	2028

[1] Team severed its relationship with the firm.

Comerica Park	Comerica Bank	Detroit Tigers	$2.2 million	2030
Compaq Center	Compaq Computer	Houston Rockets, Comets[1]	$900,000	2003
Conseco Fieldhouse	Conseco	Indiana Pacers, Fever	$2 million	2019
Continental Airlines Arena[2]	Continental Airlines	New Jersey Nets, Devils	$1.4 million	2007
Coors Field[3]	Coors Brewing	Colorado Rockies	$15 million	Indefinite
Corel Center	Corel	Ottawa Senators	$878,142	2016
Delta Center	Delta Airlines	Utah Jazz, Starzz	$1.3 million	2011
Edward Jones Dome	Edward Jones	St. Louis Rams	$3.2 million	2025
FedEx Field	Federal Express	Washington Redskins	$7.6 million	2025
FedEx Forum	Federal Express	Memphis Grizzlies	$4.5 million	2023
Fleet Center[4]	Fleet Bank	Boston Celtics, Bruins	$6 million	2025
Ford Center	Ford Motor Co.	Oklahoma City Thunder	$5 million	2012
Ford Field	Ford Motor Co.	Detroit Lions	$2 million	2022

[1] Facility replaced by Toyota Center.

[2] Renamed Izod Center when Newark's Prudential Center opened In 2007.

[3] The Coors Brewing Company made a single payment and received the right to have its name on the ball park for as long as the ball park is in operation

[4] Banking changes led to the current name, TD Garden. This facility has had more than 30 different names.

(continued)

Table 3.13 (continued)   Selected naming rights deals and North American sport facilities

Facility	Sponsor	Teams	Annual Fee	Expiration Date
Gaylord Entertainment Center	Gaylord Entertainment	Nashville Predators	$4 million	2018
General Motors Place	General Motors	Vancouver Canucks	$844,366	2015
Gillette Stadium	Gillette	New England Patriots	$7.7 million	2017
Great American Ball Park	Great American Insurance	Cincinnati Reds	$2.5 million	2033
Gund Arena[1]	Owners	Cleveland Cavs, Rockers	$700,000	2014
Heinz Field	H.J. Heinz	Pittsburgh Steelers	$2.9 million	2021
HP Pavilion	Hewlett-Packard	San Jose Sharks	$4 million	2018
Honda Center	Honda Motor Co.	Anaheim Ducks	$4 million	2021
HSBC Arena	HSBC Bank	Buffalo Sabres	$800,000	2026
Invesco Field at Mile High	Invesco Funds	Denver Broncos	$6.0 million	2021
Jobing.Com Arena	Jobing.Com	Phoenix Coyotes	$3 million	2016

[1] The naming rights to what is now Quicken Loans Arena was for 20 years, expiring in 2014. The Gund brothers had those naming rights, and when they sold the Cavaliers to Dan Gilbert, he also had the right to change the name of the facility. The naming of this facility was always complicated as the team's owners also bought the naming rights and therefore the amount paid was always an internal transfer. The Gund brothers paid the team that they owned $700,000 a year for the naming rights. In selling this right to Dan Gilbert, he is able to establish the value paid by Quicken Loans to the Cavaliers and that amount is subject to the negotiations between Gilbert and his partners.

Key Arena	Key Corp.	Seattle Supersonics,[1] Storm	$1.0 million	2010
Lincoln Financial Field	Lincoln Financial Group	Philadelphia Eagles	$6.7 million	2022
LP Field	Louisiana-Pacific	Tennessee Titans	$3 million	2016
Lucas Oil Stadium	Lucas Oil	Indianapolis Colts	$6.1 million	2028
M & T Bank Stadium	M & T Bank	Baltimore Ravens	$5.0 million	2018
MCI Center	MCI	Wash. Wizards, Caps, Mystics	$2.2 million	2017
Mellon Arena	Mellon Financial	Pittsburgh Penguins	$1.8 million	2009
Monster Park	Monster Cable	San Francisco 49ers	$1.5 million	2007
Miller Park	Miller Brewing	Milwaukee Brewers	$2.1 million	2020
Minute Maid Park	Coca Cola	Houston Astros	$3.6 million	2030
Nationwide Arena	Nationwide Insurance	Columbus Blue Jackets	[2]	[2]
Network Associates Coliseum	Network Associates	Oakland As	$1.2 million	2003
Pengrowth Saddledome	Pengrowth Management	Calgary Flames	$1 million	2016
Pepsi Center	PepsiCo	Denver Nuggets, Colorado Avalanche	$3.4 million	2019

[1] Relocated to Oklahoma City for the 2009–10 NBA season

[2] Nationwide Insurance Company built and owns the arena and reserved the naming rights. The financial plight of the arena has raised the possibility that ownership may transfer to the public sector. What becomes of the naming rights might be part of any transfer agreement should one occur.

(continued)

Table 3.13 (continued) Selected naming rights deals and North American sport facilities

Facility	Sponsor	Teams	Annual Fee	Expiration Date
PETCO Park	PETCO	San Diego Padres	$2.7 million	2026
Phillips Arena	Royal Phillips Electronics	Atlanta Hawks, Thrashers	$9.3 million	2019
PNC Park	PNC Bank	Pittsburgh Pirates	$2 million	2020
Progressive Field	Progressive Insurance Company	Cleveland Indians	$3.6 million	2023
Qualcomm Stadium	Qualcomm	San Diego Padres, Chargers	$900,000	2017
Raymond James Stadium	Raymond James Financial	Tampa Bay Buccaneers	$3.1 million	2026
RBC Center	RBC Centura Banks	Carolina Hurricanes	$4 million	2022
RCA Dome	RCA	Indianapolis Colts	$1 million	2004
Reliant Stadium	Reliant Energy	Houston Texans	$10 million	2032
Rexall Place	Katz Group	Edmonton Oilers	N/A	2013
Safeco Field	Safeco Corp.	Seattle Mariners	$2 million	2019
Savvis Center	Savvis Communications	St. Louis Blues	N/A	N/A
SBC Center	SBC Communications	San Antonio Spurs	$2.1 million	2022

N/A = Not available

SBC Park	SBC Communications	San Francisco Giants	$2.1 million	2024
Scotiabank Place	Scotiabank	Ottawa Senators	$1.3 million	2021
Staples Center	Staples	Los Angeles Lakers, Kings, Clippers, Sparks	$5.8 million	2019
St. Petersburg Times Forum	St. Petersburg Times	Tampa Bay Lightning	$2.1 million	2014
Target Center	Target	Minnesota Timberwolves, Lynx	$1.3 million	2005
Toyota Center	Toyota	Houston Rockets	$5 million	2023
Tropicana Field	Tropicana	Tampa Bay Devil Rays	$1.5 million	2026
United Center	United Airlines	Chicago Blackhawks, Bulls	$1.8 million	2014
University of Phoenix Stadium	University of Phoenix	Arizona Cardinals	$7.7 million	2027
US Airways Center[1]	U.S. Airways	Phoenix Suns, Mercury	$866,667	2019
U.S. Cellular Field	U.S. Cellular	Chicago White Sox	$3.4 million	2025
Verizon Center	Verizon Wireless	Washington Capitals, Wizards	$2.9 million	2017
Wells Fargo Center	Wells Fargo Bank	Philadelphia 76ers, Flyers	$1.4 million	2023
Xcel Energy Center	Xcel Energy	Minnesota Wild	$3 million	2024

[1] US Airways acquired America West Airways and the naming rights deal for the arena.

is equally shared by all franchise owners regardless of the size of their local market. There is no revenue sharing of money earned from local contracts.

There are two major factors that determine the magnitude of these television contracts. The first issue is simply the demand for watching sports on television. The rising demand for televised games is one explanation for the increasing revenues paid to leagues, conferences, and teams. The other major factor that affects television contracts is bargaining power. When networks first began to televise sports, there were relatively few networks and essentially as many leagues as there are today. It is not that leagues had no bargaining power, after all, if networks wanted to show professional baseball on television, they still had to go through MLB. There are, however, many more media outlets and the number of leagues has not changed. For example, a major part of Sunday afternoons in the fall for millions of Americans is watching professional football. But, if a network wants to put professional football on its Sunday schedule, it has to go through the NFL. Excluding Monday Night Football, there are still at least three networks that have NFL games on Sunday. Given that there is one major professional football league and multiple networks, this gives the NFL an advantage. Although there are multiple sports leagues, they play in different seasons and fans are often sport-specific. So, since the number of networks is increasing at a much faster rate than sports leagues, this gives leagues an advantage in bargaining power. The size of the national media contracts for each league and the rate of increase between 1960 and 2008 is illustrated in Figure 3.3.

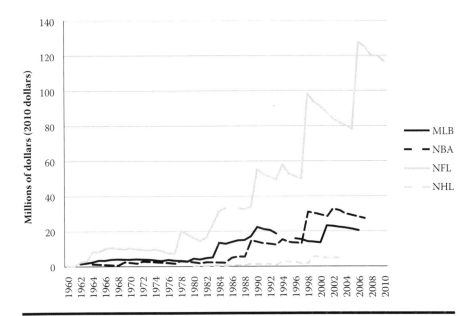

Figure 3.3 Team revenues from national media contracts, 1960–2010 (in 2010 dollars).

Player Costs

As the income statements show, there are many different costs incurred by sports teams. Things, such as marketing costs, administrative costs, travel costs, and interest payments, can certainly add up. Leagues like the NHL and MLB also can have significant player development costs. The biggest cost for most professional sports teams are their players. As Table 3.5 shows, this is not the case for universities because there are restrictions on paying college athletes. But, in a more competitive labor market, such as professional sports, players will receive a large percentage of revenues because they produce the entertainment fans want to see. In other words, players get paid a lot because their performances sell tickets and attract viewers. We will explore how league policies affect the competitiveness of the labor market later in the book, but Figure 3.4 shows how payrolls for major sports leagues have changed in the past few years.

The changes over the past few years are certainly not as dramatic as the changes over the last few decades. Team payrolls are still increasing in real terms. If we compare Figure 3.4 with Figure 3.3, it can be seen that NFL payrolls are roughly equal to their national media contract, but, in other leagues, national media contracts do not even come close to covering payrolls. The variance of team payrolls is very different depending on the league. For example, in 2009, the New York Giants had the highest NFL payroll at $138 million and the Kansas City Chiefs had the lowest at $81 million. The Giants had a 70-percent higher payroll. In 2010, the New York Yankees had a payroll of $206 million while the Pittsburgh Pirates had a payroll of $34 million. The Yankees spent more than six times what the Pirates did for players. Clearly much of the difference between leagues can be attributed to a salary cap in the NFL. This helps explain why disagreements between owners and players regarding such things as salary caps can often lead to a work stoppage.

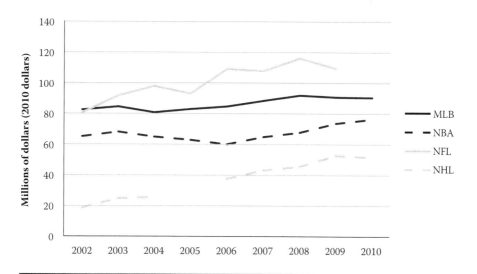

Figure 3.4   Average team payrolls, 2002–2010 (in 2010 dollars).

Chapter 4

Facilities:
"Disneyfication" and Design

Introduction

The selection of players, and their development, is the most important investment made by a team. Of almost equal importance, however, is the building and design of the arena, ballpark, or stadium in which games are played and the quality of the experience these facilities offer fans. A major part of that experience, of course, is the game on the field or court. But, the enjoyment of the game is affected by the sight lines that can be enhanced by different designs or configurations of the facilities and the inclusion of numerous other amenities. These amenities and superior views of action on the field, court, or rink can substantially enhance the revenue a team earns from its investment in players. A large number of fans are willing to pay higher ticket prices for enhanced levels of amenities, more varied experiences, excellent sight lines, and seats placed closer to the field or court. If a team fails to offer different amenity packages to the full range of its fans, then a franchise will not capitalize or realize the full potential of its investment in players. The failure to have the right mix of amenities, in essence, leaves a great deal of potential income "on the table." If a team fails to capitalize on most or all of its revenue opportunities then, in the long run, a franchise will either be less profitable (and have a lower market value) or spend less for players than teams that offer their fans a full-range of revenue generating amenities. A sports facility is a vast array of real estate and how a team designs, packages, and sells the various "locations" within its expansive holdings define the ability to maximize revenue.

It also is important to understand the value of luxury, and no one has mastered this concept more than automobile manufacturers. Consumers first and foremost want safe and dependable transportation. But, once that need is met, most automobile owners want some level of amenities, and some want every gadget and convenience available. These luxuries add profit to a manufacturer's bottom line. In a similar sense, fans want competitive teams. But, once that is available, they also want a set of amenities to enhance their experience. Those firms able to offer the most satisfying mix of packages enjoy higher profits. Those teams that play in facilities that can provide a mix of amenities at different price levels will be more financially successful than those teams that do not offer these choices to their fans. Facilities have to be considered similar to any real estate project in which a developer will offer higher priced homes and charge more for retail space in certain parts of the facility (or neighborhood) and then offer to other "buyers" lower priced seats or locations in other parts of the facility.

This chapter focuses on the design and building of facilities as well as the market dimensions that define the range of available options. It has been long realized that some fans are able and willing to pay higher admission prices to secure access to seats that offered the best available sight lines. As a result, seats closer to the field or courts have always cost more that those farther away. Fans also will pay more money for more comfortable (or wider seats). Building a facility with more comfortable seats, however, reduces the total number that can be offered (wider seats take up more space). How many wider seats should a team build at the expense of having a lower capacity? What is the appropriate balance between higher and lower priced seats given the distribution of income in the region and the amount of discretionary income that consumers can spend? Some fans also are willing to pay premium prices for luxury suites and "club seats." Suites offer adjacent and private entertainment or meeting areas. Club seats usually include access into a restricted but less private area with food and beverages at varying price points and slightly less desirable sight lines. What is the best mix of luxury and nonluxury seating that maximizes team revenues? This issue is addressed in this chapter as well.

This chapter examines the concept of *Disneyfication* (the inclusion of numerous retail outlets and entertainment activities within a facility) and its effects on revenues. The impact of building several facilities in a region on the aggregate demand for entertainment given existing levels of discretionary income is also discussed. The importance of this last point is underscored by the recent trends of building football stadiums that can host myriad sports and entertainment events (as well as conventions). The expanding supply of days on which events can be held has a direct effect on the revenues available to franchises. In New York, for example, where there are several all-purpose arenas, the Yankees announced (March 2010) that their new stadium would not only host annual college football games, but a new collegiate bowl game every year in late December. With the Mets doing the same (except for a bowl game) at Citi Field and the Giants/Jets hosting concerts and other athletic events at their brand new facility in the Meadowlands, New

York suddenly had a plethora of events and facilities each chasing the discretionary entertainment dollars available from residents and businesses. How much demand is there in any region for sports and entertainment and what happens when the supply of entertainment increases faster than demand? That, too, is considered here.

Facilities: The Early History

The initial and, in some instances, the original facilities used by teams that were built during the rise in the popularity of spectator sports in the early part of the twentieth century were paid for by team owners. Most fans reached these facilities using public transportation and owners wanted locations for the new sport venues at the nexus of transportation lines. This meant that the initial set of ballparks and arenas were designed to fit into the existing densities of urban centers. As a result, the facilities were often a bit "quirky." Some had very short home run porches (Ebbets Field, Brooklyn; left field at the Polo Grounds in New York; right field at Yankee Stadium, and "Pesky's Pole" in Boston); "Green Monsters" or very high walls to offset the short distances (Fenway Park); overhanging third decks that caught home run balls before they could fall into outfielders' gloves (Briggs Stadium, Detroit); inclines in the outfield (centerfield at Crosley Field, Cincinnati); or overly expansive center fields (Polo Grounds). The facilities with overhanging upper decks sometimes obstructed the view of the flight of the ball for fans in the lower deck. All facilities had poles to support the upper decks and those created obstructed views for some fans as well.

All of these differences or oddities became part of the urban folklore of sports in the early part of the twentieth century. Most of the facilities built were small in comparison to the facilities that would be built in the second half of the century, but there were some notable exceptions. Yankee Stadium (built in 1923 in the "suburban" Bronx) and Cleveland's Municipal Stadium built on the edge of downtown and away from that city's more densely developed residential neighborhoods each had more than 65,000 seats.

Team owners assumed complete responsibility for building the facilities they wanted. Legendary parks that are still in use include only Fenway Park (1912) and Wrigley Field (1914). Both, of course, were built by team owners and remain privately owned. The recent extensive renovations at Fenway Park were paid for by the Boston Red Sox. All of the other facilities about which legends abound were privately built as well, but have been replaced, including the original Yankee Stadium (1923), the Polo Grounds (1883), Crosley Field (1912), Comisky Park (1910), Ebbets Field (1913), and Briggs/Tiger Stadium (1912). These older facilities were characterized by Smith (2001) as jewel boxes, an allusion to the need to fit these larger urban structures into the land use patterns of late nineteenth and early twentieth century urban grid designs. They were not jewel boxes in terms of the comfort provided to fans. Indeed, even after renovations, the cramped aisles and concourses and obstructed views often compromised the romantic views many held of these ballparks and arenas. With these facilities aging and professional football emerging as another outdoor sport of increasing popularity in the 1960s, attention turned to the building of dual purpose facilities that would minimize land consumption and maximize the dates the facilities would be used. Cincinnati, New York, Philadelphia, Pittsburgh, and St. Louis each built saucer-like facilities that were homes to baseball and football teams.

The sight lines for fans of either sport were compromised in these circular stadiums given the need to fit both a diamond and rectangle into a round structure. For baseball, a majority of the action is concentrated within the 8,100 square feet defined by the infield diamond. Even balls that are hit to the outfield inevitably involve action within the 30 × 30 square yards that make up a baseball diamond. The best seats are the ones located between first and third base that circle around home plate. Football's action occurs across a space that is 100 yards from goal line to goal line and 53⅓ yards across. The best seats are at the 50-yard line with the stands pressed as close to the field as possible to ensure that those seats from the 10-yard line to the 10-yard line still offer a great view of the action. The two very different geometric shapes of the playing fields—a diamond and a rectangle—are not conducive for maximizing sight lines for fans if both baseball and football are to be played in the same venue. The compromises made to fit both playing fields into a single facility inevitably meant that the fans from one sport or the other were farther from the action on the field and that meant lower revenue levels as too much real estate for fans was too far from the action requiring lower prices to ensure the seats would be purchased. These reduced revenues led to keen interest in building separate ballparks for baseball and stadiums for football. The first area in which separate facilities were built for baseball and football teams was in Kansas City in the 1970s.

Since the opening of Arrowhead Stadium (Chiefs) and Kaufman Stadium (Royals), a new pattern of building separate facilities for baseball and football teams has been underway. With the Minnesota Twins leaving the Metrodome for Target Field in 2010, only the Oakland Athletics (baseball) and Raiders (football) now share a facility. The Athletics remain focused on building a ballpark and, through 2011, were interested in relocating to downtown San Jose and building a 37,000-seat ballpark. The Raiders will then remain at Oakland–Alameda County Coliseum.

Arenas followed a similar history in terms of initially being built and maintained by franchise owners or other entrepreneurs, followed by increasing levels of public investment in several markets. A number of new arenas, however, have been largely privately financed. One of the first publicly paid for arenas was a new home for the Zollner Pistons (NBA) in Fort Wayne, Indiana built by Allen County. After a few seasons, Fred Zollner decided to move the team to Detroit leaving the county to find another tenant and other entertainment events to generate sufficient revenues to repay the bond sold to build the War Memorial Coliseum. Arenas were initially designed for basketball and nonsports events, and then several facilities added the machinery needed to maintain ice. A hockey rink can fit into an arena designed for basketball, but sight line issues inevitably exist given the longer dimensions of the playing surface for NHL hockey compared to a basketball court. For an arena to accommodate both sports, the upper decks of seats need to have larger setbacks (the distance of the upper decks from the playing surface) so that the goal nets for hockey are not obscured from any seat. An NBA basketball court is 94 feet long and 50 feet wide (Rule No. 1). An NHL rink is 200 feet long and 85 feet wide. The additional 53 feet in length on both ends means that fans in the upper decks of an arena might not see the net if the deck was placed closer to the playing surface defined by an NBA court. Similar blind spots could exist on the sides if an arena was constructed for basketball and that team's owner wanted to ensure fans were as close to the court as possible.

Some hockey teams in regions with basketball franchises sought their own venues and found willing partners in Glendale, Arizona, and St. Paul, Minnesota. In Detroit, the Pistons built their own arena in the region's northern suburbs, but its design would permit a hockey team's presence without any obstructed views of the goals. In most areas with both an NBA and NHL franchise, however, the teams play in the same facility (e.g., Boston, Chicago, Dallas, Los Angeles, New York City, Washington, D.C.). The older arenas were built and maintained by private entrepreneurs. Today, team owners have built several facilities with limited public support (e.g., Columbus, Chicago, Los Angeles, Washington, D.C.) while other owners have benefited from substantial public sector investments (Cleveland, Dallas, Glendale, St. Paul, etc.). Later in this chapter, the implications for a region having separate arenas for basketball and hockey teams will be explored.

Why and when did the pattern of exclusive private sector responsibility for the building and maintaining of facilities change? The answer to this question lies in the ability of teams and leagues to control the supply of teams. When that level of economic and political control was combined with the growing popularity of sports and increasing levels of consumer wealth, team owners could and did make demands that led to the public sector in many regions making investments in facilities. That commitment of tax money for the building of a facility reduced owners' costs, which created the opportunity to realize higher levels of profits from team operations. There may be an appropriate reason for the public sector to make an investment in a sports facility (and the reasons for that will be detailed), but the scarcity of franchises, in many instances, has led to excessive public investments that exceed what would be appropriate given the public goods benefits created by a team's presence. How this artificial scarcity of teams came to exist and how it is maintained lies in the history of the development of the four major leagues, the various consolidations that took place, and the ultimate control over the supply and location of teams that is now vested in these leagues.

The Constrained Supply of Sports Franchises

In the early years of professional sports in the United States, teams and leagues fell into bankruptcy or ceased operations at about the same rate as other start-up businesses (Scully, 1995). These failures, despite the success of numerous other teams, convinced franchise owners to form leagues that would enhance their chances of success. There were several main purposes for these leagues, but a paramount concern was to ensure that each team would retain exclusive control of its designated local market. Further, to prevent interlopers or competitors from gaining a foothold in any market, each league member agreed not to schedule games with nonleague teams. This restricted the number of teams that would exist in any market area (in most instances, setting that number at one) and by maintaining tight control on the number of teams that existed, the owners could be sure that regions would compete with each other to attract teams. Within regions, with the number of teams restricted, cities might well also compete to be a team's home. All of this competition led to inducements or subsidies from communities that wanted a team to locate within their borders, and the frequent vehicle or form of these subsidies was to offer a team's owner use of a new facility for a cost far less than was needed to build and maintain it. This subsidy would then substantially reduce the cost of operating a franchise. The supply of teams was restricted and demand soared as the nation's population increased and became wealthier. Sports fans in cities without teams yearned for a franchise. If the leagues would not create new teams, then the next best strategy for a city to pursue was to build a new arena, ballpark or stadium and offer it to any team that might find the lure of reduced rent (or no rent) as a way to realize new profits.

In the wake of the baby boom and the economic expansion of the post-World War II years, the competition for sports teams became *the* sport for cities across the United States. The 1950s saw the relocation of four baseball teams and, in each instance, a new facility in an untapped market for professional sports was the lure. Milwaukee County (Milwaukee, Wisconsin) launched the modern era of public support for a sports facility paying 100 percent of the cost for a new ballpark. That public sector inducement lured the Braves who left Boston to their American League rivals (Red Sox). Years later, Atlanta would offer the Braves another new facility and a larger population base; the Braves moved once again to become Atlanta's team. Baltimore paid 100 percent of the cost for a ballpark that brought the Browns from St. Louis. The team left that market to the Cardinals and assumed the name of Baltimore's original baseball team, the Orioles. The original Orioles had left Baltimore to become the New York Highlanders in 1903. The Highlanders later changed their name to the Yankees and moved from Manhattan to the Bronx.

Boston and St. Louis each had two teams as a result of the founding of the American League as a competitor to the older and more established National League of Professional Baseball. In 1900, the National League contracted, eliminating teams in Baltimore, Cleveland, Louisville, and Washington, D.C. The American

League was created as a competing major league in 1901 with teams in Baltimore, Boston, Cleveland, Chicago, Detroit, Milwaukee, Philadelphia, and Washington, D.C. (The upstart league initially decided not to confront the older league in New York where the Dodgers played in Brooklyn and the Giants played in Manhattan.) New York then had teams in each of its largest population centers.* The original Milwaukee Brewers moved to the larger market of St. Louis in 1902. Cities that could not get teams often found that being home to a team from a competing league was the best way to assure the presence of professional sports. In the 1960s, the American Football League battled the NFL and brought football teams to cities that the older league had ignored. The American Basketball Association brought professional basketball to Denver and Indianapolis. In the absence of a new league, however, cities were forced to try to lure teams from other cities.

The 1950s also saw the Dodgers leave Brooklyn for Los Angeles. Los Angeles's offer of land upon which the team could build a new ballpark was a sufficient subsidy after New York's legendary civic leader, Robert Moses, thwarted the O'Malley family's dream of a new ballpark at the current site of the Barclays Center (Atlantic Yards and the Nets). The Giants joined in the move west, and San Francisco paid for Candlestick Park that became that team's home for decades. The Giants shared Candlestick Park with the city's other professional team, the NFL's 49ers. To help entice MLB back to New York, after threatening to form a third major league, New York City agreed to build a new home for an expansion franchise (the Mets). Shea Stadium also would serve as the home to the New York Jets and it was built in the area offered by Robert Moses to the Dodgers, in the borough of Queens' Flushing Meadow Park. That was the space where Moses wanted professional baseball to be played. Adjacent to one of the region's major highways, Moses's plans called for a new ballpark that would be convenient for those arriving by car and for the placement of that automobile-friendly ballpark in a location where neighborhoods like those in Brooklyn would not suffer from ballpark-generated automobile traffic.

The building of facilities to lure teams continued into the 1980s. Indianapolis built the Hoosier Dome as part of its new convention center with substantial financial support from a local foundation. Ostensibly created to enhance the city's location for conventions, the community's leadership was hardly secretive in its willingness to offer the facility and very luxurious lease terms that included retention of all income from suites to any NFL team willing to relocate to Indianapolis. The inclusion of luxury seating in facilities was, at the time, a novelty and their inclusion in the design of the Hoosier Dome was a clear incentive to pique the interest of an NFL team owner who wanted to enjoy an

---

* In terms of the general observation that leagues never placed two teams in the same city, it should be noted that when the club that would become the Dodgers (the Grays) began play (1883), Brooklyn was an independent city. Brooklyn had a professional baseball team in the first year of play of the National League (1876); that franchise was eventually expelled and replaced, first by the Hartfords and then the Grays. Brooklyn became part of New York City in 1898.

immediate boost in revenues. Robert Irsay owned the Baltimore Colts and when he could not secure a financial commitment from Baltimore for a new stadium, he chose to move the legendary franchise to Indianapolis. Numerous other communities also would respond to the scarcity in the number of franchises by offering to pay for facilities. Chicago and Illinois feared the White Sox would move to Florida and increased their investment in a new ballpark in 1992. Ironically, the White Sox threat was to move to St. Petersburg where the Tampa Bay Rays now play. The Rays have had attendance problems for years and questions remain unanswered as to the long-term viability of this region as a market for baseball. Had the White Sox moved, they likely would have encountered some of the same challenges that have plagued the Rays' efforts to attract fans. Far fewer people live in the Tampa/St. Petersburg region (2.7 million) than live in the Chicago metropolitan area (9.6 million).* Even if half of the Chicago region's fans support the Cubs, the White Sox would enjoy a market of at least 4.8 million people, considerably larger than what exists in Tampa/St. Petersburg.

Cleveland and Cuyahoga County feared the Indians would relocate to Florida, especially after MLB's commissioner said the franchise would be supported in its efforts to move if a new ballpark was not built in Cleveland (Rosentraub, 1999). Cuyahoga County's voters agreed to a subsidy in 1990 and the new ballpark opened in 1994. Cleveland then lost the Browns to Baltimore (the team changed its name to the Ravens) when Maryland offered to build a new stadium for the franchise without requiring any investment by the team's owner or any substantial rental fees. Baltimore and Maryland responded to the loss of the Colts by offering a facility just as Indianapolis had done. Cleveland rallied political support that convinced the NFL to offer the city an expansions franchise, but Cleveland and Cuyahoga County had to secure financing for a new stadium before a new Cleveland Browns could begin play. A detailed list of the early set of capitulations to ensure teams would move to a city or stay is available in Cagan and deMause's *Field of Schemes* (1998); Long's 2002 dissertation, *Full Count: The Real Cost of Public Subsidies for Major League Sports Facilities*; and Zimbalist and Long's (2006) journal article, Facility finance: Measurement, trends, and analysis. Added to the lists compiled by these authors would be the city of Arlington's taxpayer support for a new home for the Dallas Cowboys. The deal between the Cowboys and the City of Arlington was somewhat different from many of the arrangements agreed to in the early 1990s. In most of those earlier deals, the public sector was responsible for all or a substantial portion of a facility's cost. In Arlington, taxpayers invested $325 million in Cowboys Stadium. With a final cost in excess of $1 billion, the team's investment was more than twice as large as that made by taxpayers. It was, however, Arlington's willingness to provide the subsidy that convinced the team to relocate from Irving.

---

* U.S. Bureau of the Census estimates for 2009, http://www.census.gov/popest/metro/CBSA-est2009-annual.html (accessed January 27, 2011).

Legal challenges to the leagues' ability to control the supply of teams have been unsuccessful. In addition, the U.S. Congress, even when urged by various federal courts to restrain the power of the professional sports leagues, has been unwilling to pass laws that would have created an economic environment in which competitive leagues could flourish. As a result, an environment continues to exist in which cities encounter substantial challenges to attract and retain teams, and a great deal of innovative policies, practices, and politics are needed to minimize the subsidies that only enhance the wealth of team owners and players. As cities attempted to use sports franchises as tools or assets for the redevelopment of downtown areas, there was even more pressure to retain or attract teams. As described by one former U.S. senator, when St. Louis lost its NFL team (to Phoenix), the general feeling was that the city's best days were behind it because the team left (Rosentraub, 1999). That sentiment allowed team owners to become the beneficiaries of the public sector's large investment in sports facilities to ensure the continued presence of a team, or to lure a franchise from somewhere else. In later years, strategies would develop to effectively reduce the subsidies (Rosentraub, 2010), but the 1990s became a watershed period when dozens of facilities were built. The public sector in many instances paid a substantial portion of the construction costs associated with the building of arenas, ballparks, and stadiums. In several cities, the public sector also assumed a large portion of the responsibility for ongoing maintenance costs. These annual maintenance costs, after the initial few years of operations, frequently amount to several million dollars if a facility is to remain attractive and state-of-the-art relative to amenities and revenue production. The term *state-of-the-art* found its way into numerous contracts between teams and local governments and became a standard for defining what was meant by appropriate maintenance of a facility.

The magnitude of the public sector investments led to a series of analyses highly critical of the relations between teams and their host cities. In a variety of ways, researchers noted that the payments by local governments for facilities were a direct result of the constraint placed on the number of franchises by the four leagues. Zimbalist (1992) tackled this issue by noting the potential for more high-quality teams to exist as a result of the growth in the supply of high-quality athletes. He concluded that in 1903, when the American League was independent and challenging the National League for fans and players, there was one ballplayer for every 250,000 people. Given today's population of the United States and the number of teams that exist, the ratio is larger, not smaller. Today there is one ballplayer for every 400,000+ people in the United States. To be sure, there are more sports leagues (the NBA and the NFL, for example) and one could then argue that there has been a diminution of the talent available for baseball teams despite this impressive ratio. The obvious response, of course, is that MLB in the twenty-first century draws players from a much larger pool of human capital than did owners at the beginning of the twentieth century. For example, in the early part of the twentieth century, MLB did not include African-American players and so their numbers in the population in Zimbalist's ratio for 1903 included a large segment of the population that was excluded from participation. In reality, the ratio was probably closer to 200,000 people for every ballplayer than it was to 250,000. Today there are also dozens of MLB players from Central America and a score of other countries, so Zimbalist's point remains quite valid. The population has increased so much that there is no deficiency in the supply of people with the ability to play MLB. The expanded supply of potential ballplayers is more than sufficient to support a larger number of teams than currently exist.

Is there sufficient demand and consumer spending available to support more teams? With rising attendance levels for MLB and minor league baseball, there is indeed ample evidence that consumers (sports fans) would be very receptive to more teams. Of course, if there were more teams, prices might decline, as supply would increase. That might well be in the interest of fans, but it might not be in the best interest of team owners or local governments that have invested in facilities. The value of these investments—owning or hosting a team—lies in the artificial scarcity that has been created. After all, if every city that wanted a team had one, then being home to a team has less cache and less value.

Owners have an incentive to restrict supply and because MLB controls the supply of teams, their interests prevail over those of consumers. Rosentraub (1999) used the growth in the population in the United States to illustrate that more NFL and MLB teams could exist without overstressing markets with too much sports product. The Dallas/Fort Worth, New York, and Los Angeles regions, to name just three, have grown sufficiently large that each could comfortably support additional NFL and MLB franchises. As noted earlier, there is currently no NFL team in Los Angeles despite the apparent demand that exists for sports relative to the supply of tickets to all major professional sports and USC and UCLA football.

When demand increases faster than supply, prices rise, and this is exactly what has happened. The price rise has taken the form in many cities of both higher ticket prices and the participation of the public sector in financing and maintaining new arenas, ballparks, and stadiums. With supply growing far slower than demand, communities present bids to convince a team to remain or come to their region. In effect, what exists is an auction where communities present their bids that usually consist of pledges from businesses to purchase luxury seating, commitments from businesses and individuals to buy season tickets, and then an investment by the public sector in a playing facility. These investments by the public sector reduce the cost of operating a team. As a result, profits are elevated.

Disneyfication and the Location of Facilities

The contributions a facility's design can make to the production of positive externalities for a city's identity and for the attraction of human capital was already discussed. A major planning decision for a city and the teams that use a facility is the extent to which an arena, ballpark, or stadium is to have an iconic exterior design. The image benefits for a city or region of such an external design is clear. Later in this chapter, we will discuss why an iconic external design can lead to higher revenue for a team from the hosting of other events. Before turning to that issue in the section that looks at the number of facilities in a region, it is necessary to focus on "internal" design issues that must be considered to maximize revenue generation. That discussion is anchored in what has been labeled the Disneyfication of sports, tourism, and entertainment. Understanding these changes are critical for sport managers and these new design elements have created extraordinary new revenue sources that can and do dramatically change a team's financial position.

The term *Disneyfication* is used to refer to the building of facilities or locales that include a wide set of complementary activities that fans or visitors are likely to engage in when they attend a game or event. The concept, according to legend, grew from Walt Disney's conclusion after seeing the hotels and activities that other entrepreneurs built surrounding Disneyland in Southern California. A story is told and retold that Walt Disney declared that, when he built a new park, it would be large enough to include all of the activities or amenities that visitors consumed from other entrepreneurs when visiting "his" park. Such a park would require a great deal of land so that numerous hotels, restaurants, and even other parks and attractions could be built by Disney and controlled by his corporation. After rejecting a location in the St. Louis region, Walt Disney and his team chose land in the Orlando area to build his "Disney World." Disney World includes 32 hotels, a 600,000-square-foot convention center, 6 golf courses, several other entertainment parks, and scores of restaurants and retail outlets. Disney World's facilities cover more than 47 square miles or a land area approximately the size of the city of San Francisco. Disneyland was built on a 430-acre site. Disney World covers 30,500 acres, making it 71 times larger.

What Does Disneyfication Mean for the Design of Sports Facilities?

Disneyfication's meaning and impact begins with a much larger footprint (or a much larger physical structure) to include within the facility the full set of amenities a fan or visitor might enjoy on a game day or while attending a nonsports event. These amenities include restaurants, pubs, retail spaces, and even other activities that one can enjoy while the main event takes place. Because businesses use sports and entertainment to impress their clients and reward their employees, space also is needed for hosting visitors. Playing fields did not get larger (and, in numerous instances, the number of seats in the newer facilities was actually smaller to afford better site lines), but the newer "Disneyfied" facilities were far larger. For example, the new Yankee Stadium has almost twice the retail square footage of the old ballpark and 13 restaurants and pubs compared to 4 in the facility built in 1923 (and remodeled in the 1970s). The new Yankee Stadium has 56 luxury suites and 410 party suites (which can be rented for an individual game). The older facility had 19 suites. The new Yankee Stadium is 163-percent larger than the size of the facility it replaced even though the playing fields in both facilities were identical.

Lucas Oil Stadium is the new home to the Indianapolis Colts and covers 12 acres with 522,720 square feet of space. It replaced the 7.25-acre RCA Dome that included 315,820 square feet of space. The new facility is 65.5 percent larger than the one it replaced even though the size of the playing surface is unchanged. The new facility, however, includes 148 retail sites compared to 85 in the older one, and more suites and space within each suite for added amenities. As unbelievable as this might sound, and as large as Lucas Oil Stadium is, it could be placed *inside* the new stadium that serves as the home of the Dallas Cowboys. The Cowboys' new home can seat 35,000 more fans than their former home, Texas Stadium, (80,000 with expansion possibilities that permit 100,000 spectators for football games), and has 800 retail and restaurant points or sites and 2,900 video screens. The Cowboys' new stadium covers 73 acres, making its footprint six times that of Lucas Oil Stadium. The new Yankee Stadium sits on a 22-acre site, and although Citi Field has 15,000 fewer seats than the stadium it replaced, the Mets' new home is far larger than Shea Stadium and includes a rotunda as well as several clubs, restaurants, and numerous points for retail sales. Just as Walt Disney greatly expanded his concept of Disneyland to encompass the total experience of an amusement park, team owners now seek designs that encourage fans to enjoy their game or event day meals (pre- and postgame activities) at the facility while providing space for entertaining friends or clients and numerous points of sale for souvenirs. The spending that fans did outside of facilities in a bygone past now occurs within, resulting in more revenues for a team. And, with fans spending far more time at a facility, advertising or naming rights are more valuable as there is more time for people to see the messages and products of different companies. Each of these changes creates opportunities for sports managers to maximize team revenue.

The building of a new facility that can incorporate the space required to maximize revenues requires the assembly of the land needed. A new arena, to fully maximize its revenue potential, benefits from having a building site that is approximately 10 acres in size. Ballparks and stadiums, as the example of the Colts, Cowboys, and Yankees illustrate, can utilize anywhere from approximately 15 to 73 acres. The first issue in building a facility, then, is to ensure that enough land is available to maximize all the revenue streams that can be built into a facility that practices Disneyfication.

The next issue to consider is convenient fan access, and that varies quite a bit between the sports.

Where Should a Facility Be Built?

After considering the need for land (and that is nonnegotiable relative to revenue flows), the second consideration is convenience for fans. Two factors guide the convenience discussion. First, the constraints on convenience vary by sport. Second, each team has to consider the needs of customers who purchase luxury seating and those who buy seats in the other sections.

There is a large difference in what is referred to as consumption costs by sport. Consumption costs, as they relate to attendance at a sporting event, refer to the commutation expenses fans have to make to attend games. These costs are lowest for football and highest for baseball. Why? A typical NFL season involves a small number of home games, the vast majority of which are played on the weekend. A season ticket involves a commitment to be present for eight games (with two preseason games) and, if a team qualifies for the playoffs, the maximum number of games that can be hosted by any team is two. If one of those preseason games becomes a regular season contest (as was considered by the players and owners as part of their recent collective bargaining process), the total number of games played will not change. This means that a fan would make, at the most, 12 trips to a venue spread across 6 months (August through January) or an average of two trips a month for any fan. That is very different from the experience or commitment fans of any of the other major sports must make if they acquire a season ticket. Teams in the other three leagues play from 41 (basketball, hockey) to 81(baseball) regular season home games. In addition, NHL and NBA teams can play as many as 16 home playoff games, raising the total number of contests to 57 (not counting preseason games). That can mean as many as eight trips to a sporting facility per month, and, in some weeks, there are multiple home games for NHL and NBA teams. In baseball, the total number of home playoff games is 11, raising the total number of games any team can play to 92. This means there can be as many as 15 games or more in any month. How does the number of games affect where teams should locate?

Revenue maximization for teams requires catering to two groups of fans: those who buy luxury seating and those who purchase tickets for seats in the balance of a facility (often referred to as the deck). In choosing a location, it is important to understand where each group of fans or consumers is concentrated, and their "consumption costs" related to the purchase of season ticket plans (or even partial ticket plans) and individual game tickets. Starting with the NFL, with games played mostly on weekends or holidays (with the occasional weekday night game), these facilities, even if located in suburban areas away from business centers, can still be convenient locations for all fans. Those who purchase luxury seating can generally afford extra travel time for a weekend game. If there are comfortable and convenient transportation options and congestion time is minimized, the available data suggest suburban locations do not hinder consumption or restrict revenue flows. The Washington Redskins and Dallas Cowboys, for example, both have stadiums in suburban areas or cities a bit distant from the centers where businesses that typically buy luxury seating have headquarter offices. The Arizona Cardinals' new stadium is also on the northwestern edge of the Phoenix metropolitan area and luxury seating there enjoys robust sales despite its location far from downtown Phoenix and the valley's wealthy eastern suburbs.

There is greater risk for teams in the other sports to locate their facilities too far from headquarter offices of area businesses. The majority of baseball, hockey, and basketball games are played on weekdays. After a day of work, commuting a long distance to a game and then having to return home increases consumption costs. Having facilities near a concentration of headquarters offices often maximizes convenience for those fans and businesses. Downtown areas often offer this type of concentration even in decentralized areas (e.g., Dallas, Los Angeles, Phoenix) where there may be more than one business center. Downtown areas are often located at the nexus of public transportation and roadways and the concentration of parking structures. The latter is an important asset as the existence of these structures can reduce the need for the building of new parking lots. The transportation and parking advantages in downtown areas frequently means congestion levels might be less. That could reduce commuting times and make attendance even more convenient as compared to a more suburban location where parking options are constrained, mass transportation could be less available or even absent, and a smaller network of roads could lead to more congestion.

The availability of sufficient land is the most important issue when choosing a location for a new sports facility. If the needed acreage is not available to include the aspects of the Disneyfication of sports, then profitable revenue streams may be absent leading to lower levels of profitability. If the required land is available in more than one location, and one of those locations is closer to a region's central business district, then that is a more profitable location for ballparks and arenas. Football teams also might find such a location attractive, but the nature of their product offers locational options with minimal risk. For baseball, basketball, and hockey teams with their longer schedules and the high proportion of weekday games, locations farther from central business districts and employment centers carry with it more risk. That risk is reduced when the team is successful. Winning teams make fans feel more inclined to absorb consumption or travel costs. When teams go through their inevitable cycles that includes nonwinning seasons or years in which a franchise does not compete for a championship, convenience and the quality of a fan's experience at a venue can bolster attendance. Land and location, then, are the two factors that should be the main variables guiding the selection of a site, but other factors inevitably enter into the process.

Historic locations often mean that choosing another part of a region is not realistic. The Yankees and Mets might have considered alternatives, but each remained where they had played for decades. Citi Field was built in the parking lot adjacent to Shea Stadium in Flushing Meadow Park in Queens. The Yankees and New York entered into a controversial land swap allowing the new Yankee Stadium to be built on municipally owned parkland adjacent to the old stadium. The site of the former ballpark will then become a park for the neighborhood. The controversy was tied, in part, to the larger size of the new facility and, therefore, its use of more land than was immediately available to make "the swap" equal. With the building of an $800 million new ballpark in the Willets Point section of Queens by the Mets, there is renewed interest and pressure on the city to advance economic development in an area that had been allowed to deteriorate to ensure the success of the facility.

Incentives provided by the public sector in an effort to relocate economic activity to certain areas also assumes a large role in the selection of a site for a new facility. The public sector is frequently interested in enhancing the economic vitality of its downtown areas, so the incentives that are provided are frequently more politically palatable if teams agree to play in the city's center. The San Diego Padres, for example, played their home games in a suburban facility controlled by the NFL's Chargers. Its sight lines were far from ideal for baseball, but they were not as terrible as those in some other dual use facilities. The Padres preferred a suburban location for a new ballpark, but the city government's interest in a new facility and their willingness to invest in it was tied to a downtown location. In the end, the Ballpark District was built on the location chosen by the city. The resulting partnership led to more than $2 billion in new residential and commercial real estate development in the Ballpark District.

Design and the Competition for Discretionary Income

Before returning to the issue of iconic design and its effects, the next decision a team must make involves the mix of luxury seating and the overall seating capacity. What is the right number of suites and club seats, and how many seats should be included? There are certain size issues that have become benchmarks relative to sight lines. For example, ballparks with seating for approximately 45,000 have been found to maximize sight lines and offer fans the best range of amenities. Facilities of this size maximize the number of seats between first and third base and then along the foul lines, but beyond the bases. Those ballparks that offer more seating capacity must either place extra seats in a taller upper deck or in the outfield. With reduced sight lines, extra seats will only sustain lower prices. Further, if the team is not as successful, it is likely these seats will remain unsold. While it is usually considered better to play games without too many vacant seats, there is another very important reason not to build too much excess capacity. When fans know that there will always be tickets available, they are reluctant to make advance purchases. This leaves teams dependent on large walk-up crowds on the day of a game and vulnerable to the possibility that at the last moment people might decide not to attend a game. When fans are concerned that good seats for a particular game they want to see may sell out, they are more likely to make an advance purchase.

The seating capacity of all ballparks and the date the facilities were built or renovated are detailed in Table 4.1. The convergence on seating capacities for ballparks of approximately 42,000 for those built in the 1990s or later is evident. The

Table 4.1 Seating capacity at MLB ballparks

Team	Seating Capacity	Year Opened or Renovated
Arizona Diamondbacks	49,033	1998
Atlanta Braves	50,096	1996
Baltimore Orioles	48,876	1992
Boston Red Sox	39,512	2005
Chicago Cubs	41,118	2005
Chicago White Sox	40,615	1991
Cincinnati Reds	42,059	2003
Cleveland Indians	43,345	1994
Colorado Rockies	50,445	1995
Detroit Tigers	41,782	2000
Florida Marlins	37,000	2012
Houston Astros	40,950	2000
Kansas City Royals	38,030	1973
Oakland Athletics	35,067	1996
Los Angles Angels	45,050	1998
Los Angeles Dodgers	56,000	2008
Milwaukee Brewers	41,900	2001
Minnesota Twins	40,000	2010
New York Mets	41,800	2009
New York Yankees	50,086	2010
Philadelphia Phillies	43,647	2004
Pittsburgh Pirates	38,496	2001
San Diego Padres	42,445	2004
San Francisco Giants	41,503	2000
Seattle Mariners	47,116	1999
St. Louis Cardinals	46,861	2006
Tampa Bay Rays	34,078	2006
Texas Rangers	49,115	1992
Toronto Blue Jays	49,539	1989
Washington Nationals	41,888	2008

robustness of the market or demand for baseball explains the variations from this figure. As would be expected, the new Yankee Stadium has more seats. At the same time, the New York Mets, intent on building a facility more similar to the "jewel box"-era ballparks, chose a capacity of less than 42,000. The two Florida franchises, given the challenges they have had in attracting fans even in successful years, chose designs with fewer than 40,000 seats. What is critical to understand in terms of the seating capacity at a ballpark is that with less than 45,000 seats there is a concentration of high-value seats (good sight lines). Larger capacities mean the inclusion of more low-value seats and this should only be done when market demand assessments indicate those seats too will be sold on most game days.

There is even more convergence in the seating capacity for arenas. The largest seating capacities for NBA teams are to be found at the Detroit Pistons' Palace in Auburn Hills (22,076 seats) and at the Wachovia Center where 21,600 seats are available for Philadelphia 76ers' games. The New Orleans Hornets play in the facility with the fewest seats, 18,000. The average for all arenas is 19,277. The Hornets' home has 7.2 percent fewer seats than the average NBA arena and the Pistons' home offers 13.8 percent more seats. Given the larger playing surface for hockey, seating at arenas would be expected to be less. The average for NHL teams is 18,522. The Chicago Blackhawks can seat 20,500 fans at its games. The arenas home to the Edmonton Oilers and New York Islanders have the smallest seating capacities, but both teams will soon play in new facilities. In the newest arenas, it is common to find approximately 18,000 seats for hockey teams. The decision on seating capacity for an arena is driven by the same factors that shape the conversations regarding the capacity for ballparks. More seats means fans in the upper deck will be farther away and above the playing surface. These seats will command far lower prices unless the demand for tickets is relatively inelastic. In addition, when the team enjoys less success, tickets for these seats may be in relatively low demand meaning there could be empty sections. The team also would become more dependent on walk-up sales. For these reasons, the clear pattern of seating capacity of approximately 19,000 for basketball and 18,000 for hockey is the dominant pattern in newer facilities (Table 4.2).

Once the overall seating capacity is selected then the focus is on the right mix of luxury suites and club seats. The importance of this design decision is best illustrated by outcomes in Cleveland. When Progressive Field (originally Jacobs Field) was built, the team's owner, Richard Jacobs (he sold the team to the Dolan family trust), wanted an extra tier of suites. One plan included two levels of suites; a second plan installed a third level. The design built had suites on three different levels. Jacobs Field opened during a time when Richard Jacobs dramatically increased his spending for players and the team was in the midst of a series of very successful seasons culminating in two World Series appearances. The demand for tickets was at an all-time high and, in this robust environment, it seemed reasonable that a larger number of suites would sell to businesses eager to entertain their clients. Including an extra tier of suites, however, meant the upper deck would be 10 to 12 feet higher (above the playing field). Seats in this deck were thus farther from the field. The extra tier of suites led to more revenue

Table 4.2 Seating capacities for NBA and NHL teams

NBA Team	Seating Capacity	Year Built/ Renovated	NHL Team	Seating Capacity	Year Built/ Renovated
Atlanta Hawks	18,750	1999	Anaheim Ducks	18,136	1993
Boston Celtics	18,624	1995	Atlanta Thrashers	18,545	1999
Charlotte Bobcats	19,000	2005	Boston Bruins	17,565	1995
Chicago Bulls	20,917	1994	Buffalo Sabres	18,690	1996
Cleveland Cavaliers	20,562	1994	Calgary Flames	19,289	1983
Dallas Mavericks	19,200	2001	Carolina Hurricanes	18,730	1999
Denver Nuggets	19,309	1999	Chicago Blackhawks	20,500	1994
Detroit Pistons	22,076	1988	Columbus Blue Jackets	18,136	2000
Golden State Warriors	19,596	1966	Colorado Avalanche	18,007	1999
Houston Rockets	18,370	2003	Dallas Stars	18,352	2001
Indiana Pacers	18,345	1999	Detroit Red Wings	20,066	1979
Los Angeles Clippers	19,060	1999	Edmonton Oilers	16,839	1974
Los Angeles Lakers	18,997	1999	Florida Panthers	19,250	1998
Memphis Grizzlies	18,165	2004	Los Angeles Kings	18,118	1999
Miami Heat	19,600	1999	Minnesota Wild	18,064	2000

Team	Capacity	Year	Team	Capacity	Year
Milwaukee Bucks	18,717	1988	Montreal Canadians	21,273	1996
Minnesota Timberwolves	20,500	1990	Nashville Predators	17,113	1996
New Jersey Nets	18,000	2012	New Jersey Devils	17,625	2007
New Orleans Hornets	18,000	1999	New York Islanders	16,234	1972
New York Knicks	19,738	2013	New York Rangers[1]	18,200	2013
Oklahoma City Thunder	18,203	2009	Ottawa Senators	19,153	2005
Orlando Magic	18,500	2010	Philadelphia Flyers	19,519	1996
Philadelphia 76ers	21,600	1996	Pittsburgh Penguins	18,087	2010
Phoenix Suns	18,422	1992	Phoenix Coyotes	17,125	2003
Portland Trail Blazers	19,980	1995	San Jose Sharks	17,496	1993
Sacramento Kings	17,317	1988	St. Louis Blues	19,260	1994
San Antonio Spurs	18,797	2002	Tampa Bay Lightning	19,500	1996
Toronto Raptors	19,800	1999	Toronto Maple Leafs	18,819	1999
Utah Jazz	19,991	1991	Vancouver Canucks	18,630	1995
Washington Wizards	20,173	1997	Washington Capitals	18,672	1997
Average	19,277		Average	18,522	

[1] Renovations to Madison Square Garden are under way.

in the facility's earliest years even though the more distant upper deck seats commanded lower prices as they were located farther from the field. A few years after the new ballpark opened the decline in the region's economy accelerated and, with several businesses relocating to other parts of the United States, there was a sharp decline in the demand for luxury suites. The intensity of the recession combined with a decline in the team's performance further dampened demand and many of the suites went unsold for several seasons. If the region does not become home to several larger firms in the near future, these seats may remain unsold at the same time the elevation of the upper deck reduces the revenue capacity of those seats. Properly estimating the short- and long-term demand for luxury seating is critical in the design of a facility. Beginning in 2011, the Indians' owners began considering options to reuse the suites to generate more income.

How does one measure the demand for luxury seating? Market surveys can be helpful, but so can an assessment of market conditions. Figure 4.1 illustrates the number of large firms (those with at least 500 employees) in a selection of markets with teams in the four sports leagues. Table 4.3 uses these data as well as the number of suites and club seats to produce two interesting statistics: (1) the number of large firms per suite and (2) the total payroll dollars per luxury seat in each market. The total number of luxury seats was determined by using an estimate of 12 seats for each suite and then adding that total (12 times the number of suites in a region) to the number of club seats.

It is far easier to sell luxury seating when there are a number of large firms (500 or more employees). To that end, one can see the advantages that exist for teams in

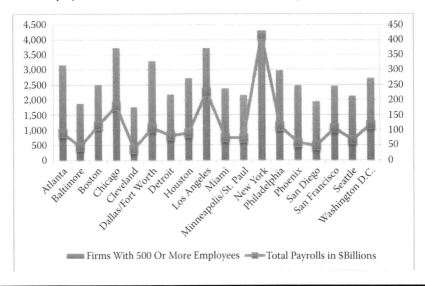

Figure 4.1 Shown is the number of large firms and total payroll in selected regions.

Table 4.3   Large firms, payroll dollars, and luxury seats in selected markets

Region	Firms with 500 Employees	Total Payroll $Billion	Number of Suites	Number of Club Seats	Firms Per Suite	Payroll $ Per Luxury Seats
Atlanta	3,176	89.8	449	10,230	7.1	57,498
Baltimore[1]	1,893	45.2	180	7,904	10.5	44,913
Boston	2,511	115.6	375	13,171	6.7	65,418
Chicago[2]	3,729	180.0	604	14,800	6.2	81,640
Cleveland	1,758	37.2	357	12,818	4.9	21,752
Detroit	2,186	81.0	494	10,000	4.4	50,854
Dallas/Fort Worth	3,299	107.2	710	23,899	4.7	33,067
Houston	2,727	90.0	341	16,100	8.0	44,572
Los Angeles	3,713	226.4	609	7,964	6.1	148,245
Miami[3]	2,391	74.1	469	12,039	5.1	41,943
Minneapolis/St. Paul	2,170	73.6	315	6,400	6.9	72,299
New York[4]	4,043	416.4	921	40,804	4.4	80,299
Philadelphia	2,985	111.5	496	21,188	6.0	41,083
Phoenix	2,476	57.5	332	15,425	7.5	29,625
San Diego[5]	1,951	47.4	163	7,882	12.0	48,181
San Francisco	2,474	105.4	300	12,200	8.3	66,709
Seattle	2,136	661.0	193	14,000	11.1	40,512
Washington, D.C.	2,727	117.0	566	23,544	4.8	38,568

[1] Club seat information was not available for the Baltimore Orioles.
[2] Club seat information was not available for the Chicago White Sox.
[3] The Florida Marlins' new ballpark's final design was not available.
[4] The Nets will move to a new arena and its final configuration was not available.
[5] Club seat information was not available for the San Diego Padres.

the Chicago, Los Angeles, and New York markets. Smaller firms, however, can be clients if their payrolls indicate there are large numbers of well-paid individuals (a proxy measure of a firm's success and the ability of individuals in a region to afford luxury seats). The advantages for clubs in the Atlanta, Dallas/Fort Worth, Houston, Philadelphia, and Washington, D.C. regions become evident as they join Chicago,

Los Angeles, and New York as valuable markets. Areas with fewer large companies and lower corporate payrolls can be excellent markets if the supply of luxury seating is appropriate for the demand. This issue is directly addressed in Table 4.3.

The absence of an NFL team in Los Angeles creates a favorable market for the selling of luxury seats with $148,245 in payroll dollars for every luxury seat. Chicago, New York, and the Minneapolis/St. Paul areas also emerge as fertile environments for the sale of luxury seats. A new facility for the Vikings, however, could change the market dramatically as the Metrodome has no club seats. At the other end of the spectrum, notice the challenges for clubs in the Cleveland and Phoenix markets. The recent economic recession has left Cleveland as the least favorable market to sell luxury seating followed by Phoenix where the owner of the NHL's Coyotes had to file for bankruptcy protection for the franchise. It is interesting as well to note that in the Dallas/Fort Worth area the inventory of luxury seating added by the building the Cowboys' new home could create problems for the other teams. The region continues to grow, but payrolls would have to substantially increase before the payroll dollars per luxury seat matched the ratios that exist in Houston (increase by 34.8 percent), Miami (increase by 26.8 percent), or Detroit (53.8 percent). There is less wealth available in the Detroit market than there is the Dallas/Fort Worth region. There are, however, far more luxury seats for sale in northcentral Texas than there are for sale in Detroit. That larger supply reduces the available payroll dollars per seat. Similarly, there are more payroll dollars in the Phoenix region than there are in the Detroit area, but the supply of luxury seating is also far larger in Arizona. These data can help one understand the problems that have beset the Phoenix Coyotes and the difficulties the NHL has had in finding a buyer to pay the price they want for the team. One also could recalculate the numbers for Minneapolis/St. Paul if the Vikings built a new facility with 10,000 club seats and 80 suites. A facility with those luxury seats would mean there would be $36,043 per luxury seat, placing the region in the lower quarter of the markets analyzed in Table 4.3. Such an increase in supply could have substantial financial effects on all teams.

There is one final point with regard to luxury seating and regional markets that must be remembered. Major college athletic programs have entered the luxury-seat market as well. The University of Michigan, the University of Minnesota, and The Ohio State University (and numerous others) have added substantial numbers of luxury seats to the inventories that exist in many different cities. The information in Table 4.3 only includes luxury seating at facilities used by professional teams. If the figures for university sports teams were added to the count, the number of payroll dollars supporting the full supply of luxury seating would be even less. As supply increases, prices can decline as each professional and collegiate team tries to sell out its inventory, raising the financial stress for all teams.

The Exterior Design of Facilities and Intrafacility Competition

The decisions made regarding the exterior of a facility are as important as those made involving the number of luxury seats in a facility. The exterior of a facility becomes a "face" of the franchise and establishes linkages to the surrounding real estate development and its competitive position in attracting nonsports events. These issues need to be explored separately as well as the implications of having several similar sports facilities in the same regional market area.

Franchise Faces

Whether it's the Green Monster in Boston, the lattice-work façade and gold lettering that symbolizes Yankee Stadium, the Indiana fieldhouse look at the home of the Pacers, or the arches that surround the Los Angeles Memorial Coliseum, iconic designs create an image for a team and the city. These unique architectural statements can turn a facility into a tourist attraction and also create a special ambience that attracts fans to athletic and nonathletic events. A venue's exterior can be so dramatic that it transforms a place into a destination that attracts other events. The spectacular scale and interior design of the new home of the Cowboys attracted the NBA's 2010 All-Star Game, numerous college football and bowl games, and the Super Bowl. The venue also will host numerous other entertainment events. The STAPLES Center in Los Angeles became a favored location for entertainers and the striking exterior glass design of the Sprint Center in Kansas City helped make it a venue of choice even in the absence of an anchor major league-level sports team. When Forest City Enterprises contemplated a new arena for the Nets in Brooklyn, the firm initially retained noted architect Frank Gehry in an effort to design a facility that would be an immediate attraction to offset the advantages of New York's Madison Square Garden. A facility like that is indeed iconic, but it may be far more expensive to build and operate than one that is a bit less dramatic. Gehry's design would have meant a facility cost of *more than* $1 billion resulting in a construction price comparable to that paid to build the far larger Yankee Stadium and the much, much larger home of the Dallas Cowboys. Cost issues required Forest City Enterprises to use a different design that will cost at least $200 million less to build.

The challenge for Forest City Enterprises and its Atlantic Yards arena (the Barclays Center) in Brooklyn will be to attract other events to this facility with its less iconic design. Those events or acts might decide that it is better to be at Madison Square Garden (New York's legendary arena) or perhaps at the Prudential

Center in Newark, New Jersey. When an area has more than one venue, the venues themselves compete to host events. Newer facilities offer more revenue streams, and that is attractive to promoters. The iconic nature of Frank Gehry's design would have inevitably attracted some events away from the Garden and the Prudential Center.* It will now remain to be seen how successful the new design and the facility's location will be in making the Barclays Center a venue of choice.

Facilities as Anchors for Real Estate Development

Chapter 6 will focus on the changing role of facilities for real estate. There are the two general roles the facility can assume. First, a facility can be an integral part of a neighborhood similar to the "jewel box" era of ballparks in the first half of the twentieth century. As will be discussed, Nationwide Arena in Columbus (Ohio), PETCO Park in San Diego, and Oriole Park at Camden Yards were designed with this element or feature in mind. These facilities are designed to fit comfortably into a design and not to dominate the area. Second, an iconic facility is designed to create through its more dominating appearance an entirely new image for an area. The STAPLES Center and LA LIVE tried to achieve that objective for downtown Los Angeles with residential and complementing development across and away from the facility as opposed to having the facility integrated into the neighborhood where it is built. Both design approaches can fit development objectives that lead to positive economic and social changes for a community. These issues will be discussed in detail as several facilities have been used as anchors of larger real estate developments. Those real estate projects also have been at the center of revitalization strategies pursued by several cities. The financial success, limitations, and lessons learned from these projects for cities and the teams involved are also detailed in Chapter 6.

Overbuilding of Facilities and Market Saturation

Every facility built increases the supply of available dates for sporting and entertainment events. Any facility development project must look at the effect of adding to the supply of performance dates that exist in a region and the demand for residential, commercial, and retail space that can surround these venues.

To maximize the financial success of any facility, it is best if approximately 150 events days are "sold" each year. An event day is one in which tickets can be sold and revenue generated. All events require setup and breakdown time. For

---

* A depiction of Frank Gehry's original design can be seen at www.nytimes.com/imagepages/ 2009/06/06/nyregion/05gehry.2.span.ready.html.

example, if an arena is home to a basketball and hockey team, a few hours, at a minimum, is needed to convert the playing surface and stands from one sport to another. The time needed might make it impossible for both teams to have a game on the same day. Similarly, if an arena hosts the circus or another entertainment event, a few days might be required to set up all of the needed equipment and then another few days could be required to remove it. Setup and takedown time reduces the days or hours during which tickets can be sold and revenue generated to cover the costs associated with building and maintaining a facility and profits. These costs have to be met if a team owner builds the facility, if the public sector pays for a new venue, or if there is a level of cost sharing between the public and private sectors. How many events are needed to meet revenue expectations? The specific number varies, of course, with the prices that can be charged for events in a particular market and the cost to construct and maintain a facility. A helpful rule of thumb might be that a favorable goal to create a level of financial comfort for the repayment of bonds and to meet maintenance costs for an arena would be 150 event days. A football stadium might host only 10 games and the occasional concert; generating sufficient revenue for a facility of that nature is, thus, a greater challenge. Ballparks host 81 games and, therefore, have a greater opportunity to spread the costs for construction and maintenance across more event days. Over the past several years, however, there has been an extensive effort to increase the event days at stadiums. When that is done, the total number of event days in a region increases and sometimes that supply can strain the finances of all facilities if regional demand for sports and entertainment is not sufficient to assure a sufficient number of event days.

Two different sets of information are provided to consider these issues. Table 4.4 identifies tickets sold for entertainment events for three-quarters of 2009. Dividing these figures by the capacity of each arena would provide an estimate of the event days at each. Because attendance can vary at every event, and the arenas themselves can be configured differently, using 15,000 as an "average capacity" for a concert event provides a glance at the range of dates sold. An adjustment was made to project anticipated 12-month averages, and then the number of event days generated by major sports tenants (NBA, NHL, or collegiate teams) was included as well. The "supply" of dates that would then be needed to reach 100 event days is illustrated.

There are a large range of events that are not included in this table. The ability to host a circus or events such as *Disney* ON ICE, or other entertainment that is not included, does provide the opportunity for many facilities to surpass 100 event days. The data, however, do illustrate the pressure on facility managers to attract events and that pressure can have a downward effect on rental fees if there are too many facilities in any region. In addition, with NFL and MLB teams increasingly interested in hosting events—and with numerous domed facilities available—arenas can find that the competition to host events is increasing and intense.

Table 4.4 Event days and selected arenas, 2009

Arena	City	Concert Tickets Sold	Estimated Concert Event Dates	Estimated Major Sports Dates	Base Number of Event Days	Short/Over 100 Target
Bell Centre	Montreal	461,622	41	43	84	–16
Madison Square Garden	New York	402,164	36	86	122	–22
Philips	Atlanta	380,373	34	86	120	–20
Sprint Center	Kansas City	376,398	33		33	–67
Allstate Arena	Rosemont	335,310	30		30	–70
St. Petersburg Times	Tampa	321,584	29	43	72	–28
Toyota Center	Houston	314,353	28	43	71	–29
Air Canada Centre	Toronto	305,702	27	86	113	–13
Rexall Place	Edmonton	305,429	27	43	70	–30
Staples Center	Los Angeles	265,473	24	129	153	53
American Airlines	Dallas	239,511	21	86	107	–7

Target Center	Minneapolis	232,667	21	43	64	-36
Verizon Center	Washington, D.C.	205,582	18	86	104	-4
Palace of Auburn Hills	Auburn Hills, MI	194,932	17	43	60	-40
Pepsi Center	Denver	154,556	14	86	100	0
Jobing.Com	Glendale	159,347	14	43	57	-43
Xcel Energy	St. Paul	147,481	13	43	56	-44
Scottrade Center	St. Louis	139,560	12	43	55	-45
United Center	Chicago	137,171	12	86	98	-2
Nationwide	Columbus	118,538	11	43	54	-46
Quicken Loans	Cleveland	116,325	10	43	53	-47
Freedom Hall	Louisville	104,027	9	30	39	-61
US Airways Center	Phoenix	101,510	9	43	52	-38
Schottenstein Center	Columbus	97,750	9	30	39	-61

Source: Some data from Pollstar Incorporated.

References

Cagan, J. and deMause, N. 1998. *Field of schemes: How the great stadium swindle turns public money into private profit.* Monroe, ME: Common Courage.

Long, J. G. 2002. Full count: The real cost of pubic funding for major league sports facilities and why some cities pay more to play. PhD dissertation, Harvard University.

Rosentraub, M. S. 1999. *Major league losers: The real cost of sports and who's paying for it.* New York: Basic Books.

Rosentraub, M. S. 2010. *Major league winners: Using sports and cultural centers as tools for economic development.* Boca Raton, FL: CRC Press.

Scully, G. 1995. *The market structure of sports.* Chicago: University of Chicago Press.

Smith, C. 2001. *Storied stadiums: Baseball's history through its ballparks.* New York: Carroll and Graf.

Zimbalist, A. 1992. *Baseball and billions: A probing look inside the big business of our national pastime.* New York: Basic Books.

Zimbalist, A. and Long, J. G. 2006. Facility finance: Measurement, trends and analysis. *International Journal of Sport Finance* 1: 201–211.

Chapter 5

Stadium Financing

Introduction

While the previous chapter briefly discussed private versus public funding of facilities, this chapter gives much more detail regarding the financing of sport facilities. What separates financing in the sports industry from that of other industries is the level of investment in facilities made by governments. Since fans do not want to see their teams move to other cities that do not have a major league franchise, and leagues limit the supply of franchises, local governments are often willing, or forced to subsidize the needed arena, ballpark or stadium. In recent years, state and local governments have invested billions of dollars in sports facilities, indicating that the demand is high relative to the supply of franchises created by the leagues. The public investment is sometimes raised through higher property and/or sales taxes, new taxes on the use of rental cars or the consumption of alcohol and tobacco products, taxes on gaming, or the diversion of tax revenues from a government's general revenue fund. In at least one instance, lottery funds were used to pay for a facility and a team was given quite a favorable lease. Many regard the use of these funds as a voluntary tax, but numerous analyses have shown that lotteries shift the burden of the public sector's investment to lower income groups (Mikesell, 2009). Some consider sports subsidies a waste of tax dollars and a result of the monopolistic powers that the sports leagues have acquired. Others point to the appropriateness of a certain level of public investment in these facilities. This public policy issue and its implications for team finances is discussed in the context of a brief history of the roles assumed by team owners and the public sector in paying for, financing, and maintaining the facilities used by professional sports teams.

Financing Tools

For any business, there are two ways to pay for investments: debt financing and equity financing. Using equity financing means selling a percentage of the firm to investors. This gives the firm cash to invest and gives investors future profits. For publicly traded corporations, equity financing means that the firm will sell shares of stock in order to raise funds. In sports, equity financing is not often used to pay for a facility's construction. Ownership restrictions and public involvement typically make equity financing less desirable and unnecessary.

Debt financing is simply borrowing funds to pay for an investment. There are different forms of debt. Debt financing could mean going to a bank and getting a loan or it could mean issuing a bond. Debt financing always involves borrowing money and then making payments to repay the principal and the associated interest charges (just like a car loan or a mortgage on a home). If a team decides to use debt financing to build a new facility, it could seek a loan from a bank; however, investments of the size needed to build a facility often involve issuing a bond. Because teams often use bonds to pay for facilities, sports managers need to understand the value of bonds. Typically, bonds require or offer to investors a periodic payment equal to the face value of the bond multiplied by the contractual interest rate. They also pay a value at maturity (usually the face value) when the bond ends. Therefore, bonds have both a periodic payment and a future value.

An example is useful in understanding the typical cash flows of a bond. Suppose that a team wants to build a new facility and issues multiple bonds with a face or par value of $1,000 with an initial maturity of 20 years and a coupon rate of 5 percent. That means that the team would receive $1,000 for each bond as soon as it was sold. They also would have to pay the bondholder $50 (5 percent of $1,000) each year and an additional $1,000 at the end of the 20 years. Table 5.1 illustrates the cash flows of such a bond. Knowing the cash flow, however, does not reveal the actual value of the bond relative to the time value of money. The present value of the bond is what we need to understand

First, as all financial analysts know well, money depreciates over time. Everyone would rather have a dollar today than the same dollar a year from today, in part because its purchasing power is likely to decline (inflation). A firm or team's depreciation rate might vary. If a team is indifferent between $1 today and $1.10 next

Table 5.1 Cash flows from a $1,000 bond

Year	0	1	2	3	...	19	20
Cash Flow	$1,000	–$50	–$50	–$50		–$50	–$1,050

year, then their depreciation rate is 10 percent. If we know a future cash flow and the depreciation rate, the net present value of that cash flow equals:

$$PV = \frac{CashFlow}{\left(1+r\right)^{N}}$$

In this equation, r is the depreciation rate and N is the number of periods (usually years) in the future when the payment is made. While a team's depreciation rate does not have to equal the interest rate, it should be close to the interest rate. For example, if the interest rate is 11 percent, then the team could loan $1 and receive $1.11 in a year. Thus, the team's depreciation rate should not be less than that. If we go back to our bond example, we can calculate the present value of each cash flow. In other words, we can calculate what each of the payments is worth in today's money.

Table 5.2 shows that with a 6 percent depreciation rate, the present value of money received 19 or 20 years later is drastically lower than money received in the near future. Now we know the value of each of the cash flows. To find the value of the entire bond, we simply need to add up the present value of each cash outflow and compare this with the $1,000 inflow. Mathematically, the value of a bond is given by:

$$NPV_{Bond} = \frac{I}{\left(1+r\right)^{1}} + \frac{I}{\left(1+r\right)^{2}} + \ldots + \frac{I}{\left(1+r\right)^{N}} + \frac{M}{\left(1+r\right)^{N}} = \sum_{t=1}^{N} \frac{I}{\left(1+r\right)^{t}} + \frac{M}{\left(1+r\right)^{N}}$$

where I is the yearly interest payment and M is the face value that is paid at the end of the bond's maturity. While this formula for a bond helps us understand how to value a bond, it can be tedious to add up all of these values. This is where financial calculators become very useful. All financial calculators have five important buttons:

PV = the present value
PMT = a constant payment made every period
N = the number of periods
I/Y = the depreciation rate (in percentage terms)
FV = the future value

Table 5.2 Present value of the cash flows from the bond (6 percent depreciation rate)

Year	0	1	2	...	19	20
NPV Cash Flow	$1,000	$\dfrac{-\$50}{1.06}$	$\dfrac{-\$50}{(1.06)^{2}}$		$\dfrac{-\$50}{(1.06)^{19}}$	$\dfrac{-\$1050}{(1.06)^{20}}$
	$1,000	−$47.17	−$44.50		−$16.53	−$327.39

If four of these values are known, the calculator will solve for the fifth. In our example, PMT = –50, N = 20, I/Y = 6, and FV = –1000. The calculator gives us a value of $885.30.*

It might seem odd that the coupon rate was different from the depreciation rate in this example. After all, when the bond is issued it would make sense that the coupon and depreciation rate both equal the market interest rate given the amount of risk involved. Because the coupon rate of a bond does not change over the life of the bond and the market rate does change over time, the value of the bond can change. This is important because bonds can be traded. As a result, the face value and present value of a bond are not always the same. If the coupon rate and the depreciation rate are, in fact, the same, then the present value is equal to the face value. If the depreciation rate is greater than the coupon rate, then the bond is said to have a discount. In our example, the bond had a discount of $114.70, because that was the difference between the face value and the present value. If the depreciation rate is less than the coupon rate, then the bond would be bought at a premium.

The coupon rate of the bond depends on the risk of defaulting on the loan. For example, recently the Memphis Redbirds (a AAA minor league baseball team) could not make full payments on their bond agreement. It is the job of many financial analysts to judge the probability of an entity or seller defaulting on a bond. The three most popular bond rating agencies are Moody's, Standard & Poors, and Fitch Ratings. The AAA ranking is the highest and D means the bond issuer is in default. Bonds with low ratings are considered junk bonds. There is a bond market that is based on the U.S. federal funds' interest rate. The difference between the bond's coupon rate and the U.S. federal funds' rate depends on how likely the firm or public entity can make payments over the life of the bond. If a firm has financial problems, they will have a low bond rating and have to issue a bond with a high coupon rate. Typically, when the federal government issues bonds, it does not have to pay a high coupon rate as the U.S. government has never defaulted on a bond. As we will discuss later in the chapter, public entities are often able to issue bonds at a much lower rate than private companies or teams. The following example, written by Greg Kinney at the Bentley Historical Library at the University of Michigan, illustrates that bonds have been used to finance stadiums for a long time.

Financing the Stadium†

Just as Fielding Yost made an extensive study of stadium design, he also thoroughly investigated methods of financing the stadium. A successful businessman himself, with interests in oil, coal, and real estate in

---

* We have to make sure our calculator settings are correct. Some common mistakes are that the payment per year (P/Y) equals 1 and, in this case, the payments should be end-of-the-year payments because a firm would start paying off the bond at the end of the first year. Furthermore, the calculator separates cash inflows and outflows. Therefore, to get a positive net present value, the outflows need to be negative.

† http://bentley.umich.edu/athdept/stadium/stadtext/bonds.htm (accessed November 10, 2010).

Tennessee and West Virginia, Yost was impressed with the University of Pittsburgh's use of bonded debt to fund its stadium. He, in particular, wanted to make certain that the university not conduct a fund drive to finance the stadium as Illinois had done. The Board in Control had realized significant profits with the growth in football attendance in the 1920s. In fact, football receipts had enabled the board to completely pay the cost of Yost Field House in just three years. By all indications, a new stadium would quickly pay for itself. The problem was how to accumulate the initial capital to fund construction.

A plan was devised, and approved by the Board in Control to finance stadium construction and the facilities called for in the Day Report through a $1,500,000 issue of 3,000 bonds at a par value of $500 at 3 percent interest. These *financial instruments* bearing the picture of a wolverine would fund not only the stadium, but all the facilities called for in the Day Committee Report (Figure 5.1).

To drum up support for his stadium proposal, Fielding Yost promoted the bonds to U-M Alumni and extended the offer to "any citizen of the State of Michigan." Yost was sure the alumni would look upon the stadium bonds as a good investment. As an added attraction, each $500 bond guaranteed the right to purchase two tickets between the 30-yard lines for a 10-year period. One person even argued that the right to purchase tickets alone was so valuable that the bonds would not have to pay interest. One-twentieth of the bonds were to be retired each year through a random drawing. The ticket privileges were guaranteed for 10 years even if a bond was redeemed. The stadium bonds went on sale August 20, 1926. A prospectus sent to each of the

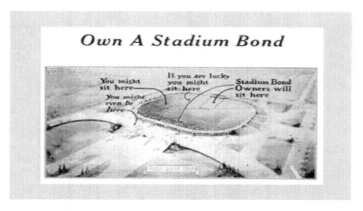

Figure 5.1   Illustration included in the Michigan Stadium Bond Prospectus from 1926. (From Bentley Historical Library [http://bentley.umich.edu/athdept/stadium/stadtext/bonds.htm]. With permission.)

63,000 alumni described the stadium and athletic building program and touted the bond's ticket buying privileges. "These bonds are reasonably certain to be taken in a very short time," football fans were warned. Bond no. 1 was purchased by former athletic director Charles Baird (Figure 5.2).

Phil Pack, the first Athletic Department publicist, assisted Yost in promoting bond sales.

For the first 10 days, sales averaged less than 15 bonds per day. By October 1st, when it had been anticipated that the issue would be nearly sold out, Yost began to worry. The alumni were not responding; only 637 bonds had been purchased. Yost and publicity director Phil Pack feverishly developed promotional plans. A new prospectus was prepared for alumni and sent to all Michigan bank presidents and chambers of commerce as well. Pack targeted all Detroit households with incomes over $10,000, the membership of the Detroit Athletic Club, and high-income Highland Park households. Suggestions were made to raise the interest rate to 4 percent and extend ticket privileges to 20 years. In a confidential letter, Yost asked newspaper editors to cooperate in promoting the bonds to the general public. "Naturally," he added, "we do not want the public to know that the bonds have

Figure 5.2   Phil Pack, the first Athletic Department publicist, assisted Yost in promoting bond sales. (From Bentley Historical Library [http://bentley.umich.edu/athdept/stadium/stadtext/bonds.htm]. With permission.)

been going disappointingly slow." In a radio broadcast over WWJ, Yost tried to dispel the notion that a larger stadium meant no sell-outs. The renewed appeal and warning succeeded as all bonds eventually sold before the 1927 season opener.

The contract for excavating a 230,000-cubic-yard hole for the stadium was issued to R .C. Merriam of Detroit in October 1926. By May, the site was ready for the Leck Construction company of Minnesota to start pouring concrete. At the same time, work was underway at Palmer Field, the women's athletic field house, and the intramural building. With Yost paying attention to every detail of construction and cost, Michigan Stadium was ready for the opening game against Ohio Wesleyan on October 1, 1927. An additional 15,000 wooden seats were erected for the dedication game against Ohio State. As Yost had predicted, all the "big games" were sold out.

The next step was to begin paying off the bonds. Between 1927 and 1930, the increased revenue from ticket sales provided the Athletic Department with ample funds to finance its regular operations, undertake additional construction, including the golf course, and to reduce its bonded debt. There were 550 bonds randomly selected for retirement by 1930. For the next six years, however, no bonds were redeemed. The onset of the great depression had significantly reduced ticket sales. The department managed a budget surplus, and never missed an interest payment in each of those years, but could not retire any bonds. Redemption of bonds resumed in 1937. By 1940, $625,000 in bonds had been retired. For many bondholders, the stadium bonds proved to be a good investment. By 1940 standards, 3 percent tax-free interest was an attractive rate. A growing number of holders whose bonds were randomly selected for retirement suggested that their bonds be returned to the pool. Eventually, many took advantage of an offer to have their bonds extended for five years at the 3 percent interest rate. The last of the stadium bonds were retired in 1951.

The $1.5 million in stadium bonds represents only a small portion of the money spent on the expansion of athletic facilities over the years. It was these bonds, however, that financed the facility that has given so much to Michigan including the revenue that has allowed Michigan to build some of the finest intercollegiate and intramural facilities in the nation.

It is not common for teams to pay for stadiums with a bank loan, but sports teams do sometimes get loans, which is another type of debt financing. In the case of a bank loan, it is typically very different with regards to the cash flows compared to a bond. Instead of only paying off interest until maturity, as in the case of a bond, a loan is typically paid off with constant payments over time with no large payment

Table 5.3 Cash flows from the loan

Year	0	1	2	...	19	20
Cash Flow	$1,000	–$80.24	–$80.24		–$80.24	–$80.24

Table 5.4 The first and last four years of the amortization table

Year	Beginning-of-Year Principal ($)	Loan Payment ($)	Interest Payment ($)	Principal Payment ($)	End-of-Year Principal ($)
1	1,000.00	80.24	50.00	30.24	969.76
2	969.76	80.24	48.49	31.75	938.01
3	938.01	80.24	46.90	33.34	904.67
4	904.67	80.24	45.23	35.01	869.66
...	—	—	—	—	—
17	284.60	80.24	14.23	66.01	218.59
18	218.59	80.24	10.93	69.31	149.28
19	149.28	80.24	7.46	72.78	76.50
20	76.50	80.24	3.83	76.41	0.09

at the end. While there are interest-only loans, generally the principal is paid off over time with each payment.

We can use a similar example for a loan as we did with a bond. Let us suppose that a team takes out a $1,000, 20-year loan with an interest rate of 5 percent. This means that the team would receive $1,000 cash inflow right away and then make periodic payments. To know how much the payments need to be, we again can use a financial calculator. Because there is not an extra payment at the end of the loan, the future value is equal to zero. In this example, PV = 1,000, N = 20, I/Y = 5, and FV = 0 and the calculator gives us a value of –$80.24 for the payment.* Table 5.3 shows the cash flows of the loan.

In this case, it is assumed that the interest rate is the same as the depreciation rate; therefore, the net present value of the loan is $1,000. Now that we know the cash flows associated with a loan, we can use an amortization table to calculate how much principal is left on the loan (Table 5.4).

---

* A typical loan might have monthly payments, but because the number of periods and interest rates are in years, this represents a yearly payment. Financial calculators can be adjusted to make monthly payments (P/Y = 12).

The information in an amortization table is important. First, it shows how much the principal is at the beginning and the end of each year. This helps calculate a firm or team's wealth because it lets the organization understand how much is owed on the loan. Second, it divides the loan payment into the interest payment, which equals the principal multiplied by the interest rate, and the principal payment. The actual interest payment is important for taxes. Notice that at the beginning of the loan, a majority of the loan payment goes toward paying the interest, but at the end of the loan nearly all of the payment goes toward the principal. Appendix 1 at the end of this chapter gives much more detail on finding the present value of different cash flows.

Financing Facilities: Who Really Pays?

The relationship between supply and demand for teams is responsible for the expanding role of the public sector in the financing of facilities. Part of the risk associated with a private investment in a professional sports team has been transferred to and accepted by the public sector. This observation does not address the key analytical issues which are: (1) who is ultimately paying for the cost of the facilities when taxes are increased to finance the public sector's investment and (2) are those payments in excess of the benefits received? A third point of interest is how do any changes in who pays influence the distribution of the benefits or profits from sports? To address these questions and to understand their dynamics it is best to initially consider the most direct and simple model or circumstance. That model is the one that existed prior to the extensive involvement of the public sector in the financing of facilities, but it might be one that fails to distribute the costs appropriately in relationship to the benefits produced.

Team owners paid for the initial facilities and the cost for building and maintaining a ballpark, stadium, or arena was then added to such things as the players' salaries, securing or owning a franchise in the league, annual team operations, spring training, player development (minor leagues), travel, and, of course, the desired profit level or margins anticipated based on the investments made. If revenues met projections, then one would observe that the costs for the ballpark were paid by the fans. If revenues declined or did not meet the anticipated goals, an owner could reduce some expenses including player salaries, but that might reduce revenues even further. If an owner could not shift the cost to labor, then reduced profit levels would result and the owner would end up paying for the facility. This in turn could force the team to relocate or simply declare bankruptcy and cease operations. Whichever of these scenarios played itself out in a city, the transaction for a facility was confined to economic exchanges between a team's fan base (or their customers), the players (labor), and the owner (capital). For some, this seems only appropriate as fans, players, and owners are seen as the only or main beneficiaries of a team's presence. But, what would happen or should happen if that logic was somewhat incomplete? Are there other beneficiaries who should pay, or more appropriately, are there others who would *lose* benefits (or technically suffer diminished levels of welfare) if the team failed to exist? Should the public sector intercede to protect that welfare as it does when other types of public goods are not produced as a result of market inefficiencies?

Sports may well generate externalities or benefits for people who do not attend games or "consume" them through broadcasts. Goods and services, as well as the actions of people, can create two different types of externalities. Those that improve life or another person's welfare are considered positive externalities, and those that make an individual's situation worse are described as negative externalities. If you drive a car, for example, initially you paid all the costs associated with the benefits you received. Those costs included those associated with ownership of the vehicle as well as the cost of building and maintaining roads (financed through gasoline taxes paid when you purchased fuel for the vehicle). In this manner, then, the transaction was limited to drivers (consumers), auto workers, those people who built the streets (labor), those who owned the manufacturing plants for cars (capital), and those who owned the companies that paved the streets and roads (capital). When your vehicle was driven, however, an externality was generated (air pollution), which creates costs in the form of reduced air quality, which can lead to breathing difficulties as well as the destruction of property (vegetation could be poisoned, property values could decline if pollution levels are too high, etc.). To reduce this negative externality, new costs were imposed on consumers (air purification systems built into cars). Another example of a negative externality is when someone throws some waste material on the road or sidewalk or on park grounds. The cost of that negative externality is evident in the expense society must allocate to clean the streets and parks. If the park or street is not cleaned, then all future users suffer the inconvenience of cleaning the area or fewer benefits from having to use a public space that is now dirty.

Sport generates externalities, too. Some see a negative externality in the form of traffic that might be generated when a large number of spectators converge on a facility or seek parking nearby and others might see a negative outcome from society's preoccupation with sports and competition. To be sure, there are people who see these same negative externalities as having positive effects. For example, traffic and congestion increases parking revenues for some property owners and others believe competition teaches important values. It seems an endless debate would ensue if one tried to conclude whether or not the positive effects outweigh the negative, or if some negative externalities are offset by the positive elements seen by others from the same effect. It is far more useful to consider a set of positive externalities that result from sports that several scholars have isolated, and then begin to think about their value and what would be lost if these benefits did not exist. Four broad categories of positive externalities have been identified.

Social capital is the first of the external benefits produced by teams and its definition was probably best described by Putnam (2000) in his popular book, *Bowling*

Alone: The Collapse and Revival of American Community. "To build bridging social capital requires that we transcend our social and political and professional identities to connect with people unlike ourselves. This is why teams provide good venues for social capital creation." When does this form of social capital exist? One can point to any of the community-wide celebrations that occur after key victories or when people from dissimilar backgrounds are able to talk about the team and, as Putnam observes, get to know people in their community who are unlike them, and who may well disagree with them on many other points. The shared common interest in the team establishes a basis for compromise, but also for recognizing that even with those with whom there are different positions or values there is still a degree of commonality and agreement. When a team wins, there is a palatable excitement "in the air," or a sort of civic celebration that is evident even if it is difficult to quantify. Everyone can remember their feelings of unity or "social capital" in New England when the Red Sox finally buried the "curse of the Bambino" in 2004. Canadians know where they were when Sidney Crosby's overtime goal against the USA netted the gold medal in 2010, just as many Americans still recall what they were doing when Team USA upset the Soviet Union in the 1980 Olympics.

What is the benefit created by this form of social capital? Sports as these and countless other examples would attest, do produce in divergent societies a sense of unity that bridges or unites people across social classes and races. This is what Putnam meant by "bridging" capital. For any society to survive and advance a common agenda, there must be a set of institutions and activities that build bridges across economic classes and races. Without that "common ground," compromise, cooperation, and solidarity may never exist. Their absence would generate substantial costs or losses from a lack of progress to, in the most extreme examples, social disintegration and conflict. Bridging capital is regarded by many social scientists as the glue that holds cities, counties, and countries together. If they are correct, ensuring that this form of social capital exists represents a substantial collective benefit and, in its absence, a society is worse off. Therefore, some form of collective payments to ensure the potential for bridging social capital exists may well exceed the costs of a tax for a ballpark.

Teams by their location can **relocate economic activity** within a region, and that movement also can create important positive externalities. In many regions, the suburbanization of businesses and residential communities has weakened the tax bases of central cities where there is, frequently, an over concentration of lower income families. If teams also locate in suburban areas, the entertainment spending that takes place will generate tax revenues for suburban governments and the part-time or other jobs that are available may not be accessible to inner city residents. Conversely, teams located in downtown areas ensure that a certain level of the region's economic activity and the tax revenues produced by that spending (and the jobs related to that spending) are concentrated in central cities. This is not a minor public policy issue for some cities, including Baltimore, Cincinnati, Cleveland, Detroit, Milwaukee, Pittsburgh, and St. Louis. Public investment to change the location of facilities to places where there are region-wide benefits relative to a redistribution of tax revenues, employment opportunities, and overall economic activity is not an inconsequential benefit. The urban economist Edwin Mills on more than one occasion observed that where something happens (in terms of economic activity) is often just as important an issue as if something happens (Mills and Hamilton, 1997). Where the economic activity generated by teams occurs is a benefit worth paying for and, in the case of a city's finances, perhaps the most important issue. A collective payment to ensure a team's facility is located where the benefits from the spending by fans improve the finances of a central city with a large concentration of a region's lower income households could well be something a region should support. The absence of the team in a downtown area or from a region could lead to a concentration of entertainment spending in suburban areas further exacerbating resource differences between cities in a region.

Teams and the facilities they use contribute to and, in some instances, help to **define the identity of a city region**. Some sports facilities create what is called a *Synecdochic* effect. A synecdoche is an image (or figure of speech) that creates an entire image. Telling someone that it is "the top of the ninth" or that to pass a test you need a "hail Mary," creates well-understood meanings or word images. Similarly, a picture of the Eiffel Tower creates an image of Paris and France. Sports facilities as Synecdochic elements are represented by "The Green Monster" in Boston (Figure 5.3) and the soccer stadium in Aveiro, Portugal (see Figure 5.4).

Indianapolis used the design of several sports facilities to help it create a new image. Conseco Fieldhouse (Figure 5.5) and Lucas Oil Stadium (Figure 5.6) replaced older facilities that were both more dated and far less architecturally

Figure 5.3   Pictured is Boston and Fenway Park's "Green Monster." (Photo courtesy of Janet Marie Smith.)

Figure 5.4   Colorful and unique Aveiro, Portugal's soccer stadium. (Photo courtesy of M. Musand, https://commons.wikimedia.org/wiki/file:Aviero_Stadium.JPG)

Figure 5.5   Indianapolis's Conseco Fieldhouse with its design to emulate a historic Indiana field house for high school basketball. (Photo courtesy of Indiana Sports Corporation.)

unique. The issue of design and image was very much on the minds of leaders when they have emphasized a desire for iconic architecture to change the brand or image of a city. The benefits of that new brand or image or the appreciation of exciting or controversial architecture is another example of the externality benefits created by the facility used by a team.

A team's performance also can elevate a city's image nationally and make residents proud to live in the area. The Packers have been synonymous with Green Bay and may well be the most distinctive aspect of that community's image. Other examples abound including the Colts and Indianapolis, and the Yankees and New York. And the success of LeBron James and the Cavaliers had a very positive effect on Cleveland's image in the midst of a substantial deterioration of that region's economy

Figure 5.6 Lucas Oil Stadium in Indianapolis. (Photo courtesy of Mark S. Rosentraub.)

and the city's loss of residents. When teams lose, they also have the potential to create a negative impression of an area and that also must be taken into account. Yet, many residents in a large number of communities believe that the "major league status" conveyed by a team's presence is an externality that has a clear value.

Economic development in the twenty-first century is driven and, in most instances, defined by the presence of a well-educated workforce and the people who are the "idea generators" behind the creation of new businesses, products, and processes. There is no debate that what is most important for economic development is the creation of educational systems that foster innovative thinking and creativity and which also provide the training needed for all workers. Companies locate now where they have the most confidence they can find the labor force they need to innovate and lead their industry. Amenities assume a role in the choices made by people. It is not entirely clear if teams or sports attract people to a region, but there are some important indicators (attendance) and a few studies that now underscore the importance of amenity packages in attracting and retaining a highly skilled workforce (Beckstead, Brown, and Gellatly, 2008; Rosentraub and Joo, 2009; Rosentraub, 2010). The contribution by a team to a region's array of amenities and its attractiveness to high-skilled labor and entrepreneurs is another potential externality generating benefits. The loss of that benefit could create financial losses and, therefore, there is collective interest in ensuring that a team remains in a region.

How much are these positive externalities worth to people? If these intangible benefits were worth just $5 or $10 a year to every household in a region, the cumulative total would be sufficient to suggest (1) that a team's absence would create lost value and (2) an investment by the public sector to ensure a franchise is in the area would be worthwhile. If that is true, then a collective payment or investment by the public sector to avoid that loss would be appropriate. Several scholars have tried to quantify the positive externalities that often emerge as intangible benefits and, in some instances, the amounts found exceeded the public sector's investment in a facility. We introduce these issues into the model not to minimize the costs imposed on fans and taxpayers as a result of a constrained supply of franchises that is controlled by team owners (usually described as monopoly rents by economists), but to point out that there are important reasons for an appropriate public investment to ensure that there is no diminishment in the level of positive externalities.

Some might be tempted to argue that there are a number of other private transactions that produce positive externalities and those externalities could occur without an investment by a government. There can be no objection to that point. What is critical, however, is that the positive externalities created by a team are known and assuring their occurrence where and when a community wants them may warrant a level of payment. That does not mean the public sector should pay 100 percent of the cost of a facility while a team retains 100 percent of the generated revenues. The challenge for a community is to provide the investment that matches the positive externalities without turning that investment into a subsidy that generates excess monopoly rents (excessive salaries and profits) for owners and players. To be sure, this is a difficult task and negotiation, but one which every city has to conduct to protect taxpayers while being sure that desirable positive externalities are not lost.

An example of the difficulty in weighing positive externalities and their value to residents (coupled with the desire to be home to two professional teams despite the relatively small size of the region) is underscored by Indianapolis's decision to build a new facility to ensure the presence of the Colts for 30 additional years. Local governments in central Indiana invested more than $750 million to build a domed stadium (Lucas Oil) that serves as the home for the Indianapolis Colts and numerous NCAA events. The annual payment on the bonds sold to finance the facility is $33.6 million, and the public sector is also responsible for maintaining the facility. The NCAA's headquarters are located in Indianapolis and, as a result of the support the organization received from a local foundation and the state to encourage its relocation from Kansas, Indianapolis hosts a robust number of NCAA events. The region's investment then secured more than just the presence of an NFL franchise, but the scale of the investment reflected the issues when a region with a population of approximately 1.7 million residents strives to be home to two franchises from the four major sports leagues. In addition, two major universities, Purdue and Indiana, draw substantial support from the same market area in which the Pacers and Colts sell their tickets. If that was not sufficient competition for residents' discretionary income and local businesses' entertainment budgets, the region is also home to the continent's largest sports event, the Indianapolis 500. There are, of course, other college teams in the region and the Indianapolis Motor Speedway hosts more than one race each year.

Both of Indianapolis' major professional teams have also encountered "troughs" where ticket sales slumped in response to poor performance. In the early 1990s, the Colts were the region's second team behind the Pacers, who were enjoying repeated runs for the Eastern Division championship in the NBA. In 2000, the Pacers lost in the NBA Finals. During the past several years, the Pacers' competitiveness has declined and so has ticket sales while the popularity of the Colts has soared. The Colts' leadership well understands the issues associated with a long-term commitment to a small market and in spurning opportunities to relocate to an area with a larger population base (Los Angeles or San Antonio, for example), the owner wanted public officials to recognize the opportunities he was willing to forego (it was never clear if the team could have moved, but what was clear was that a location elsewhere would likely mean opportunities for more income for the owner). In exchange for the public investment in the facility, the owner agreed to release the public sector from an earlier commitment to insure the team's income never declined below specified levels. Indianapolis had agreed a decade earlier to ensure that locally generated revenue levels for the Colts would reach an agreed-to amount and when they did not the public sector would make a payment to the team equal to any shortfall. That agreement was costing Indianapolis tens of millions of dollars each year. The deal for building Lucas Oil Stadium cancelled that commitment from the public sector and the team agreed to a 30-year lease and to resolve any issues related to the stadium or a decision to leave Indianapolis only in Indiana courts. For the positive externalities of having the team play its home games in downtown Indianapolis, the public sector's annual investment could approach $45 million (principal and interest as noted is $33.6 million and annual maintenance costs could easily reach and exceed $10 million). Are the externalities worth that much to Indiana's residents? Rosentraub, Swindell, and Tsvetkova (2009) using a contingent valuation survey research method found that the annual value of the team's presence to the state's residents exceeds $66 million. If that measure of the benefits accruing to residents of the state from the team's presence is accurate, then even with a $50 million annual cost (and even one that is slightly higher), the investment by the public sector generates a positive return.

In larger markets, such as Boston, Chicago, Dallas, New York, or Los Angeles, there is generally less need to pay for the positive externalities. The wealth and size of these markets are sufficient to generate substantial profits and that opportunity will attract investors willing to pay for both a franchise and a facility. Owners in these areas will still try to negotiate and secure payments for the externalities their teams generate. Local governments know that while teams might relocate within the metropolitan area (e.g., Dallas Cowboys to Arlington after 30 years in Irving; Detroit Lions to Pontiac and then back to Detroit; Pistons to Auburn Hills from Detroit, etc.) franchise owners will not move teams out of the largest markets that have the greatest potential to generate substantial profits. There, of course, are exceptions when other cities provided substantial subsidies (Houston Oilers to Nashville; Los Angeles Rams to St. Louis, etc.). Yet, it would be foolhardy to minimize the advantage larger markets have when negotiating with teams. What have been some of the payments for the positive externalities larger-market teams have generated? The owners of the Phillies and Eagles were successful in convincing Pennsylvania and Philadelphia to each contribute to the cost of building new facilities for their teams. Those generous investments seem unnecessary given the size of the Philadelphia market (5.9 million people and the fifth largest in the United States). New York City provided two levels of support in their negotiations with the Yankees and Mets. With regard to Citi Field, New York paid more than $173 million in infrastructure improvements and arranged the financing so that municipal bonds with their lower interest rates could be sold. While the team alone is completely responsible for all payments, the interest costs are lower than those that would have been associated with market-rate bonds. Should the team have been responsible for the sewers and other infrastructure costs associated with building on the site? There is no straight forward answer to that question either. New York provides streets and sewers for all business development. Were the Mets entitled to any less than what would have been done for any business enterprise? In addition, the building site has a peculiar history that explains why the appropriate infrastructure was never built. In the 1950s, local political issues led the city's planning czar, Robert Moses, to threaten property owners that the needed infrastructure would not be installed unless they complied with his plans for the Flushing Meadow area. When they refused, he carried out his threat and the appropriate infrastructure was never built. This political standoff took place long before the Mets were created and before the team's owner had formed his first business. Would it have been fair to hold the team and its owner responsible for political decisions made more than 50 years ago? Recognizing the city's investment, however, the Mets did sign a lease that requires them to be 100-percent responsible for the maintenance of the facility and 100-percent responsible for repayment of the bonds used to pay for the facility's construction. Social scientists and some community leaders might still conclude the Mets were "subsidized," but it is necessary to understand the positive externalities created by teams and then the appropriate investment that should be made to secure and retain those benefits. If there are indeed positive externalities, then the fans who attend games should not pay for the full cost of all benefits.

Facility Financing: The Team's Share

Every sports organization will look at its capital expenses a bit differently. What is germane, however, is that the team will seek to borrow money and, in doing so, will try to minimize its borrowing costs. The easiest way to accomplish that objective is to have a unit of local government borrow the money so that the interest earned by the bond holders is not subject to the federal income tax. Interest paid to investors by local governments on the bonds they sell is not subject to the U.S. federal income tax as a result of long-standing legal precedents that make it unconstitutional for one unit of government to tax the activities of another. As a result, the bonds are frequently called "tax free," which is a bit of a misnomer, but the income earned by investors is not subject to federal taxation (can be subject to state and local income taxes, however) and that enhances the return earned by bondholders. These instruments of debt attract more buyers or investors, and where there is competition there is generally lower prices. The increased number of buyers reduces interest rates and that reduces the overall cost to build and pay for a new ballpark, arena, or stadium. That is why team owners ask the public sector to help identify a unit of local government that can issue the bonds even if the team then guarantees to make all of the payments to repay the debt. If the public sector can borrow the money, the interest payment savings to a team, even if it repays the entire amount, can reduce the cost of the facility by tens of millions of dollars. The first objective in any sport facility financing plan is to determine if under existing laws tax-free bonds can be sold. If they can be sold and there is a unit of government willing to extend its credit to secure the bonds, teams save a substantial amount of money even if they are going to pay the full cost of the building of a facility.

Another advantage of using public entities to issue bonds is that they can generally get lower rates because the probability of defaulting on the bond is much lower. In some cases, the public is not actually paying the bond, but they would have to if the team could not. One reason this is done is because the local government may have a higher bond rating. In other words, municipal bonds, which are bonds issued by local, state, or federal governments, offer a lower coupon rate than corporate bonds. As Table 5.5 shows, the average default rate for corporate bonds is roughly 100 times higher than municipal bonds. Therefore, the coupon rate would be substantially less if a sports arena is backed by a municipal government. But remember, although the public is not technically paying for the stadium in this case, they are at risk and sometimes this fact is somewhat obfuscated by public officials.*

Once the annual cost of the bonds (the mortgage for the facility) is known, a team's leadership will look to new sources of revenue to meet that obligation. A team might sell naming rights or other advertising packages and use that income to help repay any bonds that have been sold. The New York Mets were able to sell the naming rights to their new ballpark to Citi Financial and, despite adverse publicity for the bank in the aftermath of their receipt of bailout money from the U.S. government, the team still receives an annual payment of $20 million to offset its obligation to repay the bonds used to pay for the $800 million ballpark. Ticket prices always increase when new teams move to new facilities. In part, this results from improved sight lines and designs that place fans closer to the playing field. Newer facilities also include many amenities that were not available in older facilities. And, of course, a new facility is an opportunity to increase prices simply because what is

---

* For example, see http://www.sabernomics.com/sabernomics/index.php/2008/04/gwinnett-countys-economist-responds/ (accessed May 15, 2011).

Table 5.5 Cumulative historic default rates (in percentage)[a]

Rating Category	Moody's		S&P	
	Muni	*Corp*	*Muni*	*Corp*
Aaa/AAA	0.00	0.52	0.00	0.60
Aa/AA	0.06	0.52	0.00	1.50
A/A	0.03	1.29	0.23	2.91
Baa/BBB	0.13	4.64	0.32	10.29
Ba/BB	2.65	19.12	1.74	29.93
B/B	11.86	43.34	8.48	53.72
Caa-C/CCC-C	16.58	69.18	44.81	69.19
Averages				
Investment grade	0.07	2.09	0.20	4.14
Noninvestment grade	4.29	31.37	7.37	42.35
All	0.10	9.70	0.29	12.98

[a] Found at http://monevator.com/2010/04/09/bond-default-rating-probability/ (accessed May 15, 2011).
Note: Muni = Municipal Bond; Corp = Corporate Bond.

Source: U.S. Municipal Bond Fairness Act, 2008.

new is generally thought to be better than what was replaced. Based on the demand for tickets to Edmonton Oilers games, if that team went forward with a facility that was a bit larger (2,000 extra seats), the improved luxury seating and the extra seats was estimated to be able to generate at least $20 million more than at an older arena (Mason and Rosentraub, 2010). New income from the enhanced sale of food and beverages and the income from other events and new advertising possibilities (including the higher value from a naming rights deal) would be in addition to this net gain. Funds of this magnitude offer important opportunities to offset the cost of building a new facility. Some have argued that naming rights should reduce the cost for the public sector. Given the scale of some of these advertising deals, however, it is easy to understand why team owners have tried to secure the right to receive the income from naming a facility for a sponsor.

Of course, differences in league structure or policy often dictate how teams will fund stadiums. In the NFL, for example, it is becoming increasingly common for teams to use personal seat licenses to help pay for stadiums. One reason teams sell personal seat licenses is because revenue from personal seat licenses is not subject to league revenue-sharing rules. A personal seat license is a one-time payment that gives a fan the right to buy season tickets. In most cases, the fan can transfer or sell the rights to buy season tickets to someone else. The NFL views teams building new stadiums as a good thing and something that creates more revenue for the league. Normally NFL teams share all of their revenue to some degree, but the league gives teams an incentive to build new facilities by letting them keep revenue from personal seat licenses. In other sports, personal seat licenses are not nearly as common, so other revenue streams are needed.

Facility Financing: A Public Sector Investment

In the above example of the revenues that could be used to meet the annual costs of repaying the bonds sold to finance the construction of a facility, the new revenues generated are retained by the team. There are examples of certain new revenue sources being dedicated to the public sector. For example, Los Angeles received parking revenue and there have been instances where the proceeds from naming rights or revenue from the sale of luxury seating (Cleveland) were assigned to a city or county to help them repay the bonds sold. The first source of funds then for the public sector is also new revenues resulting from the amenities in a new facility and attendance.

With teams negotiating to retain as much as possible from the new revenues generated by a facility, the public sector's investment frequently involves a new tax, an increase in an existing tax, or an allocation from aggregate or total tax collections. Each of these has different impacts and implications and some do not require residents paying more money. Indeed, some taxes are actually paid by the team. If, however, there are positive externalities generated, then it may be efficient and appropriate for residents to invest some of their money to ensure the desired returns or benefits are secured. There also are instances where tax money collected for a set of purposes is dedicated to a sports facility resulting only in an opportunity cost (the money is not spent on something else similar to a sport facility). Some cities, for example, have a tax on hotel rooms and that money can be used for a project that advances tourism. A new sports facility could advance tourism, but so could many other investments. The impacts (who pays), the incidence (whose wealth is actually decreased), and the distribution (is the taxing method progressive?) is explained in the discussion that follows.

Ticket Tax

Several local governments have implemented a ticket or amusement tax that is calculated either as a percent of the ticket price (similar to a sales tax) or as a flat figure ($3 or $4 per ticket or some other figure). This tax is added to the price of a ticket just like when you pay the sales tax on any purchase. The likely result of a ticket tax is an increase in the ticket price. This increase should be less than the amount of the tax. This also means that fewer fans will attend the sporting event. The magnitude of the change in price, and also the tax incidence, will depend on the slopes of the supply and demand curves. If fans are simply willing to pay the tax and still purchase tickets, then most of the tax incidence falls on the fans. If, on the other hand, fans are not willing to pay any more for tickets, then teams will pay more of the tax. While the burden on the team compared to fans depends on fans' willingness to pay, the net result of the tax is that teams receive less revenue and fans pay higher prices for tickets. The distribution of this tax depends on who exactly purchases the tickets. Lastly, as the tax does not impact nonusers, it is classified as voluntary because those who do not wish to pay the tax can decide not to attend games or events.

Parking Taxes

The same logic and effects apply to any parking taxes that are levied to offset the expense of paying for a facility. In the absence of a tax on parking, the owner of the parking lot or structure—the team or another entrepreneur—will charge what they think is the optimal price. If a portion of that fee must be transferred as a tax to the city, the price will increase. This tax is also voluntary (only attendees who use the parking structure pay the tax) and, the distribution of the tax is similar to ticket taxes.

In-Facility Sales

An additional sales or amusement tax has been placed on all transactions within a facility in some areas. Similar to the ticket or amusement tax and a tax on parking, this raises the costs to fans, businesses that entertain clients, and those advertising at the facility. Prices for souvenirs, food, beverages, and advertising would increase. This tax is again voluntary. The tax can be avoided if fans refuse to buy things at the game or event or decide not to attend, but this would hurt the team.

Sales Taxes

A number of communities have financed their investment in sports facilities with revenues collected from a small increase in the general sales tax collected on all retail sales in a city or county. Unlike the preceding three taxing tools that were voluntary because payments were made by people attending an event, parking a car in the vicinity of a facility, or buying goods and services at a facility, the use of a general sales tax affects all retail sales. The only way for a consumer to avoid the tax would be to shop for all goods and services in another city. This makes the tax somewhat involuntary as it affects nonusers of the sports facilities and, to avoid the tax, consumers must be inconvenienced (traveling and shopping in another city). If the majority of services are not subject to the tax by state and local laws, the sales tax is considered regressive. If all forms of consumption are taxed, then the tax would be described as proportional.

If that tax is involuntary and impacts nonusers, why do communities use this tool to finance their investment? There are three reasons. First, the large amount or volume of retail sales in larger cities means the increase in the sales tax rate needed to finance an investment in a sport facility is usually quite small (frequently 1 percent or less). This small increment generally does not engender a great deal of political opposition. Second, the small increment usually generates a large amount of money. The total amount of sales in a city every year is usually quite large, thus the sacrifice for any one taxpayer is quite small, but the outcome is frequently large enough to support the public sector's investment in a sports facility. Third, if a city is home to a large regional mall that attracts shoppers from many cities, a substantial portion of the tax is actually paid by nonresidents. This "exporting" of the cost of an investment in a sport facility to nonresidents in the form of their payment of the sales tax attracts local political support as it gives the impression that a portion of the costs are shifted to residents of other cities while the benefits are concentrated in the city where the facility is located. The possibility that others would pay for benefits that accrue in a city is an attractive political theme. However, even if consumers are nonlocal, the businesses are local. Since businesses are hurt by this tax, there is a local cost even when consumers are nonresidents.

Property Taxes

This tax is also nonvoluntary, but a very small increase in the rate at which real estate is taxed to support the investment in a sports facility generates a large amount of money as the assessed value of residential and business property in a city is usually quite large. The nonvoluntary aspect of the tax sometimes creates opposition from some homeowners especially those living on fixed-incomes. Other opponents have objected to using property taxes for sports facilities arguing those taxes should support education and basic services such as police and fire protection. If a community has a large base of business property, then a proportion of the tax could be exported to nonresidents. That occurs when businesses incorporate their total tax bill in the price of their goods and services. As most businesses have clients throughout a region (or state, country, and even internationally), the cost of the investment in a sports facility can be partially exported to nonresidents. In some cities where businesses account for most of the property taxes paid, the cost for an investment in a sports facility could be exported to nonresidents of a city. If business property, for example, accounts for two-thirds or more of the total valuation of property, then at least two-thirds of the cost of the investment would be paid for through the sale of those companies' products. As the property tax is generally considered mildly progressive, use of the tax instrument while sometimes politically inconvenient does distribute the burden in a progressive fashion with higher income individuals and businesses with more property supporting far more of the investment. One drawback is that it becomes harder to entice new businesses to come or to get existing businesses to stay.

Income Tax

The use of an income tax to finance an investment in a sports facility has the same benefits and liabilities found in the use of the property tax. A small increment will generate a large amount of money. The tax, however, is involuntary. The income tax is generally considered to be the most progressive of any of the taxing tools available to governments. Its use would mean the distribution of the burden could be progressive if higher-income people pay a larger portion of their income to repay the investment. Income taxes can be based on where one lives and where one works. The latter is referred to as an earnings tax, and, if that exists, suburbanites who commute to jobs in a city also would share the responsibility for an investment in a sports facility.

Tax Increment Financing

Several communities have invested in sports facilities in an effort to attract new development and to redirect spending into a specific geographic area (e.g., downtown area, etc.). That new development can include residences, office buildings, stores, restaurants, or other entertainment facilities that investors believe will complement and capitalize on the value of a close proximity to a sports facility. Baltimore, Columbus, Cleveland, Los Angeles, and San Diego are just a few of the cities that have enjoyed new levels of real estate development in the areas adjacent to sport facilities that, in turn, create new property taxes that are an *increment* to the level of taxes collected from nearby properties before the sports facility opened. The new or higher taxes paid by the owners of these properties can represent additional income for a local government and those funds can be used to pay for part of the public sector's investment in the facility. These taxes are new revenues if (1) the development that takes place near the sport facility would not have occurred without the ballpark, arena, or stadium being built, and (2) the new buildings would not have been built somewhere else in the city. Cleveland's and Columbus's efforts to attract people back to their downtown are probably the best examples of new property taxes. With declining population and investment levels in their core areas, the buildings adjacent to Progressive Field, Quicken Loans Arena, or Nationwide Arena would have taken place elsewhere in the region, but not in Cleveland or Columbus (Rosentraub, 2010). In this instance, the transfer of property taxes from the suburban areas to the central city means those other cities, in essence, are paying for part of the facility. Had the facility not been built near the central city, the investors would still have paid property taxes, but to suburban local governments. In both instances, the property taxes were new revenues and literally transferred tax money from the suburbs to the central city. The same logic can be applied to sales taxes generated in an area, and even income taxes. The use of the increment is seen as voluntary because the new income results from business activity that capitalizes on the existence of the facility and investors and consumers are free to utilize the land and amenities near a facility or elsewhere. The distribution of the tax burden would likely be progressive or, at worst, proportional. Tax increment financing has in some instances produced sufficient revenue to offset the public sector's investment (Columbus) and seems likely to do so in one other area (San Diego). In Indianapolis, the incremental revenues were, by themselves, never thought to be sufficient to produce the needed revenue.

Sports District Taxes

The state of Indiana created a sports tax district to support the building of the Conseco Fieldhouse in Indianapolis. All state income and sales tax resulting from activity within the geographic boundaries created to designate the special tax district were deflected to assist in the repayment of the bonds sold to finance the construction of the new arena. Taxes were not directly increased, but existing revenues were deflected to repay the bonds sold to build the facility. The cost or impact of this financing method was on what the state of Indiana either could not fund as a result of the deflection of the taxes or the increases in statewide taxes to meet Indiana's budget needs.

A sports district creates a voluntary tax; only those people who attend events or visit restaurants or other amenities in the district have their taxes deflected to pay for the facility. If someone does not wish to have their tax dollars used for the sports facility, they can decide to spend their money elsewhere. With the income tax the largest source of the state's revenue, its deflection underscores the progressivity of this tax method for financing sports facilities. If, however, the programs or other expenditures that a state could no longer pay for since taxes were deflected to pay for the sports facility made lower-income people worse off, the tax effect would be regressive. The political attractiveness of the district—its creation produced little adverse reaction— prompted Indiana to extend the boundaries of the district in 2009 to facilitate the building of Lucas Oil Stadium and help Indianapolis meet its responsibility for maintaining the new facility.

Sin (or Excise) Tax

A tax on the purchase and consumption of alcohol and tobacco products are popularly described as a sin tax. This tax is often seen as the least objectionable since it increases the price of products considered unhealthy and, if abused or excessively consumed, dangerous. As a result, there is little political opposition to the passage of new sin taxes to help support the public sector's investment in a sports facility. These taxes are frequently not sufficient to repay a substantial or large investment in a facility, but can be part of a group of revenue streams to repay the public sector's investment. A sin tax is considered voluntary; alcohol and tobacco products are generally not classified as necessities, and, therefore, someone could decide not to purchase either. Some of these types of taxes could be considered regressive if these products are purchased more often by individuals with lower incomes. The sin tax is essentially a special form of a sales tax (limited to a single product or a group of products) and, therefore, is also properly defined as an excise tax.

Gaming Taxes and Lotteries

Maryland used proceeds from the state lottery to finance the investment in the new stadium that convinced Art Modell to relocate the Cleveland Browns to Baltimore (Ravens). While gaming taxes and lotteries are seen as voluntary, sufficient research exists to sustain the view that in operation these taxes are regressive (Mikesell, 2009).

Tourist Taxes

Taxes on tourists or business visitors to a region engender less political opposition than some others because the immediate impact falls on nonresidents. As a result, taxes on hotel rooms and the short-term rental of cars have been used to support the public sector's investment in sports facilities in several areas. While tourist taxes make a good deal of political sense as a result of the lower levels of opposition from voters, from an economic perspective, their imposition may be inappropriate. Shifting the burden to visitors creates inefficiencies and lost revenue opportunities. At the margin, with the higher cost of hotel rooms and for rental cars, visitors could well reduce their spending on other items leaving a loss for all tourism-related businesses (hotels, restaurants, etc.). These taxes are likely to be progressive given that most tourists and business travelers have higher incomes meaning that lower income individuals are unlikely to pay the tax at all. The tax is voluntary; tourists or those on business can decide not to visit an area. Tourists might decide to reduce the number of nights they spend in an area or decide to stay with friends or family and avoid the tax.

Food and Beverage Taxes

A tax on the consumption of food and beverages sold at restaurants and pubs has emerged as a popular tax to support the public sector's investment in sports facilities. This tax is seen as voluntary (it does not apply to food purchased at markets for consumption offsite) and it is either proportional to progressive given the clientele at restaurants and the prices at more exclusive restaurants.

References

Beckstead, D., Brown, W. M., and Gellatly, G. 2008. The left brain of North American cities: Scientists and engineers and urban growth. *International Regional Science Review* 31 (3): 304–338.

Mason, D. and Rosentraub, M. S. 2010. *Financing a new arena in downtown Edmonton.* Unpublished report. City of Edmonton, Alberta: University of Alberta, Faculty of Physical Education and Recreation.

Mikesell, J. 2009. *Fiscal administration: Analysis and applications for the public sector.* Boston: Wadsworth Publishing.

Mills, E. S. and Hamilton, B. 1997. *Urban economics.* New York: Basic Books.

Putnam, R. D. 2000. *Bowling alone: The collapse and revival of American community.* New York: Simon and Schuster.

Rosentraub, M. S. 2010. *Major league winners: Using sport facilities and cultural centers for economic development.* Boca Raton, FL: CRC Press/Taylor and Francis.

Rosentraub, M. S. and Joo, M. 2009. Tourism and economic development: Which investments produce gains for regions? *Tourism Management* 30 (5): 759–770.

Rosentraub, M. S., Swindell, D., and Tsvetkova, S. 2009. Justifying public investments in sports: Measuring the intangibles. *Journal of Tourism* 9 (2): 133–159.

Appendix 1

This appendix shows more of the mathematics behind the time value of money. First, there are three types of cash flows: lump sums, annuities, and mixed streams. Lump sums are simply one payment, while an annuity is a constant payment that is made each period. A mixed stream of payments is nonconstant or is made in uneven intervals. We will first focus on lump sums, which is the same technique used to find mixed stream cash flows. To find the value of a mixed stream cash flow, each payment must be treated like a lump sum.

When making an investment with a fixed interest rate, an investor will want to know how much money they will have at the end of the investment, which is the future value. The equation for calculating the future value of a lump sum, given the principal and interest rate, is

$$FV = principal(1+r)^N$$

Where the principal is the investment, r is the interest rate and N is the number of periods of the investment. This assumes that there is a yearly compound interest rate. We also can calculate what is called a future value interest factor. The future value interest factor tells us the future value of each dollar invested in the principal. The future value interest factor is calculated by:

$$FVIF = (1+r)^N$$

Rearranging these equations, we can also find the present value of a future lump sum,

$$PV = \frac{principal}{(1+r)^N}$$

where principal in this case is a future lump sum.

The present value interest factor (the present value of one future dollar) is calculated by:

$$PVIF = \frac{1}{(1+r)^N}$$

Annuities include bonds, loan payments, and many other contracts. Companies also may want to know how much money they will have if they invest a certain amount each year. The future value of an annuity is given by:

$$FV_{Annuity} = payment(1+r)^1 + payment(1+r)^2 + \ldots$$

$$+ payment(1+r)^{N-1} + payment(1+r)^N$$

$$= \sum_{t=1}^{N} payment(1+r)^t$$

The future value interest factor for an annuity, which is the future value of one dollar invested each time period, is equal to:

$$FVIF_{Annuity} = (1+r)^1 + (1+r)^2 + \ldots + (1+r)^{N-1} + (1+r)^N = \sum_{t=1}^{N} (1+r)^t$$

It also is important to know the present value of an annuity because firms often pay or receive annuities. The present value of an annuity is given by:

$$PV_{Annuity} = \frac{payment}{(1+r)^1} + \frac{payment}{(1+r)^2} + \ldots + \frac{payment}{(1+r)^{N-1}} + \frac{payment}{(1+r)^N} = \sum_{t=1}^{N} \frac{payment}{(1+r)^t}$$

The present value interest factor for an annuity is

$$PVIF_{Annuity} = \frac{1}{(1+r)^1} + \frac{1}{(1+r)^2} + \ldots + \frac{1}{(1+r)^{N-1}} + \frac{1}{(1+r)^N} = \sum_{t=1}^{N} \frac{1}{(1+r)^t}$$

This discussion of future and present value for annuities has glossed over the difference between beginning of the year payments and end of the year payments. When calculating the future value of an annuity, beginning of the year payments were assumed and when calculating the present value of an annuity, it was assumed end of the year payments. This was done because it would be somewhat rare to calculate a future value when the first payment is in one year or calculate a present value when there is an immediate payment. For example, if a business takes out a loan, it would be odd to make the first payment at the exact same time they received the loan. So, if a calculator is being used to solve for both future values and present values of annuities, this setting must often be switched. If for some reason one is calculating the future value of an annuity with end of the year payments, the formula is

$$FV_{Annuity} = payment + payment(1+r)^1 + \ldots + payment(1+r)^{N-2} + payment(1+r)^{N-1}$$

$$= \sum_{t=0}^{N-1} payment(1+r)^t$$

The present value of an annuity with beginning of the year payments is given by:

$$PV_{Annuity} = payment + \frac{payment}{(1+r)^1} + ... + \frac{payment}{(1+r)^{N-2}} + \frac{payment}{(1+r)^{N-1}} = \sum_{t=0}^{N-1} \frac{payment}{(1+r)^t}$$

Notice that the only difference is that time periods go from 0 to N−1 instead of 1 to N.

A perpetuity is simply an annuity with an infinite life. In this case, N = ∞. While infinite payments might be unrealistic, there are annuities with a very long life span which continue until the payments cannot be made. The future value of a perpetuity is incalculable: however, the present value of an annuity is

$$PV_{Perpetuity} = \frac{payment}{(1+r)^1} + \frac{payment}{(1+r)^2} + \frac{payment}{(1+r)^3} + ... = \frac{payment}{r}$$

and the present value interest factor is:

$$PVIF_{Perpetuity} = \frac{1}{(1+r)^1} + \frac{1}{(1+r)^2} + \frac{1}{(1+r)^3} + ... = \frac{1}{r}$$

The succinctness of this mathematical formula makes valuing perpetuities easy. Also, while realistically perpetuities might not have an infinite life, this valuation technique can be very close if the annuity has a long life span of, say, 30 years or more.

Sometimes money is compounded more than annually. Occasionally, money is compounded semiannually or monthly. If money is being compounded M times a year, then this effectively increases the interest rate. This means that money is being compounded MN times and the interest gained in between compounding is at a rate of r/M. Therefore, the future value of a lump sum is

$$FV = principal \left(1 + \frac{r}{M}\right)^{NM}$$

The present value of a lump sum is

$$PV = \frac{principal}{\left(1 + \frac{r}{M}\right)^{NM}}$$

The future value of an annuity is

$$FV_{Annuity} = \sum_{t=1}^{N} payment \left(1 + \frac{r}{M}\right)^{tM}$$

And the present value of an annuity is

$$PV_{Annuity} = \sum_{t=1}^{N} \frac{payment}{\left(1 + \dfrac{r}{M}\right)^{tM}}$$

Often, interest is constantly being compounded so that it is immediately added to the principal. Daily compounding is approximately the same as continuously compounding. The future value of a lump sum payment with continuous compounding is given by:

$$FV = principal\left(e^{rt}\right)$$

where *e* is the exponential function, often labeled *exp* on calculators.

The present value of a lump sum payment with continuous compounding is

$$PV = \frac{principal}{e^{rt}}$$

An annuity with continuous compounding can be difficult because there is not a simple equation. There are a couple of ways of circumventing this problem. One is simply treating an annuity as a mixed stream cash flow and finding the future or present value of each payment. This can be extremely tedious for an annuity with many payments. Another way is to adjust the interest rate.

All interest rates can be classified into nominal and effective annual rates. A nominal annual rate is the actual interest rate charged. Thus far, we have been assuming interest rates have been nominal annual rates. The effective annual rate is the actual amount of interest that is paid over one year. For yearly compounding, nominal rates are the same as effective rates. If the interest is compounded more than once a year, the effective annual rate is higher than the nominal annual rate. For semiannual compounding, the effective annual rate is given by:

$$EAR = \left(1 + \frac{r}{m}\right)^{m} - 1$$

If the interest is being compounded continuously, then the effective annual rate is

$$EAR = e^{r} - 1$$

Therefore, if an annuity is continuously compounded, it is appropriate to first find the effective annual rate and then use that in the previous equations. For example, suppose there is a nominal annual rate of 10 percent, but it is continuously compounded.

The effective annual rate is 10.52 percent ($e^1-1 = .1052$). This rate can then be used in the equations above, or using a financial calculator, to solve for the future value or present value of an annuity.

The annual percentage rate (APR) is equal to the nominal annual rate of interest and the annual percentage yield (APY) is equal to the effective annual rate of interest. These rates must often be disclosed by banks or credit cards companies.

Chapter 6

Sports Teams and Real Estate Development, or Real Estate Development Companies with Sports Teams?

Introduction

William Dillard, the founder of Dillard's department stores, is generally credited with originating the saying that real estate's value is determined by three factors: location, location, and location. It is, of course, very difficult to attribute a popular phrase like that to any one person. *Yahoo! Answers,* instead of giving Dillard the credit for coining such profound insight, notes that late-night comedian David Letterman might be responsible for the phrase's popularity. Letterman repeatedly used the words in numerous jokes. Regardless, few disagree that location is critical to financial success and drives the value of land at any particular point in time. What is most fascinating is that the term itself is quite dynamic. Over time, the land that is lauded for its value because of its location has changed. In the early years of the rising interest in the popularity of spectator sports, the land in downtown areas and urban neighborhoods was the favored (most valuable and valued) location for ballparks and arenas. In later years, suburban sites became the land of "location, location, location," and currently downtown areas have reemerged as the most valued. What drives this back and forth phenomenon in the value of land for sports facilities?

Increasing Value of Downtown Locations for Sports Facilities

Three factors define the value of land and the meaning of "location, location, location" for new sports facilities: transportation preferences, in-facility amenities, and the increasing horizontal integration of sports with entertainment operations and real estate development. In the early years of the increasing interest in spectator sports, most fans relied on public transportation. To make it as inexpensive as possible for fans to attend games, facilities were built at the nexus of public transportation lines or in urban neighborhoods where many could walk or even ride a bicycle to a game. When fans shifted their preference from public transit to automobiles, team owners sought locations where they could surround new ballparks and football stadiums with "oceans of asphalt" and a vast number of parking spaces. People not only preferred to drive to games in the post-1960 era, but, with millions of fans relocating from central cities to the suburbs, team owners followed their customers to these newly emerging cities and built facilities with acres of adjacent parking spots. Some teams stayed in urban centers, but those that did demanded ample parking to meet their customers' preference for private as opposed to public transportation. As sports spread west in the 1950s, 1960s, and 1970s, the provision of ample parking became a necessity in the era of the ascendency of the popularity of the automobile.

The advent of luxury seating and the inclusion of other in-facility amenities enhanced the value of downtown locations. Teams like the Cleveland Cavaliers, Washington Wizards (Baltimore Bullets), and San Francisco Giants that had moved to suburban locations moved back downtown. Why? With many of the businesses interested in leasing suites and clubs seats having downtown offices (banks, law firms, real estate corporations, etc.), easy access to new facilities for these fans became critical. The other amenities offered—higher-end food and beverage services and space for pregame entertaining—also were designed to appeal to higher income fans. There was also a concentration of the consumers who worked at the service sector businesses still located in the downtown area or who lived in the emerging downtown neighborhoods filling with condominiums and townhouses. The amenity-laden sports facilities also were becoming fixtures in the mix of entertainment and cultural centers increasingly concentrated in downtown areas as revitalizing cities tried to create new and exciting core areas to redefine the image of urban America. As integral parts of the new mix defining urban entertainment zones, sports facilities benefited from the consumers attracted to a mix of pre- and postgame venues that created a new sense of liveliness in the downtown areas in Baltimore, Cleveland, Indianapolis, Los Angeles, Philadelphia, Pittsburgh, and St. Louis.

Downtown locations also became more valuable as team owners looked to horizontally integrate related entertainment businesses and real estate developments with their teams. There had always been an element of vertical integration in sports even when team owners concentrated their focus on sports as an athletic enterprise. MLB teams, for example, either owned or were affiliated with minor league teams to help develop players. Those linkages constituted vertical integration (for the production of players, which is the essential product that fans consume). Team owners became focused on horizontal linkages, or leveraging the ownership of sports with related business activities or opportunities that capitalized on the visibility or popularity of sports. For example, across the past 20 years, there has been an increasing interest in urban living and lifestyles from two different market segments. Young professionals just beginning their careers have become primary tenants in downtown neighborhoods across the country. Having decided to postpone child rearing, this growing market segment has created a demand for apartments and condominiums that offer easy access to nearby restaurants and entertainment. Developers have capitalized and built condominiums, townhouse, and apartments in downtown areas anchored by sports facilities, and some team owners became partners in residential real estate development or profited from developing new condominium towers that were adjacent to or that overlooked different facilities. Demand for this urban lifestyle is also coming from the "baby boomer" generation. Having completed their child-raising responsibilities, this large cohort of "empty nesters" has created a strong demand for condominiums and townhouses in downtown neighborhoods. Several team owners have focused on downtown locations for new facilities and used those locations to anchor related real estate investments (e.g., Brooklyn, Columbus, Denver, Los Angeles, Newark, San Diego). This is but one example of horizontal integration that has now changed the definition of which land is the most valuable for a sports facility.

Rise of Horizontal Integration, Residential Real Estate, and Entertainment Venues

Horizontal integration is synonymous with the concept of "Disneyfication." While sports entrepreneurs were focused on moving their teams closer to the growing wealth of America's booming suburbs and ensuring that every fan could park his/her car and then walk to the facility, Walt Disney revolutionized the entertainment business. He, like baseball owners, initially thought a location for his theme park adjacent to freeways and acres of parking was all that was needed to attract millions of visitors and grow his business. Disney was not sufficiently focused or even concerned with an important dimension of horizontal integration related to the hospitality sector and entertainment. What he did not account for in the 1950s in the design of Disneyland was that the popularity of the park encouraged others to invest in hotels, restaurants, and other amusement venues near his facility. Walt Disney had failed to control the land adjacent to the amenity he built that attracted millions of visitors. That oversight convinced Disney to build an even larger complex where he would have development rights to a substantial amount of land surrounding Disney World's theme parks. He challenged his corporation with the idea that, if 10 million or more visitors came, what would they imagine (in his words: "image-geneer") for the space or land around the theme parks?

Team owners slowly began to understand that because games also attract millions of visits to a specific location, they too could or should begin to imagine what could be built adjacent to a facility and what investments were best to horizontally integrate into their operations. Just like Disney, they needed to control the land adjacent to a facility at the nexus of transportation lines and to begin to think of sports teams as real estate development companies or entertainment corporations that were linked to hotels and restaurants. That control in an urban setting where young professionals and empty nesters would want to live, work, and play could lead to substantial financial returns. "Location, location, location" now means "put a sports facility where there are substantial real estate development options."

In the early 1990s, energized by some of the concepts put forward by the Baltimore Orioles' design team (which included Janet Marie Smith and team co-owner Larry Lucchino), team owners began asking what could be accomplished with the land surrounding a ballpark, stadium, or arena if a team (1) attracted millions of visits and (2) its owner had control of tracts of adjacent land. Two development approaches emerged. When sufficient acreage could be secured, new neighborhoods were built (e.g., the Ballpark District in San Diego, the Arena District in Columbus, Ohio, or the area adjacent to the Verizon Center in Washington, D.C.). Other owners focused on building new types of entertainment areas when smaller amounts of acreage were available and market conditions favored a focus on restaurants, pubs, and entertainment venues instead of residential buildings, hotels, or offices. And, when an owner was not interested in real estate development or the inclusion of other entertainment venues into his/her sports business, there was a need for a far larger "footprint" for the new ballpark, arena, or stadium. The playing field was not expanded and often the seating capacity was also smaller. The extra space was needed for the amenities built into the new facilities, which were designed to offer fans the opportunity to spend far more time at a facility and far more money on entertainment, food, and beverages when attending games. To expand the revenue streams at these new facilities, space was needed for luxury seating and to deliver higher quality food and beverages in expansive concourses where fans could linger while receiving service in a relatively short period of time. Available video displays ensured that the fans would not miss any action while they made their purchases or talked with clients, friends, or colleagues. This chapter focuses on the management of the real estate *inside* a facility and the development of real estate that *surrounds* a site. We turn first to real estate management inside the newly built megafacilities that were far bigger than the older facilities that were replaced.

Managing the Real Estate Inside a Facility

It might seem unusual to describe a facility in real estate management terms, but relative to revenues, ballparks, stadiums, and arenas offer teams large tracts of space, and maximizing team revenues requires managers to realize the potential each offers to enhance the bottom line. It is important to think of just a few examples before we "drill down" to the management issues and revenue potential that is available within a facility. The 60-yard video/scoreboard that hangs across the new home of the Dallas Cowboys provides 25,000 square feet of space across which messages can be delivered to as many as 100,000 people. Comfortable three-bedroom houses usually have approximately 2,500 square feet of living space. One could think of the Cowboys' scoreboard as being the equivalent of 10 houses. Managing these houses if they were to be rented would create enormous revenue potential. If that space did not offer sufficient new revenue possibilities for the Cowboys' business staff, the new stadium also offers 11,000 square feet of ribbon board space—electronic message boards that form a giant ring around the entire facility. That would add another four houses with revenue potential to the inventory. The Cowboys' new stadium itself encloses 3 million square feet complete with concourses that are 15,000 and 20,000 square feet in size. The new Yankee Stadium is a bit smaller than the Cowboys megafacility, but it encompasses 714,384 square feet. Its footprint is 163 percent larger than its predecessor. The new Meadowlands Stadium where the Giants and Jets play encompasses 2 million square feet. While in every instance, the playing fields account for a large proportion of the available area, there remains numerous opportunities to enhance revenues.

It is best to think of any sports facility as having six distinct pieces of real estate that can be managed to maximize revenue flows:

1. Luxury seating
2. The seating deck
3. The scoreboard and other electronic displays
4. Concourses and entrances
5. The playing surfaces
6. Overall naming rights

Within each of these six broad categories there are component parts. Those teams that are able to effectively manage the complete array of their real estate holdings will enjoy far more profits. Each of these separate real estate assets, their revenue potential, and the management issues are described below in greater detail.

Luxury Seating

The largest single change in facility management has involved the incorporation of suites and club seats into arenas, ballparks, and stadiums. It should not be surprising that people would be interested in more luxurious surroundings in which to watch games. There was a time when people did not care about amenities in their cars. Over time, convenience packages in cars have become commonplace and the amenities built into homes also improved and increased. In some ways, it is probably a bit surprising how long it took for team owners to realize that fans (individuals and businesses) would be willing to pay premium prices for private areas that offered an excellent view of play, meeting places and bathrooms, closets for clothes, temperature controlled areas, and a wide choice of premium food and beverages. Some fans might not be able to afford an entire suite, but they might be interested in the amenity package that is available in club seat areas. An important issue when designing a facility becomes in deciding the number of suites and club seats that should be built. The situation involving the Cleveland Indians and Progressive Field (previously Jacobs Field) underscores the critical nature of the design decisions that must be made.

Suites, Club Seats, and Designs for Flexibility (Or Not)

A new ballpark for the Cleveland Indians opened in 1994. The team owner, Richard Jacobs, was in the midst of substantially increasing his investment in players, and the team began to dominate the Central Division (five consecutive titles) and appeared in two World Series. During this spectacular run (that extended into the tenure of the team's new owners, the Dolans), the team sold every ticket for 494 consecutive games. Anticipating the explosion in demand for tickets, Jacobs insisted on building 122 suites and 2,024 club seats. The inclusion of an additional tier of seats increased the size of the ballpark and changed the elevation of the upper deck. The seats in the third deck are 10 to 12 feet higher and 20 to 24 feet farther back from the playing field than what would have existed had the extra tier of suites not been added. If all or most of the 122 suites were consistently sold, the increased revenue from the luxury seating would offset any losses from the reduced quality of the view from the upper deck. With these seats farther from the field, their revenue potential may well be reduced from what would exist if the seats were closer to the field.

In the years after the team's robust success, attendance has declined. To be sure, losing records was a major factor in the lower level of fan interest. In 2007, however, the team won the American League's Central Division and defeated the Yankees in the first round of the playoffs before losing to the Red Sox in seven games in the AL

Championship series. Despite that success, the team only attracted 2,275,913 fans to their home games, far less than the 4 million+ who turned out for games in the late 1990s. Why did the team attract far fewer fans? Northeast Ohio was in the midst of a substantial economic contraction that included the loss of numerous residents and businesses. Simply put, the team's market had contracted and the remaining fans and businesses had less money to spend on tickets. The success of the Cleveland Cavaliers also had a role in explaining what fans did with their dwindling levels of discretionary income.

By 2010, it became clear that it was unlikely that the team would ever again be able to lease 122 suites (or it would take a decade of growth for the number of fans to increase to the number present in the 1990s). As a result, the team decided to hire an architectural firm and a designer to present the team with ideas on how best to utilize an entire level of suites. The decision to build an extra tier left the Indians with a "dark" area (unsold suites) and thousands of square feet that are not producing revenue. The team's options are constrained by irrevocable design decisions made once an additional level of suites was added. The critical lesson from Cleveland's experience is to consider carefully the long-term demand for suites. It is important that team owners carefully assess the potential that exists within a market and then design the facility that fits best with an appropriate mix of luxury and nonluxury seats. Managers have to look carefully at the demand for luxury seating in a market and the long-term prospects for growth and demand.

How many suites should be built? Market surveys can be valuable, but so can a database that enumerates the total number of luxury seats in a market (as a result of the existence of facilities for other teams or potential facilities) and the number of larger companies and wealthier individuals. Constructing ratios that permit a consideration of the levels available in other markets (and the relative success of selling that product in the other markets) can be helpful. There is no iron rule of the desired ratio of companies to suites or how many higher-income people a region needs to ensure that suites will sell. What is important to understand is that scarcity is valuable. In other words, if a facility appears to have so many suites that buyers can patiently wait to see if the supply is consumed, then too many have been built. It is probably better to have as many as 5 or 10 firms that could buy a suite such that, if 60 were built, there is a pool of from 300 to 600 potential customers. This not only ensures that there are a sufficient number of firms and, as their fortunes rise and fall, there will always be a sufficient number to lease the available supply of suites. With 300 to 600 firms and only 60 suites, a sense of scarcity will exist and the price of a suite will be relatively high. Looking at the sales experiences when teams win smaller or larger proportions of their games in other markets can help in selecting the best possible design.

With regard to suites, as with any other seat at a sports facility, fewer means a higher price, which in turn could produce more revenue than if a larger number were created, which would leave a team with excess capacity. An additional level of suites also can require extensive remodeling costs if demand for luxury products declines.

Returning to the situation in Cleveland, with the building of a new ballpark and arena, the Indians and the Cavaliers were going to be the first teams in the market with luxury seats. As the Indians were in the midst of a surge in their on-field success, Richard Jacobs, the team's owner, correctly guessed that he would be able to exploit short-term demand and lease a large number of suites. In later years, the Cleveland Browns entered the luxury seating market with their new stadium and the Cavaliers had their own run of success during LeBron James' tenure with the club. When the Indians entered a period of decline in terms of their on-the-field success, and the regional economy contracted, there was suddenly a "glut" of unsold luxury seating.

Supply and demand issues impact large markets as well. The new Yankee Stadium has 56 suites but 4,300 club seats. Citi Field, the home of the New York Mets, has 54 suites and 7,800 seats in its club level. The far fewer number of suites (given the size of the New York market in terms of large corporations and people) further underscores that the capacity built into the Indians' ballpark was excessive. Oriole Park at Camden Yards was built at about the same time as Progressive Field and it has 72 suites. When Oriole Park opened, there was no team in Washington, D.C. As a result, the Orioles had a far larger market than did the Cleveland Indians. With the Nationals now in Washington, D.C., and given the change in the economy, the Orioles also are considering a reduction in the number of suites and the conversion of the space in some suites to other uses to extract more revenue from that real estate. What could the space be used for to generate more revenue? Some ideas include "all-you-can-eat" accommodations with seating for a few dozen fans to areas where children can have "play space" while their parents enjoy the game.

The pricing for suites is frequently more complex than the sale of tickets. Clients interested in suites may want to take advantage of advertising opportunities in the facility and their contract price for the suite may include a certain number of messages that appear on video boards or permanent signage or a set of other incentives or benefits. Suites are leased for multiple years and different payment schedules can be arranged that would change the present value of the asking price. Suites also require the purchase of food plans that range from simple fare to far more elegant meal service. The variety of points that are negotiated in the leasing of a suite and the agreed to price may include different elements for different clients.

In recent years, baseball teams have offered the equivalent of first-class (padded) luxury seating in the rows closest to the field and provided these patrons with unlimited high-end food service. The new Yankee Stadium has several rows of select super club seats. Some of these seats were marketed as being closer to the batter's box than the pitcher (less than 60 feet from home plate). For these seats with unlimited premium food and beverage service, the Yankees were charging as much as $2,500 per game. Sales were quite slow and televised games showed scores of empty seats. The image of unsold luxury seats convinced the Yankees to offer everyone an additional seat for each ticket purchased dropping the price by 50 percent. Even after winning their 27th championship the Yankees were unable to sell all of these high-priced seats. While demand might return to a level where companies would be willing to spend $1,250 for a ticket to a game, the state of the economy in 2011 does not suggest this will occur for at least an additional year. While the Yankees might have chosen a price point above what the market would support, the concept of first class-type seating and unlimited high-end food service (with the price of the food included in the ticket price) was not an impractical or inappropriate use of the real estate closest to the field. Numerous other teams copied the program and now make available first-class seats with exclusive food service to their fans. The prices for their seats in other venues are far less expensive when compared to the prices charged by the Yankees. For example, the St. Louis Cardinals charge $250 and $260 for their first-class or Cardinals Club seats (2010). The New York Mets charge $440 for their Delta Club Premium seats.

Club seats provide areas where guests (who also have club seat tickets) can be entertained and where there is usually extensive food and beverage service, but there is no private space. Club seats, as their name implies, provide access to a club and, with as many as 7,500 club seats in a facility, it is possible to gauge how crowded the "clubs" can be on game day or the size of the clubs needed to accommodate all guests. In some instances, the food service may be included in the price of the club seat ticket. Several teams have experimented with buffet-style food service in their clubs with ticket holders permitted to eat as much as they want. Other teams require club seat ticket holders to pay for the food and beverages they consume. Increasingly teams are offering a mix of both packages. Those seated in the most exclusive club seats (the front-row seats now routinely available at ballparks and the most desirable seats at some football stadiums) usually include unlimited access to very elaborate food service facilities (and wait service at the seats). Other club areas are available that might include unlimited food access to a less elaborate menu of items and opportunities for some club seat holders to pay for food and beverages that they consume. In this way, one needs to think about the club seat real estate being subdivided into different tiers much the way an apartment building or a luxury condominium building would be designed. In those buildings, there are smaller and larger units, units with terraces and other amenities, and even penthouse units. Team owners now look at the real estate in their club seat area of the facility in the same manner. This is a substantial change in the management of a facility's real estate. For example, when Progressive Field (Jacobs Field) opened, its 2,000+ club seats offered an excellent view of the playing field from an elevated deck that was along the first-base side of the field. Citi Field, built 15 years later, offers fans the ability to chose from the *Delta Sky360 Lounge*, the *Delta Sky360 Club*, the

Champions Club, *Caesars Club*, the Promenade Club, and the *Acela Club*. (Those in italics represent club areas for which the Mets receive naming rights revenues.) What is critical to appreciate is that by providing numerous club options not only is the available real estate divided to ensure that separate market points and demands are satisfied, but that numerous naming opportunities are available for other clients. Delta Air Lines chose to invest in two different naming opportunities to advertise their brand to preferred customers. Acela is the name AMTRAK uses for its exclusive express service in the Northeast Corridor (between Boston and New York City and New York City and Washington, D.C.), and Caesars is the hotel chain that has prominent properties in Atlantic City, Las Vegas, and elsewhere. As the Mets entered the 2011 season, they still had two additional naming opportunities available even after having sold the naming rights for the entire facility (Citi Field). This is another example of the aggressive marketing for additional revenue that becomes possible if a facility is designed with very careful attention to real estate management possibilities. As the Mets are part of the holdings of Sterling Equities, a leading New York-based real estate development company, their focus on a design that created numerous naming opportunities was to be expected. Facilities and the available square footage are prime examples of the need for expertise in real estate management and the resulting revenue generation that is possible when all of the real estate within a venue benefits from a strong design and management strategy. Club seats usually offer customers excellent if not the closest views of the field and, in some instances, are actually the seats closest to the field of play.

Table 6.1 lists the luxury seating currently available at each facility where a team from the NFL, MLB, NBA, and NHL plays. The Nets have not yet announced the final configuration for the Barclays Center that is still under construction. A major renovation also has been announced for the Madison Square Garden and that likely will change the mix available to Rangers and Knicks fans. Some inaccuracies also result from the changing mix of seating at ballparks where teams have added special seating that include a wide set of amenities. What is obvious from the data, however, is the importance of this real estate for club revenues. There is a substantial advantage relative to revenues if a team plays in a facility that has luxury seating and if a market exists for the product. The table also shows how quickly the sports business has changed. Prior to the 1990s, luxury seating did not exist. Its popularity and profitability spread so quickly that some teams playing in relatively new arenas requested or demanded new facilities long before communities had finished paying for the ones that had become economically obsolete (Charlotte and Dallas).

Having a supply of luxury seating is clearly important to enhance team revenues. The important management issue as each team has rushed to offer its luxury seating options to its fans, is the aggregate demand that can exist in any single market. This issue was addressed in Chapter 4; it surfaces again in this chapter as sports has undergone a boom-and-bust period cycle similar to the one experienced in the housing market. As a result, the prices for luxury seating real estate has declined. In

Table 6.1 Luxury seating and seating capacities at the venues used by the NFL, MLB, NBA, and NHL teams

Team	Facility Name	Year Opened/ Renovation Completed	Number of		Capacity
			Suites	Club Seats	
NFL Clubs					
Arizona Cardinals	University of Phoenix	2006	88	7,400	63,400
Atlanta Falcons	Georgia Dome	1992	203	5,600	71,250
Baltimore Ravens	M&T Bank Stadium	1998	108	7,904	71,008
Buffalo Bills	Ralph Wilson Stadium	1973/1999	164	6,878	73,967
Carolina Panthers	Bank of America Stadium	1994	159	11,358	73,298
Chicago Bears	Soldier Field	2003	133	8,600	61,500
Cincinnati Bengals	Paul Brown Stadium	2000	114	7,620	65,535
Cleveland Browns	Browns Stadium	1999	145	8,754	73,200
Dallas Cowboys	Cowboys Stadium	2009	300	15,000	80,000
Denver Broncos	Invesco Field at Mile High	2001	106	8,500	76,125
Detroit Lions	Ford Field	2002	120	7,000	65,000
Green Bay Packers	Lambeau Field	2003	167	6,260	72,922
Houston Texans	Reliant Stadium	2002	187	8,200	71,500

(continued)

Table 6.1 (continued)   Luxury seating and seating capacities at the venues used by the NFL, MLB, NBA, and NHL teams

| Team | Facility Name | Year Opened/ Renovation Completed | Number of | | Capacity |
			Suites	Club Seats	
Indianapolis Colts	Lucas Oil Stadium	2008	137	7,100	63,000
Jacksonville Jaguars	Alltel Stadium	1995	75	11,000	76,877
Kansas City Chiefs	Arrowhead Stadium	2001/2010	80	10,199	79,451
Miami Dolphins	Sun Life Stadium	1987	195	10,209	75,235
Minnesota Vikings	Humphrey Dome	1982	113	0	64,035
New England Patriots	Gillette Stadium	2002	87	6,600	68,756
New Orleans Saints	Superdome	1975/2008/2012	137	14,077	72,968
New York Giants	Giants/Jets Stadium	2010	217	9,300	82,500
New York Jets	Giants/Jets Stadium	2010	217	9,300	82,500
Oakland Raiders	McAfee Stadium	1966	143	9,000	63,026
Philadelphia Eagles	Lincoln Financial Field	2003	172	10,828	68,532
Pittsburgh Steelers	Heinz Field	2001	129	7,300	65,050
Saint Louis Rams	Edward Jones Dome	1995	124	6,500	65,321
San Diego Chargers	Qualcomm Stadium	1967/1984	113	7,882	71,500
San Francisco 49ers	Monster Park/Candlestick	1972/1995	93	0	70,047

Seattle Seahawks	Century Link Field	2000	111	7,000	67,000
Tampa Bay Buccaneers	Raymond James Stadium	1998	195	12,232	65,657
Tennessee Titans	LP Field	1999	175	11,800	68,798
Washington Redskins	Fed Ex Field	1997	280	15,044	91,704
MLB Clubs					
Arizona Diamondbacks	Chase Field	1998	69	4,400	48,569
Atlanta Braves	Turner Field	1996	62	5,372	50,097
Baltimore Orioles	Oriole Park, Camden Yards	1992	72	4,631	48,262
Boston Red Sox	Fenway Park	1912/2004–2008	80	1,871	37,373
Chicago Cubs	Wrigley Field	1914	67		41,160
Chicago White Sox	US Cellular Field	1991	103	1,822	40,615
Cincinnati Reds	Great American Ball Park	2003	57	2,276	42,059
Cleveland Indians	Progressive Field	1994	122	2,064	43,515
Colorado Rockies	Coors Field	1995	52	4,400	50,200
Detroit Tigers	Comerica Park	2000	108	2,000	41,070
Florida/Miami Marlins	Marlins Park	2012	60		35,521
Houston Astros	Minute Maid Park	2000	62	5,000	40,950

(continued)

Table 6.1 (continued) Luxury seating and seating capacities at the venues used by the NFL, MLB, NBA, and NHL teams

Team	Facility Name	Year Opened/ Renovation Completed	Number of		Capacity
			Suites	Club Seats	
Kansas City Royals	Kauffman Stadium	1973	19	2,487	38,177
Los Angeles Angels	Angel Stadium of Anaheim	1966	74	5,000	45,113
Los Angeles Dodgers	Dodger Stadium	1962	33	565	56,000
Milwaukee Brewers	Miller Park	2001	70	3,500	41,900
Minnesota Twins	Target Field	2010	60	3,400	40,000
New York Mets	Citi Field	2009	54	7,800	42,000
New York Yankees	Yankee Stadium	2009	47	4,374	52,325
Oakland Athletics	McAfee Stadium	1966	143	9,000	34,007
Philadelphia Phillies	Citizens Bank Park	2004	72	6,600	43,647
Pittsburgh Pirates	PNC Park	2001	65	3,374	38,496
St. Louis Cardinals	Busch Stadium	2006	63	3,600	46,700
San Diego Padres	PETCO Park	2004	50	5,000	42,500
San Francisco Giants	AT&T Park	2000	67	5,300	41,600
Seattle Mariners	SAFECO Field	1999	82	7,000	47,447
Tampa Bay Rays	Tropicana Field	1990	63	3,600	43,722

Texas Rangers	Rangers' Ballpark in Arlington	1994	122	5,699	48,911
Toronto Blue Jays	Rogers Centre	1989	120	5,700	50,516
Washington Nationals	Nationals Park	2008	66	2,500	41,222
NBA Clubs					
Atlanta Hawks	Phillips Arena	1999	92	1,866	18,750
Boston Celtics	TD Garden	1995	104	2,350	18,624
Charlotte Bobcats	Time Warner Cable Arena	2005	51	2,300	19,000
Chicago Bulls	United Center	1994	160	3,100	20,917
Cleveland Cavaliers	Quicken Loans Arena	1994	90	2,000	20,562
Dallas Mavericks	American Airlines Arena	2001	144	1,600	19,200
Denver Nuggets	Pepsi Center	1999	95	1,800	19,309
Detroit Pistons	Palace of Auburn Hills	1988	180	1,000	22,076
Golden State Warriors	Oracle Arena	1966	72	3,900	19,596
Houston Rockets	Toyota Center	2003	92	2,900	18,370
Indiana Pacers	Conseco Fieldhouse	1999	69	2,400	18,345
Los Angeles Clippers	STAPLES Center	1999	192	2,500	19,060
Los Angeles Lakers	STAPLES Center	1999	192	2,500	18,997

(continued)

Table 6.1 (continued) Luxury seating and seating capacities at the venues used by the NFL, MLB, NBA, and NHL teams

| Team | Facility Name | Year Opened/ Renovation Completed | Number of | | Capacity |
			Suites	Club Seats	
Memphis Grizzlies	FedEx Forum	2004	75	2,500	18,165
Miami Heat	American Airlines Arena	1999	144	1,600	19,600
Milwaukee Bucks	Bradley Center	1988	68	0	18,717
Minnesota Timberwolves	Target Center	1990	68	702	20,500
New Jersey Nets	Barclays Center	2012	100	TBD	18,000
New Orleans Hornets	New Orleans Arena	1999	56	2,538	18,000
New York Knicks	Madison Square Garden	1968	89	3,775	19,763
Oklahoma City Thunder	Ford Center	2002	55	3,380	19,599
Orlando Magic	Amway Center	2010	56	1,428	18,500
Philadelphia 76ers	Wachovia Center	1996	126	1,880	21,600
Phoenix Suns	US Airways Center	1992	88	2,200	18,422
Portland Trail Blazers	Rose Garden	1995	70	2,397	19,980
Sacramento Kings	ARCO Arena	1988	30	412	17,317
San Antonio Spurs	SBC Center	2002	60	1,300	18,797
Toronto Raptors	Air Canada Centre	1999	153	1,020	19,800

Utah Jazz	Energy Solutions Arena	1991	50	670	19,991
Washington Wizards	Verizon Center	1997	110	3,000	20,173
NHL Clubs					
Anaheim Ducks	Honda Center	1993	84	1,716	18,136
Atlanta Thrashers	Phillips Arena	1999	92	1,866	18,545
Boston Bruins	TD Garden	1995	104	2,350	17,565
Buffalo Sabres	HSBC Arena	1996	88	5,000	18,690
Calgary Flames	Penngrowth Management Saddledome	1983	72	1,461	19,289
Carolina Hurricanes	RBC Center	1999	66	2,000	18,730
Chicago Blackhawks	United Center	1994	160	3,100	20,500
Columbus Blue Jackets	Nationwide Arena	2000	78	3,200	18,136
Colorado Avalanche	Pepsi Center	1999	95	1,800	18,007
Dallas Stars	American Airlines Arena	2001	144	1,600	18,352
Detroit Red Wings	Joe Lewis Arena	1979	86	0	20,066
Edmonton Oilers	Rexall Place	1974	66	3,323	16,839
Florida Panthers	BankAtlantic Center	1998	70	230	19,250
Los Angeles Kings	STAPLES Center	1999	192	2,500	18,118

(continued)

Table 6.1 (continued) Luxury seating and seating capacities at the venues used by the NFL, MLB, NBA, and NHL teams

| Team | Facility Name | Year Opened/ Renovation Completed | Number of | | Capacity |
			Suites	Club Seats	
Minnesota Wild	Xcel Energy Center	2000	74	3,000	18,064
Montreal Canadians	Bell Center	1996	135	2,674	21,273
Nashville Predators	Bridgestone Arena	1996	70	1,850	17,113
New Jersey Devils	Prudential Center	2007	76	2,330	17,625
New York Islanders	Nassau Veterans	1972	32	150	16,234
New York Rangers	Madison Square Garden	1968	89	3,775	18,200
Ottawa Senators	Scotiabank Place	2005	148	2,500	19,153
Philadelphia Flyers	Wells Fargo Center	1996	126	1,880	19,519
Pittsburgh Penguins	Consol Energy Center	2010	66	2,000	18,087
Phoenix Coyotes	Jobing.Com Arena	2003	87	1,425	17,799
San Jose Sharks	HP Pavilion	1993	68	3,000	17,496
St. Louis Blues	Scottrade Center	1994	91	1,684	19,260
Tampa Bay Lightning	St. Petersburg Times Forum	1996	72	3,300	19,500
Toronto Maple Leafs	Air Canada Centre	1999	153	1,020	18,819
Vancouver Canucks	Rogers Arena	1995	75	2,195	18,630
Washington Capitals	Verizon Center	1997	110	3,000	18,672

looking at Table 6.1, it is important to realize that prior to 1990 there was little to no luxury seating in any market. Over the next 25 years, luxury seating grew as each team owner wanted to capture as much of the emerging demand as they could, fearing that the last one into the market would fail to capture new income.

It should not be surprising that there was a demand for luxury seating from fans that created an important new revenue stream for owners. Allen Sanderson, a senior lecturer in the University of Chicago's Department of Economics, observed that sports fans, like all of us, enjoy shiny new cars with luxurious amenities. He made the observation in response to a question dealing with the razing of sports facilities with good sight lines. Sanderson was neither criticizing owners for providing what fans wanted nor belittling fans who wanted more comfortable seats and spaces within which they could entertain guests or enjoy higher quality and more varied food choices. The cornerstone of his observation was that, as people's discretionary income rises, it is common to find interest in amenities, comfort, and different experiences. Sports team owners were responding to this demand. The observation that people were becoming more interested in consuming experiences rather than purchasing possessions was initially indirectly introduced by Joseph Pine and James Gilmore in their book, *The Experience Economy* (1999). Their advice to businesses was that they plan and present events so that the memory of the experience becomes the product. Collecting experiences has become important just as is the consumption of tangible goods. Enhancing the game-day experience has meant providing luxury seating and opportunities to enjoy different types of food and beverages and other forms of entertainment while at a game. Those who can afford club seats or suites get to enjoy experiences that, if not offered at sports facilities, would be consumed at venues offering other types of entertainment. An essential part of the sports business now is understanding that the game-day experience is paramount in terms of ticket sales and realizing all of the revenue potential that exists for clubs. Had new facilities with luxury seating and other amenities not been built, then both players and owners would have lost the opportunity to realize a substantially enhanced level of revenues that has led to higher salaries and profit levels. The issue in every market is to ensure that an adequate supply of luxury seating exists. Each team also needs to protect against an over supply that leaves too much real estate unsold and, therefore, does not contribute to the overall revenue picture. As markets change, the demand for luxury seating can fluctuate and that is why in the newest designs owners are seeking plans that would permit luxury seating to be converted to other uses and the ability to add luxury seating when needed. The Cleveland Indians and Baltimore Orioles appear to be the first teams actively considering plans to permanently convert some luxury seating given changes in their market. Those changes seem to suggest that alternative uses of the space would generate more money than can be earned as suites and club seats.

The Seating Deck

Chapter 10 describes the various decisions and options that must be considered by team owners and business managers as they seek to optimize profits and attendance levels. In this chapter, we want to focus on design decisions that influence the real estate management issues and ticket pricing involved with every facility's nonluxury seating, or "the deck," as the other seats are usually described.

First, and probably the most important management issue, involves the lessons learned from the circular facilities built in the 1960s and 1970s to accommodate baseball and football teams in the same facility. While having two teams in a facility is advantageous relative to the number of dates the structure is used, two different sports played in the same facility leads to compromises in sight lines that reduce the quality of a fan's experience. That reduced quality often means lower prices for seats to lure fans to the facility relative to their other entertainment options. Managers must never lose sight of the need to deliver quality game experiences to each fan and that begins with seating that provides excellent sight lines. When every seat offers fans excellent views of the field of play, revenues rise from individual ticket sales and higher and more persistent levels of demand. People will pay higher prices for better sight lines and comfortable seats. Facilities that are designed to cater to each sport (ballparks for baseball and stadiums for football) create better sight lines and fans. There are even compromises that have to be made for basketball and hockey played in the same facility, but in most metropolitan areas, hockey and basketball teams play at the same arena. Most arenas are designed to accommodate both sports even though the playing surfaces are different, requiring some seats for basketball to be farther from the court to ensure that every seat has a view of the goals in hockey.

Second, another lesson learned from those facilities that lacked amenities was that fans want enhanced comfort and are willing to pay higher prices even in the general seating deck for more improved surroundings. Customers respond positively to the availability of amenities, and new facilities that charge higher prices receive uniformly favorable responses from consumers. There is a "honeymoon" effect meaning that after the novelty of a new facility wears off, what takes place on the field in terms of competitive play reasserts itself as a primary predictor of demand. What is important for managers to realize, however, is that higher-priced tickets, when greater conveniences and amenities are provided, meet with little resistance. This does not mean that there is no upper price point when amenities are offered. The New York Yankees have had to change their pricing policies with regard to their special seats adjacent the field. That was a vivid reminder that severe price escalations can result in unsold seats although the Yankees had the misfortune of unveiling their new seating and fan experience at the height of the recession. As noted, the Yankees effectively reduced the price of the tickets by 50 percent (seats sold on a 2 for 1 basis). As the economy recovers, many will be watching to see if demand for these premium seats ($2,500 per game) increases. If indeed it does, then the observation that demand for amenities provides great pricing flexibility will be an important object lesson for all managers.

Third, the designs or exterior of the circular facilities lacked architectural appeal and the views they offered from the seats of the surrounding landscape were generally also quite poor. A sports facility as a result of its social importance and scale has a unique opportunity to contribute to a community's architectural profile. Those facilities built since the 1990s have become far more iconic and that too adds to the value enjoyed by fans and a community. Managing a facility now also includes an opportunity to ensure that the external appearance and the view of the urban landscape provided to fans adds to a facility's value to the community and its potential for advertisers who want their product and company identified with exciting and provocative architecture. Failing to emphasize architectural appeal can reduce the revenues that can be earned from advertising and that is something every manager should focus on when designs for new facilities are developed. The importance of design and architecture is best illustrated by the success of Target Field. Its success led the *Minneapolis Star Tribune* to declare the facility's architect, Earl Santee, the region's sportsman of the year. In describing the accomplishment, Jim Souhan concluded, "In one season, Target Field became for downtown Minneapolis what the North Star is to the night sky (Souhan, 2010)."

Finally, more so for baseball than football, the height of a facility matters; for all sports, the distance from the playing field is also important. Taller facilities might have more seats, but the incremental value of those seats declines. There is also a danger from building a facility with too many seats. Smaller facilities create an impression of scarcity that is absent when ballparks are so large that fans never have to fear the games will be sold out. When this occurs, there is less incentive for fans to commit to buying tickets before the day of the game. Owners benefit from advance ticket sales as the team not only has use of the cash for longer periods of time, but there is far less or no need to hire staff to sell tickets on the day of a game. When deciding on how big a facility to build, it actually is far more beneficial to have too few seats than too many. Fears of scarcity or sellouts will permit a team owner to charge higher prices and to be able to have access for a longer period of time to the money paid for tickets for weeks or days ahead of a game. If fans are convinced there will always be tickets available, then their decision to attend a game could be based on weather (for baseball) and impacted by who is playing (pitchers) or who is injured. To avoid the chance that people might not attend, building a facility that creates an impression of scarcity actually is in the owner's best interest. For this reason, it is not uncommon to find that newer facilities are smaller than a team's older home (Table 6.2).

Indeed, most baseball team owners would prefer smaller and lower facilities to create a sense of scarcity and, therefore, more interest in purchasing tickets before the day of the game. Design elements that require larger setbacks—the movement of seats and decks farther from the playing field—also reduces the value of any seat. Facilities that had running tracks around a field reduce the value of all seats and

Table 6.2 Smaller is often better: Creating a sense of scarcity and urgency in buying baseball tickets

City	Old Facility/Capacity	New Facility/Capacity
New York	Yankee Stadium[1]/67,337	Yankee Stadium/50,086
New York	Shea Stadium/57,333	Citi Field/41,800
Cleveland	Municipal Stadium/73,200	Progressive Field/45,199
Detroit	Tiger Stadium/52,416	Comerica Park/41,070
Houston	Astrodome/54,816	Minute Maid Park/40,950
Miami[2]	Sun Life/47,662-38,560	Marlins Park/37,000
Minneapolis	Metrodome (56,144)	Target Field/39,504
Philadelphia	Veterans' Stadium/62,418	Citizens Bank Park/43,647
San Francisco	Candlestick Park/59,000	AT&T Park/40,800
St. Louis	Busch Stadium/46,048	Busch Stadium/43,975

[1] The original Yankee Stadium opened in 1923 with 58,000 seats. When the third deck was completed, the capacity grew to 67,337. After being remodeled in the 1970s, the capacity declined to 56,866.

[2] The Florida Marlins have played their home games at the football stadium used by the Miami Dolphins. They have experimented with different seating capacities starting with 47,662 seats and then moving to designs with 42,531, 35,531, 36,331, and 38,560. Their new permanent home in downtown Miami will have 37,000 seats.

have been largely eliminated. Adding additional levels of luxury seating can lead to an elevated and more distant upper deck as well.

Scoreboard and Electronic Displays

Advertising on scoreboards began decades ago. The advent of high definition video and the technology that allows the presentation of multiple images substantially increased the revenue potential. Every facility manager and team must balance the value of providing fans with game and play information against the revenue that can be generated by leasing more space for advertising messages. A recent innovation is the use of ribbon boards that now adorn the upper decks in all facilities. These ribbon boards usually surround an entire arena and in ballparks and stadiums run the length of the grandstands. In between plays and during time outs, scoreboards and ribbon boards send out advertising messages.

What this means for design is attention to detail so that advertising messages are visible to everyone regardless of where they sit. The balancing of advertising messages and game information (including replays) also has become a major design issue. Some facilities, for example, have reduced game information or moved some of their auxiliary displays to make sure advertising revenues can be maximized. Too much advertising, however, can become an annoyance to dedicated fans. In planning for the use of the scoreboard, managers have to balance revenue potential with the information that fans want to see during a game and with regard to games being played elsewhere. At the college level, it should be underscored that some universities prohibit any advertising (other than that related to other university athletic events) inside a facility. Professional teams have never followed that practice, but their management teams have to balance the interest of devoted fans and the potential revenue streams from the exposures that can be offered to firms wanting to advertise or be identified with the team (Figure 6.1).

Figure 6.1   The leasing of scoreboard real estate: (top) Cleveland's Progressive Field and (bottom) the new Yankee Stadium. (Photos courtesy of Mark S. Rosentraub.)

Concourses and Entrances

Facilities are now designed to provide myriad naming or advertising opportunities. A brief 20 years ago, the concept of naming an entire facility was seen as extraordinary. Facilities designed in the twenty-first century are done with attention to the possibility of creating distinct entrances and entry points reserved for luxury seating clients. Distinct entrances with special architectural themes create an opportunity to offer interested companies a naming rights/advertising deal that would cost far less than an opportunity to purchase a name for the exterior of the facility. The number of teams that have sold naming rights to a facility and entrances or concourses underscores the popularity of named portions of a facility. Citi Field is just one example where Delta Airlines found great value in having its name on part of the facility while Citi Financial has the overall naming rights contract.

Playing Surfaces

While there has been some reluctance to create an overly labeled environment, advertising or messaging on the playing field has been steadily increasing as teams seek to enhance their revenue streams. If a sponsor has been secured for a facility or event (e.g., Air Canada Centre, Discover Orange Bowl, etc.), it is increasingly common to find the sponsor's name or brand somewhere on the playing surface. Some sports or team owners are more aggressive with regard to the placement of advertising on the playing surface, but there is an unmistakable trend. The playing surface represents a substantial amount of real estate and while it can be counted upon to drive the largest portion of revenue from the game itself, from a management perspective it seems unlikely that other income possibilities can be ignored. Electronically, the networks already offer clients the possibility to impose different graphical representations. Baseball fans routinely see advertisements on the backstop behind the catcher that are not visible in the ballpark. Different statistical boxes, replay windows, and strike zone projections are made available for advertising by the networks. Will teams and the leagues decide to adorn the playing surfaces with even more advertising in the future? That decision will probably be made relative to what fans will tolerate before becoming too alienated by the advertising messages or when sponsors believe the addition of one more message has no value as fans have become either alienated or numb to the content as a result of the bombardment of ads. Scoreboards have already become laden with advertising messages. In hockey, there is extensive use of the ice and sideboards for messaging. It is probably only a matter of a few years before more extensive advertising messages appear on the playing surfaces of each sport. The increment will involve electronic images visible only to those watching the games on television. Shortly, it can be expected that permanent messages on the playing fields will become routine.

Naming Rights

If there is a "big banana" in the effort to secure revenue from advertising, it is the naming of the facility itself. Surprisingly, naming rights is not a "new venture." William Wrigley named the stadium he built and where his Cubs played for his chewing gum company, Wrigley Field, in 1926. A proposal to rename the St. Louis Cardinals' stadium to Budweiser Stadium was opposed by then MLB Commissioner Ford Frick. Busch Memorial Stadium was acceptable as that was the name of one of the team's owners (the name was later truncated to Busch Stadium.). MLB did not interfere with the decision of the Colorado Rockies to sell the naming rights to their home field to the Coors Brewing Company and Miller Park in Milwaukee sports the name of another beer. The Schaefer Brewery had the naming rights to the home of the New England Patriots for a short period of time.

The largest amount of money ever secured for naming rights was $400 million. Citi Financial agreed to that amount (over time) for the name Citi Field. This record price was a result of the size of New York City. In addition, however, the Citi Field sign is visible from New York's Grand Central Parkway. The substantial automobile traffic on this roadway that is also adjacent to La Guardia Airport contributed to the value of the naming rights and signage given to Citi Financial.

The owners of some facilities that have earned a place in sports history have not placed corporate names on these venues. A corporate name preceding or replacing such venerable names as Fenway Park or Yankee Stadium might engender a negative reaction from consumers. That risk may well have deterred potential advertisers from even considering the value of having their name on the venue. As a result the Yankees have not sold the naming rights to the new Yankee Stadium despite the razing of their legendary home. Instead the Yankees have sold naming rights for entrances and concourses while leaving the historical moniker in place. It does appear that Jerry Jones tried to sell the naming rights to the Cowboys' new stadium. The failure of a corporate sponsor to have been named indicates either that the interest in what would be a highly publicized advertising commitment in the midst of a recession has declined, or that those firms willing to commit were only willing to pay a fraction of what Jones hoped to secure. A similar fate seems to have befallen the new home of the New York Giants and New York Jets in the Meadowlands. That stadium, too, located just across the Hudson River from Manhattan and visible from the island's west side, also remains without a corporate sponsor. As with Yankee Stadium, there are named entrances and concourses, but the new facility is referred to as New Meadowlands Stadium. Perhaps when corporations are again willing to be associated with large and luxurious sports facilities these new structures will have corporate names as well. With Citi Field securing a fee equal to $20 million a year (in nominal terms), it is reasonable to expect that the owners of the Cowboys, Giants, and Jets are anticipating at least that much and probably a bit more. Managers should be aware that naming certain facilities and events can create a level of consumer backlash that reduces the value that can

Figure 6.2 Pasadena's venerable Rose Bowl facility without a corporate sponsor is pictured. (Photo courtesy of Mark S. Rosentraub.)

be secured. When that happens, focusing on other naming right opportunities (entrances, concourses, etc.) can be far more profitable. The Rose Bowl (stadium) remains with its historical name, but the game itself is now referred to as "The Rose Bowl Presented by" with a corporate sponsor's name inserted. This began in 1999 when AT&T became the game's initial sponsor. In recent years, Citi Financial (CitiBank) was a sponsor. For 2011, Vizio affixed its name to the game, while the facility remains "The Rose Bowl" (see Figure 6.2)" The value of naming rights to teams is illustrated in Table 6.3.

A typical naming rights deal also usually includes more than just the adorning of a corporate name on a facility. The corporate name usually appears in many different places throughout the facility and the deal might also include other benefits, such as the placement of cash machines throughout the facility in the case of a bank, or exclusive food or beverage services rights (Minute Maid products, for example) for sales in the facility. In other instances, advertisements also might range from an agreed to number of exposures on ribbon boards or static (billboard type) ads placed at strategic points.

An interesting advertising issue often arises when a facility is used for NCAA championship events and that facility is also part of a naming rights agreement. In the guidelines issued that cities must follow to submit bids to host a championship,

Table 6.3 Selected naming rights deals for sports facilities

Facility Name	Sponsor	Average Annual Fee	Expires
Air Canada Centre	Air Canada	$1.5 million	2019
American Airlines Arena[a]	American Airlines	$2.1 million	2019
American Airlines Center[b]	American Airlines	$6.5 million	2031

Table 6.3 (continued)   Selected naming rights deals for sports facilities

Facility Name	Sponsor	Average Annual Fee	Expires
Bank of America Stadium	Bank of America	$7.0 million	2024
Bank One Ballpark	Bank One	$2.2 million	2028
Citi Field	Citi Financial	$20 million	2029
Citizens Bank Ballpark	Citizens Bank	$2.3 million	2028
Comerica Park	Comerica Bank	$2.2 million	2030
Conseco Fieldhouse	Conseco	$2.0 million	2019
Corel Center	Corel	$878,142	2016
Edward Jones Stadium	Edward Jones	$2.65 million	2013
FedEx Field[c]	Federal Express	$7.6 million	2025
FedEx Forum[d]	Federal Express	$4.5 million	2023
Ford Field	Ford Motor	$1 million	2042
Gaylord Center	Gaylord Communications	$4 million	2018
Great American Ballpark	Great American Insurance	$2.5 million	2033
HP Pavilion	Hewlett-Packard	$3.1 million	2016
Invesco Field	Invesco Funds	$6 million	2021
Lincoln Financial Field	Lincoln Financial Group	$6.7 million	2022
Miller Park	Miller Brewing	$2.1 million	2020
PETCO Park	PETCO	$2.7 million	2026
Qualcomm Stadium	Qualcomm	$900,000	2017
Raymond James Stadium	Raymond James Financial	$3.1 million	2026
Reliant Stadium	Reliant Energy	$10 million	2032
SBC Center	SBC Communications	$2.1 million	2022

[a] Miami, FL
[b] Dallas, TX
[c] Landover, MD (Washington, D.C. area)
[d] Memphis, TN
Source: ESPN.Com, Sports Business, and authors' research.

the NCAA requires that the following practices be adhered to regardless of preexisting advertising, naming, or licensing agreements made by a venue's owners or the team that may control advertising inside the venue (NCAA, 2010).

Advertising/Banners/Signs/Displays: No advertising, banners, signs, or displays of any kind may be hung, posted, or displayed anywhere within the general public seating/viewing area of the competition, practice, and ancillary events venue(s) (i.e., any place that can be seen from the playing surface or seats), including the scoreboard other than NCAA banners and television banners approved by the NCAA. Any permanently affixed (or previously leased) advertising banners, signs, cup holders or displays shall be covered with décor elements by the competition, practice, and ancillary event venue(s) and at the expense of the venue(s) as specified by the NCAA.

External Signs: All exterior venue corporate and/or professional franchise identification must be covered and must be covered with décor elements as specified by the NCAA.

Commercially Named Competition Venues: Commercially named competition, practice, and ancillary event venue(s) may display two preexisting interior signs with the competition, practice, and ancillary event venue(s)' name at the top of the venue (excluding the scoreboard), with placement designated by the NCAA. The competition, practice, and ancillary event venue(s) signage design and placement must be approved by the NCAA.

NCAA Corporate Champion/Partner Banners: The NCAA shall have the right to display NCAA corporate champion/partner banners and NCAA signage inside and outside of the competition, practice, and ancillary event venue(s) in various locations, including but not limited to on the concourse, within the competition bowl and venue exterior without limitation. The NCAA shall have the right to display banners and the like (e.g., inflatables, projections, kiosks, decals, window clings, lighting, street teams, logos, etc.) on the concourse (without limitation) and in other areas designated by the NCAA inside and outside the competition, practice, and ancillary event venue, identifying its corporate champions/partners.

The NCAA's interest in controlling the advertising real estate for its championship events is obvious. The NCAA wants to offer advertising rights to sponsors and does not want any interference or conflicts that would reduce the revenue it can earn. In effect, the NCAA accepts bids and will place its events only in venues where it can be assured that it has full authority to sell advertising regardless of the agreements in place at the venue. Notice that the only compromise that is made regards limited exposure for a facility for which the naming rights have been sold.

Similar conflicts exist when the Olympics are involved. The International Olympic Committee (IOC) also has a set of stringent rules and only their approved sponsors may be associated with the event or any participating athletes. Olympic

Charter Rule 51 governs advertising and is even more specific and demanding than those issued by the NCAA. Similar to the NCAA, the IOC also seeks to protect its interests and the revenues it can earn from any of the real estate it controls during the Olympic Games. That "real estate" is defined to be the venues where the games are played, the areas where athletes live, train, or practice, and even the equipment used.

The International Olympic Committee's Rule 51

Advertising, Demonstrations, Propaganda

1. The IOC Executive Board determines the principles and conditions under which any form of advertising or other publicity may be authorised.
2. No form of advertising or other publicity shall be allowed in and above the stadiums, venues and other competition areas which are considered as part of the Olympic sites. Commercial installations and advertising signs shall not be allowed in the stadiums, venues or other sports grounds.
3. No kind of demonstration or political, religious or racial propaganda is permitted in any Olympic sites, venues or other areas.

By-Law to Rule 51

1. No form of publicity or propaganda, commercial or otherwise, may appear on persons, on sportswear, accessories or, more generally, on any article of clothing or equipment whatsoever worn or used by the athletes or other participants in the Olympic Games, except for the identification—as defined in paragraph 8 below— of the manufacturer of the article or equipment concerned, provided that such identification shall not be marked conspicuously for advertising purposes.
   1.1 The identification of the manufacturer shall not appear more than once per item of clothing and equipment.
   1.2 Equipment: any manufacturer's identification that is greater than 10% of the surface area of the equipment that is exposed during competition shall be deemed to be marked conspicuously. However, there shall be no manufacturer's identification greater than 60 cm^2.
   1.3 Headgear (e.g., hats, helmets, sunglasses, goggles) and gloves: any manufacturer's identification over 6 cm^2 shall be deemed to be marked conspicuously.

1.4 Clothing (e.g., T-shirts, shorts, sweat tops and sweat pants): any manufacturer's identification which is greater than 20 cm² shall be deemed to be marked conspicuously.

1.5 Shoes: it is acceptable that there appear the normal distinctive design pattern of the manufacturer. The manufacturer's name and/or logo may also appear, up to a maximum of 6 cm², either as part of the normal distinctive design pattern or independent of the normal distinctive design pattern.

1.6 In case of special rules adopted by an International Sports Federation, exceptions to the rules mentioned above may be approved by the IOC Executive Board. Any violation of the provisions of the present clause may result in disqualification or withdrawal of the accreditation of the person concerned. The decisions of the IOC Executive Board regarding this matter shall be final. The numbers worn by competitors may not display publicity of any kind and must bear the Olympic emblem of the OCOG.

2. To be valid, all contracts of the OCOG containing any element whatsoever of advertising, including the right or license to use the emblem or the mascot of the Olympic Games, must be in conformity with the Olympic Charter and must comply with the instructions given by the IOC Executive Board. The same shall apply to contracts relating to the timing equipment, the scoreboards, and to the injection of any identification signal in television programmes. Breaches of these regulations come under the authority of the IOC Executive Board.

3. Any mascot created for the Olympic Games shall be considered to be an Olympic emblem, the design of which must be submitted by the OCOG to the IOC Executive Board for its approval. Such mascot may not be used for commercial purposes in the country of an NOC without the latter's prior written approval.

4. The OCOG shall ensure the protection of the property of the emblem and the mascot of the Olympic Games for the benefit of the IOC, both nationally and internationally. However, the OCOG alone and, after the OCOG has been wound up, the NOC of the host country, may exploit such emblem and mascot, as well as other marks, designs, badges, posters, objects and documents connected with the Olympic Games during their preparation, during their holding and during a period terminating not later than the end of the calendar year during which such Olympic Games are held. Upon the expiry of this period, all rights in or relating to such emblem, mascot and other marks, designs, badges, posters, objects and documents shall thereafter

belong entirely to the IOC. The OCOG and/or the NOC, as the case may be and to the extent necessary, shall act as trustees (in a fiduciary capacity) for the sole benefit of the IOC in this respect.

5. The provisions of this by-law also apply, *mutatis mutandis*, to all contracts signed by the organising committee of a Session or an Olympic Congress.

6. The uniforms of the competitors and of all persons holding an official position may include the flag or Olympic emblem of their NOC or, with the consent of the OCOG, the OCOG Olympic emblem. The IF officials may wear the uniform and the emblem of their federations.

7. The identification on all technical gear, installations and other apparatus, which are neither worn nor used by athletes or other participants at the Olympic Games, including timing equipment and scoreboards, may on no account be larger than 1/10th of the height of the equipment, installation or apparatus in question, and shall not be greater than 10 centimeters high.

8. The word "identification" means the normal display of the name, designation, trademark, logo or any other distinctive sign of the manufacturer of the item, appearing not more than once per item.

9. The OCOG, all participants and all other persons accredited at the Olympic Games and all other persons or parties concerned shall comply with the manuals, guides, or guidelines, and all other instructions of the IOC Executive Board, in respect of all matters subject to Rule 51 and this By-Law.

(International Olympic Committee, http://assets.usoc.org/assets/documents/attached_file/filename/1045/Olympic_Charter_Rule_51.pdf (accessed December 13, 2010).

Uniforms or "Kits"

While the four major North American sports leagues have not decided to classify the uniforms (or kits as they are referred to elsewhere) as real estate for advertising, that is not the rule in automobile racing or in many soccer/football leagues. The uniforms worn by drivers (as well as their cars) are adorned with advertising messages. Manchester United's players have long worn jerseys with sponsor's names (currently AON with the Nike "swoosh" prominently visible; Chelsea's uniform is adorned with Samsung and Adidas' logos, and the Seattle Sounders of the MLS have XBOX 360 emblazoned on their jerseys, for example). The visibility of a team's uniform during games watched by millions of people can produce an important revenue stream. While the four major team sport leagues have resisted expanding their revenue streams when uniforms are considered, it is perhaps only a matter of a few years before one owner tries to determine how much money can be realized from placing a sponsor's name on a uniform.[*]

Value of Internal Real Estate Management

A quick look at revenue earned by some selected MLB teams in new facilities illustrates the importance of managing the internal real estate. Similar tables including teams from other leagues could be added. It must be remembered that the data here include team revenues from all sources, so it is possible that income from local media sources influence the outcome. Despite that reservation, the pattern is obvious. The new facilities have additional revenue possibilities and, as teams enhance their abilities to manage all aspects of the expanded real estate and assess market demand, revenues increase. Notice in Table 6.4 that the elevated revenue levels are sustained even after the novelty effects of the new facility have passed. It is not surprising that there is a large jump as all of the new advertising and consumption opportunities become visible to businesses and fans. By including several different teams, it also becomes evident that while winning matters relative to escalating revenues, even teams that were less successful were able to sustain their elevated revenue levels (e.g., San Diego Padres). Revenue earned from real estate operations outside of the facility are not included as those funds accrue to other businesses that may be owned by the same individuals that own the teams, but are distinct and separate from the operations of the franchise (Table 6.4).

Managing the Real Estate Outside the Facility: The Increasing Value of Sports Venues as Anchors for Development

Walt Disney recognized what Rome's city planners understood more than 2,000 years earlier. Spectacles and the facilities built to host those events attract crowds. And, as a result, the large numbers of people present create opportunities to develop adjacent properties. That development can redevelop or define a downtown area, or create an entirely new area filled with amenities. In both settings, profits can be earned and the public sector's objectives for new development and tax revenues can be realized. These development opportunities are shaped by the answer to two very simple questions. First, if you knew that a half-a-million (arenas or football stadiums) or more visits (ballpark) were going to take place at a specific geographic

---

[*] Each year the leading Premiership teams sell between 1.2 and 1.5 million uniform shirts which, in turn, become "walking billboards" for the corporate sponsors (Alex Miller, Sporting Intelligence, http://www.sportingintelligence.com/2010/08/31/exclusive-manchester-united-lead-global-shirt-sales-list-liverpool-chase-as-england%E2%80%99s-second-best-310805/, accessed June 30, 2011.)

Table 6.4 The revenues earned by select MLB teams during the last season in an older facility and the years after in a new facility

Team	Old Facility	New Facility Opens	Year after New Facility Opens						
			2nd	3rd	4th	5th	6th	7th	8th
Annual Team Revenues in Millions of Dollars as Reported by Forbes									
Philadelphia Phillies	97	115	167	176	183	192	216		
St. Louis Cardinals	151	165	184	194	195				
San Francisco Giants	72	139	142	159	153	159	171	184	197
New York Mets	235	261							
New York Yankees	327	375							
Houston Astros	93	122	125	121	128	155	173	184	193
Seattle Mariners		112	138	166	167	169	173	179	182
Washington Nationals	144	153	184						
San Diego Padres	98	106	150	158	160	167	174		

place, what would you build in the immediate area that would appeal to these crowds and others? Second, how can a real estate development plan capitalize on the presence of crowds attracted to games and other events hosted at facilities?

Sport team owners were not as focused on external real estate development as they were on maximizing within-facility revenues. Indeed, Disneyfication within the sports business in the late 1980s and early 1990s was focused on creating dining and shopping venues inside a facility to deflect spending away from adjacent locations controlled by other entrepreneurs. Team owners saw more profit potential from absorbing all of the entertainment and hospitality spending from fans' game day experiences. That could be accomplished by building larger facilities replete with restaurants and other retail outlets capable of driving spending into a facility to maximize a team's revenues. Pursuing that option, however, reduced the value of the facility to the city or neighborhood where the arena, stadium, or ballpark was located. Ironically if owners' followed their revenue maximization strategy and pushed all fan-related spending into a venue, a sort of economic black hole for a city would exist. That black hole would be defined by crowds coming to a facility, and spending all of their money inside what was essentially nothing more than a "tourist bubble." The area adjacent to the facility could be devoid of activity resulting in no discernible effect on the city and the adjacent neighborhood (Judd and Fainstein, 1999). Some pointed to the Texas Rangers' Ballpark in Arlington as an example of the tourist bubble with no discernible effect on the host city or any one of its neighborhoods. The lack of attention to external development and a plan to integrate the facility with the neighborhood led to no real improvements for the immediate area (Swindell and Rosentraub, 2009).

The lack of results in Arlington stood in sharp contrast to impressions that Indianapolis and Baltimore had substantial success linking sports and entertainment facilities to comprehensive redevelopment strategies. In both cities, a portion of the downtown areas benefitted from substantial private sector investments to complement those made by the public sector in sports, entertainment, and cultural centers. Indianapolis's sports strategy for its downtown area produced a redeveloped area about four square miles in size that featured a domed facility for football and an arena for an NBA franchise plus other entertainment events, a convention center, a new shopping mall, thousands of hotel rooms, and myriad restaurants. Baltimore's Inner Harbor, launched with a focus on culture, entertainment, and restaurants, added Oriole Park and a football stadium.

The development of new facilities, commercial space, and residential areas in both downtown areas were indicators of success for many advocates of the use and value of sports, entertainment, and culture for redevelopment. Critics, however, challenged a definition of success that only included new buildings and pointed to important economic development goals that were not achieved (Rosentraub, 1999; Levine, 2000). For example, some of the hoped-for goals included population growth (or a stabilization of population levels), the attraction and retention of residents with higher incomes to stabilize the tax base, the attraction of more job opportunities, an overall increment in the local tax base, and the improvement of neighboring communities. Some progress on these points was made. Some neighborhoods, however, saw no benefits. Despite any shortcomings and shortfalls for some inner-city neighborhoods, the crowds and vibrancy that filled downtown areas that for decades were in decline and decay was seen by many public and community leaders as sufficiently valuable to warrant the investment of tax dollars. While debates ensued regarding the appropriate levels of public and private investments that should be part of these redevelopment efforts, a new perspective became firmly entrenched. Instead of simply building a facility (whether paid for by the team or the public sector, or through some degree of cost sharing between the team and governments), the issue became: How can an arena, ballpark, or stadium be incorporated into a redevelopment plan or strategy to realize a set of goals or objectives established by local governments while also producing profits for team owners and other private sector investors? Debates would ensue regarding the public and private investment shares and returns but, what is important to recognize is that what took place in Baltimore, Indianapolis, San Diego, and then Los Angeles altered the public debates regarding expectations when sport facilities were built. In particular, what took place in San Diego and Los Angeles changed the sports business. Outcomes there, when added to the changes taking place in Indianapolis and Baltimore, created an entirely new public policy approach to sports and development. The profits made by investors in San Diego and Los Angeles illustrated how team owners and cities could both benefit and profit from the building of a sport facility. Expectations were restructured and team owners realized their franchises could be the anchor for the formation of a real estate development firm or an entertainment corporation on a never before envisioned scale. The case studies below illustrate this change and its implications for sport managers and cities.

Case Study 1

The San Diego Padres, JMI Realty, and the Ballpark District*

The San Diego Padres were long-term tenants in a stadium controlled by the San Diego Chargers. Qualcomm Stadium opened in 1967 (as San Diego Stadium). In 1980, after the death of the legendary sports writer who convinced Barron Hilton to relocate the Los Angeles Chargers to San Diego, the facility became known as San Diego Jack Murphy Stadium. To enhance the revenue streams for the Chargers, the team was given the right to sell naming rights to the facility in

---

* A more detailed history and analysis of San Diego's Ballpark District, and the conflicting planning and development perspectives that surround the concept of extensive and rapid redevelopment is contained in Chapter 4 of Mark S. Rosentraub's (2010) *Major league winners: Using sports and cultural centers as tools for economic development.* Boca Raton, FL: CRC Press/Taylor and Francis.

the 1990s and the Qualcomm Corporation pays the Chargers $900,000 a year through 2017 (the public sector receives none of this income). The Padres began play in 1969 and since the stadium was controlled by the Chargers, there was little revenue the team could earn from in-facility operations. Fan support was a challenge as the team lost 100 or more games in its initial six years in the National League. The team almost moved to Washington, D.C. in 1974 before Ray Kroc (McDonald's owner) bought the team. After Kroc's death, his widow controlled the team, but eventually sold the franchise to local business leaders. Financial problems ensued and after another change in ownership, John Moores acquired the franchise in 1996. Early on, he recognized that no business plan could make the team financially viable if the Padres continued to play at Qualcomm Stadium. Even in 1998 when the Padres advanced to the World Series, the team lost money. Financial viability would lie in a baseball-only facility with excellent sight lines and amenities for fans where the Padres would control all revenues.*

During the time that the Padres were undergoing several ownership changes, the Chargers were making a series of demands that ended with San Diego paying for a substantial renovation to the stadium and guaranteeing team revenues through a commitment to purchase unsold tickets. The public's negative reaction to these investments intensified when stories continued to surface that the Chargers were interested in moving north to Los Angeles or Orange County. With voters and community leaders jaundiced with regard to any deal with any professional sports team, a public investment in a new ballpark for the Padres would have to involve (1) clear financial and public policy benefits for San Diego and (2) a substantial private sector investment from or led by the team and its owner.

As discussions began between the team and the city's elected leaders, the Padres' owner, John Moores, made his preference clear that the new ballpark should be built in the Mission Valley area near Qualcomm Stadium. The area was attractive because it includes an East-West freeway (Interstate 8 or the Mission Valley Freeway), and two North-South freeways (Interstate 15 and Interstate 805). With fans already comfortable commuting to this area and the nearby population densities, it is easy to appreciate the attractiveness of the location (Figure 6.3).

The City of San Diego's professional staff and many elected officials had no interest in a new ballpark in the Mission Valley area. Market forces would certainly operate to ensure private investments would take place in this part of San Diego. The city's staff and elected leaders were focused on the continuing redevelopment of the downtown area and a large increment in the number of hotel rooms near San Diego's Convention Center. The public sector's preferred location for a new ballpark was an area known as the East Village just south and east of the successful Gaslamp Quarter (entertainment and retail venues) and the convention center. If a downtown location was where the ballpark had to be, the team's owner wanted an area adjacent to the waterfront. The city would not offer a waterfront location

---

* These observations were made by John Moores in discussions with the author in October 2010.

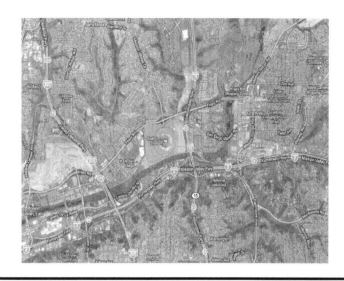

Figure 6.3 Shown is Qualcomm Stadium and the Mission Valley area of San Diego. (From Google Maps.)

Figure 6.4 Shown is PETCO Park and the San Diego Convention Center. (From Google Maps.)

for the ballpark. Its preference was for the East Village and that was the only area that would be politically palatable. Figure 6.4 illustrates PETCO Park's location across from the convention center. The desired waterfront locations were the sites immediately south of the convention center (see Figure 6.4).

John Moores wanted to limit his investment in the new ballpark to $150 million. The new ballpark with enhanced revenue streams would then produce enough annual income to (1) support competitive salaries for players, (2) repay the loan for the team's investment in the facility, (3) enable a sufficient rent payment to ensure that no public funds would be required for the maintenance of the ballpark, and (4) ensure that the team's revenues would exceed its operational expenses (or generate a profit). With an anticipated cost of $411 million for the ballpark, the Padres were essentially asking the public sector to invest $261 million. A public investment of that magnitude with the team assuming responsibility only for slightly more than one-third of the project's cost *was not* politically viable. The years of conflict with the San Diego Chargers had soured voters on deals where it was seen that the public benefits were far less than those enjoyed by the team. Something more than accepting the public sector's preferred location was going to be required from Moores. What emerged, which was unprecedented at the time, was that Moores would guarantee a level of real estate development in the area adjacent to the ballpark sufficient to generate the property tax revenues to repay the bonds sold to support San Diego's investment in the ballpark. Across two phases of development Moores was responsible for $487 million in new development in the area designated as the Ballpark District. In addition, he was required to build a headquarters hotel for the convention center that would add at least 1,000 additional rooms to the inventory in the immediate area. In the end, more than 1,000 rooms would be added to the inventory, but these rooms would be part of four smaller hotels.

Some have criticized the Ballpark District development (and the virtual replacement of buildings that were a favored location for artists and for people interested in live–work space to initiate their businesses), the size of the public sector's investment in the Padres' new home ballpark, and the politics surrounding the vote on the plan (Chapin, 2002; Erie, Kogna, and MacKenzie, 2010; Hitchcock, undated). Relative to this book and chapter, it is not essential to refute or sustain the criticisms. What is essential in understanding the role of sports teams as anchors for real estate development is what was built and how the entire partnership contributed to a changing view of the expectations of teams and for sports facilities in redevelopment strategies. It is also important to recognize the vibrant real estate business that John Moores created that profited from the building of the Ballpark District. JMI (John Moores Investments) Realty today has a portfolio of almost $600 million. While JMI Realty was created in 1992, its flagship project and what built the firm was the $3 billion in private sector investments connected with the Ballpark District. JMI Realty showed every sports franchise owner what could be accomplished when a team and its facility served as an anchor for redevelopment. It was no longer feasible to suggest that a new facility might attract investment. With JMI Realty designated as the master developer for the entire project, thousands of residential units and more than 1,000 hotel rooms were built. And, John Moores and JMI Realty were able to build a new neighborhood, exceed each of the requirements established by the City of San Diego, and still earn a substantial profit.

The total cost for the new ballpark was $483.1 million. The Padres invested $187.4 million; San Diego spent $191.6 million. The downtown redevelopment authority invested $83.1 million and the Port of San Diego gave the project $21 million. How was this presented as a public/private partnership when the public sector was responsible for more than 60 percent of the project's cost? The private side of the partnership was the guarantee from Moores that not less than $487 million (market value) in new real estate would be built in an area designated as the Ballpark District (which surrounded the ballpark itself). That investment, together with the amount of money invested in the ballpark by the team meant Moores and his real estate development company (JMI), would be spending far more than the public sector entities. San Diego's voters approved the deal and, by the end of Phase II, JMI and its partners had built and sold approximately $2.87 billion of real estate or almost six times what had been guaranteed.

There are important policy questions that need to be addressed when analyzing the benefit of the Ballpark District. For example, if the real estate would have been built elsewhere in San Diego, is the $2.87 billon new development or just a transfer within the city? In response to that possibility, it can be noted that San Diego wanted the East Village redeveloped to fulfill certain public policy goals and was willing to recognize or accept that there could be some substitution effects. Seeking to reduce commutation patterns and sprawl, and wanting to increase the residential population of the downtown area, the city's leadership was willing to accept the transfer of development as a net gain. The real achievements in San Diego, however, were (1) for the first time ever a team owner guaranteed a level of real estate development as part of the public/private partnership and (2) a ballpark was used as anchor to design an entirely new urban neighborhood. These goals where accomplished and the team owner was able to make a substantial profit from his real estate activities. While many may have always looked to sports facilities as anchors for real estate development, the Ballpark District in San Diego firmly established that if sports teams were not real estate development corporations, there was a profound new level of horizontal integration taking place. More than 7,000 residential units were built, and the neighborhood included a "park within the park." This area serves residents throughout the year. On game days, entrance to the park area is restricted and requires a ticket. But this area, with a low admission price, provides space where children can play in a sand box just behind the right center field fence as their parents sit on blankets and watch the games.

Figure 6.5 details each of these elements regarding PETCO Park and the Ballpark District. First, surrounding the field are a number of residential buildings with several offering residents a view of the field. What is important is that PETCO Park is not the tallest structure and it was designed to fit into a neighborhood. The ballpark is clearly the anchor, but it is ringed by taller structures. Second, to the right of the darkened area in center field (the black backdrop at all ballparks is designed to provide batters with the contrast needed to have a better view of each pitch) is the area where children can play in a sand box while their family members

Figure 6.5 Pictured is San Diego's PETCO Park and the surrounding Ballpark District. (Photo courtesy of Mark S. Rosentraub.)

watch the game from a set of stone steps or the park land where blanket seating is available. On days when games are not played people can use the park area, the small baseball field built for children, and even watch team practices. The financial success of the Ballpark District for JMI has helped to convince other owners of the value of incorporating real estate development as part of their sports business. In a very real sense, John Moores' success changed sports organizations. While some have criticized the profits John Moores earned from the real estate developed and sold, those gains must be balanced by the risks taken. The Memorandum of Understanding he signed with San Diego required the development of almost $500 million of new real estate and, if that commitment was not fulfilled, John Moores was responsible for the taxes that property would have generated. He was the first sports team owner to make such a financial commitment linked to the building of a sports facility and while he did profit from the building and sale of the real estate, he alone assumed the risks for the failure to develop and sell the real estate.

This new horizontal integration not only changed the sports business, but it illustrated for public officials as well the value of sport facilities and a team for their development and design policies and practices. The value of a team and its facility does not rest with the jobs created or the spending on food and beverages. Teams and facilities create very few jobs and the consumption of food and beverages (and souvenirs) is merely a transfer of economic activity within a region. While that transfer may have important and valuable policy consequences, the real economic benefit is to be found in the way in which a facility anchors redesign and redevelopment strategies that change civic images, create new or revitalized neighborhoods, or bring new wealth to a neighborhood and perhaps the city itself. Those interested in evaluations and reviews of what was accomplished in San Diego should read the contrasting perspectives provided by Erie, Kogan, and MacKenzie (2010); Rosentraub (2010); and Newman (2006).

Case Study 2

The STAPLES Center, LA LIVE, and Downtown Los Angeles*

In 1993, Richard Riordan, a Republican, was elected mayor of Los Angeles. A Republican had not led this city for more than 30 years. But, in the aftermath of police officers attacking Rodney King, numerous riots, and a fear that the Los Angeles police department was out of control, voters wanted change. The magnitude of the violence of the riots and the image of police officers unable to protect citizens caught amidst ransacking mobs presented the world with an image of a city drowning in its own chaos. While some thought things could not be worse, downtown was seen as deteriorating, crime-laden, and overrun by the homeless. A convention center built in the downtown area to attract visitors was a financial disaster, and the city's school system was seen as a model of failure. Richard Riordan, a successful business man, spent several million dollars of his own money convincing voters he alone was tough enough to handle Los Angeles' problems, violence, and deterioration. He defeated a Democratic member of the city council for the mayoralty in a city increasingly dominated by Asian, Black, and Hispanic minorities. The image he presented was that while white, he was a business leader who was too wealthy to be bribed, and tough enough to both clean up Los Angeles and reestablish its positive image.

To deal with the convention center and downtown Los Angeles, Mayor Riordan turned to Charles Isgar, a trusted aid with a doctorate in public administration. Isgar was given the seemingly impossible task of figuring out how to salvage the convention center and halt the annual revenue losses. If, along the way to reducing the public sector's operating losses for the convention center, he could also figure out a way to revive a portion of the downtown area, that too would be appreciated. Riordan was a Republican mayor pitted against a hostile city council that was controlled by members of the Democratic Party still smarting over the loss of the mayor's race by one of their own. As local politics is a contact sport, the council was eager to portray Richard Riordan as just another (white) real estate developer primed to reward his friends at taxpayers' expense. Mayor Riordan needed solutions and a progressive way to improve downtown without using taxpayer subsidies.

---

* A more detailed history and analysis of the building of STAPLES Centre and LA LIVE, and the conflicting planning and development perspectives that surround the concept of extensive and rapid redevelopment is contained in Chapter 2 and Chapter 5 of Mark S. Rosentraub's (2010) *Major League Winners: Using Sports and Cultural Centers as Tools for Economic Development*. Boca Raton, FL: CRC Press/Taylor and Francis.

Isgar was aware that the ownership of the Lakers and Kings was interested in a new arena. The teams played at the Fabulous Forum in suburban Inglewood.* Built in 1967 with an exterior designed to recall the grandeur of ancient Rome, the facility was indeed fabulous, but lacked suites, club seats, and other revenue-generating amenities that were becoming common in the new arenas built by other NBA and NHL teams. Isgar approached the teams with the idea of building their new arena downtown adjacent to the convention center. When his concept was soundly rejected (another suburban location was preferred), Isgar recruited a well-known local developer, Steve Soboroff, to serve as a volunteer deputy mayor ($1/year in salary) to help convince the Lakers and the Kings that their best destiny was to build a new arena in downtown Los Angeles. To many, it now seemed two dreamers had been chosen to implement an unworkable plan and were destined to fail.

Downtown Los Angeles, as uninviting a location as it must have appeared to many people, did have several assets. First, there was sufficient land available to build the exact sort of facility the teams wanted. The facility the teams ultimately constructed had more than three times the square footage or footprint of the Great Western Forum. Finding sufficient land in the suburbs for a facility of this scale with ample land for parking was no small challenge. While the teams might well have preferred a suburban location, the scarcity of available land there elevated the value of downtown Los Angeles as a potential site. The advantage of having the land needed for a facility laden with revenue-producing luxury seats and other amenities was not lost on Isgar and Soboroff. Second, downtown Los Angeles had convenient freeway access. The excellent access to both an East-West (Interstate 10) and North-South (Harbor/Pasadena) freeway for fans accustomed to driving to athletic events made the downtown area an intriguing possibility. Downtown Los Angeles had two assets that few if any other sites anywhere else in the county could offer. The teams could have the land they needed to build the very large arena envisioned, and the facility would be adjacent to one of the main junctions for Los Angeles' network of freeways.

The advantages of what became the location for the new arena (visible at the corner of Chick Hearn Court and South Figueroa Street) and LA LIVE, the area immediately north of Chick Hearn Court, are evident in Figure 6.6. The intersection of Interstates 10 and 110 are visible, as is the parking structure adjacent to Interstate 110 at Cherry Street and several surface parking lots along South Figueroa Street. The freeway access and the land to build the arena, a parking structure, and what came to be called LA LIVE suddenly turned everyone's attention toward downtown Los Angeles. Now what was needed was a plan where the teams' ownership would pay for the complete cost of the facilities and the taxpayers would be protected from any obligations. Before focusing on how the LA LIVE project

---

* The arena was popularly referred to as "The Fabulous Forum." The naming rights to the facility, however, had been sold and the formal name was the Great Western Forum.

Figure 6.6   Location and land make downtown the logical choice for the new arena. (From Google Maps.)

changed the horizontal integration of teams and sports organizations, the element that made the financial aspects of the deal possible are summarized.

To fulfill Mayor Riordan's objective of having the teams pay for the facilities, the City of Los Angeles did agree to permit the building of two advertising towers with exposures facing the I-110 and I-10 freeways. The average daily vehicle count at the juncture of these freeways was approximately 325,000. By allowing the business that would own the arena and LA LIVE the right to receive all advertising revenues from the two towers, it was agreed (1) that the private sector partners would spend not less than $325 million for the new arena and (2) that a dedicated revenue stream from the facility would pay for the city's infrastructure investments. If that revenue stream were ever insufficient to repay the bonds sold by Los Angeles for its investment, the teams would provide the necessary funds. That inevitability never arose and Los Angeles retired its obligation, but continues to receive the funds from the dedicated revenue stream. One of the advertising towers that was pivotal to the building of the STAPLES Center is pictured in Figure 6.7. In addition, the private sector partnership that owned and operated STAPLES Center would be responsible for paying an annual fee for using the public lands upon which the arena stood. That fee is equal to the property taxes that would have been owed had the Lakers and Kings owned the land.

To pay for the infrastructure costs needed for LA LIVE, the owners of the complex agreed to pay all local property taxes. Los Angeles did not grant an abatement of any property or use of property taxes associated with either the arena or

Figure 6.7   Shown is an advertising tower built on public land and visible from I-110. (Photo courtesy of Mark S. Rosentraub.)

the LA LIVE project.* A City of Los Angeles redevelopment corporation also provided $12.6 million in support for the STAPLES Center; no revenue streams from the arena were pledged to offset that investment. The return for the Community Redevelopment Authority was from the incremental property tax gains from new residential construction in the area. With more than 7,000 units built in the downtown area, the property taxes generated easily offset the Community Redevelopment Authority's investment. Would the housing have been built without the STAPLES Center? The area had languished for years and it is unlikely new housing starts would have been as robust without the new arena. If that logic is accepted, then the public sector investment was completely recovered from the new property taxes collected.

When the market for new hotels in the downtown area weakened, the owners of LA LIVE asked Los Angeles to agree to use the hotel tax revenue it would receive from the project for 25 years and to pay for all of the needed infrastructure improvements. The present value of the public sector's investment in LA LIVE is $167.6 million. For this investment, the project's owner agreed their investment would be approximately $2.5 billion. Los Angeles decided the public sector investment to offset the decline in the market was worthwhile as it was securing more than $2 billion in private investments in the downtown area.

---

* The public sector owns the land upon which the STAPLES Center was built. The arena owners pay a fee for use of publicly owned land, and technically it is not a property tax, but a use of property fee or assessment. The owners of LA LIVE also own the land upon which it is built and are responsible for all property taxes.

The most substantial accomplishment and innovation associated with the move of the Los Angeles Lakers and Kings (followed by the Clippers) to the downtown area was the building of LA LIVE. What is LA LIVE? It is an entertainment, retail, commercial, and residential complex that includes 19 restaurants, 8 different entertainment venues, the STAPLES Center, 2 hotels, luxury condominiums, and ESPN's West Coast broadcast center. The entire complex includes 5.6 million square feet of development across 27 acres of downtown Los Angeles. ESPN's broadcast center uses 12,300 square feet of space.

LA LIVE illustrated how sports teams can be anchors for a large-scale entertainment center that also includes residences and commercial space. The STAPLES Center with its three sports teams as tenants ensures that there will be more than 2 million visits to the area each year. When the concerts and other entertainment events held at the arena or when the facilities at LA LIVE are added to the mix, there is a base of roughly 3 million visits to the area every year. That crowd now has the opportunity to spend pre- and postevent time in the area creating additional revenue potential. In this manner, entertainment and commercial development have become part of the horizontal integration of the sports business. The controlling entity for the STAPLES Center and LA LIVE is AEG (the Anshutz Entertainment Group), itself part of the Anshutz Company. Sports has become horizontally integrated into their business operations. The holding company owns or operates facilities and teams across the United States and Europe and is developing LA LIVE-type projects in China and Europe. They are joined by Comcast SPECTACOR, Forest City Enterprises, Patriot Place, and management companies, such as SMG, in integrating sports in large-scale entertainment and commercial projects that frequently include residential development. These large-scale projects provide insight into the revenue opportunities for teams that have revolutionized the sports business. Today numerous teams are purchased by real estate development firms, partner with real estate development companies, or create their own real estate development and entertainment divisions to capitalize on the opportunities created by the crowds attracted to sports.

John Moores, the Ballpark District, AEG, and LA LIVE redefined the sports business and today most team owners are focused on the entertainment or real estate development opportunities created by their teams. Jerry Jones chose to build an extraordinary multipurpose stadium and the Dallas Cowboys now anchor a large entertainment corporation. Forest City Enterprises acquired the New Jersey Nets to anchor their Atlantic Yards project in Brooklyn. The New England Patriots created an opportunity for Robert Kraft to build Patriot Place, a shopping mall and entertainment center with more than 60 different retail outlets adjacent to Gillette Stadium. Teams are no longer just franchises, and real estate development and management, as well as entertainment, are now an integral part of what is sports management in real time.

References

Chapin, T. 2002. Beyond the entrepreneurial city: Municipal capitalism in San Diego. *Journal of Urban Affairs*, 24 (5) 565–581.

Erie, S. P., Kogan, V., and MacKenzie, S. A. 2010. Redevelopment, San Diego style: The limits of public-private partnerships. *Urban Affairs Review*, 45 (5) 644–678.

Judd, D. R. and Fainstein, S. S. 1999, eds. *The tourist city*. New Haven, CT: Yale University Press.

Hitchcock, M. Undated. Welcome to PETCO Park: Home of your Enron-by-the-sea Padres. *BerkeleyLaw, University of California Boalt Hall*, http://www.law.berkeley.edu/sugarman/PETCO_Park_and_the_Padres_____Mark_Hitchcock.pdf (accessed December 18, 2010).

Levine, M. V. 2000. A third world city in the first world: Social exclusion, racial inequality, and sustainable development in Baltimore, Maryland. In *The social sustainability of cities: Diversity and the management of change*, eds. M. Polese and R. Stren, 123-156.

NCAA 2011-2014 Champtionship host city bid specification. 2010. Retrieved from http://www.ncaa.org/wps/portal/ncaahome?WCM_GLOBAL_CONTEXT=/ncaa/ncaa/sports+and+championship/general+information/championships+administration/general+bid+template+(oct+2010)

Newman, M. 2006. The neighborhood that the ballpark built. *The New York Times*, April 26, online edition, http://www.nytimes.com/2006/04/26/business/26ballpark.html (accessed December 18, 2010).

Pines, B. J. and Gilmore, J. 1999. *The experience economy: Work is theater & and every business onstage*. Boston: Harvard Business School Press.

Souhan, J. 2010. Earl Santee: He built it. *Minneapolis Star Tribune*, December 26, online edition, http://www.startribune.com/sports/twins/112415774.html (accessed December 29, 2010).

Swindell, D. and Rosentraub, M. S. 2009. Doing better: Sports economic impact analysis, and schools of public policy and administration, *Journal of Public Administration Education*, 15 (2) 219–242.

Chapter 7

Media and Sports Management

Introduction

The 1990s and the building of facilities with luxury seating, improved site lines, expanded retail outlets, and new advertising (naming) opportunities made in-facility real estate management a new enterprise for every team. External real estate development also became a major profit center horizontally linked to the operations of numerous teams. These fundamental shifts were matched and, in some cases, exceeded by the ways in which media revolutionized the business of sports. The media have always been integral to the financial success of teams, but what was at first a medium for attracting fans to facilities has now become a defining financial component of team operations. A brief review will illustrate the change from a tool used by teams to advertise their basic product in an effort to recruit fans to the arena, ballpark, and stadium into a revenue source escalating team values and players' salaries. The past 20 years have seen teams form their own networks as the media became vertically integrated into the operations of most franchises. These networks, in some instances, have capitalized values that make them worth more than the team itself (e.g., The YES Network and the Yankees and Sports Times Ohio and the Cleveland Indians). Just as it was unlikely that anyone would imagine that real estate holdings adjacent to a ballpark or arena would be worth more than the team and its facility, the new business of sports involves a realization that the media networks and opportunities created, if not more valuable than the team, is an integral component of profitability.

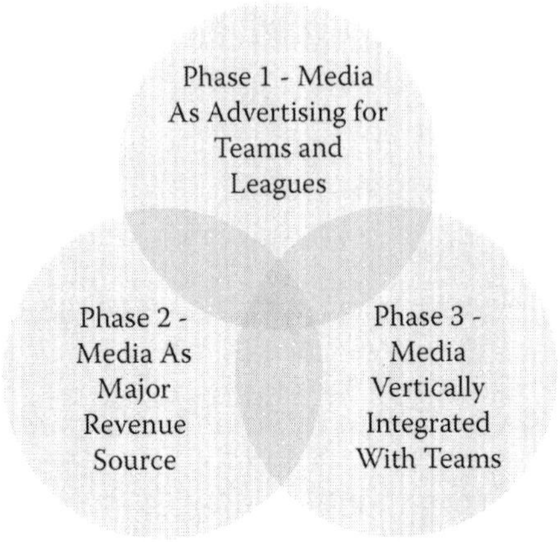

Phase 1 - Media
As Advertising for
Teams and
Leagues

Phase 2 -
Media As
Major
Revenue
Source

Phase 3 -
Media
Vertically
Integrated
With Teams

Figure 7.1   The three phases of the media's relationship with teams and sports is illustrated.

To understand the ways in which the relationship between the media and teams has changed, it is perhaps easiest to consider the evolution of this linkage as comprised of three phases (Figure 7.1). Initially the media were used to advertise teams through stories about the games and players as well as the publication of statistics. Next, with the radio and then television sets becoming staples in every household, teams began to realize they could essentially have paying fans in the stands and at home. This was followed by the complete vertical integration of sports into team operations. An off-shoot from this third phase, considered in the final parts of this chapter, is the rise of merged distribution systems (cable, air wave broadcast, and Internet delivery systems) and advanced media that relies on the Internet to deliver games to millions of fans across the globe in real time. In this context, there is also the emergence of fantasy sports that creates new demand for viewing multiple games and having instant access to statistics on players' performance (Figure 7.2). Each phase and the rise of revenue possibilities through the Internet are considered in this chapter.

Sports and the Media: Brief History

At first, the media was a vehicle for teams to publicize or advertise their sport and the entertainment value provided to fans (consumers). Teams relied on the media for publicity (through reports on the games and their outcomes and the reporting of player statistics on their prowess and accomplishments) and for maintaining fan interest in games. The means to these ends was to make it as convenient and profitable as possible for newspapers to report on a team. Teams built press boxes to provide reporters with excellent views of games and a convenient place to write their stories. Reporters also were provided with access to players and coaches (managers) in an effort to advance the

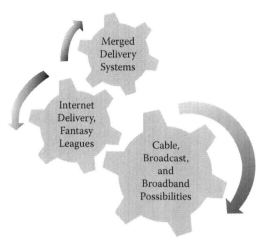

Figure 7.2   The future media issues and revenue potential emerging from Phase 3 is shown.

image of sports, highlighting the entertainment value provided, and the importance of the team to a community and its image. The initial goal for team owners was to ensure that newspapers would deliver myriad favorable and exciting stories to readers who would then become fans. The relationship with the media was designed to extend the image of the team and its players and describe the entertainment that sports would provide to potential fans. As people's interest in teams grew, a demand was created for game and player statistics as well as insights in team management and affairs. Newspapers responded to this growing interest with the expansion of sports sections. Providing information and a positive image of players and the game was essential to build the identity and popularity of sports that in the early years of the twentieth century was seeking to establish itself as a prime choice for the consumption driven by the emerging middle class' discretionary income. This was critical because at the same time that team sports and leagues were emerging so were other forms of entertainment (e.g., motion pictures, amusement parks) and each was trying to attract the discretionary income from the emerging middle class and the concentration of large population bases in America's growing cities. These large population bases established the critical mass of potential fans needed to make sports profitable. But, what was essential for the success of the fledging entertainment business of professional team sports was publicity. Favorable newspaper coverage was essential.

Phase 1: Media and Team Relationships

The early relationship between media and teams (during Phase 1) had a mutually beneficial link that may have compromised or tempered the production of stories that did not flatter a team and its players. Teams and sports needed the media to deliver information and positive images to fans. At the same time as the popularity of sports grew, it also became more and more important to the profitability of newspapers. The growing importance and interest in sports attracted more readers, and, with more readers, newspapers enjoyed more advertising revenue. Sport is a high-profit area for newspapers because it is relatively low cost to cover. Reporters can be hired to follow the team and, even though there are travel expenses associated with covering away games, the teams provide ready access to the players and owners. A great deal of "copy" is generated at relatively low cost and with readers eager for statistics and insights, advertisers flocked to have their messages printed in the sports section of daily newspapers. Through the 1980s, it was not uncommon for newspapers to have their largest runs (number of copies of papers printed) prior to or after important games. Some papers would report their highest circulation days were those prior to or after a Super Bowl when the home team appeared in the game. Similar outcomes were noted for World Series games. Others noted their highest sales existed when special sections were included in the daily newspapers prior to the start of a season (Rosentraub, 1997).

With both sides benefiting from favorable stories (negative reports might not attract fans and could even lead to some people losing interest in a team and then ignoring the sports section of the newspaper), there were concerns that stories would ignore or minimize any unfavorable items or critical insights into team operations or the world of a particular sport. If people's interest in sports declined, team and newspaper owners would both see lower profits. Looking back at the newspaper coverage of sports, most could observe that some of the behavior of legendary players (e.g., Mickey Mantle) and even some issues (e.g., steroids) were ignored or given passing attention. Today, the ubiquitous nature of Internet-based news sources turns any positive or negative incident into an instant story minimizing this possibility. Yet, as will be discussed below, despite evidence of head trauma in football existing for decades, it was not until 2010 that it became a mainstream news story. During Phase 1, when attention was directed at attracting customers, positive coverage was a desired goal and there were incentives for newspapers to minimize negative insights.

Returning to the central point, however, the initial relationship between teams and the media (Phase 1) was one of financial reciprocity. Teams benefitted from the coverage provided and to achieve their goal provided access to games, players, and managers. Newspapers benefitted from the increased advertising that was sold in response to the enhanced readership levels and the level of dedicated readers. The advent of the Internet has not substantially altered this relationship. Reporters who distribute their stories electronically are accorded the same or similar access as those reporters from the print media. Changes in the way in which people consume information about sports, however, has not altered the basic relationship between reporters, teams, and digital or newsprint owners; the relationship would still be considered financially reciprocal. Each benefits from the exposure provided through print or electronic journalism. The wide-ranging number of news outlets, pundits, and bloggers created by the Internet has made the suppression of negative stories and insights virtually impossible. Yet, even though there was widespread evidence in the early 1990s that helmets either did not protect NFL players or were being used to inflict injuries, the life-threatening and life-altering injuries incurred were largely ignored by the media. There was little criticism of the NFL, the NCAA, or of high school athletic associations for lax attitudes toward the diagnosis and treatment of head injuries and concussions. Such injuries were often comically referred to as a player having "his or her bell rung." This underplayed the severity of the situation and perhaps too many players were encouraged to return to play too soon after a "bell ringing" resulting in permanent and disabling conditions that emerged in later years. The issue of head trauma and its treatment did not become a centerpiece issue for the media or the sport leagues until 2010 (http://www.headinjury.com/sports.htm (accessed April 6, 2011)). From a revenue standpoint, however, Phase 1 involved an indirect relationship between the media and teams. Teams do earn income from the media, but it is through the creation of new fans and the provision of information to all fans and their decision to buy tickets that revenues rose. The receipt of money from media distribution services begins in Phase 2, which did overlap with Phase 1, but soon emerged to be a fountain of wealth.

Phase 2: Large Scale Revenue from the Sale of Media Rights

Phase 2, and with it the advent of large amounts of direct revenue for teams from the broadcast of games first through radio transmissions and then on television, actually began before radios were a common household appliance. Few people realize that before the advent of radio's popularity and affordability as instruments of entertainment for households, teams were receiving income from telegraphic transmissions. Michael J. Haupert notes that Western Union offered free telegraph service to teams in exchange for the right to transmit updates on games to bars (saloons) in the 1890s. The popularity of these updates grew to the point where in 1913 Western Union paid each team $17,000 per year ($374,515 in 2010 dollars) for the rights to transmit game descriptions. In those instances, however, someone on the receiving end of the telegraph had to recount to those gathered what had happened. There are numerous stories of Western Union hiring readers to embellish what was received to create a degree of excitement from the mechanical descriptions that came through to fans as the telegraph's system of dots and dashes (Morse code). What is critical for the business of sports is that even in 1913 and even before fans could hear or see instantaneous reports about games, the value of sports to the consumers and of the media to teams was apparent. Broadcast fees for some events of approximately $375,000 would be respectable today. Given incomes and the population size of cities the fact that retransmission rights had a value of $374,515 underscores the value of sports to people.

Motion picture entrepreneurs bought the rights to film the 1910 World Series and then distributed those images for $500 in 1910. This was again a delayed retransmission of the games. The demand for those images, however, allowed MLB to receive $3,500 ($77,236 in 2010 dollars) for the rights to the 1912 World Series (Haupert, 2011, http://eh.net/encyclopedia/article/haupert.mlb (accessed December 20, 2010)). Baseball's growing popularity and the demand for sports was ripe to explode into people's homes as soon as the technology would expand to permit the live transmission of games.

Radio broadcasts of baseball began in 1921 over the air waves of the first commercial radio station, KDKA in Pittsburgh. As radio's popularity grew so did the broadcasting of games. The 1921 World Series was transmitted to Pittsburgh (from New York) and in 1923 the station that would become WNBC broadcast the World Series. Chicago's baseball fans began enjoying baseball games in 1924 and in 1938 the New York Giants, Brooklyn Dodgers, and New York Yankees agreed their games could be broadcast on the radio. Some owners had feared that radio broadcasts might reduce attendance and that loss might not offset the revenues gained by allowing games to be broadcast. As that fear was eliminated (radio created more baseball fans), the number of broadcasts increased. Every team entered into a contract with local radio stations and MLB itself sold the rights to the World Series with revenues shared by every club. Revenues began to escalate and with it the value of franchises. The real bonanza, however, was on the horizon and, in the post-World War II years, televised games and television sharply increased revenues.

The 1950s marked the beginning of the television era, even though the first telecast of a game took place on August 26, 1939 to a small audience in New York (Cincinnati Reds versus Brooklyn Dodgers televised in the New York area by the station that was the forerunner to WNBC). Later that same year, that same station also televised the first NFL game from Ebbets Field. That game between the Brooklyn Dodgers and the Philadelphia Eagles was played before 13,050 fans. The overcast skies reduced the available lighting and parts of the game were literally "blacked out." At the time of these first telecasts, there were approximately 500 television sets that had been purchased by households in the New York City region. In 1947, the first World Series was televised and, in 1948, WGN in Chicago began televising White Sox and Cubs games. Some worried that the proliferation of televised games would lead to fewer fans buying tickets at the ballpark, but MLB's attendance increased even as more and more games were available to fans on television. By bringing games to many more people, television may have actually helped to expand the market for baseball. In 1951 the first baseball game was televised in full color and those with televisions across America could actually watch the final game of the Dodgers–Giants legendary playoff series (Bobby Thompson's home run won the pennant for the Giants). The color telecast could be seen in a handful of laboratories with access to televisions that could reproduce those images.

In the post-World War II years, with the rising wealth of the middle class and the advancing technology that would lead to lower effective prices, televisions became a staple of life; the rapid spread of this technology in the United States is illustrated in Table 7.1 and Table 7.2. Most importantly, in 1950, less than 1 in 10 households

Table 7.1   The rising presence of televisions in the United States, 1939–1959

Year	Total Televisions Sold	Cumulative Total of Televisions In Service
1939–1941	7,000	7,000
1942–1949	Not available	3,602,872
1950	6,132,000	9,734,872
1951	5,905,000	15,639,872
1952	6,144,989	21,784,861
1953	6,370,571	28,155,432
1954	7,317,034	35,472,466
1955	7,421,084	42,893,550
1956	6,804,783	49,698,333
1957	6,560,220	56,258,553
1958	5,140,000	61,396,000
1959	5,749,000	67,145,000

Source: www.tvhistory.tv/stats.htm

Table 7.2   Proportion of U.S. households with televisions, selected years, 1950–1975

Year	Households with at Least One Television	Percent of All Households with a Television
1950	3,880,000	9.0
1952	15,300,000	34.2
1954	26,000,000	55.7
1956	34,900,000	71.8
1960	45,750,000	87.1
1965	52,700,000	92.6
1970	59,550,000	95.2
1975	68,500,000	97.0
Source: www.tvhistory.tv/stats.htm		

had a television, but by 1960, almost 9 out of every 10 households had at least one television. This rapid surge created a demand for programs or content to be broadcast. With its supply of games, sports had content that met the needs of emerging televisions stations; soon a strong and permanent relationship would form between teams and stations and then between leagues and networks of stations. The presence of televisions in almost 90 percent of all U.S. homes by 1960 (and virtually all by 1975), the large supply of content (games) controlled by teams and leagues, and the sustained popularity of sports created the opportunity for extremely profitable partnerships between teams, leagues, and networks. This profitability took a giant step forward with an idea presented to all NFL team owners by the league's young commissioner, Pete Rozelle, in 1961.

Impact of Phase 2: The Profitability and Revenue Power of Television, the NFL, and Revenue Sharing

Two football games are usually identified or singled out as changing the profile and perhaps the status of the NFL in the mindset of the American public: the 1958 overtime championship game between the Baltimore Colts and the New York Giants and the 1960 championship game between the Philadelphia Eagles and Green Bay Packers. Both games were exciting and a country growing attached to its televisions found the games enticing and well organized for at-home entertainment (sufficient timeouts for commercials and, yet, long periods of sustained play that was relatively easy to telecast and easy to follow). Observing this growing interest in the sport and the conversion of profitability and technology (commercials that generated income that could be shown during convenient breaks in play coupled with the growing affordability of televisions), and eager to promote a unified league where each team would be profitable and competitive regardless of the size of the local market, Rozelle suggested teams should surrender their television rights to the league. The NFL would then sell the rights to a network and each team would receive an identical share. That would mean the team in the largest market (New York Giants) would receive the same amount of media income from television as the team in the smallest market (Green Bay). Rozelle argued that if all teams were financially stable the league would be able to deliver a large number of competitive games every week. Telecasting these games across the country would lead to more money than any owner could earn, even if their team was dominant and playing in a large market area. In essence, Rozelle believed that a truly competitive league where each team could win on any given Sunday would produce more revenue for teams in New York, Chicago, and Los Angeles (the league's largest markets) than those teams would earn from the telecast of games in a league where their teams were dominant. Table 7.3 provides insight into the success generated for the NFL from the Rozelle concept of shared revenues and

Table 7.3 Media revenue and the NFL, 1960–2013 (in $thousands)

| Contract Period/Year | Network or Media Company | | | | | | | | Total Contract Value |
	CBS	NBC	ABC	FOX	Cable	ESPN	TBS	DirecTV	
1960–1961									
1960	300								300
1961	300								300
Total	600								600
1962–1963									
1962	4,485	229							4,714
1963	4,815	1,001							5,816
Total	9,300	1,230							10,530
1964–1965									
1964	16,125	75							16,200
1965	16,175								16,750
Total	32,875	75							32,950

(continued)

Table 7.3 (continued) Media revenue and the NFL, 1960–2013 (in $thousands)

Contract Period/Year	CBS	NBC	ABC	FOX	Cable	ESPN	TBS	DirecTV	Total Contract Value
1966–1969									
1966	21,850								21,850
1967	25,700								25,700
1968	25,200								25,200
1969	25,700								25,700
Total	98,500								98,450
1970–1973									
1970	21,000	17,500	8,500						47,000
1971	22,500	16,000	8,500						47,000
1972	21,000	17,500	8,500						47,000
1973	22,500	16,000	8,560						47,060
Total	87,000	67,000	34,060						188,060
1974–1977									
1974	22,000	19,600	13,000						54,600
1975	25,000	16,600	13,000						54,600
1976	22,000	19,600	13,000						54,600

					Strike Year	
1977	26,000	16,600	11,500			54,100
Total	95,000	72,400	50,500			217,900
1978–1981						
1978	51,000	51,000	59,700			161,700
1979	57,000	45,000	59,700			161,700
1980	51,000	51,000	59,700			161,700
1981	57,000	45,000	59,700			161,700
Total	216,000	192,000	238,800			646,800
1982–1985						
1982	72,000	63,000	65,000			200,000
1983	108,000	94,000	98,000			300,000
1984	150,000	130,000	135,000			415,000
1985	150,000	140,000	160,000			450,000
Total	480,000	427,000	458,000			1,365,000
1986–1989						
1986						
1987	150,000	120,000	160,000		46,000	476,000
1988	156,000	143,000	135,000		51,000	485,000

(continued)

Table 7.3 (continued) Media revenue and the NFL, 1960–2013 (in $thousands)

Contract Period/Year	Network or Media Company								Total Contract Value
	CBS	NBC	ABC	FOX	Cable	ESPN	TBS	DirecTV	
1989	194,000	146,000	135,000		56,000				531,000
Total	500,000	409,000	430,000		153,000				1,492,000
1990–1993									
	265,000	188,000	225,000			111,250	111,250		3,642,000
1994–1997									
		217,000	230,000	395,000		131,000	124,000		4,388,000
1998–2005									
	500,000		550,000	550,000		600,000			17,600,000
2006–2010									
								700,000	3,500,000
2006–2011									
	622,500	600,000		712,500					11,610,000
2006–2013									
						1,100,000			8,800,000
Total									23,910,000

Source: www.rodneyfort.com (accessed January 11, 2011).

a single media contract. Indeed the popularity of the league has led ESPN to offer it an annual payment of $1.1 billion for its package of telecasts for each year from 2006 through 2013. CBS is paying $622.5 million per year for AFC games (2006–2011), and Fox pays $712.5 million for the right to televise NFC games (2006–2011). DirecTV's satellite package costs the company $700 million per year (2006–2010).

At first glance, and realizing that the NFL will have earned almost $24 billion in collective television revenues between 1960 and 2013, it would seem that Rozelle was correct. Pooled media rights and the creation of numerous competitive teams produced more revenue than most if not all owners realized was possible. Furthermore, selling media rights collectively eliminates competition between the individual teams. Recognizing this revenue growth, however, does not answer the question of the value or benefit for larger-market teams. Would the Giants and Bears, among other larger-market teams, have earned more money if they controlled their media rights in a manner similar to what exists in MLB? It is impossible to answer that question. The NFL appears to remain committed to sharing its largest source of revenue equally among every team. The Jacksonville Jaguars, Indianapolis Colts, and Green Bay Packers play in the league's smallest markets, yet their share of the television contracts is equal to that received by teams in the largest markets. Does that mean, however, that a league that does not divide its largest revenue sources equally between all teams will lead to domination by those franchises in the largest markets? If that domination occurs, will both fan interest and media revenues decline? Surprisingly, the answer might well be "no."

In England's Premiership, there is little sharing of media revenues and each club can spend as much as it wishes on players without incurring a penalty or a fine. Over the past 15 years, only four teams (Manchester United, Arsenal, Chelsea, and Liverpool) have finished first. A fifth club appears ready to enter this top echelon, Manchester City, as a wealthy new owner has the ability to spend quite a bit of money to attract and retain superior players. His commitment allowed Manchester City to emerge as one of the Premiership's elite teams in 2010 and 2011. One might then observe that the Premiership operates within a philosophy that is the antithesis of NFL's "on any given Sunday any team can win" philosophy. Indeed, it is probably safe to conclude that the teams that can emerge in first place and those that will not are known not only for next season, but for numerous seasons to come. Yet, despite a very limited uncertainty parameter (some teams can simply never compete for the title), Premiership games remain popular, earning billions of dollars (pounds) in media revenue each year.

In MLB, there also are substantial differences in media earnings; there is a national package that is divided equally among the clubs, but each team retains the right to sell their games that are not nationally televised in their local markets. As a result, the Boston Red Sox, Chicago Cubs, Chicago White Sox, Los Angeles Dodgers, New York Yankees, New York Mets, and Texas Rangers earn far more than several other clubs. Despite these revenue differentials, however, over the past 10 years, *nine* different teams have won the World Series and attendance levels for the league have remained robust throughout the recession. There is far more competitiveness than one might imagine or suspect given the different media markets available to teams. MLB does not have a salary cap and owners can spend as much as they wish for players. There is a luxury tax payment if too much is spent by any one club. Yet, despite far lower levels of revenue sharing than exists in the NFL, and very different earnings levels, there has been a sharing of the wealth when it comes to championships. There is, though, a higher level of consistency in MLB regarding the teams that are in the playoffs. For example, the Yankees have missed the postseason playoffs only once in the twenty-first century (through 2010). Given attendance and television ratings, however, there is no evidence that the repeated appearances by the Yankees in MLB's playoffs (or the Patriots and Colts in the NFL's playoffs) have had a depressive effect on fan interest or demand. As we will see in Chapter 12, the relationship between team revenues and team quality is not always straightforward.

The important point is that what fans want and what attracts them varies. The NFL's model of success based on the sharing of media revenue has contributed to its popularity, but different models have worked well for other sports that also have maintained high levels of popularity. Yet, what is clear in every instance is that media revenue is vital and robust and, while its direct effect on winning, uncertainty of outcomes, and championships varies, what has not is the overall rise in team values and salaries. Team owners and players have reaped substantial financial rewards from growing media contracts and team values have increased as well. This is not an outcome that has shortchanged fans. In the United States, for example, every game played can be seen by any fan (if they purchase the appropriate media package). This provides ample evidence that consumers, owners, and labor have each benefitted from the televising of games and that leagues have remained popular even when some teams consistently do not appear in the playoffs.*

An example of the benefits accruing to players is provided in Table 7.4 where the change in players' average salaries from 1989 to 2010 is analyzed. Two factors contributed to rising team revenues that supported the observed increases. New facilities produced more revenues as did local and national media contracts. For each season, the actual (or nominal) average salary is presented followed by the value of the average salary in 2010 dollars. The year-to-year percent change and the percent change from each year to the average salary in 2010 is also included.

---

* Certainly policies such as the salary cap affect competitive balance in the NFL. This leads to factors other than payroll that create team success. For example, management also matters given the high level of success, across time, of franchises, such as the Pittsburgh Steelers and Indianapolis Colts. When their success is contrasted with the lack of success of some larger market teams (e.g., New York Jets) it is apparent that something other than equal revenues contributes to on-the-field success.

Table 7.4   Average MLB salaries, 1989–2010

Year	Average Salary ($)	Average Salary in 2010 Dollars	Annual Percent Change	Percent Change from Year to 2010
1989	512,804	993,558		231.92
1990	578,930	986,090	(0.75)	234.43
1991	891,188	1,436,759	45.70	129.53
1992	1,084,408	1,703,958	18.60	93.54
1993	1,120,254	1,704,734	0.05	93.45
1994	1,188,679	1,764,318	3.50	86.92
1995	1,071,029	1,546,329	(12.36)	113.27
1996	1,176,967	1,654,157	6.97	99.37
1997	1,383,578	1,887,093	14.08	74.76
1998	1,441,406	1,935,551	2.57	70.38
1999	1,720,050	2,271,764	17.37	45.17
2000	1,998,034	2,568,563	13.06	28.39
2001	2,264,403	2,806,256	9.25	17.52
2002	2,383,235	2,920,169	4.06	12.93
2003	2,555,476	3,051,944	4.51	8.06
2004	2,486,609	2,913,575	(4.53)	13.19
2005	2,632,655	2,995,732	2.82	10.08
2006	2,866,544	3,136,864	4.71	5.13
2007	2,944,556	3,156,960	0.64	4.46
2008	3,154,845	3,243,019	2.73	1.69
2009	3,240,206	3,332,345	2.75	(1.04)
2010	3,297,828	3,297,828	(1.04)	

Source: CBS Sports, http://www.cbssports.com/mlb/salaries/avgsalaries (accessed January 11, 2011) and authors' calculations.

From 1989 to 2010, average salaries increased more than 230 percent, meaning the average player in 2010 earned three times more than the average player in 1989. There also have been years in which average salaries declined (indicated by figures in parentheses). Smaller annual increments can be seen in recent years, as the effects of the recession have been severe in several markets. The main point, however, from expanding revenue steams from the media and from new ballparks has been increasing salaries for players.

To illustrate the benefits that have accrued to owners, the changing value of sport franchises is summarized in Table 7.5; these figures also are discussed in Chapter 8, but they are important to briefly reconsider here in terms of understanding the effect of revenue from media and facilities on franchise values. Again, it is important to remember that media and facility revenues are both increasing across the past two decades and both have contributed to increases in franchise values.

NFL franchises have enjoyed robust growth across the past two decades resulting from the revenues generated by new facilities and rapidly escalating contracts with broadcast networks, a satellite television service, and the development of the NFL network. In some instances, values increased four- and five-fold from 1991 (in real terms or adjusted dollars). Teams worth approximately $200 million back then are valued today at more than $1 billion. The value of the Washington Redskins increased 669 percent in real terms from 1991 to 2010. While the chart does not isolate facility and media effects, suffice to note that the management of the real estate within facilities and income from the media combined to dramatically change the business of the NFL at what is likely an unprecedented rate relative to any sport franchise business. The small rate of growth for the Oakland Raiders is related to their return to Oakland from Los Angeles. The benchmark year for measuring the growth in value the team enjoyed was not from 1991, but from their return to Oakland for the 1995 season. New facilities and the media have catapulted numerous NFL franchises into billion-dollar companies, with a large number worth just slightly less than a billion dollars (see Table 7.5).

MLB franchises have seen very robust real growth rates as well, although the changes are far less than those enjoyed by NFL franchises (Table 7.6). Notice the increments in value enjoyed by teams that own (or are part owners of) their own

Table 7.5   **NFL team value growth (in $millions)**

Team	Value in 2010 ($)	Value in 1991 or First Year (in 2010 Dollars)	Percent Change
Atlanta Falcons	831	182	357.0
Baltimore Ravens	1,073	282	279.8
Buffalo Bills	799	202	294.6
Carolina Panthers	1,037	232	346.1
Chicago Bears	1,067	203	425.3
Cincinnati Bengals	905	202	349.1
Cleveland Browns	1,015	234	334.2

Table 7.5 (continued)   NFL team value growth (in $millions)

Team	Value in 2010 ($)	Value in 1991 or First Year (in 2010 Dollars)	Percent Change
Dallas Cowboys	1,805	290	522.0
Denver Broncos	1,049	183	474.3
Detroit Lions	817	187	338.0
Green Bay Packers	1,018	322	215.7
Houston Oilers/Texans	1,171	192	508.8
Indianapolis Colts	1,040	187	456.1
Jacksonville Jaguars	725	204	255.8
Kansas City Chiefs	965	197	389.0
Miami Dolphins	1,011	330	205.9
Minnesota Vikings	774	192	303.1
New England Patriots	1,367	161	749.6
New Orleans Saints	955	200	377.7
New York Giants	1,182	242	388.8
New York Jets	1,144	202	467.7
Oakland Raiders	758	316	140.2
Philadelphia Eagles	1,119	227	391.9
Arizona Cardinals	919	192	378.6
Pittsburgh Steelers	996	181	450.1
San Diego Chargers	907	183	396.1
San Francisco 49ers	925	242	282.5
Seattle Seahawks	989	209	372.3
St. Louis Rams	779	432	80.2
Tampa Bay Buccaneers	1,032	184	461.0
Tennessee Titans	994	431	130.6
Washington Redskins	1,550	202	669.1

Source: Forbes/Financial World, authors' calculations.

Table 7.6 Growth in team values in MLB (in $millions)

Team	Value in 2010	Value in 1991 or first Year (in 2010 Dollars)	Percent Change
Arizona Diamondbacks	379	384	−1.4
Atlanta Braves	450	145	210.8
Baltimore Orioles	376	170	120.7
Boston Red Sox	870	221	292.9
Anaheim/LA Angels	521	247	110.9
Chicago Cubs	726	230	215.7
Chicago White Sox	466	196	137.9
Cincinnati Reds	331	153	115.9
Cleveland Indians	391	145	170.1
Colorado Rockies	384	163	135.2
Detroit Tigers	375	187	100.1
Florida Marlins	317	120	163.7
Houston Astros	453	179	153.3
Kansas City Royals	341	204	66.8
Los Angeles Dodgers	727	298	143.9
Milwaukee Brewers	351	145	142.4
Minnesota Twins	405	162	150.3
New York Mets	858	298	187.8
New York Yankees	1,600	341	369.7
Oakland Athletics	295	145	103.8
Philadelphia Phillies	537	238	125.2
Pittsburgh Pirates	289	145	99.6
San Diego Padres	408	145	181.8
San Francisco Giants	483	145	233.6
Seattle Mariners	439	153	186.4
St. Louis Cardinals	488	238	104.6

Table 7.6 (continued)   Growth in team values in MLB (in $millions)

Team	Value in 2010	Value in 1991 or first Year (in 2010 Dollars)	Percent Change
Tampa Bay Rays	316	297	6.3
Texas Rangers	451	170	164.8
Toronto Blue Jays	326	247	32.0
Washington Nationals	387	353	9.7

Source: Forbes/Financial World, authors' calculations.

networks (New York Yankees, New York Mets, Boston Red Sox, and Cleveland Indians). The growth in value of the Indians is quite instructive given the team's poor on-the-field performance in 2008–2010 and the slow economic growth in Northeast Ohio. The team's owners, however, developed Sports Time Ohio (STO) and, long after the effects of the revenue streams from the new ballpark had been reduced, the team's value is still robust. One franchise has lost value, the Arizona Diamondbacks, even though the team plays in a very modern facility. The economic decline in the state took a toll and is reflected in the local revenue that the Diamondbacks can realize. The Tampa Bay Rays also face challenges as a result of the recent declines in Florida's economy and playing in the market with the lowest population density. The sprawling nature of the region means fans must travel greater distances to reach the ballpark where the Rays play, and these travel costs may be taking a toll on support for the team as well.

Phase 3: The Vertical Integration of Teams and the Media

The dramatic increase in revenue earned by teams from media contracts elevated salaries and team values. As important as these funds are for teams, players, and fans who now had more games to enjoy, two unrelated watershed events signaled the beginning of the third phase of the relationship between teams and the media. These events—poorly understood or under appreciated at the time they took place— would be seen in retrospect to having "changed everything." These unrelated events are wrapped into the values reported in the preceding tables. Their impact on the sports business cannot be minimized, and, in essence, begins with what seemed to be a minor business decision by the New York Yankees and the New Jersey Nets. The other event took place in the 1980s, but the importance of what took place as a result of the meeting between the Yankees and Nets elevates its stature in terms of defining what is Phase 3 and how the sports business was irrevocably altered.

In 1999, the Yankees and Nets agreed to what initially seemed to be a relatively inconsequential merger of both teams' business operations. The goal of the merger was to improve the business offices of both clubs and through the realization of some efficiencies and the removal of duplicate operations, increase profitability. There also was interest in merging or creating cooperative marketing efforts to leverage increased revenues from the local broadcast of both team's games. These goals seemed hardly revolutionary or likely to substantially change the games of baseball and/or basketball or sports in general. What the merger did lead to, however, was nothing short of a quantum shift in the organization and structure of the sports business and an extraordinary surge in revenues for teams. With business operations merged and a cooperative marketing agreement, both teams focused on enhanced revenues from the sale of their broadcast rights to New York City's largest cable television operator, Cablevision. Initially both teams just wanted higher revenues. But, in the course of exploring what was the real value of their broadcast rights, the teams began to consider the feasibility of establishing their own independent network. Cablevision enjoyed control of the distribution of local broadcast rights to all seven of the region's MLB, NBA, and NHL teams. Unified, the Yankees and Nets believed they would be able to entertain a variety of offers and opportunities when it came time to renew their contracts.

After considering all of their options, the two teams decided to form their own network with financing provided through an investment by Goldman Sachs. When the New Jersey Nets were sold to Bruce Ratner (Forest City Enterprises), the stake in Yankees–Nets was not included. The Steinbrenner family has wrapped their share of The Yankee Entertainment and Sports (YES) Network into Yankee Global Enterprises LLC that operates the New York Yankees and the family's interest in the television network. The value of the network was placed at more than $3 billion in 2007 when Goldman Sachs expressed interest in selling their share. In 2010, *Forbes* magazine estimated that the Yankees were worth $1.6 billion. It is conceivable that the network today is worth twice as much as the ballclub.*

The notion that teams could form their own network begins a bit earlier than 1999. Some might argue that Ted Turner's linking of the Braves to his television empire was the first example of a team forming or being used to establish a network. The Braves were an important part of TBS and its success, but Turner acquired the local broadcast rights to the team's games in 1972, four years before acquiring complete ownership of the team. It seems more appropriate to conclude that Ted

---

* The Steinbrenner family owns approximately 34 percent of the YES Network with other shares owned by Goldman Sachs (46 percent). One-fifth of the network was owned by the Nets and was not included in the sale of the basketball team to Bruce Ratner (Forest City Enterprises), leaving that share controlled by the original YankeesNets partnership. Goldman Sachs has had its stake for sale for several years, but through the end of 2010 no purchase had been announced.

Turner acquired the team to bolster the network rather than having a franchise and then choosing the option of forming a network with the team as its core product. What is clear, however, is that the owners of the Boston Red Sox and Boston Bruins established the New England Sports Network (NESN) in 1984 beginning in earnest the era of teams and then sports leagues creating their own television networks and media distribution systems. These networks would then negotiate with cable television operators and satellite providers to deliver their network and its content just as do ABC, NBC, Lifetime, CNN, or ESPN. The teams could use the popularity of their games as a way to entice the highest possible fees for the right to carry their games. The Red Sox own 80 percent of the NESN network and the Bruins retain the balance. In 2009, when *The New York Times* was interested in selling its stake in NESN (The Times Corporation is a minority owner of the Boston Red Sox and, therefore, owns a portion of NESN), the network was valued at $443 million (Farrell, 2009). The Red Sox's stake in NESN is actually owned by New England Sports Ventures, which owns the baseball team, the 80 percent share of NESN, FC Liverpool, Fenway Park, and the Fenway Sports Group, which is a marketing, management, and real estate company that also has ownership interests in an auto racing business. These collective interests make the Red Sox part of a business empire that, while less valuable than the one that includes the New York Yankees and the YES Network, is far more diversified.

The first part of the twenty-first century also would see the advent of college conference networks. The prospect of additional revenues from media sales prompted realignments with universities joining other conferences to ensure that conference championship games could be played and that additional media markets would be added to a network's inventory.

The fact that some baseball teams have created their own networks has helped others receive very lucrative contracts from Fox Sports to offset their possible interest in following in the footsteps of the Red Sox, Yankees, Mets, and Indians. For example, the Los Angeles Dodgers' contract with Fox Sports involved payments of $35 million in 2011, $37 million in 2012, and $39 million in 2013. The Texas Rangers' local market in the growing northcentral Texas region, is home to more than 6.6 million residents. In 2010 Fox Sports Southwest paid $1.6 billion for a 20-year contract with the Rangers. The $80 million a year payment certainly suggests that when the Dodgers' contract expires that franchise's owners may well anticipate an extraordinary increment or they, too, could join the growing number of teams creating their own network.

The success enjoyed by the Red Sox and the Yankees has translated into far higher revenues for all teams. Had those franchises not founded their own independent networks, it is likely that Fox Sports and other distributors would have had little incentive to come forward with media deals that less than 10 years ago would have seemed outlandish and unprofitable. While it still remains to be seen how much profit Fox Sports realizes from its exclusive control of the local broadcast rights to numerous teams, the Rangers have far more money available to invest in their franchise or retain as profits. If rights to televise Rangers' games are worth $80 million, it is reasonable to expect that the Dodgers might be looking forward to a 100 percent increase in the $39 million fee charged for 2013 when that contract expires. There is clear value for each team threatening to form a network to understand the value of their team and their games to Fox Sports or other distributors.*

The relationship between television networks and sports teams has produced other issues. For example, during the divorce proceedings between Jamie and Frank McCourt (owners of the Los Angeles Dodgers), not only were questionable spending patterns disclosed, but Fox Sports advanced payments to the Dodgers in response to a request from Frank McCourt to help maintain the team's liquidity. Some speculated that a Rangers-like extension to the media contract was likely to provide the money needed for one McCourt to buy out the ownership interests of the other (Shaikin, 2011). The use of media funds to settle ownership issues would leave the team with less money for team operations. Fearing this possibility and the loss of operating funds for the team, MLB Commissioner Bud Selig appointed a representative of his office to oversee all business operations of the Dodgers in April 2011.

Media funds and their use are also at the heart of the labor conflict in the NFL. The scale and importance of the revenues earned by the NFL from its broadcast partners has made these contracts critical to the players as they are the centerpiece of the revenue dedicated to player salaries. With their salaries inexorably linked to the size of the contracts negotiated by the league with its media partners, the players' union agreed with the NFL owners in the White Stipulation and Settlement Agreement (SSA) that owners alone would be depended upon to negotiate the best possible contracts with their media partners to assure the richest possible pool of revenues for players' salaries. The intent of the agreement was to ensure that the NFL would act in accordance with the best interests of both the players and owners in terms of maximizing revenues from the broadcast partners. In exchange, the players agreed that the negotiations with the media partners would be left to the Commissioner's office and the owners.

The players' perspective is that this agreement restrains the NFL and the owners from having interests in media corporations and then accepting lower broadcast fees to elevate the profits of the media corporations. In addition, the agreement serves to ensure that the owners would never have any interest other than in maximizing the revenues received from the broadcast partners.

This agreement became a controversial centerpiece in the 2011 labor dispute when it was disclosed the NFL would continue to receive payments from the broadcast partners *even if games were not played in 2011* as a result of a "lockout" or a

---

* Forbes reports that nine MLB teams have equity positions in regional television networks. The value of the rights to televise Dodgers' games was at the center of controversy that led to the team's owner filing for bankruptcy in 2011.

strike by the players. The players union argued that by accepting this benefit the value of the contracts was likely diminished or less than what they would have been if prepayments tied to a lockout of the players by the owners were not included. "In TV deals made while the SSA was in effect, the players contend the owners failed to obtain the maximum revenues the agreement requires. Instead of using remarkable increases in television ratings to extract greater fees from the networks, the players assert, the owners accepted less money in return for payments during a lockout (Munson, 2010)." The union's blunt assertion was that money had been left on the table that will lead to lower salaries for the players. The players filed a grievance against the NFL and the owners arguing that accepting guaranteed payments even if games were not played was a violation of the SSA and constituted an unfair labor practice with regard to the maintenance of a fair environment in which negotiations would occur. If the owners receive media revenues even if games are not played, they clearly enjoy an economic benefit not available to the players. In April 2011, a court found the owners had indeed violated the SSA and the players were entitled to damages and additional compensation.

Media revenues are benefits of ownership. But, in the NFL, those revenues have entered the collective bargaining process because of their importance to the salary pool that supports players' salaries as agreed to by the players and owners in their previous contracts. Now the question becomes whether their use by the owners to bolster their negotiating position is a breach of an existing contract and agreement and constitutes an unfair bargaining tactic. Or, as it could be argued, if the collective bargaining agreement expires, are owners able to pursue their selfinterest even if that amounts to undoing previous agreements?

In the McCourt case, is an owner free to do as he or she sees fit relative to the use of media revenues? The collective bargaining agreement with the players in that league does not specify which revenues are used for salaries, but a commissioner can try to use that office's power to restrain how these revenues are used if he concludes the best interests of baseball are not being represented. If the media revenues are used to settle questions of ownership, there is, however, a potential for an adverse effect for fans (a team of less quality) and those players who do not receive contracts from other teams. But, in this instance, neither the fans nor the players have legal standing to challenge the use of the funds. The players can rely on free agency to secure better deals from other clubs. Fans can exercise their disappointment through lower attendance levels, but that indirect response is their only tool besides expressing outrage. That latter strategy has been employed as local pundits and fans have argued MLB should force the McCourts to sell the team. If that was to occur (or, as some argued, the MLB commissioner tried to force the McCourts to sell the team), the new owners might not be able to meet fans' expectations any better than if one McCourt ended up with the team.

In summary, some teams have added media corporations to their holdings and have vertically integrated television and radio into their operations. The Yankees, Mets, Red Sox, Bruins, Indians, Rangers, and Knicks are no longer just sports teams. They are media corporations with sports teams, or sports teams intertwined with a media network such that where one ends and the other begins is indistinguishable. The teams that do not have their own networks have benefitted from the transformation of other franchises through the far larger media contracts they have enjoyed. Without several teams acting on the threat to create a network, it is highly unlikely Fox Sports would have paid the price it did for rights to broadcast Texas Rangers' baseball or been as interested in prepaying for the rights to Dodgers' games. In this manner, the vertical integration of television with sports teams has changed or transformed the sports business by clearly establishing the value of local media rights and the transfer of more of that value from the owners of television and radio systems to team owners. The escalating revenues have led to players trying to collectively and individually gain larger shares of the income. At the same time, some owners have tried to use their expanding revenue source to increase profits and settle ownership issues in ways that displeased other owners.

Phase 3 Continues: College Conference Networks

No discussion of Phase 3 of media and the sports business is complete without a review of the changes taking place in the NCAA. College sports never went through the period where the media was relied upon to expand the popularity or fan base for athletics. Decades before the NFL established its identity and dominance, college football was attracting large crowds to its games. Ohio State and Michigan each had attracted more than 70,000 fans to football games by the late 1920s and early 1930s, and the men's NCAA basketball tournament attracted sellout crowds long before Brent Musburger employed the term "March Madness" in 1982 during the CBS telecast of tournament games (the term appears to have been used first to describe the state high school basketball tournament in Illinois in the 1930s).

Before the NCAA tournament was a staple on America's sports calendar, the National Invitational Tournament (NIT) with its final games at Madison Square Garden in New York was played before sellout crowds. Lastly, each of America's major universities had rivalry games that frequently attracted large crowds (e.g., Harvard–Yale, Army–Navy, Texas–Texas A&M, Texas–Oklahoma, Michigan–Ohio State, USC–UCLA) that required no additional exposure from the media to ensure fans would attend.

The initial issue for collegiate sports was not the role of the media in popularizing games, but it involved the control the NCAA would or could have to regulate the number of times any one team could appear on television. Prior to 1984, the NCAA limited the number of appearances any team could make on national television and the number of games any university could televise of its football team. The NCAA would argue in court that too many televised games of any one team would lead to adverse effects on attendance. The NCAA had entered into contracts with CBS and ABC to televise football games and it set the schedule with the networks. The University of Oklahoma challenged the NCAA's authority claiming it violated the Sherman Anti-Trust Act. In *NCAA v. Board of Regents of University of Oklahoma* (468 U.S. 85, 1984), the Supreme Court agreed with the University of Oklahoma that the NCAA's television plan violated the antitrust law and that universities were free to televise as many or as few games as the market would demand and support noting:

> The NCAA television plan on its face constitutes a restraint upon the operation of a free market, and the District Court's findings establish that the plan has operated to raise price and reduce output, both of which are unresponsive to consumer preference. Under the Rule of Reason, these hallmarks of anticompetitive behavior place upon the NCAA a heavy burden of establishing an affirmative defense that competitively justifies this apparent deviation from the operations of a free market. The NCAA's argument that its television plan can have no significant anticompetitive effect since it has no market power must be rejected. As a matter of law, the absence of proof of market power does not justify a naked restriction on price or output and, as a factual matter, it is evident from the record that the NCAA does possess market power.... The record does not support the NCAA's proffered justification for its television plan that it constitutes a cooperative "joint venture," which assists in the marketing of broadcast rights and, hence, is pro competitive. The District Court's contrary findings undermine such a justification.*

The ending of the NCAA's control on the telecast of collegiate events created a surge in the supply of games that could be televised. The increase in televised games did not have a negative effect on attendance levels. Records maintained by the NCAA on its website indicate that since 2003 at least 38.2 million fans attended Division 1A or 1AA games in every year through 2009 (Table 7.7). This is an important time period to analyze (2003 through 2009) as it includes the creation of the Big 10 Network and several special sports stations created by cable companies and television networks (e.g., Versus, Comcast Sports) to support the telecast of even more games. While there was variation in attendance levels, the number of televised games cannot explain the differences as the highest attendance levels were reported in 2008 and 2009 at the same time that all of the games

---

* Readers interested in the Court's complete decision can review the decision at http://caselaw. lp.findlaw.com/scripts/getcase.pl?court=us&vol=468&invol=85. The importance of this case for collegiate sports and the media makes a careful reading of the decision very important.

Table 7.7 Annual attendance at NCAA Division I and I-AA football fames, 2003–2009

Year	Attendance
2003	41.2 million
2004	38.2 million
2005	38.1 million
2006	42.5 million
2007	43.0 million
2008	43.5 million
2009	43.0 million

Source: National Collegiate Athletic Association website http://www.ncaa.org/wps/wcm/connect/public/ NCAA/Resources/Stats/Football/Attendance/ index.html (accessed January 18, 2011).

of every major collegiate team were telecast. As an example, despite relatively poor on-the-field performances (3–9 in 2008 and 5–7 in 2009) and the telecast of each of its home (and away games) to its local market, the University of Michigan continued to attract more than 110,000 fans to each of it games at Michigan Stadium (The Big House).

Just as the vertical integration of networks and teams was a "this changes everything" event with regard to the revenues earned by professional teams, a seemingly innocuous announcement by the Big 10 Conference had a very similar effect on collegiate sports. On June 21, 2006, the Big 10 Conference announced that a 10-year extension of its contract with ABC/ESPN for football games was not part of the national package and, far more importantly, it announced a 20-year joint project with the Fox Entertainment Group called The Big 10 Network. The Conference would own 51 percent of the network and provide all of its programming, including games and matches not televised as part of any national or league contract. This included, but was not limited to, football, hockey, softball, volleyball, and lacrosse games as well as all other matches. The Fox Entertainment Group would own 49 percent of the network and provide the hardware and distributional mechanism required. Within one year of its creation, the Big 10 Network was available in 30 million homes and by 2010 the network reached 75 million homes in 19 of America's 20 largest media markets. The Big 10 Network also was available across Canada. Canadians' appetite for following the exploits of their young men and women who ventured south to play Division I hockey was sufficient to make the network an attraction for Canada's cable television providers. Currently the Big 10 Network has distribution agreements with 300 cable and satellite providers including AT&T U-Verse, Cablevision, Comcast, DirecTV, DISH Network, and Time Warner. Some people might have thought that the Big 10 Network would find a following only in states with Big 10 universities. With alumni across the continent, however, there was a national and even an international demand for Big 10 sports.

The Big 10 Network pays $60 million each year to the Big 10 Conference for the rights to the games, matches, and other programs produced by the Conference and its member universities. That means each school receives $5.45 million from the Big 10 network *plus* an equal share of any profits. In 2010, the *Minneapolis Star Tribune* reported the profits made were $66 million, providing each member university with an additional $6 million in revenue (Miller, 2010). The University of Nebraska will join the Big 10 Conference in 2011. This will likely lead to additional profits given the national following of that university, and the Conference has indicated that further expansion is a possibility. The Big 10 has long coveted an association with Notre Dame, but that school has elected to continue its independent status with regard to its football program while its other athletic teams compete within the Big East. While it was believed that if Notre Dame would consider an all-sports association that the Big 10 was the best fit, the Big East's admission of TCU (Texas Christian University) might increase the appeal of that conference to Notre Dame. The Big East now serves several of the nation's largest media markets including those in Texas, and those revenue possibilities might eventually lure Notre Dame's football program away from its long-cherished independent status.

In terms of the importance of media revenues for university athletic budgets, the annual revenues for the University of Michigan's athletic departments were estimated at $105 million. Total operating expenses were anticipated to be $100.3 million (Vernellis, 2010). Revenues from the Big 10 Network, ABC/ESPN, and other contracts were expected to exceed $22 million. This would mean media revenues account for approximately 21 percent of all revenues and support 22 percent of all expenses. If the success of the Big 10 Network leads to more profits, it is reasonable to anticipate that media sales will play a larger role in the financing of collegiate sports.

The success of the Big 10 Network attracted substantial interest from other conferences that either launched networks of their own, expanded their membership to enhance their media presence and create a football conference championship game, or expanded their efforts to televise more games and matches. Most notable was the PAC-10's expansion effort that initially seemed to focus on the University of Texas and other institutions in the Big 12 Conference. When Texas spurned both the Pac-10 and the Big 10, the Pac-10 invited the University of Colorado and the University of Utah to join the eight university members located in states that are adjacent to the Pacific Ocean and two universities from Arizona, creating the PAC 12. Utah's decision to leave the Mountain West Conference encouraged that league to invite Boise State University to be a member, and then the Big East Conference reached out to TCU to extend its media footprint into Texas. It is likely that in 2011 or 2012 other universities will realign. The Pac-12 has declared its interest in a 16-team configuration. A 16-team conference was also an option that some media commentators speculated was in the grand scheme for the Big 10 (now also with 12 university members). Some athletic directors in the Big 10 debated the value of including one of Canada's largest universities (to attract even more viewers from Ontario and Quebec Provinces). The admission of a Canadian university into an NCAA athletic conference would require a change in emphasis for that institution as their athletic programs are not as extensive as what exists at all Big 10 universities. In addition, there would have to be an alignment with NCAA policies and practices by the Canadian universities including acceptance of the definition of amateur status. Nevertheless, the consideration of an extension of a conference's boundaries into Canada merely underscores the value of media markets in terms of planning for future revenue growth.

The Big 10 Network and the Pac-12 Networks have the advantage of programming from a larger group of universities and, therefore, are able to offer viewers a complete package of athletic events and features developed by 11- and now 12-member institutions. In January 2011, the sports media business world was again redefined when a single institution, The University of Texas, announced a $300 million, 20-year deal with ESPN to create the Longhorn Network. "ESPN will own and operate the network and pay $300 million over 20 years, two-thirds to the university and one-third to IMG College, which already owns some of the university's rights. . . . The Texas network plans to show 200 sports events a year, including at least one football game and eight men's basketball games" (Sandomir, 2011). The university also received a $10 million, upfront payment. By this decision, The University of Texas joins the New York Yankees, New York Mets, Cleveland Indians, and the Boston Red Sox and Bruins as sport organizations with their own network. An issue will be the amount of programming The University of Texas can generate to sustain a full-time network. It is possible the Longhorn Network will only operate a few hours each day, and, on some days, the Longhorn Network might not offer any programs. The Longhorn Network also plans to rebroadcast games originally offered on ESPN or ABC. The Big 10 Network has used the strength of the alumni base of all of its universities to secure itself in 19 of the 20 largest media markets. The demand for the Longhorn Network could be less, but three of the largest media markets in the United States are in Texas (Dallas/Fort Worth, Houston–Galveston, and San Antonio). These markets will give the new network a valuable base or backbone and each of these markets is growing and there are other excellent market areas in the state (e.g., Austin and El Paso).

The University of Texas will receive approximately the same amount of money as each of the Big 10 Network universities (in 2010, each Big 10 Network member university received approximately $11.45 million). What makes The University of Texas deal more lucrative, however, was the upfront payment of $10 million. The University of Texas could receive more money in future years if the Longhorn

Network's profits increase. That provision or opportunity also exists for each member of the Big 10 Network. The University of Texas will receive approximately $14 million as well through the Big 12 Conference contracts for games sold through the conference (Smith, 2011a). That would mean a potential media income stream approaching $26 million, surpassing the $24 million realized by each of the Big 10 universities (Smith, 2011b). In May 2011 the Pac-12 announced a $3 billion, 12-year deal with ESPN and Fox to create its own network. This deal will give each member university $20.8 million per year.

The creation of collegiate networks set in motion a wide-ranging series of management and business changes that are still reverberating and creating issues and opportunities for athletic directors and university presidents. It is likely that by the time you read this chapter, new conference alignments will have taken place. The payout from collegiate networks creates many new options and opportunities for their university members. These potential opportunities make it more and more difficult for any aspiring or growing athletic program to avoid an alliance with one of these new networks. The scale of The University of Texas's deal with ESPN was a "game changer." The Big 10 Universities changed the game and profited from the creation of their own network. Now, just five years after announcing the first collegiate network, The University of Texas has ventured out taking a page from the Yankees, Mets, and Red Sox playbook. The PAC-12 deal assures each of its members a staggering $20 million of income each year. All of these universities will now receive more revenue from media than these other schools. Most importantly for students, however, is that these contracts come within five years of the Big 10 universities announcing the creation of a network. The next five years may see even more innovations and media revenues generating an even larger portion of a university's total athletic budget.

Media, Sports, and the Future: Emerging Competition in the Delivery of Games to Fans and Advanced (Internet) Media

No discussion of the role of media in the transformation of the sports business is complete without some reference to the strategies of the megadistribution/media organizations led by Disney, Comcast, and Fox Sports and "Advanced" or Internet media. Turning first to the delivery of games and matches to fans, leagues and teams in the 1950s through the 1980s focused on the three major networks, ABC, CBS, and NBC. Slowly new broadcast networks and cable television providers emerged (e.g., WTBS, ESPN, Fox). The landscape for the decades ahead is dramatically different. Two of the original three major networks are now part of much larger media corporations. ABC is now part of the Disney Corporation that also acquired ESPN; the Comcast cable corporation acquired NBC. CBS remains an independent network. Fox has expanded with numerous regional sports affiliates. Delivering sports programming into households is now led by Disney/ESPN/ABC, Comcast/NBC, CBS, and Fox Sports and its affiliated regional sports network groups. In some areas, there are other merged regional organizations, such as MSG/Cablevision (New York City metropolitan area). The strategy being followed by these distribution giants is to essentially control as much of the "track" or mechanisms by which consumers access sports content. Comcast is the nation's largest cable television company serving almost 23 million households. Its acquisition of NBC Universal means it has its own movie studio as well as several other networks (CNBC, Bravo, Telemundo, and Oxygen). The 23 million subscriber households also means Comcast/NBC has a huge base of customers that rely upon it for Internet connections. Comcast with its control of the "tracks" over which sports and entertainment are delivered to approximately 23 million households across numerous networks that it also owns gives it a substantial distribution base of interest to the sports leagues and college conferences.

Disney's acquisition of ESPN and ABC gives it control of 23 network ventures involving ESPN and two involving ABC that can be used to distribute games and programs. Disney itself has a set of entertainment networks illustrating their strategy of controlling "tracks" that reach millions of viewers. The Fox Corporation includes 20 owned networks and 5 affiliated networks. They, too, control or participate in operating 24 different distributional systems over which countless hours of sports programming can be delivered to most if not all households in North America.

Relative to the distribution of televised games, the competitive environment in the future will be between these megadistributional networks and teams, leagues (e.g., MLB Network, NFL Network), and conference networks, and the threat that teams or college conferences will create their own networks independent of each or any of the megadistributional systems. The existence of the team and league networks will maintain a competitive environment, as evidenced by The University of Texas's recent agreement.

The escalating revenue figures might lead some to wonder if a media "bubble" exists. Real estate values plummeted in the aftermath of the collapse of the housing market and the severe recession between 2008 and 2010. Are escalating media deals another example of Shiller's irrational exuberance (Shiller, 2005), meaning that a massive market correction in values is inevitable? It is certainly possible that prices will decline, but the escalating value of sports as a media product lies in (1) its ability to consistently attract large audiences, (2) the need of advertisers to place their product messages before large numbers of people, and (3) consumers' willingness to pay fees through their cable and satellite providers for the entertainment provided by sports.

Sports' value as an advertising medium has benefitted from the fragmentation and expansion of the number of video options available to consumers. Not only are there many channels on every cable and satellite system, but the distribution of movies through DVDs eliminates the possibility of a large number of viewers waiting for films to be shown on television. Add to all of the cable and satellite options those available on the Internet, and it seems more appropriate to describe the televising of entertainment as "narrow casting" rather than "broad casting" or the term used to refer to the televising of programs to large audiences. The fragmentation and expanding number of entertainment choices has elevated the value of sports. Games are the televised events that attract the largest number of viewers, and that ability is what continues to pique the interest of advertisers. As long as the popularity of sports endures, televised sports events will attract a multitude of viewers and encourage consumers to pay cable and satellite fees. Their consumption of sports will make games the most valuable medium from which to distribute advertising messages. Throughout the prolonged recession, the popularity of sports has endured. While an extended period of labor disputes in the professional sports leagues could convince some fans to focus on other entertainment options, in the absence of scandals that threaten the sense of competition (athletes purposely playing poorly), the popularity of sports seems recession proof. While it is imprudent to suggest that there is no irrational exuberance resulting in over-priced deals involving sports and the media, there is also evidence to show that the popularity of sports has weathered economic cycles and as a product consumed through the media will continue to enjoy considerable popularity.

This next phase of sports and the media, then, will involve the competition for games between integrated cable providers and networks and the individual networks created by teams and leagues. That competition will lead to higher revenues for teams and leagues and, over time, elevated player salaries. At the same time, consumers will be better off as more sports will be available at very affordable prices. Given the improved images delivered by HD and 3D television, the quality of the fan experience from watching games in their homes seems poised to enjoy considerable increments. The growing financial returns to teams and the media outlets may well be based on sound supply and demand factors and not an irrational exuberance.

The term *advanced media* is used to describe the use of the Internet to deliver sports to consumers and the advent of fantasy leagues and computer-generated games. MLB has established early leadership in the use of the Internet to grow revenues and joined its MLB Network (MLBN) to its subsidiary, MLBAM (Major League Baseball Advanced Media). Each owner of a MLB franchise invested an equal share in these ventures and the profits are divided into equal shares. In 2001, MLBAM generated $36 million in income. By 2005, MLBAM was producing $236 million in profits, and it was estimated that for 2009, MLB's franchise owners were able to divide $450 million from MLBAM (Brown, 2009). If revenues reached that level of profitability, MLBAM would be returning approximately $15 million to each club every year. It is clear that Internet-based distribution of games and other material is an expanding market. The years ahead will see more games available on the Internet and consumers will be allowed to design their own packages and purchase only those games they want to view. The Big 10 Network offers a package of each university's games and matches, or all Big 10 games and matches for a particular sport. A consumer can buy all of the games of one or more teams or the entire league and access that video through the Internet. In essence, what each league and team will experiment with in the years ahead is personalized networks that consumers create through the Internet for their favorite teams.

Fantasy sports also has grown into a megaindustry with important revenue opportunities through advertising as those involved in the games visit the required websites. The estimate of the number of people involved in Fantasy Football range from 15 to 50 million suggesting that no validated number exists. ESPN has noted simply that tens of thousands play Fantasy Baseball on its website. EA Sports has noted that John Madden's Football Game has sold more than 85 million copies. The number of people involved in fantasy sports or computer-generated games has established this form of sport consumption as another valuable revenue producing outlet. When advertising possibilities are linked to these attractions, the potential for additional revenue for team owners and players seems poised to increase yet again.

References

Brown, M. 2009. Understanding the real value of MLBAM and MLB Network. The Biz of Baseball, January 19, http://bizofbaseball.com/index.php?option=com_content&view=article&id=2878:understanding-the-real-value-of-mlbam-and-mlb-network&catid=26:editorials&Itemid=39 (accessed January 19, 2011).

Farrell, M. 2009. New York Times puts NESN on block. *Multichannel News*, http://www.multichannel.com/article/162920-New_York_Times_Puts_NESN_Stake_On_Block.php (accessed January 3, 2011).

Haupert, M. J. 2010. The economic history of Major League Baseball. *EH.net*, February 1, http://eh.net/encyclopedia/article/haupert.mlb (accessed December 20, 2010).

Miller, P. 2010. Big Ten Network: Big man on campus. *Minneapolis Star Tribune*, May 5, online edition, http://www.startribune.com/sports/gophers/92558764.html (accessed January 18, 2011).

Munson, L. 2010. NFL's lockout-likelihood plot thickens. *Courtside Seat*, http://sports.espn.go.com/espn/commentary/news/story?page=munson/100617 (accessed January 17, 2011).

Rosentraub, M. S. 1997. *Major league losers: The real cost of sports and who's paying for it*. New York: Basic Books.

Sandomir, R. 2011. University of Texas will create its own sports network with ESPN. *The New York Times College Sports Blog*, January 19, http://thequad.blogs.nytimes.com/2011/01/19/university-of-texas-will-create-its-own-sports-network-withespn/?ref=sports (accessed January 20, 2011).

Shaikin, B. 2011. Fox advances Frank McCourt money to help cover Dodgers' operating expenses. *Los Angeles Times*, January 15, online edition, http://www.latimes.com/sports/la-sp-0115-mccourt-dodgers-20110115,0,7861995.story (accessed January 17, 2011).

Shiller, R. 2005. *Irrational exuberance*. New York: Random House.

Smith, E. 2011a. Texas, ESPN reach $300 million deal to air Longhorn Network. *USA Today*, January 19, online edition, http://content.usatoday.com/communities/campusrivalry/post/2011/01/texas-espn-agreement-longhorn-network/1 (accessed January 19, 2011).

Smith, E. 2011b. Report: ESPN will pay Texas $12 million per year to distribute the Longhorn Network. *USAToday.Com*, January 19, http://content.usatoday.com/communities/campusrivalry/post/2010/11/report-espn-will-pay-texas-12-million-per-year-to-distributethe-longhorn-network/1 (accessed January 19, 2011).

Vernellis, B. 2010. Michigan athletic department projects revenues to top $100 million in 2010-11. *AnnArbor.Com*, June 17, http://www.annarbor.com/sports/athletic-department-projects-revenues-to-top-100-million-in-2010-11/ (accessed January 19, 2011).

Chapter 8

What Are Teams Worth? Team Valuation

Introduction

This chapter focuses on the private valuation of sports franchises. While the financial techniques used in this chapter can be applied to find the value of bonds used to finance facilities, preferred stock, or common stock, most of this chapter applies valuation techniques to the value of sports teams. Many financial analysts spend most of their time valuing companies. Creating a value from a stock's price is one valid method because that price represents the market's values of "shares" of a company. A stock price should represent the net present value of all future dividends. For the most part, sports teams are no different. The value of a team should represent all of the discounted future profits.* Some would argue that owners purchase a sports franchise for fun or for the prestige of controlling something that is so popular and important to so many people. If that is true, this welfare benefit could account for a substantial portion of the value of a team and could be far greater than the future value of anticipated or expected profits. Even if that is the case, the financial value should still be affected by the discounted value of future profits. Valuing firms, however, is always easier said than done.

---

* While there are various valuation techniques including liquidation and accounting, relative, and contingent claim techniques, this chapter mainly focuses on discounted cash flow techniques.

There is also an important political reason to focus on valuations. In the midst of recent confrontations between players and owners in the NFL, for example, the Players Association was careful to point out that the owners' claims of failing business models and the need to reduce compensation levels seemed difficult to accept when even franchises in smaller-market teams, such as the Indianapolis Colts, were estimated to be worth in excess of $1 billion. The value of the Colts was estimated by *Forbes* to be $332 million ($427 million in 2010 dollars) in 2000. With a 2010 value of $1.04 billion, franchise owner James Irsay has seen the value of his asset rise 144 percent in real terms in a decade. To be fair, the value of the team had shrunk from an apex of $1.076 billion in 2008, but that loss in the midst of the severe recession, to the Players Association was an indicator of a successful business model, not one that needed substantial changes to attract investors or ensure owners of a substantial return on their investment.

Establishing a Team's Market Value: Basic Observations

Valuing teams can have some familiar obstacles for financial analysts. In any industry, it is difficult to guess or estimate future profits. In that way, valuing firms is very different from establishing the value of a financial asset for which all cash flows are known barring default. Because firms entail much more risk and uncertainty than bonds, future profits are difficult to estimate. This increased level of risk should increase the required return for investors. If a firm faces more risk, this will decrease the value relative to another firm with the same expected profits and less risk. Also, future discount rates can be difficult to estimate because they are constantly changing. Furthermore, it can be difficult to obtain accurate financial data for most teams and we usually have to rely on estimates of data. Finally, the value of a company can depend on how much of a company the investor owns. For example, often investors will purchase 51 percent of a company. This is called a "controlling interest" and that individual or partnership will have complete control of the firm's decisions. This could drastically increase the value to that majority owner.

Valuing sports teams also can have some unique obstacles for financial analysts. First, some owners might view owning a team as "consumption," or something, as noted earlier, acquired to gain prestige. That means that the owner did not buy the team to maximize profits or for financial returns on the investment. Rather, the buyer is seeking to maximize a set of intangible, but valuable, gains. If team owners buy a sports team because they think it is useful for a community, creates prestige, or is simply fun, then it can be hard to put a price tag on the team using financial tools.

Second, because teams are becoming part of entertainment, real estate, or media conglomerates, it is not always easy to know how the team contributes to the profits of the related businesses. For example, some team owners own multiple teams as well as media, food, or other entertainment companies. If this is the case, there can be efficiencies to owning multiple teams. If a media company owns the team, it may be easier to get the team's games on television, which could help both the media company and the team. Certainly a food or beverage company will sponsor the team in some way or at least sell their products in the facility. If an entertainment company owns a team, the same facility can sometimes be used for other nonsports events. So, it can be difficult to determine the value of the contribution of the team to the corporation's bottom line. This also means that the team can have a different value depending on who buys the team.

This type of relationship is even more complex in college athletics. A successful college team can increase donations to the university (although the effect on donations to academics is ambiguous) and attract more students. Furthermore, an athletic team can completely change the image of a school, good or bad. It is hard to know what the value of that is. While most college athletic departments lose money and many are subsidized by the school's general fund, a similar observation could be made regarding many academic departments. For example, excess revenues from a successful professional school could be used to ensure that a philosophy or foreign language department continues to provide opportunities to students. In many cases, the entire value of an athletic department comes from ancillary benefits it brings to the university.

Third, given the league structure, policies can dramatically affect a team's value. Salary caps, luxury taxes, revenue sharing, and player drafts all have a large impact on a team's value. All of these policies help small-market teams and some probably increase franchise values of all teams. Some leagues, like the NFL, share most of their revenue. Because of this, most of the team values are relatively close together. In some other major sports leagues, there is not as much revenue sharing and the profit level can vary dramatically. This implies that the team values also will vary dramatically.

An overview of financial theory precedes the actual assessment of valuation techniques to provide you, the sports manager, with an understanding of the ways to think about team values. Even if the available data make it difficult to use the equations introduced below, the different models illustrate the crucial factors that enter into a valuation estimate. Lastly, the values of the major professional leagues and some college teams are examined.

Valuation Models

If the profits generated by a team were known and it also was clear how the team affected other businesses owned by the same individual, partners, or conglomerate, then with the application of an appropriate discount rate, an accurate value could be established. The one exception to this is if an owner is buying the team to secure intangible benefits (e.g., prestige, fun, or to advance a community without any pecuniary gain for the team owner). If a purchase is made to secure intangible benefits, there is little need to perform a financial valuation of the franchise. Assuming the team is bought as a financial investment, the value of the team is equal to the present value of all future profits the team expects to gain over an infinite horizon. This equation is given by:

$$Value = \frac{\pi_1}{\left(1+r\right)^1} + \frac{\pi_2}{\left(1+r\right)^2} + \dots + \frac{\pi_\infty}{\left(1+r\right)^\infty} = \sum_{t=1}^{\infty} \frac{\pi_t}{\left(1+r\right)^t}$$

where π_t is the team's profit's in year t and r is the required return. The required return represents the owner's discount rate. Of course, the problem with this model is that an analyst does not know exactly what future profits will be. Therefore, typically financial models are used that assume certain things about future profits. Another possibility is that firms are valued by using some kind of industry standard. What follows are a few of the more common valuation techniques.

Multiple Earnings

One basic valuation model that is occasionally discussed in the sports industry is the multiple earnings approach. This approach is rarely, if at all, mentioned in general finance texts because it is not very useful. The only reason to use this is when there is very little data available, which is often the case in sports. Even in sports, however, while there is little data available to the outside observer, potential buyers may have far more information. Therefore, this method is typically used to simply generate a gross estimate of the team's value. Using the multiple earnings approach, the value of a team is considered to be some multiple (an industry rule of thumb) of revenue. The formula for the multiple earnings approach is

$$Value = Multiple \cdot Revenue$$

where *Multiple* simply represents some number.

The limitations of this approach are clear. Most obviously, costs are not taken into account. Also, the growth of future revenues or profits is not considered. In order for this method to be remotely accurate, the analyst must be comparing two very similar teams. For example, suppose the revenue for the New York Islanders was $100 million last year and they were sold for $600 million. In this case, the multiple is 6. Now suppose the New York Rangers had revenues of $150 million last year. The best guess might be that the Rangers were worth $900 million (150 × 6). This would assume, however, that costs were proportional for both teams and their future growth rates are expected to be identical. It is clear as well that the *Multiple* changes for leagues over time. So, while this approach might yield an approximate value with additional financial data, a more accurate franchise value could be projected.

Zero Growth Model

The zero growth model is only slightly more sophisticated than the multiple earnings approach. For some assets, however, it is more appropriate. As the name implies, this model assumes that any cash flow (in our case, profits) does not change. As with the multiple earnings approach, there are clear drawbacks with using this model to value a firm. There are some assets that give a constant return, such as annuities. Annuities can include bond payments or some stock dividends. These have a fixed payment. The problem is that a team's profits are usually not constant. On the other hand, one's best guess might be that, on average, a team's profits might not change much in the foreseeable future. Or, even if one expects profits to change, it is completely unclear if profits will increase or decrease. If this is the case, the following equation can be used:

$$Value = \frac{\pi}{\left(1+r\right)^1} + \frac{\pi}{\left(1+r\right)^2} + \dots + \frac{\pi}{\left(1+r\right)^\infty} = \sum_{t=1}^{\infty} \frac{\pi}{\left(1+r\right)^t} = \frac{\pi}{r}$$

The big advantage of using a zero growth model is that mathematically it is very simple to use. The value equals the yearly profits divided by the discount rate (or required return). If the discount rate is 10 percent (.1), then the value of a firm will be 10 times their yearly profits. If the discount rate is 5 percent, the value will be 20 times yearly profits.

Establishing Discount Rates and Value

Risk-free discount rates are typically (but not always) around 5 to 10 percent. This means that 1 divided by the discount rate is roughly 10 to 20. If we know the value and profits for a firm or team are known, then that tells a manager something about what people expect future profits to be. If the value divided by profits is less than 10, then people expect profits to decrease (either that or it is undervalued). If value divided by profits is more than 20, profits are expected to grow.

For example, there have been spikes in oil prices over the past few years. When the price of oil rises sharply, profits for many oil companies increase. When this has happened, however, the price to earnings ratio (analogous to value divided by profits) was around 3 or 4 for some of the oil companies. This implied that the market did not expect high profits to last and there would be a negative growth rate of profits in the future. So, even though the price of these stocks increased, they did not increase proportionately to the increase in profits.

Historically, the average price to earnings ratio for the S&P 500 since 1920 has been approximately 16.* But, in 1920, the average price to earnings ratio hit a low of 4.78 and in 1999 reached 44. This either means that investors expected very high growth rates in 1999 or stocks were overpriced. It is easy to look back and argue that stocks were probably overpriced, but at the time many were arguing that profits would dramatically increase. Even today, one could make the case that stocks were not overpriced given the information investors had. It could be that there was "irrational exuberance" in the market, or maybe there was great potential that was not realized.

A similar situation might exist for professional sports. The value of sports franchises seem to be much more than 20 times their profit. In fact, sometimes the teams lose money and are still valued highly. This relationship between value and profits implies one of three things. First, the team's profits may not include all of the benefits of owning a team (consumption value, effect on other related businesses, etc.). Second, owners and potential buyers may expect profits to dramatically increase in the future. That may not be a bad assumption and, in some cases, that has happened with sports teams. The other explanation is that owners are simply paying too much for franchises. While this explanation may seem appealing to some, owners usually did not become wealthy by making bad investments.

Constant Growth Model

A useful approach to valuing stocks or firms is the constant growth model, otherwise known as the Gordon model. The reason this is so useful is that a financial analyst can use it to try and predict the future growth of profits. This methodology might not be as useful for very young firms, but it works quite well for more established businesses. The zero growth model is actually a special case of the constant growth model; it assumes that the profit growth is zero. Growth estimates of profits are almost always wrong, but, more often than not, they should be more accurate than assuming a growth rate of zero. If profits grow at a constant rate, the value of a firm can be given by:

$$Value = \frac{\pi(1 + g)}{(1 + r)^1} + \frac{\pi(1 + g)^2}{(1 + r)^2} + \ldots + \frac{\pi(1 + g)^\infty}{(1 + r)^\infty} = \sum_{t=1}^{\infty} \frac{\pi}{(1 + r)^t} = \frac{\pi}{r - g}$$

---

* http://www.multpl.com/

where g is the expected growth rate of profits.* Using a constant growth rate, the value is the profits divided by the difference of the required return and the growth rate. If a team can grow their profits close to the required rate of return, their franchise value would be very high.

One drawback of this model is that it does assume one growth rate. This model is not as useful if the growth rate varies from year to year. Because it can be a challenge to estimate a constant rate of growth, it can be nearly impossible to know if the actual growth rate will increase or decrease. Another drawback is that it is not very useful if a team is currently experiencing a loss. It is not uncommon for sports teams to be experiencing a loss, but expecting profits in the future.

Capital Asset Pricing Model (CAPM)

The most sophisticated model examined in this chapter is the CAPM. This model is often used for stocks, which represent a firm's value. The model can also be used to find a team's value. Furthermore, even if the exact equations of the CAPM are not used, there is value in understanding how risk affects value. The benefit of this model is that it takes into account risk. Essentially, if risk is higher, then the required return (discount rate) also should be higher. In other words, investors or potential buyers do not like assets that have highly variable returns. If a team's profits are very different year to year, then that team's value will be smaller than a team with constant profits (assuming their average profits are the same).

The drawback is that estimating risk can be more difficult than estimating future profits. If the level of risk for an asset or firm is known, the CAPM works well. If the level of risk is hard to determine, then other models might work better. Typically risk is measured by past performance. If a financial analyst knows past profits, then they should also know the variation of those profits. Research has shown that a company's past returns often have little correlation with their historical risk level (Fama and French, 1992). But again, at the very least, this model helps us understand the relationship between risk and value.

The CAPM model is somewhat similar to the constant growth model, but the difference is in the required return. In the CAPM, the required return is given by:

$$r_{required} = r_{risk\,free} + \beta(r_{market} - r_{risk\,free})$$

where $r_{required}$ is the required return, $r_{risk\,free}$ is the risk-free rate, β is the beta value and r_{market} is the market rate. The risk-free rate is the return that investors can get with no risk to themselves. Investments with the least amount of risk are usually bonds or treasury bills. Therefore, the risk-free rate is equal to the returns on these types of investments. The market rate is the return on the market portfolio of all

---

* Mathematically, it is important to note that the growth rate cannot be bigger than the required return. If this were the case, the firm or team would have an infinite value.

traded securities. This represents the average return on all investments in a market. Sometimes this can be represented by some stock market index.

The beta value represents risk. Specifically, the beta value indicates how risky an investment is compared to the market average. For example, if an investment's beta value is 2, then that asset is twice as risky as the market average. The return of an investment that is twice as responsive as the market should change 2 percent for every 1 percent change in the market's return. If the market increases by 3 percent, then an investment with a beta of 2 should increase by 6 percent. By definition, the average beta value is 1. If an investment has a beta value of less than one, then it is not as risky as an average investment. A risk-free investment has a beta value of 0. Some investments have negative beta values. That is, they are countercyclical. When the market increases, some investments decrease. Countercyclical investments are good to have if the economy is in decline. The CAPM shows that if returns or profits are risky, then the required return is higher. In other words, investors need to expect a higher return if they are taking on more risk. This model helps us understand the tradeoff between risk and reward.

Now that we know what determines the required return, we can use that to find a team's value. We simply use the required return and put it into the constant growth model so the value is determined by:

$$Value = \frac{\pi}{r_{risk\ free} + \beta(r_{market} - r_{risk\ free}) - g} = \frac{\pi}{r_{required} - g}$$

As stated before, if the risk increases, the required return increases. Because the required return is in the denominator. If the required return goes up, the value of the firm decreases. More risk means lower value. This implies that teams should try to decrease their risk as much as possible in order to increase the value of their franchise.

Free Cash Flow Model

Another valuation technique is the free cash flow model. Free cash flow is defined as the available cash flow that investors can access. "Investors" include all providers of debt and equity. More formally, free cash flow is the difference between cash flows from operations and capital expenditures. This method might be preferred over the others if a team is not as established. Older teams have a history of profits, which can be used to estimate valuations (although outside analysts have a hard time getting reliable profit values). The free cash flow is similar to other models that use profit or dividends in that it estimates the present value of money, but it uses free cash flows instead of profits. Mathematically, the free cash flow models are similar to models that use profits.

Other Factors Affecting Value

While financial models create an understanding of the factors that are considered in (1) owning a team and then (2) determining its value, there are other things that need to be taken into consideration. The ownership structures described earlier in the book identify many of these factors. Because many teams have become the cornerstone for entertainment complexes, much of the value of these teams can come from ensuring the success or value of other capital assets. For example, the Yankees increase the value of the YES network and numerous teams increase profits for businesses around a facility. The Lakers and Kings create value for LA LIVE. These values may or may not show up on the team's income statements, but these are very real values that can be leveraged by an owner.

Having majority ownership, or a controlling interest, is often important. The majority owner does not need anyone's permission to make business decisions. This flexibility can be important especially when owners are involved in other businesses related to the team. That could mean a franchise's value might be greater for someone who also owns other businesses that capitalize on the team's operations. Also, if an entrepreneur owns other sports teams, it might be more efficient to be a multiple team owner. Another example is that a team might be more valuable to a media company. Sports teams and media companies often merge and use each other to increase profits. Given the extraordinary public image or "footprint" of a sports team, and the increasingly complex ownership structures, much of the value of a team can be derived from multiple uses.

Another problem with valuing sports teams is that it is difficult getting accurate financial data. Although some data are available, these are usually estimates, meaning the resulting valuations are approximations. Furthermore, when accurate data are available, the full value may still be unclear as money and profits can be shifted between related businesses (e.g., the Lakers and LA LIVE or the Detroit Tigers and Olympia Entertainment). If a media company owns a team, it could either pay too much or too little for broadcast rights fees so that the team's financial statements show either artificially inflated or deflated revenues. Typically, team owners have an incentive to show a financial loss or low levels of operating profits as underscored by the recent confrontations by various players' associations and team owners. Claiming a loss is one way owners can portray players as greedy. Recent disclosures of the financial records of the Florida Marlins and Los Angeles Dodgers illustrated that some owners entered their own salaries and salaries of family members as expenses thereby lowering profits (and illustrating operating losses). It is often very difficult to estimate profits as teams can obscure costs and shift revenues to other entities.

Other benefits to team owners that do not show up on financial statements are tax shelters from owning a team. For example, the roster depreciation allowance is clearly worth quite a bit to owners, but the financial statements show this as a depreciation of the players. In other words, while they might show losses on their tax forms, they might actually be making quite a bit of profit.

Yet another issue with valuing sports teams is the variety of league policies and franchise fees. Policies, such as revenue sharing, luxury taxes, and salary caps, can have a profound impact on a team's value and will affect small-market teams much differently than large-market teams. Also, if the league is successful, then new teams will be created and incumbent teams can expect payments in the form of franchise fees. League policies and future franchise fees can be difficult to predict.

What Is the Value of NFL, MLB, NBA, and NHL Franchises?

The price of a major sports franchise has certainly increased across the past few decades. This is true for all NFL, MLB, NBA, and NHL teams. Furthermore, when the changes in valuation are analyzed, it should be noted that most analysts have to disregard any profits taken out of the company. Just because team value increases or decreases, does not imply that the team was a good or bad investment. In other words, if owners are receiving a profit every year, then an increase in franchise value is only part of the return on their investment. Still, it is certainly worthwhile to look at how values have changed.

Most teams have enjoyed large increases in revenue streams, especially media contracts that have created elevated franchise values and sale prices. While NHL franchise values also have seen tremendous growth across the past few decades, they have not enjoyed the same level of media income as teams in other leagues. Nonetheless, NHL teams have seen dramatic increases in franchise values. As the theoretical models show, revenues and profits are key in determining franchise values. Therefore, everything that affects revenues affects values. Revenues (for each team) in the NFL are somewhat homogeneous. With salary caps and a high amount of revenue sharing, there is not as much difference in the relative values of NFL franchises. Therefore, it is harder to find team-specific determinants. Alexander and Kern (2004) found that team performance is still important for NFL franchise values. Variables, such as regional population and a new stadium, do not significantly increase values in the NFL to the extent that it does in other professional sports leagues.

In other leagues, revenues are more heterogeneous. In the NBA, NHL, and MLB there is a large difference between the most valuable team and lease valuable team in the league. In addition, the NFL does not allow its owners to own other teams in an NFL city. In the other leagues, cross-ownership is permitted. Owners can use the same infrastructure to operate multiple teams, which decreases cost and increases franchise value (Fort, 2006).

With the increase in size of facilities and with the addition of luxury seating, revenues are increasing, which, in turn, further elevates franchise values. A smaller percentage of facility-based revenue is coming from the typical ticket sales and more revenue is coming from luxury seating, advertising, and sponsorships. In addition, with some new massive facilities being built, owners of some NFL teams are seeing a larger percentage of their revenues coming from non-NFL events in their stadiums.

Because facility revenues affect franchise values, how the building was financed is also important. A new facility should always increase revenues, but at what cost? Because professional sports teams often receive some level of public support, how the stadium is paid for is also important. For instance, if the team completely owns the facility or retains all revenues with little or no obligations for construction or maintenance, profits will increase more than if the public still owns the facility and assigns responsibility for maintenance to the team. In MLB, at least, the increase in revenue from completely owning the stadium is not enough to offset the cost of the public financing (Miller, 2007). While building a new facility may or may not be a good investment if the team has to pay for it, it is always a good investment for the team if the public pays for it.

As noted earlier, financial data for sports teams can be difficult to obtain. While much of their revenue that comes from national television contracts are known, there are other revenue streams that are not publicly disclosed. Without this crucial data, only estimated values can be included in the financial models. The nature of the Green Bay Packers ownership requires more disclosure, but the lack of data for other teams can make it difficult to know how to properly estimate the value of a franchise. Nonetheless, people are buying sports teams and their value must be determined. This chapter will compare and contrast four different ways of estimating a franchise's value. These methods are using actual sale data, *Financial World* and *Forbes* valuations, a multiple earnings approach, and present value models. There are strengths and weaknesses with each of these methods.

Sale Prices

The obvious advantage of examining actual sale prices is that this is what people are willing to pay to own a team. These values should include any ancillary benefits as well as any consumption values realized by the new owner. Ultimately, any company is worth what investors are willing to pay. The drawback of using actual sale data is that there are few observations and the sale price of one team may not be transferable to other teams. Furthermore, the exact structure of the sale might not be known and even if it is known, it is difficult to separate the team from other things, such as the facility and terms for its use, and land or other assets related to the team. Not only are the exact details of a deal frequently not known, sometimes the dollar figures that are reported in the media are disputed. The disclosure in 2011 that the Wilpon family was considering the sale of part of the Mets illustrates the complexity of valuation. The family repeatedly stated that the network of which the team is a part would not be included in the sale even though several potential buyers noted the network was a more valuable asset to the team.

The NFL has been relatively successful since the 1920s. The sale price of NFL franchises proves that the league has clearly been a robust financial success. Over the past two decades, profits have dramatically increased. The NFL is the most valuable sports league in the world and *Forbes* estimated that in 2010 the average NFL team was worth more than $1 billion. Media contracts in the NFL have been growing at a very rapid pace and larger stadiums were built in numerous cities. Quirk and Fort (1992) give a useful history of sports franchise values from the 1920s through 1990 and show that franchise values had extremely high growth rates since the NFL's beginning in the 1920s. The average annual return from 1920 to 1990 for an NFL team was about 20 percent. In 1926, the Duluth Kellys (later the Washington Redskins) were bought for one dollar and the team's debts. While the team's debt may have been significant, buying the Redskins for a dollar was not a bad investment since *Forbes* estimates the 2010 value of the franchise to be $1.55 billion. This would mean a yearly return of more than 28 percent sustained across 83 years. Given this rate of return, complicated financial theory is not needed to illustrate that values have dramatically increased, even compared with other investments. While one can find investments with higher growth rates (across the past 25 years, the growth in Microsoft® stock has been about 42 percent, but then again, one would still need 23-percent growth for 59 years to equal the Redskins' rate for 84 years), buying an NFL team in the 1920s was a good investment by any standard. On the other hand, it should be noted that most of this massive growth took place in the 1920s. While buying an NFL team in today's market might be a good investment, it is not likely the goldmine it was when the NFL first started.

Table 8.1 shows NFL franchise sales across the past 20 years; there have been 26 sales since 1991. As the limited details of these transactions show, NFL teams can be part of a relatively complicated ownership structure. For example, regarding the 2009 partial sale of the Pittsburgh Steelers, the percentage sold is not even known. Therefore, the values can be difficult to ascertain. Nevertheless, the fifth column in Table 8.1 creates an estimated value of the team by taking the sale price divided by the percentage of the team that was sold. Table 8.1 also compares the sale prices with *Financial World/Forbes* estimated values; those numbers will be discussed later.

The growth rate in the value of MLB franchises was not quite as impressive as those for NFL franchises during the twentieth century, in part because the league was established earlier. Although MLB values did grow quite rapidly during the 1960s, 1970s, and 1980s, the average annual growth rate of from 1901 to 1990 was 7.5 percent (Quirk and Fort, 1992). While this seems paltry compared to the NFL, 7.5 percent is still a respectable growth rate and it is for a longer time period. Across this time period, there are many instances of team values rapidly changing in both positive and negative directions. For example, it has been reported that George Steinbrenner bought the New York Yankees for $8.8 million ($44 million in 2010 dollars) in 1973. Given that in 2010, *Forbes* estimated the Yankees to be worth $1.6 billion, this is a growth rate of more than 15 percent for 37 years.

Table 8.1 Sale prices of NFL teams, 1991–2010

Year	Team	Price ($millions)	Percentage Sold[a]	Implied Value	Financial World/Forbes Estimate (Year if Different)	Percentage Difference
1991	New York Giants	75	50	150	150	0.0
1991	Minnesota Vikings	52	51	102	119	16.8
1993	Carolina Panthers	140	100, Expansion fee	140	161 (1995)	15.0
1993	Jacksonville Jaguars	140	100, Expansion fee	140	145 (1996)	3.6
1994	Miami Dolphins	109	85, Some debt	128	161	25.5
1994	Philadelphia Eagles	185	100, Some debt	185	172	–7.0
1994	New England Patriots	158	100	158	142	–10.1
1995	Tampa Bay Buccaneers	192	100	192	151	–21.4
1995	St. Louis Rams	60	30	200	186	–7.0
1997	Baltimore Ravens	32	9	356	235	–33.9
1997	Seattle Seahawks	200	100	200	171	–14.5
1998	Minnesota Vikings	206	96, Some debt	215	232	8.1
1998	Cleveland Browns	476	100, Expansion fee	476	557 (2000)	17.0
1998	St. Louis Rams	20	10	200	322	61.0
1999	Baltimore Ravens	275	49	561	408	–27.3

(continued)

Table 8.1 (continued) Sale prices of NFL teams, 1991–2010

Year	Team	Price ($millions)	Percentage Sold[a]	Implied Value	Financial World/Forbes Estimate (Year if Different)	Percentage Difference
1999	Washington Redskins	800	100	800	607	−24.1
1999	Houston Texans	700	100, Expansion fee	700	791 (2003)	13.0
2000	New York Jets	635	100	635	384	−39.5
2001	Atlanta Falcons	545	100	545	338	−38.0
2002	Atlanta Falcons	27	5	540	407	−24.6
2003	Washington Redskins	200	20	1,000	952	−4.8
2004	Baltimore Ravens	325	51	637	776	21.8
2005	Minnesota Vikings	600	100	600	658	9.7
2008	Miami Dolphins	550	100	1,100	1044	−5.1
2009	Pittsburgh Steelers	250	Not known	Not known	1020	
2009	Miami Dolphins	550	45	1,222	1015	−17.0

Average −3.3

Correlation between sale price and estimate = .947

[a] Although this lists the percentage of the team bought, there are typically many more details that should be considered. For example, there are often team debts that are assumed. Often there are also land or stadium issues involved with the sale. Many times owners are purchasing a larger percentage of a team of which they were part owner. Sometimes there are also other estimates of the amount paid.

Table 8.2 shows MLB franchise sales across the past 20 years. Since 1990, there have been 43 sales (or partial sales). MLB teams, on average, are not quite as valuable as NFL teams. In addition, the values of MLB franchises seem to vary more than those of NFL teams. For example, in 2002, the Boston Red Sox were sold for almost six times as much as the Montreal Expos were worth. Given that MLB does not share as much revenue as the NFL, the Red Sox are obviously able to capitalize on their large market and loyal fan base (Red Sox Nation).

The NBA historically has had growth rates more similar to the NFL, but it is not nearly as old. On average, franchise values grew at a rate of 16.5 percent from 1950 to 1990 (Quirk and Fort, 1992). Again, this is quite a remarkable rate of growth. At that rate, every dollar invested in a team in 1950 would be worth $450 dollars in 1990. Table 8.3 shows that NBA team prices are somewhat similar to those paid for MLB teams, but on average, they tend to be a bit lower. This is especially true on the high end. The most expensive teams are not as valuable; however, the Los Angeles Lakers have not been sold since 1979. The New York Knicks are a valuable team and are on the list, but their sale price involves ownership of Madison Square Garden and Cablevision, complicating interpretation of the team's value.

While there is less information about historical sale prices of NHL teams, Table 8.4 shows sale prices for NHL franchises across the past couple of decades. The variation in franchise values looks more like MLB and NBA than for teams in the NFL. Some teams, like the Montreal Canadiens, are worth much more than many of the other teams. On average, the value of NHL teams is the lowest of the four major North American sports leagues.

It is easy to look at Table 8.1 through Table 8.4 and observe that values have increased. The interesting question is by how much. With only a few observations, it is difficult to obtain a robust analysis, but it is possible to estimate growth rates. A regression analysis provides an estimate of how much franchise values increased across the past 20 years.*

Table 8.5 shows the estimated growth rates for each league. This basic analysis shows a 14.2 rate of growth for the NFL and between 8 and 10 percent for the other leagues. The average NHL team seems to be worth slightly more than half the value of MLB and NBA teams. As usual, there are many critiques of this basic analysis. One obvious problem is that only teams that were sold are included in the sample. This could give us flawed results. It is, however, interesting to see how the leagues compare with each other. A return of 14.2 percent in nominal terms across an 18-year period is

---

* A regression was done using logged franchise value as the dependent variable and the year as the only independent variable. By logging the estimated franchise values, we can calculate the growth rate easily. Therefore, we will use the following model,

$$\ln(value) = \beta_0 + \beta_1 YEAR + \varepsilon$$

A basic OLS regression was done (and assuming $YEAR = 1$ in 1991) and gives us the results in Table 8.5.

Table 8.2 Actual sale prices of MLB teams

Year	Team	Price ($millions)	Percentage Sold[a]	Implied Value	Financial World/Forbes Estimate (Year if Different)	Percentage Difference
1990	Montreal Expos	86	100	86	100	16.3
1990	San Diego Padres	75	100	75	85	13.3
1991	Florida Marlins	95	100, Expansion fee	95	81 (1994)	−14.7
1991	Toronto Blue Jays	60.3	45	134	178	33.1
1992	Colorado Rockies	95	100, Expansion fee	95	110 (1994)	15.8
1992	Houston Astros	115	100	115	95	−17.4
1992	Seattle Mariners	106	60	177	79	−55.4
1992	San Francisco Giants	100	100	100	99	−1.0
1993	Baltimore Orioles	173	100	173	130	−24.9
1993	Detroit Tigers	80	100	80	97	21.3
1994	San Diego Padres	94	100	94	85	−9.6
1995	Oakland A's	85	100	85	101	18.8
1996	Pittsburgh Pirates	90	100	90	62	−31.1
1996	St. Louis Cardinals	150	100	150	112	−25.3
1998	Arizona Diamondbacks	130	100, Expansion Fee	130	291 (1999)	123.8

1998	Los Angeles Dodgers	311	100	311	237	-23.8
1998	Tampa Bay Rays	130	100, Expansion fee	130	225 (1999)	73.1
1998	Texas Rangers	250	100	250	253	1.3
1999	Anaheim Angels	140	75	187	195	4.3
1999	Cincinnati Reds	183	Not known	Not known	163	
1999	Florida Marlins	158.5	100	159	153	-3.8
1999	Montreal Expos	50	35	143	84	-41.3
1999	New York Yankees	225	38	600	491	-18.2
2000	Cleveland Indians	323	100	323	364	12.7
2000	Kansas City Royals	96	100	96	122	27.1
2000	Toronto Blue Jays	112	80	140	162	15.7
2001	Colorado Rockies	35	24	148	334	125.7
2002	Boston Red Sox	700	100	700	428	-38.8
2002	Florida Marlins	158.5	100	159	137	-13.6
2002	Montreal Expos	120	100	120	108	-10.3
2002	New York Mets	150	50	300	483	61.2
2003	Anaheim Angels	184	100	184	225	22.3

(continued)

Table 8.2 (continued)   Actual sale prices of MLB teams

Year	Team	Price ($millions)	Percentage Sold[a]	Implied Value	Financial World/Forbes Estimate (Year if Different)	Percentage Difference
2004	Los Angeles Dodgers	371	100	371	399	7.5
2004	Arizona Diamondbacks	Not known	100	Not known	276	
2004	Cincinnati Reds	6.1	7	91	245	169.2
2004	Colorado Rockies	20	14	143	285	99.3
2005	Milwaukee Brewers	220	100, Some debt	220	208	−5.5
2005	Oakland A's	180	Not Known	Not Known	185	
2006	Cincinnati Reds	270	100	270	274	1.5
2006	Washington Nationals	450	100	450	440	−2.2
2007	Atlanta Braves	450	100	450	458	1.8
2009	Chicago Cubs	845	95	845	700	−17.2
2010	Texas Rangers	593	100	593	451	−23.9

Average 12.2

Correlation between sale price and estimate = 0.879

[a] Although this lists the percentage of the team bought, there are typically many more details that should be considered. For example, there are often team debts that are assumed. Often there are also land or facility issues involved with the sale. Many times minority or majority owners are purchasing a larger percentage of a team. Sometimes there are also other estimates of the amount paid.

Table 8.3 Sale prices of NBA teams

Year	Team	Price ($millions)	Percentage Sold[a]	Implied Value	Financial World/Forbes Estimate (Year if Different)	Percentage Difference
1991	Denver Nuggets	70	100	70	41	−42.0
1991	Orlando Magic	85	100	85	61	−28.5
1992	Golden State Warriors	21	25	84	63	−25.0
1992	Sacramento Kings	140	53	264	63	−76.1
1993	Houston Rockets	85	100	85	58	−31.8
1993	San Antonio Spurs	75	100	75	65	−13.3
1995	Golden State Warriors	95	75	127	83	−34.5
1995	Miami Heat	60	Not known	Not known	88	
1995	Minnesota Timberwolves	88.5	Not known	Not known	99	
1995	New York Knicks	1,100	Not known	Not known	173	
1996	Minnesota Timberwolves	6	10	60	110	83.3
1996	Philadelphia 76ers	125	100	125	93	−25.6
1997	New York Knicks	850	Not known	Not known	250	
1998	New Jersey Nets	123	82	150	157	4.4

(continued)

Table 8.3 (continued)   Sale prices of NBA teams

Year	Team	Price ($millions)	Percentage Sold[a]	Implied Value	Financial World/Forbes Estimate (Year if Different)	Percentage Difference
1998	Sacramento Kings	250	53	472	119	−74.8
1998	Toronto Raptors	408	100	408	121	−70.3
1999	Charlotte Hornets	80	35	229	136	−40.5
1999	New York Knicks	1,430	Not known	Not known	334	
2000	Dallas Mavericks	280	54	519	167	−67.8
2000	Denver Nuggets	450	Not known	Not known	175	
2000	Vancouver Grizzlies	170	100	170	118	−30.6
2001	Atlanta Hawks	184	100	184	199	8.2
2001	Seattle Supersonics	200	100	200	200	0.0
2002	Boston Celtics	360	100	360	274	−23.9
2003	Toronto Raptors	71	Not known	Not known	249	

Year	Team					
2003	Charlotte Bobcats	300	100	300	225 (2004)	−25.0
2004	Atlanta Hawks	208	100	208	232	11.5
2004	New Jersey Nets	300	100	300	296	−1.3
2004	Phoenix Suns	401	100	401	356	−11.2
2004	Charlotte Hornets	65	35	186	225 (2005)	21.2
2005	Cleveland Cavaliers	375	100	375	356	−5.1
2006	Seattle Supersonics	350	100	350	268	−23.4
2010	Charlotte Bobcats	300	Not known	Not known	281	
2010	Golden State Warriors	450	100	450	363	−19.3
2010	Washington Wizards	170	56	304	322	5.9
						Average −19.8

Correlation between sale price and estimate = 0.628

a Although this lists the percentage of the team bought, there are typically many more details that should be considered. For example, there are often team debts that are assumed. Often there are also land or facility issues involved with the sale. Many times minority or majority owners are purchasing a larger percentage of a team. Sometimes there are also other estimates of the amount paid.

Table 8.4   Actual sale prices of NHL teams

Year	Team	Price ($millions)	Percentage Sold[a]	Implied Value	Financial World/Forbes Estimate (Year if Different)	Percentage Difference
1990	Minnesota North Stars	38.2	100	38	30 (1991)	−21.5
1990	Minnesota North Stars[b]	24.6	100	25	30 (1991)	22.1
1990	San Jose Sharks	45	100, Expansion fee	45	43 (1993)	−4.4
1991	Ottawa Senators	45	100, Expansion fee	45	50 (1994)	11.1
1991	Tampa Bay Lightning	45	100, Expansion fee	45	39 (1994)	−13.3
1992	Florida Panthers	50	100, Expansion fee	50	47 (1995)	−6.0
1992	Anaheim Mighty Ducks	50	100, Expansion fee	50	108 (1995)	116.0
1994	Hartford Whalers	47.5	100	48	46	−3.2
1994	Toronto Maple Leafs	54.9	Not known	Not known	77	
1995	Dallas Stars	84	100	84	50	−40.5
1995	Los Angeles Kings	113.3	100	113	81	−28.5
1995	Vancouver Canucks	80.2	Not known	Not known	87	
1996	Philadelphia Flyers	250	100	250	102	−59.2
1997	Atlanta Thrashers	80	100, Expansion fee	80	138 (2000)	72.5
1997	Columbus Blue Jackets	80	100, Expansion fee	80	145 (2001)	81.3

1997	Minnesota Wild	80	80	100, Expansion fee	135 (2001)	68.8
1997	Nashville Predators	80	80	100, Expansion fee	130 (1999)	62.9
1997	New York Rangers	195	195	100	147	−24.6
1998	Edmonton Oilers	68.8	69	100	67	−2.6
1998	Buffalo Sabres	76	76	100	91	19.7
1999	Pittsburgh Penguins	70	70	100	99	41.8
1999	St. Louis Blues	100	100	100	137	37.4
1999	Tampa Bay Lightning	115	115	100	113	−2.1
1999	Washington Capitals	85	85	100	144	69.5
2000	Colorado Avalanche	450	Not known	Not known	198	
2000	New Jersey Devils	175	Not known	Not known	163	
2000	New York Islanders	190	190	100	139	−26.8
2000	Phoenix Coyotes	125	125	100	86	-31.2
2001	Florida Panthers	104.7	105	100	115	9.8
2001	Montreal Canadiens	183	228	80	182	−20.3
2002	San Jose Sharks	80	94	85, Some debt	158	67.9
2003	Buffalo Sabres	92	92	100	95	3.3
2003	Toronto Maple Leafs	71	Not known	Not known	263	

(continued)

Table 8.4 (continued) Actual sale prices of NHL teams

Year	Team	Price ($millions)	Percentage Sold[a]	Implied Value	Financial World/Forbes Estimate (Year if Different)	Percentage Difference
2003	Ottawa Senators	100	100	100	117	17.0
2004	Atlanta Thrashers	250	85, Some debt	294	106	–64.0
2004	New Jersey Devils	125	100	125	124	–0.8
2005	Anaheim Mighty Ducks	75	100	75	157	109.3
2006	St. Louis Blues	150	100	150	144 (2007)	–4.0
2006	Vancouver Canucks	150	50	300	211 (2007)	–29.7
2007	Nashville Predators	193	100	193	143	–25.9
2007	Tampa Bay Lightning	206	100	206	199	–3.4
2008	Edmonton Oilers	200	100	200	175	–12.5
2009	Montreal Canadiens	575	100	575	339	–41.0

Average 9.1

Correlation between sale price and estimate = 0.792

[a] Although this lists the percentage of the team bought, there are typically many more details that should be considered. For example, there are often team debts that are assumed. Often there are also land or facility issues involved with the sale. Many times minority or majority owners are purchasing a larger percentage of a team. Sometimes there are also other estimates of the amount paid.

[b] The Minnesota North Stars were sold twice in 1990.

Table 8.5   Estimated franchise value growth rates from actual sales

League	Growth Rate (In Percent)	Number of Sales with Known Value
NFL	14.2	25
MLB	8.2	40
NBA	9.2	26
NHL	9.6	38

extraordinarily high. In fact, the rate of growth of the Dow Jones Industrial Average from January 1, 1991 to January 1, 2009, was 9.4 percent and for the NASDAQ it was 8.3 percent. Even MLB's growth rate of 8.2 percent is in a similar range.

Financial World *and* Forbes *Data*

Financial World provided valuation estimates for sports franchises from 1991 to 1997. *Forbes* has produced these estimates since 1998. The strength of the *Financial World/ Forbes* data is that it estimates values for teams for each year. Also, the authors of these estimates have some information on facility-based revenue, and then input that data into their proprietary formulae. The drawback is that much of the *Financial World/ Forbes* analysis is a "black box" or unknown. Furthermore, it is not clear that the revenue data that *Financial World/Forbes* uses are reliable. As previously stated, revenue data can be difficult to find. Even if revenue data are found, that may not show all of the benefits of owning a team. Of course, the valuation estimates can be compared with sales data to see how accurate those estimates have been.

Table 8.6 shows the Forbes valuations for 2010 and various growth rates for each team in the NFL using both *Financial World* and *Forbes* data. This data show an 11.4-percent return across the 19-year time period (compared to 14.2 using actual sale data). What is remarkable about the values is the lack of variability from team to team. The most valuable team is the Dallas Cowboys at $1.805 billion and the least valuable is the Jacksonville Jaguars at $725 million. While this range is larger than it has been in the past, the relative variation is much higher in other sports leagues. It is important to remember that most of the revenue is from national broadcasting agreements that are shared equally among the teams. The *Financial World/Forbes* data also compared with actual sale prices in Table 8.1. While the values can be incorrect by as much as 61 percent (Stan Kroenke paid $20 million for 10 percent of the Rams when it was valued at $322 million), on average, the valuation estimates are fairly accurate. On average, the estimates were 3.3 percent less than the actual sale value.

Table 8.7 shows the *Financial World/Forbes* data for MLB teams. The average value ($491 million) is actually less than half than that of NFL teams. What stands

Table 8.6 *Financial World/Forbes* valuation for the NFL

Team	2010 Value (in $millions)	Growth Rates (in percent)				
		1 year	3 year	5 year	10 year	19 year
Atlanta Falcons	831	-2.92	1.44	3.79	9.98	11.08
Baltimore Ravens (Browns)	1,073	-0.56	3.60	4.43	8.40	11.11
Buffalo Bills	799	-12.10	-0.90	2.45	8.15	10.23
Carolina Panthers	1,037	-1.14	2.75	3.38	7.29	
Chicago Bears	1,067	-1.39	2.74	4.14	12.83	11.90
Cincinnati Bengals	905	-5.04	-0.26	4.80	7.90	10.98
Cleveland Browns	1,015	-1.65	1.56	2.62	6.18	
Dallas Cowboys	1,805	9.39	6.36	11.17	9.73	12.90
Denver Broncos	1,049	-2.96	1.81	2.95	8.34	12.43
Detroit Lions	817	-6.31	-2.07	0.93	8.01	10.84
Green Bay Packers	1,018	-0.10	3.17	3.70	11.69	8.94
Houston Texans	1,171	1.83	3.51	4.36		
Indianapolis Colts	1,040	1.46	4.51	7.78	12.10	12.24
Jacksonville Jaguars	725	-16.28	-3.67	0.97	4.65	
Kansas City Chiefs	965	-6.04	0.17	4.84	10.15	11.48

Miami Dolphins	1,011	-0.39	2.38	3.38	7.91	8.76
Minnesota Vikings	774	-7.31	-0.34	3.30	9.17	10.35
New England Patriots	1,367	0.44	4.47	5.62	11.41	14.77
New Orleans Saints	955	1.38	3.80	5.87	11.42	11.34
New York Giants	1,182	-0.08	6.66	7.96	11.81	11.48
New York Jets	1,144	-2.22	5.76	9.13	11.53	12.36
Oakland (LA) Raiders	758	-4.89	-2.27	2.32	9.18	9.51
Philadelphia Eagles	1,119	-0.36	2.08	3.29	13.02	11.51
Phoenix/Arizona Cardinals	919	-1.71	1.15	6.43	11.66	11.31
Pittsburgh Steelers	996	-2.35	2.35	3.97	9.18	12.17
San Diego Chargers	907	-1.09	3.17	5.99	8.72	11.56
San Francisco 49ers	925	5.71	5.00	5.76	9.33	10.05
Seattle Seahawks	989	-0.50	2.40	3.74	9.28	11.28
St. Louis (LA) Rams	779	-14.68	-4.98	0.57	6.42	9.66
Tampa Bay Buccaneers	1,032	-4.88	2.33	3.31	6.85	12.29
Tennessee Titans (Oilers)	994	-0.60	2.54	3.45	6.99	11.80
Washington Redskins	1,550	0.00	1.85	4.16	7.66	14.17
Averages	1,022.4	-2.42	1.97	4.39	9.26	11.38

Table 8.7   Financial World/Forbes valuation for MLB

Team	2010 Value (in $millions)	Growth Rates (in percent)					
		1 year	3 year	5 year	10 year	20 year
Arizona Diamondbacks	379	-2.82	3.79	5.79	3.53	
Atlanta Braves	450	0.90	-0.59	3.33	1.49	8.69
Baltimore Orioles	376	-6.00	-1.63	1.97	0.81	6.85
Boston Red Sox	870	4.44	6.31	9.09	11.85	9.97
California/Anaheim/LA Angels	521	2.36	6.53	12.12	10.33	6.60
Chicago Cubs	726	3.71	7.04	12.77	11.61	8.78
Chicago White Sox	466	3.56	6.94	12.21	10.87	7.25
Cincinnati Reds	331	-3.22	2.54	5.36	6.58	6.73
Cleveland Indians	391	-2.01	2.41	4.15	0.72	7.93
Colorado Rockies	384	2.95	6.60	5.78	2.33	
Detroit Tigers	375	1.08	1.65	9.43	6.49	6.32
Florida Marlins	317	14.44	9.12	9.00	9.75	
Houston Astros	453	1.80	0.82	4.88	4.93	7.58
Kansas City Royals	341	8.60	6.54	12.77	10.83	5.36

Los Angeles Dodgers	727	0.69	4.78	11.39	8.38	7.38
Milwaukee Brewers	351	1.15	6.94	11.03	7.71	7.35
Minnesota Twins	405	13.76	12.04	17.87	16.10	7.52
New York Mets	858	-5.92	5.25	11.18	10.57	8.27
New York Yankees	1,600	6.67	10.06	10.99	11.31	10.96
Oakland Athletics	295	-7.52	0.34	9.78	8.21	6.42
Philadelphia Phillies	537	8.27	5.52	6.50	13.60	6.95
Pittsburgh Pirates	289	0.35	1.79	5.80	6.02	6.31
San Diego Padres	408	1.75	3.59	4.40	7.55	8.16
San Francisco Giants	483	2.55	1.71	4.86	7.38	9.08
Seattle Mariners	439	3.05	0.23	1.13	4.23	8.25
St. Louis Cardinals	488	0.41	1.99	5.69	8.34	6.44
Tampa Bay Devil Rays	316	-1.25	5.78	12.42	6.84	
Texas Rangers	451	11.36	7.31	6.71	4.37	7.82
Toronto Blue Jays	326	-7.65	-1.78	8.78	7.24	4.13
Washington Nationals (Expos)	387	-4.68	-4.69	4.54	15.83	7.00
Averages	491	1.76	3.96	8.06	7.86	7.47

out is the New York Yankees. Their value ($1.6 billion) is more than double that of most teams and more than five times the Pittsburgh Pirates. Table 8.7 also shows that the average growth rate across the past few decades has been less than the NFL, but the growth rate across the past five years has actually been higher than the NFL. Across the last 20 years, 7.5 percent is still a reasonably high growth rate (but not the 8.22 percent estimated using sale data). Comparing the *Financial World/ Forbes* value estimates with actual sale prices shows that the estimates are typically 13.1 percent higher than the actual price.

Table 8.8 shows the value estimates for NBA teams. The average 2010 value of an NBA team is $369 million while the most highly valued team (New York Knicks) is estimated to be worth $655 million. The NBA seems to have less variation than MLB. The Milwaukee Bucks are the least valued team at $258 million. While the recent downturn on the economy seems to have had a somewhat larger impact on NBA franchise values, across the past 19 years teams have had an average growth rate of nearly 10 percent, which is a high rate (slightly higher than the 9.2 percent estimated using sale data). Looking back at Table 8.3, what is striking is that the *Financial World/Forbes* data seems to consistently underestimate the value of NBA teams. On average, the estimates are 19.8 percent less than the actual sale value. Some of these deals include things like facilities, but that is true of the other leagues as well. It is not clear why these teams seem to be consistently undervalued.

Table 8.9 shows the valuations for NHL teams. The Toronto Maple Leafs are the most valuable team at $505 million while the Phoenix Coyotes are the least valuable at $134 million. The value of the Maple Leafs is less than all NFL teams, slightly more than the average MLB team, and lower than a number of NBA teams. The average value is "only" $228 million for NHL teams. Compared to the other three leagues, NHL franchises are certainly the least valuable. The average growth rate for NHL teams across 19 years is 9.4 percent (which is very close to our growth estimate of 9.6 percent for sale prices). While this is not as high as the NFL or NBA, it is higher than MLB, and most investors would accept a return of 9.4 percent.

Figure 8.1 shows the average *Financial World/Forbes* values for the four sports leagues across the past two decades. In Figure 8.1 the valuations are all in 2010 dollars. Notice that values have doubled in real terms across the past two decades. Considering there are many industries that have not grown at all in these years, major professional sports teams have been quite successful. The NFL has clearly been the most successful, benefitting from large television contracts.

Figure 8.2 shows the growth rates of average teams over time from the *Financial World/Forbes* data. In 1998, the NFL, MLB, and NHL all saw tremendous growth rates. This probably illustrates a problem with the data. In 1998, *Forbes* started calculating franchise values separate from *Financial World*. The graph does show some interesting things. Figure 8.2 actually tells an interesting story of recent NFL economic history. First, there is a spike in 1994. This is the year NFL owners successfully negotiated a salary cap. Ignoring 1998, there is still a large spike in 1999. Revenues from media contracts skyrocketed during this period. It is also interesting

Table 8.8 Financial World/Forbes valuation for the NBA

Team	2010 Value (in $millions)	Growth Rate (in percent)				
		1 year	3 year	5 year	10 year	19 year
Atlanta Hawks	295	-3.59	1.04	2.40	4.83	9.40
Boston Celtics	452	4.39	4.95	5.07	7.86	4.97
Charlotte Bobcats	281	1.08	-0.70	-1.30		
Chicago Bulls	511	0.00	0.73	4.55	4.99	8.96
Cleveland Cavaliers	355	-25.42	-7.94	-0.06	6.73	9.70
Dallas Mavericks	438	-1.79	-1.69	1.68	10.12	11.60
Denver Nuggets	316	-1.56	-0.52	2.23	6.09	11.40
Detroit Pistons	360	-24.84	-8.95	-2.18	4.31	4.72
Golden State Warriors	363	15.24	5.52	8.36	8.01	10.92
Houston Rockets	443	-5.74	-1.39	0.98	7.96	11.29
Indiana Pacers	269	-4.27	-6.87	-3.65	1.49	11.62
Los Angeles Clippers	305	3.39	1.23	4.22	7.07	10.88
Los Angeles Lakers	643	5.93	4.71	3.98	5.97	6.34
Memphis (Vancouver) Grizzlies	266	3.50	-4.35	-1.98	8.47	
Miami Heat	425	16.76	0.56	3.26	6.57	10.99

(continued)

Table 8.8 (continued) Financial World/Forbes valuation for the NBA

Team	2010 Value (in $millions)	Growth Rate (in percent)					
		1 year	3 year	5 year	10 year	19 year
Milwaukee Bucks	258	1.57	−0.76	2.24	7.01	8.63
Minnesota Timberwolves	264	−1.49	−5.01	−2.72	4.56	9.02
New Jersey Nets	312	15.99	−2.63	2.86	5.71	11.05
New Orleans (Charlotte) Hornets	280	4.87	0.97	4.47	6.88	8.48
New York Knicks	655	11.77	2.51	3.82	5.19	10.40
Oklahoma City Thunder (Supersonics)	329	6.13	6.94	7.05	5.81	12.14
Orlando Magic	385	6.65	6.14	9.28	8.84	10.20
Philadelphia 76ers	330	−4.07	−4.59	−1.23	3.54	8.11
Phoenix Suns	411	−4.20	−2.90	0.80	5.01	7.78
Portland Trail Blazers	356	5.33	12.06	9.42	2.73	9.83
Sacramento Kings	293	−3.93	−8.70	−3.21	5.11	9.86
San Antonio Spurs	404	1.51	−0.08	2.91	7.89	12.05
Toronto Raptors	399	3.37	2.27	7.49	10.43	
Utah Jazz	343	0.00	0.10	4.59	4.26	11.30
Washington Wizards	322	2.88	−2.56	0.25	4.37	11.98
Averages	368.8	0.98	−0.33	2.52	6.13	9.76

Table 8.9 *Financial World/Forbes valuation for the NHL*

Team	2010 Value (in $millions)	Growth Rate (in percent)				
		1 year	3 year	5 year	10 year	19 year
Anaheim Mighty Ducks	188	-8.74	-1.55	3.67	4.95	
Atlanta Thrashers	135	-5.59	-3.02	1.07	-0.22	
Boston Bruins	302	11.44	7.51	5.14	3.36	9.13
Buffalo Sabres	169	-0.59	1.42	2.55	5.71	8.32
Calgary Flames	206	3.00	7.90	8.82	9.65	7.51
Carolina Hurricanes (Hartford)	162	-8.47	1.27	2.38	7.45	6.92
Chicago Blackhawks	300	16.28	18.78	12.30	4.30	10.50
Colorado Avalanche (Quebec)	198	-3.41	-2.56	-2.00	0.00	8.11
Columbus Blue Jackets	153	-7.27	0.66	1.94		
Dallas Stars (Minnesota)	227	-7.72	-3.68	-1.75	2.23	11.24
Detroit Red Wings	315	-6.53	2.44	4.07	3.75	10.96
Edmonton Oilers	183	10.24	5.24	4.62	9.04	6.89
Florida Panthers	168	5.66	3.62	3.42	1.34	
Los Angeles Kings	215	3.37	0.95	0.96	3.00	8.58
Minnesota Wild	202	-3.81	3.92	4.38		

(continued)

Table 8.9 (continued)   Financial World/Forbes valuation for the NHL

Team	2010 Value (in $millions)	Growth Rate (in percent)				
		1 year	3 year	5 year	10 year	19 year
Montreal Canadiens	408	20.35	12.97	12.15	7.89	10.69
Nashville Predators	148	−5.13	1.15	2.01	1.38	
New Jersey Devils	218	−2.24	3.79	8.05	2.95	10.11
New York Islanders	151	1.34	0.45	1.52	0.83	5.79
New York Rangers	461	10.82	8.09	8.54	5.77	11.90
Ottawa Senators	196	−0.51	1.76	4.27	8.84	
Philadelphia Flyers	301	10.26	7.25	4.12	2.29	10.81
Phoenix Coyotes (Winnipeg)	134	−2.90	−3.04	−1.29	4.53	8.20
Pittsburgh Penguins	235	5.86	14.88	12.06	5.94	9.56
San Jose Sharks	194	5.43	5.55	6.00	3.24	
St Louis Blues	165	−6.25	4.64	1.92	1.95	9.09
Tampa Bay Lightning	145	−24.08	−10.01	−3.36	3.09	
Toronto Maple Leafs	505	7.45	6.93	8.75	9.54	13.54
Vancouver Canucks	262	9.62	7.48	6.41	10.11	10.17
Washington Capitals	197	7.65	10.76	9.18	3.93	9.05
Average	228.1	1.18	3.85	4.40	4.53	9.38

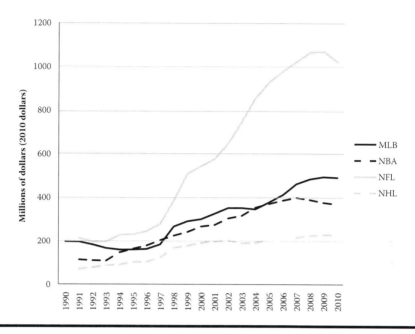

Figure 8.1   Average franchise values, all leagues.

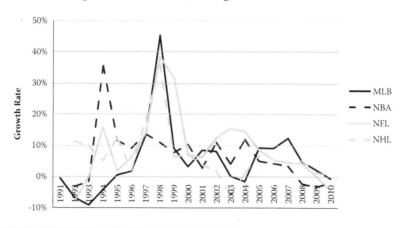

Figure 8.2   Real growth rates of average franchise values.

looking at MLB. Their franchise values were very flat in the early 1990s. This may be due to labor strife during this period. The NBA saw an increase in franchise values in 1994. This is probably largely due to a new league television contract. All leagues experienced low growth in 2008 and 2009, which shows the effect of the recession on sports.

Finally, Figure 8.3 illustrates a measure of relative dispersion in team values for the four leagues. Specifically, it shows the coefficient of variation for each league.

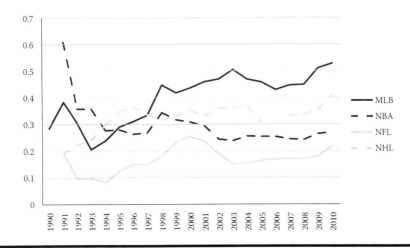

Figure 8.3 Coefficient of variation of franchise values.

The coefficient of variation is the standard deviation of team values divided by the average value. This gives a measure of the relative variability of team values. The NFL consistently has the lowest coefficient of variation, meaning that the team values do not differ much from each other. This makes sense because they share a great deal of their revenue. MLB has the highest coefficient of variation. Presumably this is because they share relatively little revenue and also MLB does not have any kind of salary cap that would tend to equalize revenue. Also interesting, while a sluggish economy has certainly made average team values stagnant, the coefficient of variation seems to be creeping up. This means that some teams are being affected much more than other teams by a poor economy.

When one looks at the *Financial World/Forbes* data compared to the actual sale prices, it is natural to ask: Is *Financial World/Forbes* right or do buyers have a better sense of the value? Often when buyers "overpay" relative to these estimates pundits wonder why they paid so much. Potential buyers may have more information or better analysts. Also, remember that these deals are often complicated (not just the team is sold) and the value often depends on the owners other holdings and assets.

Multiple Earnings

Another valuation technique that is sometimes used in sports is the multiple of earnings approach. This approach simply multiplies revenue by some number to find the value of the firm. In 2001, when Bud Selig testified before the U.S. Congress, he gave values for all Major League Baseball franchises. Most baseball franchise values were quite close to twice their annual revenue. Also, on *Forbes's* website, Badenhausen, Ozanian, and Settimi (2009) reported in their opening paragraph that the 2009 economy had decreased "the average revenue multiple used to value teams from 4.7 to 4.4." It seems to be accepted by everyone that sports franchise values should be based on a multiple of their revenues. The benefits of this approach are that it is quick and easy and only revenue data are needed. The drawback is that costs and growth rates are not taken into account. Clearly cost, growth rates, and depreciation rates are important, but essentially this method is assuming that costs (as a percentage of revenue) and growth rates are similar for all teams. Given that owners use their teams very differently and in different types of ownership structures, it is difficult to see how all teams can have the same ratio between value and revenue.

Using the *Financial World/Forbes* data, Figure 8.4 shows the ratios between franchise values and revenues for the four major sports leagues. Most of the time an average team is worth about two to three times its revenue, but there are a couple of exceptions. This ratio goes up when revenues are low due to a work stoppage. This makes sense because even though there may be a shortened season, analysts know this is not a long-term effect. If a league loses half of a season, and half of its revenues, this in no way means team values should be cut in half. It also is interesting to note that this ratio has increased in the NFL since the mid-1990s. It may not be a coincidence that this is around the time the NFL installed a salary cap thereby limiting costs.

If an analyst has some idea of what a typical multiple earnings value is for a league, it might be used to find future values of teams. If an investor is attempting to find an estimate of the value of team in 2009 and only knows the revenue of the team, it might be useful to know that, on average, teams were worth 4.4 times their revenue. Given what this technique omits, many financial analysts would shudder at using a multiple earnings approach to valuing teams.

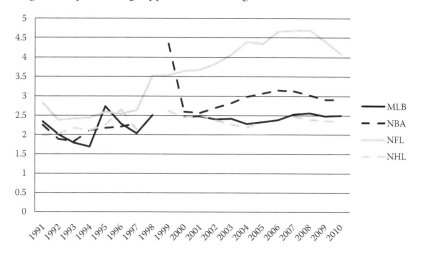

Figure 8.4 Multiples of earnings.

Constant Growth Pricing Model

The final valuation method discussed is a constant growth present value model. Finding the net present value of future profits should give an investor the value of that asset. As stated earlier in the chapter, a basic constant growth model is as follows:

$$Value = \frac{\pi}{r - g}$$

where π is the team's profit, r is the required return, and g is the growth rate of the team's profit. Although, theoretically, this is a better valuation technique than the multiple of earnings approach, the main problem is getting reliable data. While estimates of team values, revenues, and costs are available for the past 20 or more years,[*] there are still problems with using a constant growth pricing model. First, growth rates of profit are not realistically constant. Because growth rates are estimated anyway, this simplifying assumption is not too detrimental. Guessing what average growth rates are going to be in the foreseeable future is always extremely difficult. Second, while revenues and costs are available, they are not necessarily perfectly accurate, especially when those teams are part of a bigger entertainment complex. As noted, many revenues do not show up on the team's income statement. Third, the required return or depreciation rate is not always obvious. Analysts would like to include the level of risk in the depreciation rate, which implies the CAPM might be best to estimate values. Finding the level of risk compared to the market average is not always easy. In fact, even finding a risk-free depreciation rate can be difficult.[†] Finally, the net present value of a team also does not take into account any consumption value the owner may have or any assets or debt that are not a part of yearly profits.

While realizing that valuing teams can be difficult, going through the process is still very useful. Furthermore, because our most reliable data are for values and profits, we can use that data to estimate the difference between the depreciation rate and growth rate. In other words, we can manipulate the model so that we estimate the following equation:

$$r - g = \frac{\pi}{Value}$$

---

[*] Revenue and cost data are available for most leagues from 1990 to 2009, which correspond to the franchise value information that is available from 1991 to 2010.

[†] For more information regarding depreciation rates, see Damodaran, A. 2008. What is the risk-free rate? A search for the basic building block. Working paper. Stern School of Business, New York University.

This will allow an analyst to determine if the valuation estimates seem reasonable. One further complication is that the *Financial World/Forbes* data are actually an estimate of earnings before interest, taxes, depreciation, and amortization (EBITDA). Since EBITDA can be a fair amount larger than profits after interest payments, taxes, depreciation, and amortization, one has to try to figure out the comparison between the two. Examining the Packers' documents, it appears that profits are, on average, 75 percent of EBITDA. Some recent MLB financial documents have an average of profits equaling 36 percent of EBITDA. In the interest of conciseness, we will show examples of profits equaling EBITDA and profits equaling half of EBITDA.

Table 8.10 shows various financial statistics for the NFL, MLB, NBA, and NHL. The average EBITDA ranges from 1.6 percent to 3.3 percent of the average franchise value. That means if profits are half of EBITDA, then profits range from 0.8 percent to 1.7 percent of value. Using the constant growth model, this implies that the difference between the expected future growth rate and the depreciation rate is approximately 1 to 1.5 percent (ignoring the other benefits of ownership that do not show up on income statements). Table 8.10 also shows nominal and real past growth rates of EBITDA, which should be similar to the growth rates for profits. While past growth rates do not guarantee future growth rates, this is used as the best guess for future growth rates. The final two columns provide estimates of the nominal and real depreciation rates.

If the depreciation rates in Table 8.10 seem high, this means the values might actually be too low. Conversely, if the depreciation rates seem too low, this means the valuations might be too high. The estimated depreciation rates show that NBA teams are clear outliers. This table provides evidence that MLB teams are underpriced relative to NBA teams. It also is reasonable to argue that MLB teams will not

Table 8.10   Average EBITDA ranges

League	Average 2010 Value[a]	Average 2009 EBITDA	EBITDA/Value	.5 Times EBITDA/ Value	Nominal EBITDA Growth Rate[b]	Real EBITDA Growth Rate	Implied Nominal Depreciation Rate	Implied Real Depreciation Rate
NFL	1,022.4	33.4	0.0327	0.0163	9.8%	7.1%	11.38%	8.7%
MLB	491.3	16.3	0.0331	0.0165	13.0%	10.2%	14.65%	11.9%
NBA	368.8	6.1	0.0165	0.0082	2.1%	−0.4%	2.96%	0.5%
NHL	228.1	5.3	0.0234	0.0117	11.27%	8.4%	12.34%	9.6%

[a] in $millions

[b] The nominal and real EBITDA growth rates are past growth rates calculated from *Financial World/Forbes* data from the past two decades.

have the nearly 13-percent growth rates in the future while NBA teams might very well have higher than 2-percent growth rates. But, even if it is assumed all leagues are going to have the same growth rates, MLB teams are still a better deal than NBA teams as evidenced by the ratio of EBITDA to estimated value.* One must also remember that one bad or good year can significantly change these results. To make this analysis more robust, it would be useful to do the same exercise for different years. Again, it could also be the case that NBA teams have more ancillary benefits than MLB teams.

Other Sports

The focus on the four major North American sports leagues is not meant to dismiss the large values of teams in other leagues. Even though most NFL teams are estimated to be among the 50 most valuable sports teams, *Forbes* estimates that the English soccer team Manchester United is the most valuable sports team in the world at $1.83 billion. Ferrari Motorsports has been estimated to be worth $1.05 billion. Hendrick Motorsports, a NASCAR team, is estimated to be worth $380 million. The Sacramento River Cats, a minor league baseball team, is valued at $29.8 million by *Forbes*. There are even Indian cricket teams that have been sold for as much as $370 million. In 2008, *Forbes* estimated that the Major League Soccer (MLS) team, the Los Angeles Galaxy, was worth $100 million. The average value for an MLS team is $37 million. Table 8.11 shows the valuations for all MLS teams.

It is clear that many different sports leagues have teams with substantial values. But how these teams generate their values can greatly differ. Some leagues, like MLS, might get most of their value from potential growth. Most teams in MLS do not generate huge profits. If fan interest grows and is similar to what is found in other parts of the world, the value of MLS franchises will escalate. Minor league baseball teams, on the other hand, may not have the same growth potential because they will never offer fans the best athletes and, while some minor league teams have small media contracts, major league sports will always dominate in terms of media revenue.

College Sports

As alluded to earlier in the chapter, the value of college sports are almost impossible to calculate. As many analysts point out, a large number of college athletic departments typically operate at a loss. Virtually no college athletic department is a

---

* If one knew exactly what depreciation rates should be, then a similar exercise calculating implied growth rates for teams could be calculated.

Table 8.11 *Forbes's* **2008 valuations of major league soccer teams**

Team	Valuation (in $millions)
Chicago Fire	41
Chivas USA	24
Colorado Rapids	31
Columbus Crew	23
D.C. United	35
FC Dallas	39
Houston Dynamo	33
Kansas City Wizards	22
Los Angeles Galaxy	100
New England Revolution	27
New York Red Bulls	36
Real Salt Lake	30
Toronto FC	44
Average	37.3

major source of profits for the school and most athletic departments are subsidized. While some athletic departments do have high revenues, their costs are typically just as high. If one looks at the athletic departments separately, sports teams have very little financial value.

At the end of 2009, *Forbes* valued the football team at the University of Texas at $119 million. This value came from both direct and indirect contributions to the school and local area. If professional sports can be difficult to value, then college sports teams are nearly impossible. Just as in professional sports, college sports teams must be looked at as part of a larger organization. In fact, college sports teams are much more associated with a larger entity than professional sports teams. Universities and colleges use these sports teams as a marketing tool. It is an amenity used to attract students and donors to the school. Often young children know what university they would like to attend because their athletic loyalties have already been formed. But the question is: What is the value of this type of marketing? Since college sports are so much a part of the school, basic financial analysis is of little use. If one could estimate how many students came to the school because of the athletics, then an analyst could try to make a financial calculation based on tuition rates. Sometimes the effect on enrollment is zero because enrollment is capped. Even in this case, there is still a benefit because if there are more student applications, then the school will end up with a higher quality student. But again, this is almost impossible to value. College sports also has an impact on donations. Universities often try to generate donations by providing donors with tickets to games. The problem is that while it seems that athletics, especially successful athletic teams, generate more in donations, it is not at all clear that they increase donations to the academic side of a university. In other words, if the point of an athletic department is to help the rest of the school, one drawback is that it could actually be siphoning away donations from academics to the athletic department.

While it is virtually impossible to correctly value athletic departments, it is clear that universities value them differently. Some schools, like the University of Chicago, have decided to pursue athletics without scholarship athletes and compete at a different level than the universities with major athletic programs. The leaders of these institutions believe the value of an athletic department to them is less than do the leaders of the University of Texas and those at Big 10 Conference schools. Even though some schools view athletic departments differently, this does not mean one side is wrong. It seems to be the case that some schools try to cater to students that do not need or want large-scale sports teams while other schools are trying to entice students with sports. It makes sense that each school has its own niche.

Conclusion

This chapter provided an overview of basic valuation techniques and analyzed franchise values for sports teams. Using *Financial World* and *Forbes* data, sports franchise values have increased dramatically across the past 20 years. In fact, it appears that franchise values have increased faster than profits. There are a few possible explanations for this. First, owners are leveraging their teams more than they have in the past. Sports teams are becoming part of large entertainment complexes. These additional profits would not show up in the available data. Second, it might be that expected future growth rates are larger than they once were. Other factors that can increase firm values relative to profits are a decrease in risk or a decrease in the required return. Because interest rates are currently low, this may be a partial explanation.

References

Alexander, D. and Kern, W. 2004. The economic determinants of professional sports franchise values. *Journal of Sports Economics* 5: 51–66.

Badenhausen, K., Ozanian, M. K., and Settimi, C. 2009. Recession tackles NFL team values, *Forbes*, September 2, on-line edition, http://www.forbes.com/2009/09/02/nfl-pro-football-business-sportsmoney-football-values-09-values.html (accessed May 13, 2011).

Damodaran, A. 2008. What is the risk-free rate? A search for the basic building block, (working paper). Retrieved from Stern School of Business, New York University.

Fama, E. F. and French, K. R. 1992. The cross section of expected stock returns. *Journal of Finance*, (47) 427–465.

Fort, R. 2006. The value of major league baseball ownership. *International Journal of Sport Finance* 1 (1) 3–8.

Miller, P. 2007. Private financing and sports franchise values: The case of Major League Baseball. *Journal of Sports Economics*, (8) 449–467.

Quirk, J. and Fort, R. D. 1992. *Pay dirt: The business of professional team sports*. Princeton, NJ: Princeton University Press.

Chapter 9

Demand and the Sports Business:
What Does the Customer Want and How Does a Team Owner Provide It?

Introduction

Every business owner understands that profitability depends on delivering to their customers exactly what they want in the manner in which they want it. There are some particularly unique elements to the sports industry that make its business affairs and the assessment of consumer demand unlike any other. For example, car manufacturers or computer makers would love to be the only purveyors of their product in a given market. If all competitors were eliminated from a particular market, then it becomes infinitely easier to be profitable. No computer maker or car company needs a competitor in the market to ensure that their product is purchased. While competition between companies might improve the quality of a product and lower the price, these benefits accrue more to consumers than to business owners. Yet, every sports team and every athlete in an individual sport, such as golf, tennis, or boxing, needs other competitors to sell their product. The need for competitors is what makes sports unlike most, if not all, other businesses. Furthermore, people involved in the business of sports need to figure out how much competition fans want.

Sports differs in another important way from many other businesses. When you buy a car or computer, its use of consumption is limited or controlled by one person. While you can drive others to different places and show people things on your computer, the driver controls the car's direction and use and what the computer shows or how it is used is controlled by the person at the keyboard (assuming no virus has infected the machine). Sports, on the other hand, can be enjoyed live by tens of thousands and hundreds of millions through the broadcast of a game, and each of these consumers is engaged in using the same product at the same time. The sports business is defined and described by conjoint production (requires at least two producers) and conjoint consumption (the experience is usually far better when one watches or enjoys a game with others). Within this complex environment, the owner faces the challenge of understanding what it is that should be maximized for consumers. At first glance, what can be maximized is proximity and comfort (better seats and more comfortable seating environments), and the demand for these amenities can be differentially priced.

That observation should focus sports managers on understanding what it is about the experience that can be differentiated and priced relative to demand, and what cannot be separated out from the conjoint experience. Demand can change depending on the proximity to the field or different levels of luxury seating and services at the game. Luxury car makers also must understand the demand for amenities that are added to the basic transportation function of an automobile. That differs from the sports business in that no one else enjoys the car when it is driven besides the owner and his/her passengers. At a ballgame, however, there may be 30,000 fans in nonluxury seats and 3,000 in suites and club seats. Sports owners must create a private experience to satisfy the demand for luxury seating while still ensuring that other fans are willing to attend in nonluxury seating. Satisfying these different demand functions within sets of fans implies a careful understanding of the market as the design of facilities is impacted by the number of suites that are built. More luxury seating also means other seats are pushed farther and farther from the playing field reducing their value. Balancing the different demand functions for the design of a facility is another way the business of sports differs.

One thing is clear, however. Sports teams are no different when it comes to maximizing revenues and providing different groups of consumers or fans what they want. Businesses increase revenues by giving each of their groups of consumers what they want and increasing demand for their product. Every team owner wants to understand what each of the different groups of consumers who attend games seeks and to ensure that the appropriate number of products and services are available to each group.

Some components of the analysis of fans and their behavior are obvious—larger regions usually have more fans and more corporate clients. Both individual and corporate fans want to see a winning team, and both groups enjoy the amenities of new and well-maintained facilities. Some things, however, are not so obvious. Will fans pay to see a marquee player, even if he is past his prime playing years? Do fans care about the nationality of players? Do fans care about uncertainty in the sporting event or do they just want their team to dominate? These are important questions that teams and leagues must ask and each has an impact on the level of demand for each team's revenue streams. What are the determinants of the demand for sports teams and each of the different products they offer? These are the issues addressed in this chapter.

Defining Demand

Before delving too far into the case of sports, managers must be clear on the definition of the demand function. Demand is defined as the relationship between price and quantity of a product. The law of demand states that when prices increase, consumers will want less of a good. In Chapter 10, price changes are discussed, which implies a movement along the demand curve. In this chapter, the focus is on preferences that shift the demand curve up or down. Movements upward imply there is more demand for a good or service; movements downward highlight less consumer interest.

Figure 9.1 shows demand and how it can shift either up or down.

This chapter focuses on things (besides price) that will create new fans for a team (increase demand) or make existing fans buy more tickets or buy better seats (increased demand) and, therefore, pay more money to the team. But, first, what do sports teams produce? In other words, what is the quantity of each product that a sports team should produce?

This is not as straightforward as some people might think. At one level, teams produce games, merchandise, and fan "experiences" within their facilities. In this chapter, the focus is on the demand for games, which is reflected in attendance and television ratings. It must be underscored, however, that demand can be differentiated into different types of attendance. Even when simply considering overall attendance levels, a team actually produces many different components including victories, exciting games, and the fan experience inside the facility. For example, the Chicago Cubs and Wrigley Field have provided fans with an extraordinary game

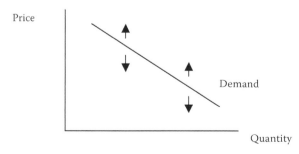

Figure 9.1 Demand and how it can shift either up or down.

day experience. The quality of that experience has contributed to high attendance levels even though it has been more than 100 years since the team won the World Series. Even in years when the team has had little chance of winning a division title, attendance levels have remained robust. This is just one example of a team that is able to offer fans something of extreme value besides winning that leads to high attendance levels and robust levels of demand even when the team has been unsuccessful on the field. Teams also offer a variety of seating plans and options from general seating to suites, and these are marketed or sold to very different groups of consumers seeking different products. It must be remembered that demand is not the same for all of the products offered by a team, and there are several different consumer groups to which a team must market.

There are five factors that affect demand for any good:

1. Tastes and preferences
2. Income levels of consumers (individuals and businesses)
3. Population size
4. The price of substitutes
5. Future expectations

Regarding sports teams, there is a great deal of specificity that can be applied to the factors of demand. For example, differences in regional wealth and the presence of economic competitors, winning percentages, new facilities, superstars, the types of players and their performances, game-specific determinants, marketing, work stoppages, and competitive balance each can impact demand. These determinants are divided into long- and short-run factors. This chapter also provides insight into which factors are most important and the magnitude of some of these effects. Empirical evidence is introduced to illustrate how different factors influence revenue streams.

Long Run Demand for Sports

Regional Wealth

A primary issue for any team to assess is the wealth available in its local market for each of its seating products. In a similar vein, investors interested in bringing a new team to a community also must understand how much competition there is for the discretionary income that households possess to spend on sports. The biggest long-run factor for a team is its location, and the fundamental question is always: What will the market bear? To answer that question, one must first understand how much wealth exists to buy tickets and to place that demand in the context of the total supply of sports and entertainment produced for a region.

The importance of this part of the consideration of demand is underscored by the 2009 bankruptcy of the Phoenix Coyotes, the financial problems encountered by the Columbus Blue Jackets and Indiana Pacers, and the declining attendance levels at Cleveland Indians' games. However, the issue of declining attendance and increasing competition for the discretionary entertainment dollars in households is not limited to smaller markets or regions enduring particularly long and deep economic contractions. The issue of the supply of available entertainment and sport options and household demand represented by consumers' discretionary income exists also in larger markets. For example, Forest City Enterprises acquired the NBA's New Jersey Nets to be the anchor tenant in a new arena to be built in Brooklyn (the Barclays Center at Atlantic Yards). Had the Nets remained in New Jersey, they likely would have moved permanently into the Prudential Center in Newark (where they played the 2010–2011 season), the new home of the NHL's New Jersey Devils. The building of the new arena in Brooklyn at the same time that Madison Square Garden, the Prudential Center, and the Nassau Coliseum (New York Islanders) exist (not to mention the Izod Center at the Meadowlands) means the New York metropolitan area is served by four or five indoor arenas. Is there sufficient disposable income in the New York market to buy all the tickets for all of the sporting events, shows, and other events held at these and other venues (Radio City Music Hall, Carnegie Hall, Lincoln Center, etc.)? What does a new facility have to offer to be competitive with these other venues, and what does the manager of an older venue do to keep it competitive, attractive, and providing fans with the event-day experience they expect? Understanding overall demand levels is critical, especially since the new homes for the Yankees, Mets, and the Jets/Giants each can host concert events several months each year and a major renovation is underway for Madison Square Garden. In addition, the New York Islanders also are looking to replace their aging home. With each renovation and with the building of a new facility, there is an expansion in the supply of venue dates available to host events. At what point is a market even as large as New York saturated? The strains in markets, such as Phoenix and Minneapolis/St. Paul, are even greater where domed facilities exist that can compete with arenas for indoor events.

How does one measure the demand for sports and entertainment? While no one can accurately predict recessions or boom times, or the severity of a recession or how long an economic expansion will last, the size of a market and the money consumers and companies have for purchasing tickets can be measured. This is vital for teams that are considering entering or leaving a market. Wealth measurements indicate the size of the market and can provide insight into risk and what might happen during a recession when businesses and consumers have less discretionary income. Population statistics and the supply of sports in a region can be compared. This allows a team owner to see how different markets compare to each other.

In addition, the U.S. Department of Commerce's Bureau of Labor Statistics conducts an annual survey to understand what consumers buy and how much money they have available for entertainment and sports. The Department of Commerce also looks at annual changes in household income in an effort to understand how consumers are being affected by current economic trends. Other government agencies collect data on population growth, the number of businesses in a community and the number of their employees (larger firms, for example, might be more interested in entertaining clients at sporting events), and the overall payroll size (firms paying employees more might similarly have larger entertainment budgets). Understanding how these different measures of wealth compare and contrast across numerous regions provides a careful assessment of the variety of opportunities for teams. It also illustrates the varying degrees of difficulty teams have in different markets due to such factors as rising levels of unemployment and reduced consumer spending. To illustrate the factors that should be considered, a variety of these measures are used to describe the market for professional sports in 18 different regions and the wealth available to purchase what is supplied.

Figure 9.2 provides an overview of the markets in 18 different metropolitan areas. The bars in the graph represent the total number of tickets to professional sports games available for sale. This number was produced by simply multiplying the number of games home teams play by the number of seats in the arena, stadium, or ballpark used by the team. Each baseball team plays 81 home games, hockey and basketball teams play 41 home games, each NFL team plays 8 home games and it is expected that season ticket holders buy tickets to 2 preseason games. The regions with the most tickets for sale are New York (2 baseball, football, and basketball teams and three hockey teams) and Chicago (2 baseball teams and 1 team in each of the other major sports leagues). Los Angeles, excluding Anaheim, does not have an NFL team, but there are 2 basketball teams, a baseball team, and a hockey team playing in the region.

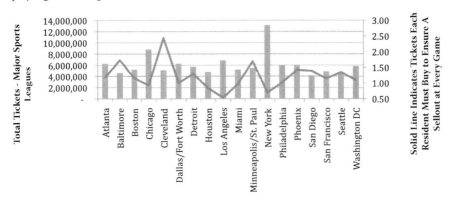

Figure 9.2 **The supply of tickets to major league sports (bars, left axis) and the sales per capita (line, right axis) required to sell out all major sports league games in selected metropolitan areas. Note: Major league sports include regular season games for teams in the NFL, (and up to two preseason games), MLB, the NBA, and the NHL.**

The bars provide a measure of the supply in each region. The line above or passing through each bar connected provides a broad measure of demand for the available tickets to professional sports based only on the population size of the region. The points within or above each bar where the line crosses the bar reflects the number of tickets that must be sold to every resident of the region *if* every ticket to every professional sports game is sold. This provides a quick glance into the challenge each team in each region would face to sell its tickets. For example, notice in Cleveland that while the supply of tickets is far below the supply in other regions, for all these tickets to be sold, every resident would have to buy more than 2 tickets. Every team knows that some residents will not buy any tickets and that some residents are either too young or unable to attend games. That means that each team in the Cleveland metropolitan region has to work much harder to find more people willing to buy far more than two tickets if all games are to be sold out. If income levels are stagnant or declining, or if a region such as Cleveland was losing population, the stress levels would be even greater to sell out every game.

In this sample of 18 markets for sports and entertainment, only Cleveland and Detroit lost residents from 2000 and 2008. The Cleveland metropolitan area lost 2.8 percent of its 2000 population base, and the decline, while small, was continuous (and in each year). This trend indicates that with fewer people in the region and lower levels of economic growth, all teams will have a harder time selling all of their tickets (Table 9.1). When the Indians were highly successful in the late 1990s through 2001, the team sold out every home game. After a few unsuccessful years, the team rebounded and won the AL Central Division in 2007. By then, however, the recession had already begun in the region and the Cavaliers, led by LeBron James, were emerging as a potential championship team. As a result, in that year, the Indians sold 2,275,912 tickets or 1 million *less* than they sold each season from 1996 through 2001. Regional economic conditions and the popularity of other teams in the area can have a decisive effect on attendance levels.

In New York, where the supply of tickets exceeds 13 million, the teams need to sell less than one ticket to each resident to secure sellouts. Teams in New York have a less difficult task than teams in other regions trying to sell out their games. This does not mean that fans in New York would necessarily support a team regardless of its performance. But, it does suggest that a winning team in New York would have an easier time selling tickets than teams with similar records in most other markets. In most, if not all, markets, championship teams will sell out. The value of having more wealth in a larger market comes when a team is competitive, but fails to win a championship. In these instances, a team in New York would likely be far more profitable than one from any other market. Similarly, the teams in the Los Angeles area would appear to have the least work to secure high ticket sales as compared to teams in other regions.

It is not surprising that large markets have fewer seats to sell per capita. Leagues clearly do not want teams competing with each other in large markets. Many small-market teams would move to New York or Los Angeles if they could, but this might

Table 9.1 Population changes in selected metropolitan regions, 2000–2008

Metropolitan Area	Percent Change, 2000–2008
Atlanta	25.6
Baltimore	4.3
Boston	2.7
Chicago	5.0
Cleveland	–2.8
Dallas/Fort Worth	21.2
Detroit	–0.7
Houston	20.9
Los Angeles	3.8
Miami	7.7
Minneapolis/St. Paul	8.3
New York	3.6
Philadelphia	2.6
Phoenix	30.6
San Diego	6.2
San Francisco	3.3
Seattle	9.6
Washington D.C.	11.1

not be what is best for the league. Regardless, this does show the obstacles for small-market teams.

These data also provide insight into the capacity for each region to consume tickets for additional games or teams. For example, a new league or sports product would seem to have a greater chance for success in Chicago or the Dallas/Fort Worth area than in Baltimore, Minneapolis/St. Paul, or Phoenix. Why? In Chicago and in the Dallas/Fort Worth area the number of tickets that have to be purchased by each resident for sellouts is far below what is needed in the Baltimore, Minneapolis/St. Paul, or Phoenix regions. The lower the line (Figure 9.2 and Figure 9.3), the more capacity exists for households to buy tickets despite the supply of tickets in the market. The data in Figure 9.2, however, focused only on professional sports.

What happens when major college sports are introduced? Figure 9.3 shows the small changes when the supply of tickets available for major college football games in each market is included.

College football has varying effects on different markets. For example, the situation does not deteriorate for the major professional sports teams in the Cleveland metropolitan area as the home games for The Ohio State University were excluded. While fans from the Cleveland region do attend football games in Columbus because it is a separate market region and the university draws fans from across the state and country, no additional stress was introduced into the figures for professional teams from Cleveland.

Notice, however, that the financial stress levels have changed for Baltimore, Detroit, the Minneapolis/St. Paul region, in metropolitan Phoenix, in the Seattle region, and even in the Washington, D.C. area. Some recent events involving teams in these markets become easier to understand in light of these data. For example, it is perhaps not surprising that the popularity of the Seattle Supersonics declined after the team failed to qualify for the playoffs in three consecutive years (2005/2006 season through the 2007/2008 season). The combination of nonplayoff seasons and the inability of the team to secure public support for a new arena prompted a sale of the franchise to an owner who wanted to move the team to Oklahoma City. The Seattle Supersonics became the Oklahoma City Thunder for the 2008/2009 season, but did not qualify for the playoffs in that inaugural season. The relocation of the NBA franchise, in the long run, may be a positive outcome for the two sports

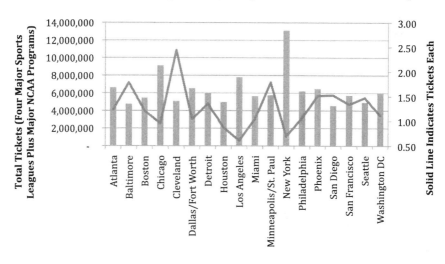

Figure 9.3 **The supply of tickets to major league sports and major college football tickets (bars, left axis) and the sales per capita (line, right axis) required to sell out all games.**

franchises that remain in the Seattle region as there is now less competition for the entertainment spending by residents.*

Similarly, it is perhaps now not difficult to understand the pressures facing franchises in the Minneapolis/St. Paul area and the bankruptcy of the Phoenix Coyotes. Both of these regions may have had too much supply and too little demand to ensure that every sports enterprise would be successful. Increasing attention to the issues involved with the supply of entertainment in the Phoenix region and the impact of the national recession on that region's economy have contributed to a lengthy process as the NHL seeks to find a new ownership group willing to maintain the team in the region. At the other end of the spectrum, even including the available tickets for USC and UCLA football, the Los Angeles region still offers its professional sports teams a robust market within which to sell all of their tickets. This would lead to the observation that any NFL team relocating to the area—or a newly created franchise for Los Angeles—would appear to have a clear route to high levels of revenue generation and profitability even with sustaining levels of interest in USC and UCLA football, and in the area's two NBA teams, a MLB franchise, and an NHL team.

The New York region, without any major collegiate football power, remains the most attractive and profitable market for professional sports. That projection might shift if a new chart was created that included all forms of entertainment, such as Broadway shows and concerts. New York, however, also attracts a large number of tourists who buy a substantial portion of those entertainment tickets. The point here, though, is that every sports business and entrepreneur needs to focus on the supply and demand factors related to other activities that compete for the discretionary spending of a region's residents. There are oversaturated markets and, in booming economic times or when teams are winning, these regions might be able to support all teams. The data in Figure 9.2 and Figure 9.3 illustrate the issues that team owners and investors initially should consider when asking the question: What is the demand for tickets in our market?

Perhaps that question should have been asked before new franchises were awarded to or moved to the Minneapolis/St. Paul or Phoenix regions. Similarly, it is not surprising that the Seattle Supersonics under new ownership chose to leave. Investors and the political leadership in that region might well be cautioned against actively seeking another NBA team to replace the Supersonics. Adding in the supply of football tickets from the University of Washington shifted the consumption required to one of the highest among the 18 regions analyzed. If the tickets to an NBA season were added to what already exists in the Seattle region, the total number of tickets in the market would increase by 738,000 and further saturate a market that would already be considered saturated. The financial collapse of several women's professional basketball teams in saturated markets (e.g., Cleveland, Detroit), after the WNBA embarked on a rapid expansion plan that increased the number of teams from 8 to 16, is also hardly surprising after a look at the data in Figure 9.3. At the

---

* Seattle has also been home to a popular Major League Soccer team since 2009.

conclusion of the 2010 season, there were 14 teams left in the WNBA, with the future for a few unsettled if not quite tenuous (e.g., the Indiana Fever, Phoenix Mercury). When you look at Figure 9.3, you also can begin to think about the sports tickets not included in the measure of supply: WNBA, minor league sports, other college sports, and nearby college sports teams that are not in the immediate market areas. You can think as well about factors not included in the measure of demand, such as population outside of the city and regional preferences. Those increments might lead some to conclude that some markets are supersaturated.

Another helpful way to evaluate markets is to look at penetration rates across teams in the same sport. There are several slightly different definitions of market penetration rates. One definition focuses on a product's sale compared to the sale of all similar products in a market. Translated to a particular team, this could mean looking at its ticket sales relative to all tickets sold by sports teams or all tickets sold to entertainment events in their area. Another measure of market penetration focuses on the volume of product sales in a particular market compared to the same product in different markets. This would involve looking at a team's total ticket sales as a percent of a measure of population (total population, all sports fans, etc.) in each region. Within this perspective, the concern is the extent to which the potential market of all consumers has bought a particular product compared to that product's performance in other regional markets.

To illustrate the usefulness of the concept, the analysis below looks at market penetration rates for all baseball teams from 2000 to 2009. Market penetration in this exercise was calculated by taking the total number of tickets sold by each club and dividing that figure by the population of the metropolitan statistical area (MSA) as defined and reported by the U.S. Bureau of the Census. With MSAs as the unit defining market sizes, the teams in Chicago and New York were each assumed to share or divide the market. In the other regions with more than one team, each plays in a separate MSA. Teams, of course, sell tickets to fans living outside of their MSA and to fans of other teams. This is expected to be the same for each team although one could think of several differences related to tourism (e.g., far more visitors to New York City than Kansas City) or the presence of historic ballparks (e.g., Fenway Park, Wrigley Field) or the opening of a new facility. Each of those differences would impact total sales. Other factors influencing demand could involve a team's winning percentage and the relative number of other competitors for consumers' entertainment dollars or discretionary spending.

The approach presented here is done to illustrate the usefulness of market penetration analyses to help understand the influence of different factors and the value of this approach. These data assess the relative popularity of a single product, MLB, in different markets without controlling for any other factors. This depiction, then, does not introduce any degree of complexity relative to the influence of other factors on attendance. Yet, if a consistent market penetration rate existed in a particular region across time, then it might be possible to observe which regions, if any, have a higher demand for baseball than others. The data also might help analysts identify other issues or questions needed for further analysis. To introduce the issue of market penetration, several different perspectives for the 2000 through 2009 seasons are presented.

Figure 9.4 and Figure 9.5 look separately at the market penetration rates for American and National League teams. This separation was done to make the figures somewhat easier to depict. It also could be interesting to array the data by market size or by region of the country. It is important to remember that there are a variety of market penetration questions that sports managers should investigate. The value of a large market is evident from the Yankees' penetration. The New York club had the second-lowest penetration rate, but as will be seen shortly, even with a consistently lower market penetration rate the Yankees have sold more tickets than any other club. What is particularly important in this presentation, however, is the consistency that some clubs enjoy while others have seen their popularity rise and fall. When the Cleveland Indians dominated the American League Central Division and challenged for the pennant, the team's market penetration rate was the highest in the league. That rate declined sharply when the team was less successful, but then rose again when it became competitive. In 2009, even with a lackluster performance (the team finished 32 games below .500) and with the region mired in the depths of the recession with one of the highest

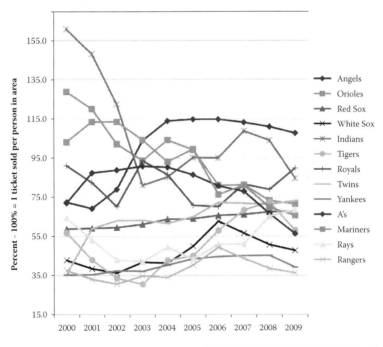

Figure 9.4 Market penetration rates of American League teams, 2000–2009. (From attendance reported by ESPN, *USA Today*, and *Sports Illustrated*; MSA population figures from the U.S. Bureau of the Census.)

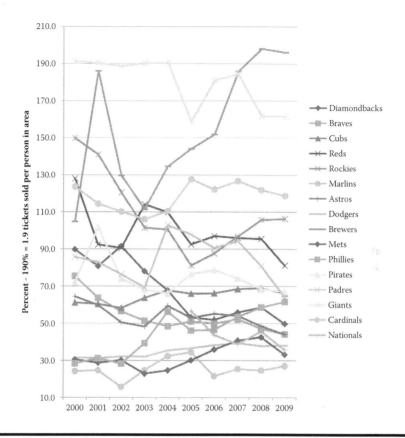

Figure 9.5   Market penetration rates of National League teams, 2000–2009. (From attendance reported by ESPN, *USA Today*, and *Sports Illustrated*; MSA population figures from the U.S. Bureau of the Census.)

unemployment and population loss rates in the United States, the team's market penetration rate was still the *third best* among all American League teams.[*]

Unlike Cleveland, the Baltimore Orioles have seen their market share decline. Part of that loss is explained by the presence of the Washington Nationals. The presence of a new franchise in Washington, D.C. led to fewer ticket sales for the Orioles. As you look at Figure 9.4, you can find interesting questions to ask about what happened to each team as their popularity increased and decreased. It is important to note that

---

[*] Despite leading the American League's Central Division in July 5, 2011, average attendance at Cleveland Indians games was the fourth smallest in MLB (through July 5, 2011). Fans may have feared the team would falter and the lingering effects of the recession could also have contributed to a reluctance to purchase tickets despite a vastly improved on-the-field record. Demand for tickets is related to fans' expectations and the economy suggesting increments in both would be needed to bolster attendance levels at Progressive Field (http://espn.go.com/mlb/attendance, accessed July 5, 2011).

the Kansas City Royals have had a consistently high market penetration rate despite relatively poor on-the-field performances. Clearly, it is easier to have a high penetration rate in a small market, but this could indicate that the Kansas City market is an area where baseball is popular and that an owner can rely on a high market penetration even when performance does not improve (or remains consistently below that of other clubs). This implies that the owner may have to wonder and worry if paying more for players and an improved on-the-field performance level would lead to the needed attendance levels to offset that investment in a market that is far smaller than the ones available to other teams. The Cleveland Indians were able to attract more than 3 million fans to their games when they challenged each year for the American League pennant. Richard Jacobs was able to retain the needed players as a result of the new revenue streams created from a new largely publicly financed ballpark. He then capitalized on his investment when the team was sold (Rosentraub, 2010). The new owners, having paid the capitalized value of those revenue streams in their purchase price, have less flexibility or need dramatically increased levels of demand to ensure that their investment in the team and players generates a profit. The Kansas City market is smaller than the one available to the Indians and their existing ballpark does not offer new revenue streams to the team's owner. Hence, it is not surprising to find lower expenditures for players, and it is far more difficult to elevate demand and generate the revenue needed to pay the salaries of established star athletes. It makes more sense for owners in these situations to trade away higher-priced players and exploit the profit possible from higher performing, younger and less costly athletes.

The market penetration rates of the Los Angeles Angels of Anaheim offer insight into the behavior of different types of owners. Notice that the team's market penetration rates were sustained at a high level during the period the team was owned by the Disney Corporation and after it was sold to an individual. The Disney Corporation also substantially remodeled the ballpark in an effort to both attract more fans and enhance revenue streams. This is an interesting example of where a team succeeded on the field and at the ticket office with both corporate and individual owners.

The market penetration rates for National League clubs also make some interesting points. For example, the San Francisco Giants had a very high market penetration rate from 2000 to 2004, riding the crest of excitement created by a new ballpark, Barry Bonds' single-season home run record, and then Barry Bond's effort to surpass Henry Aaron's career home run record. Even after the excitement of a new ballpark had waned and the home run chase ended, the Giants still had a very high market penetration level. The team has succeeded in making the San Francisco market a very strong one for MLB, exceeding the expectations of many who in the aftermath of the Giants' move from New York City thought the region was not as valuable as others. The Milwaukee Brewers also have enjoyed a substantial increase in their market penetration rates probably related to a new ballpark and improved winning percentages. If the Brewers sustain interest, they might surpass the Cardinals' success in terms of the length of time a consistent penetration rate has been sustained. The St. Louis Cardinals have long sustained a high level of success on the field with high market penetration rates extending across the entire time period (with very little variation). Indeed, across the entire time period, their average penetration rate is second only to the Giants. This is again notable given the effects of the national recession. The St. Louis market, similar to the one in Kansas City, seems to be in "baseball country."* The Chicago Cubs have had a market penetration that is more robust than the level enjoyed by their American League counterpart just as the Yankees have had a larger market penetration in New York than the Mets (see Figure 9.5). In 2010, the Cubs were able to capitalize on their market penetration by offering seats to individual games at prices that were 10 to 20 percent above the stated or printed sale price prior to the beginning of the season. Demand for tickets to Cubs games is so high that the team decided to capitalize on the potential for even higher profits and to capture the returns made by resellers who use services such as StubHub, eBay, or Craig's List. In this manner, the Cubs captured the income made by people who bought tickets at "face value" and resold them for higher prices. The team, with a broad understanding of its market penetration rate capitalized on its popularity and successfully charged a premium price (see Figure 9.5). From the data presented, do you see other markets where teams might be successful in offering tickets for more than "face value"?

A third and final view of the penetration rates is provided in Table 9.2 and Table 9.3. In these tables, the penetration rates for each team are displayed together with the total attendance figures for each season. These data illustrate the value of large markets. In several large population centers, teams had penetration rates below those of franchises in smaller markets, but often sold more tickets. Relative to a range of sports management issues including the effort each team makes to attract fans, maintain profitability, maximize revenue streams, and ensure its product is affordable, there are important league-wide issues raised by these data. For example, if two teams in different size markets have similar penetration rates, but one attracts far more fans, should salary caps be instituted to equalize each owner's ability to attract the best players? Or, do the owners of teams in the larger markets effectively pay higher prices to own their franchise? If they did pay more for the franchise because of the larger market size and the resulting lower penetration rate needed to attract larger crowds, then the extra dollars earned from having more fans merely offsets the higher costs of ownership and no revenue sharing is needed to equalize profitability. One can imagine the owners of teams in smaller markets, such as Kansas City or Tampa/St. Petersburg, taking exception to that logic and claiming the Yankees, Red Sox, and Dodgers have a clear advantage. Certainly many issues can be raised when looking at the data in Table 9.2 and Table 9.3.

In summary, these figures provide important insights into the challenges teams and regions encounter to remain profitable in the face of a recession. Cleveland's

---

* While the St. Louis Cardinals have had one of the highest penetration rates in MLB, the Royals outdrew the Cardinals from 1976 through 1982. Perhaps all of Missouri (and parts of Kansas and Illinois) should be described as "Baseball Country," although winning might be more important in Kansas City than it is in St. Louis relative to overall attendance.

Table 9.2 Market penetration rates (in percent) and attendance (in thousands): American League clubs, 2000–2009 (100 percent = 1 ticket sold per person in the market area)

Team		Season									
		2000	2001	2002	2003	2004	2005	2006	2007	2008	2009
Angels		72.3	69.2	78.9	103.9	113.8	114.7	114.7	113.1	110.8	107.6
	Attendance	2,067	2,001	2,306	3,061	3,376	3,405	3,407	3,366	3,337	3,241
Orioles		128.9	120.1	102.2	93.7	104.1	99.2	81.0	81.3	73.1	71.5
		3,295	3,095	2,656	2,455	2,744	2,625	2,153	2,165	1,950	1,907
Red Sox		58.7	59.1	59.5	61.1	63.7	63.9	65.6	66.1	67.4	67.7
		2,586	2,625	2,651	2,724	2,838	2,848	2,931	2,971	3,048	3,063
White Sox		42.7	38.4	36.2	41.7	41.3	49.9	62.7	56.5	50.7	47.7
		1,948	1,766	1,676	1,940	1,931	2,343	2,957	2,685	2,425	2,284
Indians		160.9	148.1	122.5	81.0	85.3	95.2	95.0	108.6	103.9	84.6
		3,457	3,176	2,622	1,730	1,814	2,014	1,998	2,276	2,170	1,766
Tigers		56.8	42.9	33.5	30.5	42.6	45.0	57.9	68.4	72.4	58.0
		2,534	1,921	1,503	1,368	1,917	2,024	2,596	3,047	3,203	2,567

Royals	91.1	82.4	70.2	93.6	86.5	70.8	70.1	81.6	78.9	89.8
	1,678	1,537	1,323	1,780	1,662	1,371	1,373	1,617	1,579	1,798
Twins	35.5	59.0	63.0	63.2	61.5	65.0	72.2	71.8	71.3	73.1
	1,060	1,783	1,924	1,946	1,912	2,034	2,285	2,297	2,302	2,362
Yankees	35.2	35.3	37.3	37.1	40.3	43.5	44.6	45.1	45.2	39.1
	3,227	3,265	3,466	3,466	3,775	4,091	4,201	4,271	4,299	3,719
A's	17.6	87.4	88.8	90.8	90.3	86.4	80.7	77.9	66.5	56.3
	1,729	2,133	2,170	2,217	2,202	2,109	1,977	1,922	1,666	1,409
Mariners	71.9	113.4	113.4	104.2	93.0	99.5	76.2	81.0	69.7	65.6
	3,148	3,507	3,540	3,269	2,941	3,181	2,481	2,672	2,330	2,195
Rays	64.4	53.2	42.9	42.0	49.5	43.3	50.9	51.1	65.1	68.6
	1,549	1,298	1,066	1,059	1,275	1,142	1,369	1,388	1,781	1,875
Rangers	37.5	33.0	30.6	34.7	33.9	40.3	49.3	43.6	38.5	36.3
	2,800	2,831	2,352	2,094	2,514	2,525	2,389	2,354	1,946	2,156

Table 9.3 Market penetration rates (in percent) and attendance (in thousands): National League clubs, 2000–2009 (100 percent = 1 ticket sold per person in the market area)

Team	Season									
	2000	2001	2002	2003	2004	2005	2006	2007	2008	2009
Diamondbacks	89.7	80.8	91.5	78.0	67.8	53.2	51.8	55.8	58.6	49.7
Attendance	2,943	2,737	3,199	2,806	2,520	2,059	2,092	2,325	2,510	2,129
Braves	75.5	63.7	56.4	51.4	48.5	51.0	49.9	52.2	47.1	44.2
	3,234	2,824	2,568	2,401	2,328	2,521	2,550	2,745	2,533	2,374
Cubs	61.2	60.5	58.3	63.7	67.8	66.0	66.2	68.5	69.0	66.2
	2,790	2,780	2,695	2,963	3,170	3,100	3,123	3,253	3,300	3,169
Reds	127.9	92.4	90.5	114.0	109.8	92.5	97.0	96.0	95.5	81.1
	2,577	1,890	1,856	2,355	2,287	1,943	2,135	2,059	2,059	1,748
Rockies	149.8	140.9	120.4	101.5	100.6	81.2	87.6	96.9	105.7	106.3
	3,286	3,167	2,741	2,334	2,338	1,914	2,106	2,377	2,650	2,665
Marlins	24.2	24.7	15.7	24.9	32.4	34.5	21.6	25.4	24.7	27.0
	1,218	1,261	813	1,303	1,723	1,853	1,165	1,371	1,335	1,464
Astros	64.5	59.9	50.4	48.3	59.5	52.9	55.1	54.0	48.5	44.0
	3,056	2,904	2,512	2,454	3,088	2,805	3,023	3,020	2,780	2,521

Dodgers	31.5	31.3	32.2	32.0	35.4	36.6	38.2	39.3	37.8	38.1
	3,011	3,017	3,131	3,139	3,488	3,604	3,758	3,857	3,731	3,762
Brewers	104.8	186.1	129.6	111.4	134.6	144.1	151.8	185.9	198.1	196.1
	1,574	2,811	1,969	1,700	2,062	2,211	2,336	2,869	3,069	3,038
Mets	30.5	28.8	30.2	22.9	24.7	30.1	35.9	40.7	42.5	33.2
	2,800	2,658	2,805	2,141	2,319	2,830	3,380	3,854	4,042	3,154
Phillies	28.3	31.2	28.2	39.3	56.3	46.1	46.5	53.4	58.6	61.7
	1,613	1,782	1,619	2,260	3,250	2,665	2,702	3,108	3,423	3,601
Pirates	72.0	101.9	74.1	68.2	66.2	76.6	78.9	74.3	68.4	67.1
	1,749	2,465	1,785	1,637	1,580	1,817	1,862	1,749	1,609	1,578
Padres	85.8	82.9	76.4	69.3	103.0	97.9	90.6	94.3	80.9	64.1
	2,423	2,378	2,221	2,030	3,017	2,870	2,660	2,790	2,428	1,923
Giants	191.2	190.4	188.6	190.3	190.4	158.8	181.1	184.4	161.8	161.6
	3,315	3,312	3,253	3,265	3,257	2,726	3,130	3,223	2,864	2,861
Cardinals	123.5	114.4	110.2	106.1	110.5	127.6	122.1	126.6	121.8	118.7
	3,337	3,110	3,012	2,910	3,048	3,539	3,407	3,552	3,431	3,343
Nationals						56.7	43.7	38.8	45.6	35.7
						2,732	2,153	1,944	2,320	1,818

Began Play in Washington, D.C. in 2005

professional teams have to exceed the market penetration rates of many others by a considerable amount to reach their revenue goals. In the midst of a recession and with one team enjoying far more success on the playing court than the others (Cavaliers, until LeBron James signed with the Miami Heat, relative to the Browns and Indians), the Browns and Indians might face declining revenue bases. The financial stress also is robust in markets such as Baltimore, Detroit, Minneapolis/St. Paul, Phoenix, and Seattle. Teams in the Los Angeles, New York, and Chicago regions would still be disadvantaged in a recession, but in a far better situation. The effects of a recession on their operations would not be anywhere as severe as those faced by the teams in the other markets where the line indicating how many tickets each person needs to buy to achieve sellouts is almost as high or higher than the supply bars.

Thinking about the player trades different clubs have made in recent years, it was hardly surprising that the Cleveland Indians elected to trade higher-cost athletes during the 2009 season to reduce their payroll at the height of the recent national recession. The Indians sent players to the Boston Red Sox and Philadelphia Phillies, teams in two areas where far lower efforts are required based on population sizes to sell tickets and regions that seemed to recover more quickly from the national recession. These figures can help project where one would expect winning teams and free agents to be located given the demand for and supply of tickets to professional sports and college football games.

Figure 9.4 and Figure 9.5 looked only at the supply of tickets and population sizes. That is important, but so too is wealth in a region. In other words, it might be possible for a smaller area with wealthier residents and a substantial number of large firms to be able to buy a sufficient number of tickets and luxury seating to allow a team to reach its financial goals. Figure 9.6 provides data describing the total amount of money households in different regions spend for sports activities (including all spectator sports) and the total corporate payrolls in the region. Corporate payroll data provide a measure (or an important indicator) of the wealth available

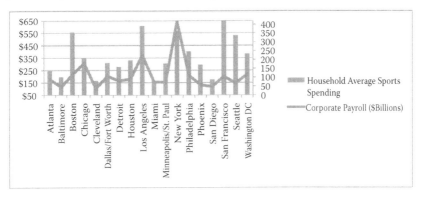

Figure 9.6 Household spending for sports (bars, left axis) and total corporate payroll (line, right axis) for selected metropolitan areas.

to purchase luxury suites and club seats. There are some individuals who buy these products or amenities, but businesses are the primary clients that teams look to when selling their suites and club seats. Regions with a larger number of businesses with robust corporate payrolls are likely to purchase more suites. The cities where the average household has the most amount of money available to spend on sports include Boston, Los Angeles, New York, and Seattle. Corporate payrolls were highest in New York, Los Angeles, and Chicago. Notice again that in the Cleveland area household spending and corporate payrolls were far below those in other region. In the Phoenix area, households had a reasonably robust level of income available to spend for sports tickets, but corporate payroll levels were more similar to what existed in Cleveland and Baltimore. Households in the Minneapolis/St. Paul region also had a fairly high level of income available to spend for sports, but, in comparison to other regions, had lower levels of corporate payrolls. Those areas with lower numbers of firms with large corporate payrolls will face a far more difficult challenge selling luxury seating and, as a result, have less available revenue to secure a desired return on their investment while also meeting the market prices for the best players.

These data also provide important insight into demand issues that relate to the revenue possibilities for clubs in different regions. Notice that household spending for sports is highest in Los Angeles and San Francisco. The three regions with the next highest levels of household spending were Boston, New York, and Seattle. This might provide some additional support for the possibilities for a new NBA team in Seattle. The household spending data, however, does not separate spectator from participatory sports. In other words, some of the sports spending reported by respondents from Seattle could have been for outdoor activities. More important, and of concern in the Seattle market would be the low level of corporate payrolls compared with other regions. Among the 18 regions, Seattle was in the bottom third in terms of corporate payrolls suggesting again the challenges each team encounters finding a sufficient number of buyers for all of the luxury seating available in the region. While New York was not the number one region with regard to household spending on sports, it ranked first in corporate payrolls. Los Angeles was second, illustrating once again the potential that would exist relative to demand if the NFL created additional supply in this region.

Economic Competition

The Miami Heat may be the only NBA team in the Greater Miami area, but they are not the only sports experience. The Greater Miami area offers fans access to MLB, NFL, and NHL games and numerous games played by various universities. There are also annual college bowl games, various tournaments, and MLB preseason games played within a drive of less than two hours from the Greater Miami metropolitan area. A demand issue for every team and sports entrepreneur to understand is what the substitutes are in a particular region. When there are too many teams and too many facilities in a particular region, it is possible that one team might become unprofitable. If a region builds too many facilities, there is elevated competition between the venues to host teams and events. An important issue for every manager is the demand in a particular market relative to other amenities and activities that compete for the discretionary income of residents. The number of substitutes and economic competitors can have a dramatic affect on a team's revenue potential. How much sports and entertainment can a region support? What is the number of teams and events that can be economically viable in a particular market area?

Sports teams are substitutes for all other forms of entertainment spending undertaken by a household. If people attend an Indians' game in the Cleveland metropolitan region or a Red Sox game in Boston, then they are not spending money for tickets to see the games of other sports teams and they are not enjoying other forms of entertainment. Similarly, if people do not attend a game, then it is quite likely they are spending their discretionary income for a movie, a concert, or for some other form of entertainment. For example, some people make the decision between going to a game and going to the movies. Sports teams are usually closer substitutes for each other. There is no doubt that there would be more New York Mets fans if the Yankees did not exist or played their home games in another region. Every sports team in a market is competing with each other for fans. The presence of another team—professional or collegiate—will affect any existing team's attendance. Research has explicitly shown that MLB teams have significantly less attendance if another team is nearby, especially if the nearby teams are successful (Winfree, McCluskey, Mittelhammer, and Fort, 2004; Miller, 2008). This point was underscored earlier in this chapter when the graphs focusing on the aggregate number of tickets to sporting events and the demand indicated the stress that existed in some markets.

The effect of other sports teams on the demand for a given team can best be illustrated by examining when teams enter or leave a market. Although all sports teams within a region compete economically, the effect is biggest when teams are in the same league. Table 9.4 shows the data when a team in the same league enter a market.

This table shows that, while differences exist, when a new team enters a market, other franchises experience a decline in attendance. When the Raiders first moved to Los Angeles, however, it was in the midst of a strike and when the owners decided to use replacement players. As a result, the decrease in the Rams' attendance cannot be attributed to the presence of the Raiders. Excluding that example, an entering team typically leads to a 6-percent decrease in the attendance of games of the already existing franchise. Table 9.5 shows the effect for teams across leagues when teams from another league (sport) move into a market where teams from other sports are already established.

There is very little fan substitution when teams from different sports enter a market with existing teams from other sports. Clearly other elements, such as winning percentage, will affect a team's attendance, but it looks like teams in other leagues have a relatively small effect.

What happens to attendance levels in a region when a team leaves? This is addressed in Table 9.6.

Table 9.4 Attendance effects when an additional team enters a market (1950–2010)

League	Entry Year	New Team	Existing Team	Attendance Year before Move	Attendance Year after Move	Percent Change
MLB	1954	Baltimore Orioles	Washington Nationals	880,242	1,039,698	18.1
MLB	1961	Los Angeles Angels	Los Angeles Dodgers	2,253,887	1,804,250	−19.9
MLB	1962	New York Mets	New York Yankees	1,747,725	1,493,574	−14.5
MLB	1968	Oakland Athletics	San Francisco Giants	1,242,480	837,220	−32.6
MLB	2005	Washington Nationals	Baltimore Orioles	2,744,018	2,624,740	−4.3
NBA	1976–7	New Jersey Nets	New York Knicks	672,745	644,811	−4.2
NBA	1984–5	Los Angeles Clippers	Los Angeles Lakers	622,398	613,826	−1.4
NFL	1982	Los Angeles Raiders	Los Angeles Rams	493,964	258,421	−47.7
NFL	1995	Oakland Raiders	San Francisco 49ers	516,808	518,928	0.4
NFL	1996	Baltimore Ravens	Washington Redskins	413,150	427,750	3.5
					Average =	−10.3

Table 9.5 Attendance changes when competitors in a different league enter a market (2000–2010)

Entering Team's League	First Year in Market	Entering Team	Existing Team's League	Year	Existing Team	Attendance Year before Entry	Attendance Year after Entry	Percent Change
MLB	2005	Washington Nationals	NBA	2004–05	Washington Wizards	628,159	705,069	12.2
			NFL	2005	Washington Redskins	702,670	716,999	2.0
			NFL	2005	Baltimore Ravens	558,594	563,076	0.8
			NHL	2004–05	Washington Capitals	603,528	lockout	
NBA	2002–3	New Orleans Hornets	NFL	2002	New Orleans Saints	560,472	542,796	–3.2
NBA	2004–5	Charlotte Hornets	NFL	2004	Carolina Panthers	582,566	586,259	0.6
NFL	2002	Houston Texans	MLB	2002	Houston Astros	2,904,277	2,512,357	–13.5
			NBA	2002–3	Houston Rockets	481,227	565,166	17.4
NHL	2000–1	Minnesota Wild	MLB	2000	Minnesota Twins	1,202,829	1,059,715	–11.9
			NFL	2000	Minnesota Vikings	513,051	513,394	0.1
			NBA	2000–1	Minnesota Timberwolves	655,999	717,371	9.4
							Average = 1.4	

Table 9.6 Attendance effects when economic competitors in the same league leave a market, 1950–2010*

League	First Year in New Area	Exiting Team	Remaining Team	Attendance Year before Move, Remaining Team	Attendance Year after Move, Remaining Team	Percent Change
MLB	1953	Milwaukee Braves	Boston Red Sox	1,115,750	1,026,133	−8.0
MLB	1954	Baltimore Orioles	St. Louis Cardinals	880,242	1,039,698	18.1
MLB	1955	Kansas City Athletics	Philadelphia Phillies	738,991	922,886	24.9
MLB	1958	Los Angeles Dodgers	New York Yankees	1,497,134	1,428,438	−4.6
		San Francisco Giants				
NFL	1952	Dallas Texans	New York Giants	174,076	203,090	16.7
NFL	1960	St. Louis Cardinals	Chicago Bears	270,000	278,843	3.3
NFL	1982	Los Angeles Raiders	San Francisco 49ers	435,182	274,837	−36.8
NFL	1984	Indianapolis Colts	Washington Redskins	416,512	421,500	1.2

Average = 1.9

* Not included were moves of American Football League teams out of markets and the effect on attendance at National Football League games. Those examples would be the Dallas Texans moving to Kansas City (Chiefs) leaving the Dallas Cowboys in the Dallas/Fort Worth region and the Los Angeles Chargers moving to San Diego and leaving the Los Angeles market to the Rams.

When teams in the same league leave an area, there is a very slight effect on attendance; the remaining franchise, on average, had a 2-percent increase in attendance. Removing the Raiders to blunt the effect of the 1982 season and the use of replacement players, the increase jumps to 7 percent. There are too few examples to make a strong claim, but it does appear that reducing the competition elevates attendance. Table 9.7 shows this same effect when the team leaving is from another league (sport).

Again there are only a few examples of teams leaving within the past 10 years, but there does appear to be a slight boost when teams leave, even if they are in a different league. It should be noted, however, that the only team that actually did increase attendance right after a team left was the Vancouver Canucks (NHL) when the Grizzlies (NBA) left. Because NFL teams have typically sold out their games in recent years, it is not surprising there has been little effect on NFL teams when other teams leave the market.

Examining fluctuations in attendance among various teams in one city also can assess the economic competition among sports teams. Outcomes in the Cleveland metropolitan area show that across nine years there has been very little change in the total aggregate demand for sports. Notice in Table 9.8 that at the apex of the Indians' popularity, a total of 4.6 million tickets to sporting events were sold. As the Indians' popularity waned and the Cavaliers became more competitive, fans' consumption patterns shifted away from baseball and toward basketball, but never reached the aggregate totals that existed in the early part of the decade. While it is obvious that the loss of residents could explain some of the decline in purchasing tickets to sporting events, it is more likely residents just decided to enjoy other forms of entertainment.

In the short run, between 5 and 15 percent of one team's fans will switch allegiances to another team of the same league if that team leaves or enters a city. Another 2 or 3 percent will switch their allegiances or interest to minor league sports in the absence of major league teams (Winfree and Fort, 2008). For example, if a league is having a work stoppage, 2 to 3 percent of their fans will start attending the games of minor league teams. Very few fans will switch their loyalties to rival leagues or other sports in the short run; long-run support is less clear.

The importance of understanding the supply of event days at different facilities and regional demand for sports and entertainment events is underscored by outcomes in three different cities. In the Phoenix metropolitan area, the NHL franchise, the Coyotes, had to seek bankruptcy protection. The Coyotes had moved from an arena in downtown Phoenix shared with the NBA's Suns to a new arena built for them in the Northwestern suburb of Glendale. Glendale faces a difficult financial situation if the team stays or leaves the area. The team's prospective new owner demanded improved lease terms at the city-owned arena and that meant an even larger public subsidy and reduced income from the facility for Glendale. This means the city will have to rely on other revenues to pay for the bonds sold to build the facility. The city's general revenue funds will be tapped as well to ensure that the

Table 9.7 Attendance effects on the remaining team when economic competitors from another league leave a market, 2000–2010

Exiting Team's League	First Year in New Area	Exiting Team	Existing Team's League	Year	Team	Remaining Team's Attendance Year before Move	Remaining Team's Attendance Year after Move	Percent Change
MLB	2005	Montreal Expos	NHL	2004–5	Montreal Canadiens	842,767	lockout	
NBA	2000–1	Vancouver Grizzlies	NHL	2000–1	Vancouver Canucks	600,313	697,717	16.2
NBA	2002–3	Charlotte Hornets	NFL	2002	Carolina Panthers	573,377	572,015	–0.2
NBA	2008–9	Seattle Supersonics	MLB	2009	Seattle Mariners	2,329,702	2,195,284	–5.8
			NFL	2008	Seattle Seahawks	545,551	543,965	–0.3
							Average = 2.5	

Table 9.8 Demand for sports tickets in Greater Cleveland, 2000–2009

	Cleveland's Professional Sports Teams								
	Indians		Cavaliers		Browns		Total Tickets Sold	Metropolitan Area Population
Season	Tickets	Capacity	Tickets	Capacity	Tickets	Capacity		
2000	3,456,278	98.4	603,702	71.6	581,544	99.3	4,641,524	2,147,944
2001	3,182,523	90.6	650,775	77.2	583,094	99.6	4,416,392	2,143,980
2002	2,616,940	74.5	596,115	70.7	586,294	100.1	3,799,349	2,139,550
2003	1,730,002	49.3	471,374	55.9	585,564	100.0	2,786,940	2,134,689
2004	1,814,401	51.7	749,790	88.9	584,840	99.9	3,149,031	2,127,333
2005	1,973,185	56.2	784,249	93.0	578,330	98.8	3,335,764	2,116,304
2006	1,998,070	56.9	792,391	94.0	578,672	98.8	3,369,133	2,103,850
2007	2,275,911	64.8	837,883	99.4	584,006	99.7	3,697,800	2,094,885
2008	2,169,780	61.8	839,074	99.5	582,230	99.4	3,591,084	2,094,051
2009	1,766,242	50.3	820,439	97.3	551,110	94.1	3,137,791	2,091,286

arena is properly maintained. The arena in Glendale will then continue to compete for nonsports events with two domed stadiums (the homes to the Diamondbacks and the Cardinals) and the arena in downtown Phoenix. In addition, Arizona State University has an arena that can host myriad concerts and shows, making the Phoenix market one of the most competitive in the nation for the hosting of sports and entertainment events.

Indianapolis is the smallest metropolitan region in the United States that is home to two professional sports teams from the four major leagues. With the region mired in the national recession (although Indiana's growth was more robust than the surrounding states through 2010) and with the Pacers struggling on the court, the NBA franchise lost money as did its subsidiary that operates the arena. The Conseco Fieldhouse was built with substantial financial support from the public sector, but the financial losses being sustained by the Indiana Pacers and Pacer Entertainment forced the team to demand that Indianapolis reconsider how much money the team can pay for use of the Conseco Fieldhouse and to reduce its financial responsibilities for maintaining the facility. Indianapolis might be forced to increase its investment (or subsidy) or face the loss of the team.

In Columbus, Ohio, where private investors built an arena for an NHL franchise while The Ohio State University built one for its own use, the sudden substantial increase in the supply of event days has led to fiscal losses for the private investors. Both of the arenas in Columbus added to a growing supply of event days across several cities in the Midwest (Cincinnati, Indianapolis, and Louisville). The total number of residents in this region is 14.3 million.* Five large arenas, one domed stadium, and a number of smaller venues for concerts and entertainment now serve this part of the Midwest. In contrast, the New York City region has 17.9 million residents in a far more dense setting, meaning people have to travel less far to get to a facility. The New York City region has four arenas (with a fifth under construction, but one of the older ones will probably close), but does not have a domed stadium capable of hosting some of the same events that might be held at an arena. The contrast with the supply in the Midwest and the greater distances people would have to travel to get to facilities in Columbus, Indianapolis, Cincinnati, and Louisville indicates again that supply and demand may be poorly aligned. This became critical during the recession leading to fiscal problems in three of the four cities. Only Louisville seemed to have temporarily avoided the problem, but with a new arena opening in 2010, it too encountered financial problems and in 2011 insufficient earnings meant required tax payments could not be made.

The issue of the supply of event days and the demand for sports and entertainment as reflected by household spending is depicted in Table 9.9 and Figure 9.7. In Table 9.9, the breakdown illustrates the number of regions where sharing of a facility

---

* Population figures is the summation of the U.S. Bureau of the Census 2008 estimates for all metropolitan statistical and micropolitan areas served by the facilities in Cincinnati, Columbus, Indianapolis, and Louisville.

Table 9.9 Household spending on entertainment (in billions of 2008 dollars), population (in millions), and the number of major league teams and facilities in selected regions[a]

Metropolitan Area	Entertainment Spending ($billions)	Population (millions)	Teams	Facilities
Atlanta	4.92	5.38	4	3
Baltimore	2.80	2.67	2	2
Boston	9.15	4.52	4	3
Chicago	9.76	9.57	4	3
Cleveland	2.67	2.09	3	3
Dallas/Fort Worth	6.16	6.30	4	3
Detroit	5.09	4.43	4	4
Houston	4.99	5.73	3	3
Los Angeles	13.29	12.9	6	4
Miami	2.73	5.41	4	4[b]
Minneapolis/St. Paul	5.35	3.23	4	4
New York	24.45	19.0	7	6
Philadelphia	7.39	5.84	4	3
Phoenix	5.73	4.28	4	4
San Diego	2.33	3.00	2	2
San Francisco	10.12	4.28	5	4
Seattle	7.52	3.35	2	2
Washington, D.C.	6.89	5.36	4	3

[a] The areas included are those for which consumer spending were available from the Bureau for Labor Statistics; teams in any of the four major sports leagues are counted as major league.
[b] The Marlins new ballpark is included.
Source: Survey of Consumer Expenditures, 2008, Bureau of Labor Statistics, U.S. Department of Commerce, http://www.bls.gov/cex/ (accessed January 18, 2009).

exists (number of teams is larger than the number of facilities) and the areas where each team has its own facility (number of teams is equal to the number of facilities).

When the number of facilities is equal to the number of teams, then there is a far larger challenge ensuring there are sufficient revenues to cover the capital cost of building each facility and the costs of annual maintenance.

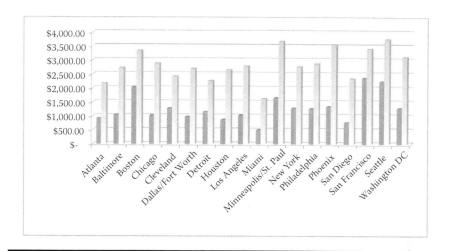

Figure 9.7   Per capita (dark bars) and household spending (lighter bars) for entertainment in selected regions (2008 dollars).

In Figure 9.7, the dark bars indicate per capita spending on entertainment (including sports) and the lighter bars represent household spending. The household spending may be more important because it adjusts for different concentrations of households without children. For example, when the unit of analysis is household spending, those living in the Phoenix and Minneapolis/St. Paul areas actually spent more for entertainment than households in New York, Boston, Chicago, and Los Angeles. Household spending in Seattle was the highest among all of the regions analyzed. At the other extreme, in the Miami region, there is reason for concern that with four teams in four facilities, there will be a challenge to generate the needed revenues. Spending in the Cleveland region was more similar to what takes place in several areas, but still at the lower end. Each of these charts and tables provides a different perspective on how substitutes and more economic competition affect demand for sports.

New Sports Facilities

Another factor that can contribute to higher levels of attendance is the facility used by a team, and this does vary among the different sports. Frequently, there is also an increment in attendance in the last year of an old facility that contains important memories for longer-term fans. For example, both the Mets and Yankees enjoyed attendance surges in their last year at the "old" Yankee Stadium and in Shea Stadium despite the fact that both teams failed to meet their fans' expectations for wins (or a division championship) in the 2008 season (Clapp and Hakes, 2005).* It also appears

---

* MLB teams that did not have a "classic" stadium had a drop in attendance of 14.4 percent during the last year of the old stadium. Teams with a "classic" ballpark had an increase of 8.1 percent in the first year of operation.

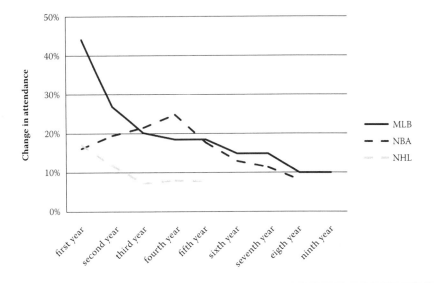

Figure 9.8 The "honeymoon" attendance effects of new facilities.

that new facilities have a "honeymoon" or "novelty" effect. The Mets certainly enjoyed that during their first season in Citi Field despite the team's poor on-the-field performance. New facilities will increase attendance, but then attendance reverts to what it was in the old facility and the importance of winning and meeting or exceeding fans' expectations returns to dominate or explain variations in ticket sales.

Figure 9.8 shows the "honeymoon" effects for new facilities used by MLB, NBA, and NHL teams. Including NFL teams in this analysis would not add any explanatory power because these teams sell most if not all of their seats every year regardless of the age of the facility. These estimates come from Clapp and Hakes (2005) for MLB (using years 1950–2002),[*] Leadley and Zygmont (2005)[†] for the NBA (using years 1971–2000), and Leadley and Zygmont (2006) for the NHL (using years 1970–2003)[‡,§]. The first year of a MLB stadium typically increases attendance by 44 percent when compared to average attendance in the old stadium. This percentage gradually decreases until attendance is essentially the same as the old stadium after 9 years. The NBA is different in that there is not a huge effect in the first couple of years, but it does have a statistically significant effect for 8 years. The honeymoon effect only lasts for 5 years in the NHL.

Now that we know these effects, we can calculate the net present value of a new stadium (using a lot of assumptions). Table 9.10 translates the percent changes in

[*] See Clapp and Hakes, 2005.
[†] See Leadley and Zygmont, 2005.
[‡] See Leadley and Zygmont, 2006.
[§] See Coates and Humphreys, 2005.

attendance into additional ticket revenue over time using average attendance and ticket prices for all clubs for the 2010 season.

A new facility will, on average, increase ticket revenue by $101 million for MLB teams, $39 million for NBA teams, and $17 million for NHL teams. This is *much less* than the cost of most new facilities, but concession sales and revenues from advertising will grow at the new facility as well. In addition, ticket prices nearly always increase in a new facility, so the estimate of new ticket revenue provided is quite conservative. There are some limitations or issues with this analysis. First, just because an average increase in attendance was calculated, it does not mean that is what will happen for each team. The change will depend on things, such as sight lines, other amenities, and team quality. The new Yankee Stadium is smaller than the facility it replaced and, despite winning the World Series, the Yankees sold fewer tickets (at much higher prices) in 2009 than they did in 2008. All teams are different, especially when we are comparing single versus multipurpose facilities.

Second, attendance and ticket prices, as already noted, usually rise when a new facility opens, and 2010 values were used to calculate attendance and revenue changes. Third, what is estimated is only regular season ticket revenue—income from parking, concessions and merchandise sold at the facility, and the sale of tickets to

Table 9.10   Expected increase in ticket revenue from a new facility

Year Team in New Ballpark	Percent Change in Attendance from Old Ballpark	Absolute Change in Attendance	Change in Ticket Revenue ($)	Discounted Revenue ($) at 5 Percent
Major League Baseball and New Ballparks				
1	44.1	1,073,891	28,715,846	28,715,846
2	26.9	655,049	17,516,015	16,681,919
3	20.2	491,896	13,153,290	11,930,422
4	18.5	450,498	12,046,330	10,406,073
5	18.5	450,498	12,046,330	9,910,545
6	14.9	362,834	9,702,179	7,601,911
7	14.9	362,834	9,702,179	7,239,915
8	10.0	243,513	6,511,530	4,627,623
9	10.0	243,513	6,511,530	4,407,260
Total		4,334,526	115,905,227	101,521,512

(continued)

Table 9.10 (continued)   Expected increase in ticket revenue from a new facility

Year Team in New Ballpark	Percent Change in Attendance from Old Ballpark	Absolute Change in Attendance	Change in Ticket Revenue ($)	Discounted Revenue ($) at 5 Percent
National Basketball Association and New Arenas				
1	16.2	113,908	5,570,087	5,570,087
2	19.5	137,111	6,704,734	6,385,461
3	21.5	151,174	7,392,399	6,705,124
4	24.9	175,080	8,561,430	7,395,685
5	17.7	124,455	6,085,836	5,006,832
6	13.0	91,407	4,469,823	3,502,223
7	11.4	80,157	3,919,691	2,924,934
8	8.1	56,954	2,785,043	1,979,278
Totals		930,246	45,489,043	39,469,625
National Hockey League and New Arenas				
1	17.1	119,170	6,109,858	6,109,858
2	11.9	82,931	4,251,890	4,049,419
3	7.3	50,874	2,608,302	2,365,807
4	8.0	55,752	2,858,413	2,469,205
5	7.7	53,661	2,751,223	2,263,438
Totals		362,389	18,579,686	17,257,727

Note: The following average prices and attendance levels were used to make these projections: MLB, 2.4 million and $26.74; NBA, 703,134 and $48.90; NHL, 696,902 and $51.27. Averages from the last completed season.

postseason games or nonsports events that the venue might host—is not included. Newer facilities have become favored locations for concerts and, in some instances, games from other sports (e.g., an outdoor hockey game or a college football game). Fourth, the analysis also assumes that the old facility in the absence of a new one would maintain a certain attendance level. While this might be true for some facilities if a team sustained its winning ways, it is not true of all and, in some instances, it would be realistic to expect that as a facility ages, there could be a slight decline in attendance. This is especially true if the older facility is already showing signs of age and is deteriorating in the absence of substantial investments to maintain or renovate it. In those situations, the new facility would be worth more than $101 million. Fifth, just because effects are not detectable after 9 years does not mean there will not be small incremental revenue effects for the very long term. There also are more subtle issues, such as what will the effect of a new facility be on television audiences? Lastly, higher income levels may be part of a league's revenue sharing program and that could change the distribution of the gains. While it is important to do an analysis as described in Table 9.10, it is also important to consider the limitations that should be included in the shortcomings of such an analysis and try to improve on the estimate from what one knows about a specific team or city.

Short Run Issues in the Demand for Tickets

Attendance

Attendance can certainly change in the short run. Furthermore, the factors that affect attendance indirectly impact other revenue streams. If more people come to a game, concession and parking revenues are likely to increase. Also, the value of advertising inside a facility increases as many of those agreements are based or indexed to attendance levels. Finally, businesses around the facility, sometimes owned by the team, also may enjoy increased revenues if more fans attend games. Looking for variations in attendance for NFL clubs is made more difficult by the game's overall popularity. Currently, for most, but not all teams, every game is a sellout. Variation in the pattern of sellouts has been related to on-the-field performance and the economic situation of the area. This pattern is most obvious from the increasing number of games that are not locally televised (the NFL permits games to be blacked out in local markets if all tickets are not sold within 72 hours of the anticipated kick-off). The Detroit Lions after unsuccessful seasons in 2008 and 2009 and the bankruptcy of two of the three automobile firms headquartered in the region had several games that were not locally televised. Jacksonville's economy also suffered in 2009 and the team's performance did not convince residents to spend their lower levels of discretionary income on tickets. It is not surprising that team performance or quality, coupled with a declining economy, leads to lower ticket sales. There is, however, an important set of management issues that result from the structure of professional football as compared to the other leagues. We turn to these after recognizing the obvious effects of on-the-field performance and the state of a region's economy.

Through 2010, NFL teams played eight regular season home games and a maximum number of two home playoff games. Even if teams required ticket holders to purchase seats to two preseason games, a season ticket would involve required purchases for 10 games with an option for a maximum of two playoff contests. Most of the games are played on weekends with the occasional weekday night game or daytime holiday contest. Notice how different that is compared to the other sports. For MLB clubs, there are 81 home games each season, and a majority of those are played on weekdays. In addition, if a team qualifies for the playoffs, an additional 11 games could be hosted leading to the sale of 92 games as part of a season ticket (playoff seats are always optional purchases). For basketball and hockey, there are 41 home games and there could be an additional 16 home playoff games for a total of 57 events. Selling packages of 10 to 12 weekend events as opposed to tickets for 50 to 92 games with a majority played on weekdays provides teams from the four major professional leagues with vastly differing marketing and management challenges. Equally successful football and baseball teams in the same market might be expected to have very different demand functions related to the number of games each plays. This can be best illustrated by looking at a comparison of attendance levels for MLB's Mets and the NFL's Jets, for the Kansas City's Chiefs (NFL) and Royals (MLB), and the Minnesota Twins (MLB) and Vikings (NFL) that played in the same facility through 2009. Numbers in bold refer to years that the teams qualified for the playoffs. A quick inspection of the data in Table 9.11 illustrates that NFL teams more often play before sellout crowds than do baseball teams, regardless of won–loss records. Notice that when the Jets won just one-quarter of their games, they sold 97.7 percent of their tickets. When the Mets won just under 60 percent of their games, they did not even sell three-quarters of the tickets to their home games.

Similar observations can be made for the teams in Kansas City. The NFL's Chiefs have had winning percentages that have varied between 12.5 and 81.3 percent, but attendance has never fallen below 93 percent of capacity. Conversely, the Royals have never sold more than 55 percent of their tickets even when their winning percentage was about 50 percent. The prolonged period of their poor performance contrasted to the Chiefs' one appearance in the playoffs in the decade is hardly sufficient to explain the difference in attendance patterns. The Twins have appeared in the play-offs four times in the decade and yet never sold as many as 60 percent of their seats. The Vikings appeared in the playoffs three times in the decade, but consistently sold out almost every one of their games. The experiences of these six teams highlights the importance of the different number of games each team plays and the days of the week those games are played in assuring high levels of ticket purchases.

The variation in attendance at NBA, NHL, and MLB permits the testing of different management decisions to understand what leads to higher levels of attendance, but there are some important caveats. Facility seating falls into two broad categories: luxury and "the deck." Luxury seating is comprised of suites, club seats, and special seating that offer a combination of extreme proximity to the action on the field, extra comfortable seats, and luxurious food and beverage choices and service. Several baseball teams offer "dugout-level suites and seating," and NBA teams place folding chairs at floor level and adjacent to the court as a sign of distinction. Ironically, given the height of the players these seats might not offer the best view of the action, but their proximity certainly offers fans a unique perspective and assures that other fans will be envious of the location. Both the Mets and Yankees provided their fans with

Table 9.11   Attendance and won–loss records of baseball and football teams in the same markets

Season	New York Mets			New York Jets		
	Winning Percentage	Total Attendance	Percent Capacity	Winning Percentage	Total Attendance	Percent Capacity
2009	.432	3,154,262	93.2	**.563**	**616,420**	**96.0**
2008	.549	4,042,047	87.0	.563	627,858	99.7
2007	.543	3,853,955	83.0	.250	616,855	97.9
2006	**.599**	**3,379,551**	**72.8**	**.625**	**618,575**	**98.2**
2005	.512	2,782,212	59.9	.250	619,958	96.6
2004	.438	2,313,321	49.8	**.625**	**623,181**	**97.1**
2003	.410	2,140,599	46.1	.375	622,255	96.9
2002	.466	2,804,838	60.4	**.563**	**628,773**	**97.9**
2001	.506	2,658,330	57.2	**.625**	**627,203**	**97.7**
2000	**.580**	**2,820,530**	**60.7**	.563	623,948	97.2
	Minnesota Twins			Minnesota Vikings		
2009	**.534**	**2,416,237**	**53.1**	**.750**	**510,203**	**99.5**
2008	.540	2,302,431	50.6	**.625**	**506,136**	**98.7**
2007	.488	2,296,383	50.5	.500	506,046	98.7
2006	**.593**	**2,285,018**	**50.2**	.375	509,743	99.4
2005	.512	2,013,453	44.3	.531	511,960	99.8

(continued)

Table 9.11 (continued) Attendance and won–loss records of baseball and football teams in the same markets

Season	Minnesota Twins / Kansas City Royals			Minnesota Vikings / Kansas City Chiefs		
	Winning Percentage	Total Attendance	Percent Capacity	Winning Percentage	Total Attendance	Percent Capacity
2004	.568	1,911,418	42.0	.500	512,969	100.0
2003	.556	1,946,011	42.8	.563	513,437	100.1
2002	.580	1,924,473	42.3	.375	512,517	99.9
2001	.525	1,782,926	39.2	.313	513,344	100.1
2000	.426	1,000,760	22.0	.688	513,394	100.1
	Kansas City Royals			Kansas City Chiefs		
2009	.401	1,797,887	54.6	.250	540,114	88.0
2008	.463	1,578,922	48.0	.125	592,622	93.2
2007	.426	1,616,867	49.1	.250	614,217	96.6
2006	.383	1,372,684	41.7	.563	623,275	98.1
2005	.346	1,371,181	41.7	.625	623,325	98.1
2004	.358	1,661,478	50.5	.438	623,010	98.0
2003	.512	1,779,895	54.1	.813	627,840	98.8
2002	.383	1,323,034	40.2	.500	625,503	98.4
2001	.401	1,536,101	46.7	.375	617,488	97.1
2000	.475	1,564,847	47.6	.438	626,974	98.6

an expanded set of luxury seating choices in their new ballparks (with vastly higher prices compared to what was paid for the most prestigious seats at the older ballparks) to complement an array of suites that had become standard in all facilities built since 1994. The new luxury seats were seen as an elevated amenity with more benefits. All teams playing in facilities built since 1994 also offer club seats. These are usually more luxurious seats, which provide access to an exclusive club where there is a wide selection of food and beverages provided in a setting where people can mingle and clients can be entertained. Suites have private meeting areas and bathrooms attached to each unit that can include as few as eight seats, but as many as 24 in some facilities. These, too, are now commonplace in facilities built in the 1990s or later.

Winning

Short of moving to another area and attracting new fans or building a new facility, the fastest way to increase the demand for tickets is for a team to win more games. While a winning team might pick up some fans for the long run, typically if a team starts losing, fans disappear. With few exceptions, winning cures all ills for a team. When a team wins, not only is there a clear, intangible benefit from an enhanced feeling of satisfaction in a community or region, but more fans attend games when teams win. (In terms of the intangible benefits of winning, think back to the 2010 Olympic Games and the mood across Canada after its men's hockey team lost to the USA and then defeated Russia in a semifinal game less than a week later.) This is even true, although to a much lesser extent, for minor league teams (Gitter and Rhoads, 2008; Winfree and Fort, 2008). In the four major sports leagues, however, the effect of winning on attendance can vary dramatically for different teams within a league (Davis, 2009). Winning also creates effects that can last from one season to the next. For example, a winning season typically creates high expectations for the next season and attendance will be high at the beginning of the next season. Winning seasons also create more loyal fans who might follow a team across many years and that, too, can lead to higher revenue levels.

There are many studies that estimate the effect of winning on attendance. While every study shows that winning leads to elevated levels of demand for tickets, these studies have relied on different data, different specifications of the models used to test for the effects of winning, and many have focused on different time periods. The varying methods obscure the effects of events or outcomes that do not occur every year (such as winning a championship). This requires some caution in the amalgamation of these studies to look for consistent patterns. A basic analysis illustrates the relationship between winning and attendance. First, Figure 9.9 plots the team's attendance for the season with their winning percentage for each team in MLB, the NHL, the NBA, and the NFL for each year from 2000 to 2010.

This figure illustrates several important points. MLB teams, for example, have a much higher seasonal attendance than the other leagues, a result of the many games played, and winning has a much larger effect on attendance for baseball

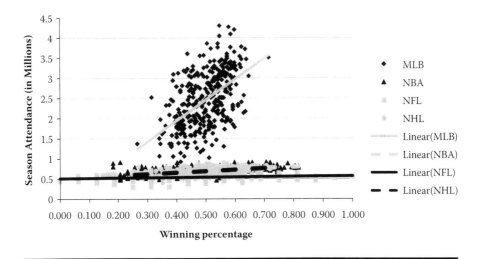

Figure 9.9 The impact of winning on attendance levels.

teams compared to other sports. That certainly does not mean that winning does not increase attendance, or demand, for other leagues. Because fans often purchase tickets far in advance, winning also increases the next season's attendance. Figure 9.10 illustrates the effect of winning on attendance for the current year and the next year. While the analysis could be improved,* it does show the basic relationship between winning and attendance from 2000 to 2010 and corresponds with the results with numerous studies. The figure also shows the percentage change in regular season attendance resulting from additional wins compared to the expectations for a team for the four major professional sports leagues that won half its games. Four of the lines represent the added attendance likely in the subsequent year based on the team's performance in the preceding season.

Interestingly, in MLB, winning actually has a slightly larger effect on a team's attendance in the following season than it does in the year in which they won the games. This takes place because, if a team is good in one year, it creates high expectations for the next year (if the most important players return) and fans base their future ticket buying habits on what took place in the preceding year. If the team does not get off to a good start when the new season begins, however, that good will and feeling can be quickly lost and ticket sales can plunge. The experience of the Cleveland Indians in 2007 and 2008 illustrate this point. In 2007, the team won the Central Division title, defeated the Yankees in the first round of the playoffs, and then lost to the Boston Red Sox, four games to three, in the American League championship series. In 2007, the team drew 2,275,911 fans and, for 2008, fans

---

* EGLS was used with the log of attendance as the dependent variable. Winning percentage, last year's winning percentage, year fixed effects, and team fixed effects were the only independent variables used.

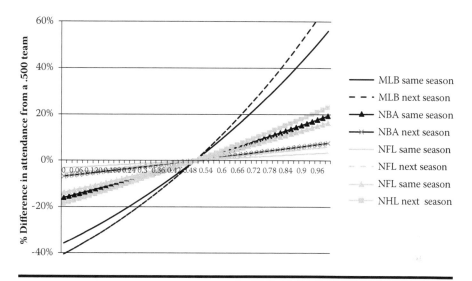

Figure 9.10   The effects of winning on that season and the next.

had high expectations for continued success. When the team faltered, attendance waned in the latter months of the season and, for 2008, the Indians sold only 2,169,760 tickets. Finally, if a team wins a few games at the end of the season, there may be too few left for attendance levels to dramatically change in that season.

Table 9.12 calculates the changes in attendance and revenue from the fitted line in Figure 9.10. This table uses 2010 average ticket prices from the four major sports leagues ($26.74 for MLB, $76.47 for the NFL, $48.90 for the NBA, and $51.27 for the NHL) to calculate the change in ticket revenue. For example, if a MLB team has a winning percentage of .400, then winning an extra game would increase attendance that year by 11,760 fans and would increase attendance the next year by 13,574 fans on average. This would mean an increase in regular season ticket revenue of $660,136. For these calculations, we used an average MLB ticket price of $26.74 and then discounted next year's revenue by 5 percent (11,760 × $26.74 + 13,574 × $26.74/1.05 = $660,136). If the team is better, has a winning percentage of, say, .600, then another win is worth an additional $801,253. This implies a win is actually worth more for a good team.

Some care has to be taken with the results in Table 9.12. The revenue estimate is for regular season ticket revenue only and does not include money earned from concessions, parking, playoff games, advertising, media outlets, or the sale of merchandise. Certainly winning has an effect on these revenue streams. If a win means that a team makes the playoffs, that win could be worth millions of dollars. These numbers only show an increasingly small part of a team's bottom line. For example, some economists claim that the winning of an extra game in MLB is worth about $2 million, maybe slightly less for an average team. This implies that our numbers

Table 9.12 Increments in attendance and ticket revenues from an additional win

Winning Percentage	MLB			NFL		
	Additional Fans That Season from One Win	Additional Fans Next Season from One Win	Discounted (5%) Ticket Revenue ($) from One Win	Additional Fans That Season from One Win	Additional Fans Next Season from One Win	Discounted (5%) Ticket Revenue ($) from One Win
10	9,009	9,933	493,876	2,164	3,664	432,345
20	9,846	11,023	543,999	2,179	3,706	436,522
30	10,760	12,232	599,243	2,193	3,749	440,742
40	11,760	13,574	660,136	2,208	3,792	445,005
50	12,852	15,063	727,259	2,223	3,836	449,312
60	14,045	16,715	801,253	2,237	3,880	453,662
70	15,349	18,549	882,828	2,252	3,925	458,058
80	16,775	20,584	972,764	2,267	3,970	462,499
90	18,333	22,842	1,071,924	2,282	4,016	466,985

(continued)

Table 9.12 (continued)   Increments in attendance and ticket revenues from an additional win

| Winning Percentage | NBA | | | | NHL | | |
	Additional Fans That Season from One Win	Additional Fans Next Season from One Win	Discounted (5%) Ticket Revenue ($) from One Win	Additional Fans That Season from One Win	Additional Fans Next Season from One Win	Discounted (5%) Ticket Revenue ($) from One Win
10	2,603	1,161	181,377	2,220	2,909	255,884
20	2,697	1,178	186,729	2,288	3,032	265,363
30	2,793	1,195	192,255	2,358	3,160	275,203
40	2,893	1,213	197,962	2,430	3,294	285,416
50	2,997	1,230	203,856	2,504	3,433	296,017
60	3,105	1,248	209,945	2,581	3,578	307,022
70	3,216	1,266	216,234	2,660	3,729	318,445
80	3,331	1,285	222,730	2,741	3,886	330,304
90	3,451	1,304	229,441	2,825	4,050	342,615

only represent about half or one-third of the effect that winning has on revenues. If we added other revenue streams, the numbers might indicate that a win is worth close to $2 million. Also, this is for an average team. The numbers might be much larger for large-market teams and smaller for small-market teams. Furthermore, winning can have a very long-term effect if it creates fans for life, and they continue to spend for tickets and memorabilia. In addition, increasing numbers of fans will lead to more advertising revenue.

While it is important for sports managers, to have an idea of how much winning is worth to your team, the actual value is not the main focus of this discussion. The main point of this analysis is to show how winning affects demand and revenue, and what sports managers must study and assess for their team. It is not good enough for managers to simply think that winning is better than losing. Winning comes at a financial cost (which we will explore later) and sports managers should understand how the financial benefit comes about. It also is useful to compare different leagues and how fans respond to winning.

Attendance: Other Factors

Many sports fans might argue (and some sports managers believe) that having a "superstar" player dramatically increases attendance. While having big-name players does increase attendance, the effect is actually relatively small. It is true that teams with more superstars have higher attendance levels, but those teams win more. Teams with star players that lose, typically do not draw that well. The Chicago Cubs did not draw that well when superstar shortstop Ernie Banks was part of the team in the 1950s and 1960s, but there are exceptions. When Michael Jordan was playing for the Washington Wizards, they played in front of large crowds at home and away even though the team was not that successful (Berri and Schmidt, 2006; Hausman and Leonard, 1997).

Players from different countries can change attendance levels and create new markets of fans. The Seattle Mariners enjoy a huge following in Japan because of Ichiro Suzuki. Although having fans in another country will not dramatically increase attendance, it can bolster other revenue streams. It's also possible for foreign players to alienate domestic fans who want to see domestic players on teams. Presumably this is the reason for limits on foreign players in the Canadian Football League as well as in other leagues. There is some evidence that foreign players were associated with decreasing levels of attendance for MLB teams, but that pattern has now been reversed (Tainsky and Winfree, 2010). The race of players also, at one time, changed attendance levels. Teams with a larger number of black players had lower attendance levels (Scully, 1974). Research has found similar outcomes in the NBA using more recent data (Kahn and Sherer, 1988; Brown, Spiro, and Keenan, 1991). In the NHL, there is some evidence that English Canadians discriminate against French Canadians. While some research shows evidence of the race of players affecting demand, other research shows no effect. It appears that if there is some discrimination from consumers, the effect is now relatively small (Longley, 1995).

Teams that generate more offense also tend to have slightly higher attendance at their games even after won/loss records are taken into account. This is one reason why leagues might change the rules such that offense and scoring will increase, and why some have wondered if there was an interest in tolerating or ignoring the use of performance enhancement drugs. For instance, when scoring was too low in the NHL, the league reduced the size of the pads goalies could wear. Typically fans do not want the fundamental nature of the game to change even though more scoring is preferred. For example, after the 1961 season (a very prolific year for hitters), MLB raised the pitcher's mound and that advantage reduced the scoring and led in 1968 to a year in which pitchers dominated. After that season, MLB lowered the mound. Fans also want to see exciting plays (and enjoy higher-scoring games) and for that reason the NBA and the NCAA use shot clocks to reduce the possibilities that teams will simply pass the ball. Before the advent of the shot clock, low-scoring games were commonplace. The NFL also has tried to limit touchbacks so there are more chances for returns for a touchdown. After injury rates increased, the NFL decided to modify its kickoff return rules.

Sports fans also like to see record-breaking performances. Many credit Mark McGwire and Sammy Sosa's race to set the season record for home runs as the decisive element that restored MLB's popularity after the 1994–1995 work stoppage. The excitement generated led some to ask if there was a lack of interest or vigilance in determining if steroids or other enhancements were responsible for the sudden surge in home runs. While work stoppages typically do not affect future demand, there is no doubt that the home run chase, and eventual record, increased the demand for baseball and for St. Louis Cardinals and Chicago Cubs games in particular (home and away). This is a short-term effect, however, since in subsequent years the number of players hitting 50 home runs in a season substantially declined. Some have attributed the decline to the crackdown on steroid use, but, in the end, no one is quite sure why 50 home runs became the plateau reached by many and, quickly, a goal few achieved. What is clear, however, is that when more home runs were hit, attendance soared. While record-breaking performances seem to be more important in MLB, record-breaking performances by Wayne Gretzky and, more recently, Brett Favre certainly increased demand for some games. Fans also prefer to see the same players on their team from year to year (Kahane and Shmanske, 1997). It is certainly understandable that fans become attached to certain players, and, when a team is constantly changing players, fewer fans will attend games. It seems that this effect is not very large and there may not be any effect in the NBA (Morse, Shapiro, McEvoy, and Rascher, 2008).

Game-Specific Determinants of Attendance and Other Factors

Until now the discussion has focused on winning, players, market size, and competition issues as they affect attendance. There are marketing or other short-term variables that can bolster attendance. It should be no surprise that more fans attend weekend games, or attend at certain times of day. Also, the home team's opponent makes a big difference. If there is a high demand for the visiting team, this will help the home team's attendance. Sometimes it is because the visiting team has a good fan base. For instance, the Yankees draw large attendances wherever they play. Attendance is usually higher when the Yankees are visiting compared with most other teams. Other times, home fans like to see rivalry games or visiting teams that have a high winning percentage.

One factor that can have long-term or short-term effects is marketing. For instance, marketing can help build a brand that creates loyal fans and helps elevate ticket demand for many years. On the other hand, other kinds of marketing, such as promotions can increase demand for a particular game. Although promotions, such as bat day, clearly help increase attendance, the question is if it simply substitutes fans away from some other game. In other words, are fans who come for bobble head day simply coming on that day when they would have gone to a different game? Although we do not focus on marketing, it can clearly have a big impact on demand.

Bill Veeck and the Birth of Sports Marketing

Bill Veeck (1914–1986) was a genius at increasing demand through marketing activities. His ideas are still practiced at most ballparks today. Other ideas were short lived, but are still well known. While working for the Chicago Cubs, he planted the famous ivy at Wrigley Field that now covers the outfield wall. As owner of the St. Louis Browns, he played 3 foot 7 inch Eddie Gaedel who walked on four pitches. Later, for one game, he let fans make all managerial decisions. He also developed the idea of "bat day" in St. Louis. As part owner of the Chicago White Sox, Veeck also started shooting fireworks when one of the White Sox players hit a home run and started putting player's names on the back of their jerseys. Of course, some of his marketing efforts, such as making the players wear shorts, did not work out so well.

Obviously sports leagues lose money during a work stoppage. The effect of a work stoppage on long-run demand, however, is less clear. Even though fans and leagues are often concerned about any long-term effects, the available evidence suggests any resentment from fans is short-lived. There are always fans of a league that will say during a work stoppage, "I'll never go to another game." Data do not typically show a drop in attendance after a lockout or strike. After the NHL lost an entire season due to a lockout, attendance levels were not substantially depressed. Fans may threaten that they will not return, but they do. Maybe the attendance is a result of "die hard" fans who could attend more games after being deprived of their ability to see their favorite team. Or, maybe fans just have short memories. While some research shows there are not long-run losses,[*] other research suggests that there are some losses from work stoppages that are being offset by new stadiums.[†]

Competitive Balance

An important aspect of the product that sport teams and athletes sell is the unpredictability of outcomes in games and matches. No matter how good the Yankees play baseball and no matter how dominant LeBron James is as a basketball player, each requires competitive teams to stage games that create the excitement and offer a degree of uncertainty with regard to the outcome. It is that uncertainty that attracts fans. When highly skilled athletes or teams play against noncompetitive squads or amateurs, the resulting exhibitions attract far fewer spectators than when the Yankees play the Red Sox or when LeBron James and the Miami Heat played Kobe Bryant and the Los Angeles Lakers. The Miami Heat is the only NBA team in the Greater Miami market, but without a league of other teams to play, the Heat would not satisfy the sports fans' demand for uncertainty of outcomes. It is crucial for the success of the sport business that fans believe every team can win and when upsets occur—as in Super Bowl XLIV when the Saints beat the favored Colts—demand is met, tickets are sold, and viewership soars. The issue is no different for sports that involve individuals instead of teams. Tiger Woods needs Phil Mickelson and Lorena Ochoa needed Michelle Wie and other competitive golfers. Roger Federer needs Rafael Nadal just as fellow tennis star Serena Williams needs Maria Sharapova.

Fans and pundits alike debate the impact the competitiveness of teams has on attendance. The argument that is made is that because fans want uncertainty and exciting outcomes, if every team has an equal chance of winning, more fans will attend. Does competitive balance lead to more fan interest and higher levels of attendance? It is difficult to answer that question because it seems people know competitive balance when they see it, but no one is quite sure of its meaning or definition. Consider the following anomalies when trying to define or describe competitive balance.

In 2009, the American League teams with the worst records were the Kansas City Royals, Cleveland Indians, and Baltimore Orioles. The Yankees had the best record. Kansas City won two of the six games played against the Yankees. Cleveland won three of the eight games played against New York, including one where they scored more than 20 runs. Baltimore played the Yankees 18 times and won 5 games. Against several teams, had the Yankees lost one more game, their

---

[*] See Schmidt and Berri, 2002; 2004.
[†] See Matheson, 2006.

"weaker" opponents would have had a winning record for the season. The Yankees paid a small handful of players more than some franchises spent on their entire team while winning 103 games (and losing 59 times to clubs with smaller payrolls). But, given the individual performances against each team, can one argue uncertainty does indeed exist? Just how large is the competitive balance problem and how far away are teams that lose from having a winning record?

In an abstract sense, competitive balance refers to the homogeneity of team quality. In practice, there can be many measures of competitive balance. If competitive balance means different teams win the championship every year, then both MLB and the NFL could sustain an argument that a high level of competitive balance has been achieved. Nine different teams have won the Super Bowl since 2000 and eight different franchises have won the World Series.

Some think competitive balance should mean different combinations of teams with the highest winning percentages in different seasons, or that a team that does very poorly in one season has a chance to win in the next. Even though teams with smaller payrolls such as the Royals and Pirates always win some games against teams with larger payrolls and might even appear in the playoffs in some years, few believe either will be consistent winners like the Yankees, Red Sox, or other large market teams. Economists have grouped measures of competitive balance into three categories: game uncertainty, playoff uncertainty, and consecutive season uncertainty (Sloane, 1976).

It is not obvious that high levels of competitive balance are good for a league. While most fans might argue that uncertainty is needed, that does not necessarily mean that a lot of uncertainty is needed. At certain college football games, there is little doubt about the outcome, but demand is high none the less. Also, while small-market fans might lament the success of some large-market teams, leagues would rather make the large number of large-market fans happy as opposed to the smaller population bases in small markets. Some fans also like to see the David versus Goliath games. Many college basketball fans want to see the low seeds win. Some fans love upsets. If a league was perfectly balanced, this could not happen. So, the optimal level of balance is ultimately a question to be answered. The academic literature is somewhat mixed on the effect of uncertainty on demand. Most studies show that fans want some uncertainty, but it does not affect attendance that much (Szymanski, 2003). Given that teams with smaller payrolls annually win some games against higher-payroll rivals, it is clear that some level of uncertainty exists. Most importantly, however, as the payrolls of larger-market teams has escalated in the past few years, so has league-wide attendance levels, suggesting that there is sufficient uncertainty to attract fans.

Television, Attendance, and Demand

As we discussed in the last chapter, television, as well as other media outlets, is increasingly important. For many sports teams, television revenue is more important than stadium revenue. Unfortunately, less is known about what creates television audiences because the data are not always easy to collect.

Many of the factors of demand for attendance are very similar to the factors of demand for television. Although studies that focus on television demand for North American sports are few and far between, some insights are available. Hausman and Leonard,[*] studying television's effect on NBA viewership levels, found a "superstar" can attract viewers, levels, but more viewers did not mean fewer tickets sold (at least when the superstar is Michael Jordan). In an analysis of the 1996–1997 NBA season, Kanazawa and Funk[†] showed that winning clearly affects local television ratings. While a high-quality visiting team will increase the ratings, the biggest effect is the winning percentage of the home team. If the team's winning percentage increases by .1, this will increase ratings by about 1.8 rating points. This represents an additional 11,600 to 121,000 households, depending on the market size. The effect of a similar increase in the winning percentage of the visiting team has about one-sixth of the effect (1,804 to 18,822 households). Games telecast on weekends have higher ratings and teams with more white players had higher television ratings than other teams. Tainsky[‡] produced an analysis of television ratings in the NFL. It is no surprise that winning percentage increases ratings for both the year the team wins and the next year. The quality of the opponent helps television ratings too. Also, both the NBA and NFL studies show that games have higher ratings when they are shown in primetime.

One question that sports managers have faced for decades is how does attendance affect television audiences and vice versa. Many owners have assumed that fans will switch between going to sporting events and watching them on television, but there is little evidence to support this. It's certainly possible that fans switch between watching a game on television or going to the game. On the other hand, it also could be the case that when fans go to some games, they have more fun later when they watch the team on television. It also could be the case that television viewers prefer to watch games where there are more fans. For example, camera operators always try to film the most expressive fans to make it appear that everyone is having a great experience at the game. Teams have even resorted to putting fans on one side of the field, the side that is being filmed on television. Evidence on the substitution for sports television and watching a game on television has had varied results. It seems that attendance is not greatly affected if the game is televised. This research has focused on European football fans,[§] rugby fans,[¶] college football fans,[**] and National Football League fans.[††]

---

[*] See Hausman and Leonard, 1997.
[†] See Kanzawa and Funk, 2001.
[‡] See Tainsky, undated.
[§] See Allan and Roy, 2008; Buraimo, 2008; Buraimo, Forest, and Simmons, 2006; Forrest, Simmons, and Szymanski, 2004; Baimbridge, Cameron, and Dawson, 1996; Allan, 2004).
[¶] See Carmichael, Millington, and Simmons, 1999; Baimbridge, Cameron, and Dawson, 1995.
[**] See Kaempfer and Pacey, 1986; Fizel and Bennett, 1989.
[††] See Putsis and Sen, 2000; Zuber and Gander, 1988; Siegfried and Hinshaw, 1979.

Reference

Allan, S. 2004. Satellite television and football attendance: The not so super effect. *Applied Economics Letter*, 11 (2) 123–125.

Allan, G. and Roy, G. 2008. Does television crowd out spectators? New evidence from the Scottish Premier League. *Journal of Sports Economics*, 9 (6) 592–605.

Baimbridge, M., Cameron, S., and Dawson, P. 1995. Satellite broadcasting and match attendance: The case of rugby league. *Applied Economics Letters* 2 (10) 343–346.

Baimbridge, M., Cameron, S., and Dawson, P. 1996. Satellite television and the demand for football: A whole new ball game. *Scottish Journal of Political Economy*, 43 (3) 317–333.

Berri, D. and Schmidt, M. B. 2006. On the road with the National Basketball Association's superstar externality. *Journal of Sports Economics*, 7 (4) 347.

Brown, E., Spiro, R., and Keenan, D. 1991. Wage and nonwage discrimination in professional basketball: do fans affect it? *American Journal of Economics and Sociology*, 50 (3) 333–345.

Buraimo, B. 2008. Stadium attendance and television audience demand in English League Football. *Managerial and Decision Economics*, 29 (6) 513.

Buraimo, B., Forrest, D. and Simmons, R. 2006. Robust estimates of the impact of broadcasting on match attendance in football (working paper). Retrieved from Lancaster University Management School, England website: http://www.lums.lancs.ac.uk/publications/viewpdf/003093/

Carmichael, F., Millington, J., and Simmons, R. 1999. Elasticity of demand for rugby league attendance and the impact of BskyB. *Applied Economics Letters*, 6 (12) 797–800.

Clapp, C. M. and Hakes, J. K. 2005. How long a honeymoon? The effect of new stadiums on attendance in Major League Baseball. *Journal of Sports Economics*, 6 (3) 237–263.

Coates, D. and Humphreys, B. R. 2005. Novelty effects of new facilities on attendance at professional sporting events. *Contemporary Economic Policy*, 23 (3) 436–455.

Davis, M. C. 2009. Analyzing the relationship between team success and MLB attendance with GARCH effects. *Journal of Sports Economics*, 10 (1) 44–58.

Fizel, J. and Bennett, R. 1989. The impact of college football telecast on college football attendance. *Social Science Quarterly*, 70 (4) 980–988.

Forrest, D. Simmons, R. and Szymanski, S. 2004. Broadcasting, attendance and the inefficiency of cartel. *Review of Industrial Organization*, 24 (3) 243–265.

Gitter, S. and Rhoads, T. 2008. If you win they will come: Fans care about winning in minor league baseball (working paper). Retrieved from Towson University website: http://pages.towson.edu/trhoads/Gitter%20and%20Rhoads%20WEA08.pdf

Hausman, J. A. and Leonard, G. K. 1997. Superstars in the National Basketball Association: Economic value and policy. *Journal of Labor Economics*, 15 (4) 586–624.

Kaempfer, W. and Pacey, P. 1986. Televising college football: The complementarity of attendance and viewing. *Social Science Quarterly*, 67 (1) 176–185.

Kahane, L. and Shmanske. 1997. Team roster turnover and attendance in Major League Baseball. *Applied Economics*, (29) 425–431.

Kahn, L. M. and Sherer, P. 1988. Racial differences in professional basketball players' compensation. *Journal of Labor Economics*, 6 (1) 40–61.

Kanazawa, M. T. and Funk, J. P. 2001. Racial discrimination in professional basketball: Evidence from Nielsen Ratings. *Economic Inquiry*, 39 (4) 599–608.

Leadley, J. C. and Zygmont, Z. X. 2005. When is the honeymoon over? National Basketball Association attendance 1971–2000. *Journal of Sports Economics*, 6 (2) 203–221.

Leadley, J. C. and Zygmont, Z. X. 2006. When is the honeymoon over? National Hockey League attendance 1970–2003. *Canadian Public Policy/Analyse de Politiques*, 32 (2) 213–232.

Longley, N. 1995. Salary discrimination in the National Hockey League: The effects of team location. *Canadian Public Policy*, 21 (4) 413–422.

Longley, N. 2006. Racial discrimination. In *Handbook on the economics of sport*, Ed. W. Andreff and S. Szymanski, 757–765. Northampton, MA: Edward Elgar.

Matheson, V. A. 2006. The effects of labour strikes on consumer demand in professional sports: revisited. *Applied Economics*, 28 (10) 1173–1179.

Miller, P. 2008. Major league duopolists: When baseball clubs play in two-team cities, (working paper). Retrieved from Minnesota State University, Mankato website: http://krypton.mnsu.edu/~millep1/papers/Major%20League%20Duopolists%20%20May%202006.pdf

Morse, A. L., Shapiro, S. L., McEvoy, C. D., and Rascher, D. A. 2008. The effects of roster turnover on demand in the National Basketball Association. *International Journal of Sport Finance*, (3) 8–18.

Putsis, W. and Sen, S. 2000. Should NFL blackouts be banned? *Applied Economics*, 32 (12) 1495–1507.

Rosentraub, M. S. 2010. *Major league winners: Using sports and cultural centers as tools for economic development.* Boca Raton, FL: CRC Press.

Schmidt, M. B. and Berri, D. J. 2002. The impact of the 1981 and 1994-1995 strikes on Major League Baseball attendance: a time-series analysis. *Applied Economics*, 34 (4) 471–478.

Schmidt, M. B. and Berri, D. J. 2004. The impact of labor strikes on consumer demand: An application to professional sports. *American Economic Review*, 94 (1) 344–357.

Scully, G. W. 1974a. Discrimination: The case of baseball. In *Government and the sports business*, Ed. R. Noll, 221–273. Washington D.C.: The Brookings Institution.

Siegfried, J. and Hinshaw, C. E. 1979. The effect of lifting television blackouts on professional football no-shows. *Journal of Economics and Business*, (32) 1–13.

Sloane, P. J. 1976. Restrictions on competition in professional team sports. *Bulletin of Economic Research*, 28 (1) 3–22.

Szymanski, S. 2003. The economic design of sporting contests. *Journal of Economic Literature*, 41 (4) 1137–1187.

Tainsky, S. Undated. Derived demand in the National Football League. *Journal of Sports Economics* (forthcoming).

Tainsky, S. and Winfree, J. 2010. Discrimination and demand: The effect of international players on attendance in Major League Baseball. *Social Science Quarterly*, 91 (1) 117–128.

Winfree, J. and Fort, R. 2008. Fan substitution and the 2004-05 NHL lock out. *Journal of Sports Economics*, 9 (4) 425–434.

Winfree, J., McCluskey, J., Mittelhammer, R., and Fort, R. 2004. Location and attendance in Major League Baseball. *Applied Economics*, (36) 2117–2124.

Zuber, R. and Gandar, J. 1988. Lifting the TV blackout on no-shows at football games. *Atlantic Economic Journal*, 16 (2) 63–73.

Chapter 10

Pricing Strategies

Introduction

One of the most important financial decisions that any team makes is the price charged for each of its products. If a team charges a high price for any of its products, it is likely that fewer units will be sold. If products have low prices, then more units are sold. As discussed in Chapter 9, demand is affected by many factors. This means that the optimal price also is affected by those same factors. For example, teams will charge a higher ticket price when they have a new facility. Those higher prices are a reflection of the improvements that range from better sight lines to improved technology that enhances each fan's experience while attending a game to wider seats and concourses that make it easier and far more pleasant to be at an arena or a stadium or ballpark.

Pricing in sports quickly becomes more complicated, however, when one thinks about all of the various effects of prices on consumption and the contribution of each aspect of a fan's consumption to gross revenues and profits. For example, because revenues come from various sources, teams must decide on prices for many different components. A team could price tickets lower, hoping that fans impressed with "bargain" admissions prices decide to spend more for food, beverages, and souvenirs sold at the facility, which have high profit margins. Managers must remember that sports products are not sold in a vacuum, but are part of a fan's "game day experience" and their relationship to and with the team. The goal is to maximize fan spending inside the facility and to ensure a long-term commitment to the team. That commitment is critical because there will be years when a team wins fewer games and it is imperative even in those seasons to be sure fans still want to attend games.

At the same time, managers have to remember that those fans who are spending premium prices for seats or food and beverages may insist upon or expect segregated entrances, clubs, and seating that offers far better sight lines than those available to fans seated in areas with far lower ticket prices. Placing luxury seating too close to the grandstands reduces the value produced and the prices that can be charged. Simply put, premium or higher-priced seats have to offer far better sight lines, exclusivity (segregated from other fans), and amenities to protect the demand for that product. In addition, every team is focused on growing its fan base as ticket revenue is declining as a percentage of total revenue for sports teams (however, it is still important). Sports managers have to be focused on efforts to create fans. Each league, for example, has developed programs designed to appeal to women and new facilities often have improved women's restroom facilities. MLB has implemented a program to reengage inner city youth in baseball in an effort to "grow their fan base." Teams in each of the leagues are actively engaged in youth sports programs and these community service activities not only create goodwill but new fans. Several MLB teams offer day game seats to youth groups at discount prices to build their fan bases.

Every team is also sensitive to its ticket pricing structure ensuring that there is an appropriate mix of expensive premium seats and an adequate supply of relatively inexpensive seats. In this way, far more people can afford to attend a game. Every NBA team offers tickets that cost as little as $10 to ensure that the game is affordable to a large segment of the population base. This might create a situation where revenue will increase in both the short run and long run. This chapter examines how prices have evolved over the past few years, the various types of pricing strategies, and the factors that prices affect.

Ticket Prices

Ticket pricing is a complex task because all too often teams do not hold auctions to understand how much fans will pay. In most instances, prices are established by the team. Sports managers have to estimate demand and then price tickets accordingly to be sure that the maximum number of fans can or will attend. Although not increasing as fast as some other revenue streams, the income earned from ticket sales can be a large factor in a team's financial stability and in determining its profitability. Over the years, it has become more expensive to attend a game. For example, in 2010, the average ticket price for a regular season Boston Red Sox game was $52.32. This is compared with an average ticket price of $9.33 in 1991. This is an increase of more than 9 percent a year. Across that same time period, average ticket prices in the NFL have increased from slightly more than $25 to approximately $75. This is not simply a change related to inflation. Fans are constantly describing how it is more and more difficult to bring a family to a game. For the 2008–2009 season, the Fan Cost Index (the cost of a family of four to go to a game) for the Los Angeles

Lakers was $479. In fact, a Lakers ticket by the bench for the 2008 NBA finals was priced at more than $27,000. When the Yankees opened their new stadium in 2009, there was a huge outcry over what many considered outrageous ticket prices. Premium seats for regular season games were priced at $2,500 per game and that was during a severe recession. While this would be an expensive ticket at any time, this seems especially high in a recessionary period. Quantity demanded at this price was not as high as the Yankees hoped and prices were reduced to $1,250 during the 2009 season (Yankees actually offered two seats for the price of one, maintaining the face value of $2,500 but increasing the number of seats and tickets a customer received).

Figure 10.1 shows the average ticket price in the past two decades for the four major sports leagues.

This chart supports several important observations. First, MLB ticket prices are quite a bit less than tickets to games in the other leagues. Presumably this is because MLB has more games than the other leagues and cannot expect fans to pay as much when the supply is so much greater. NFL teams play 10 home games (including preseason). MLB teams play eight times as many games at their home ballparks. Second, while ticket prices for NHL and NBA games were at the same level as the NFL through the 1990s, the NFL is now quite a bit more expensive. The reason for this divergence is not entirely clear. While the NFL has certainly been successful in recent years, it is unclear that there was a divergence of demand of the magnitude suggested by the price increase. Third, NFL and MLB teams have been increasing prices for the most part across the past few decades, even in real terms.

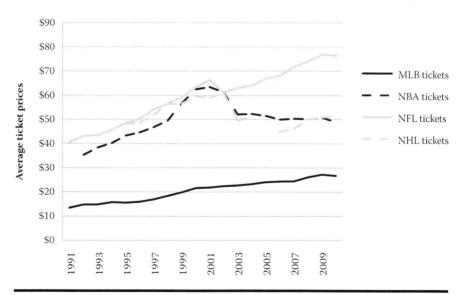

Figure 10.1   Average ticket prices in 2010 dollars, 1991–2010.

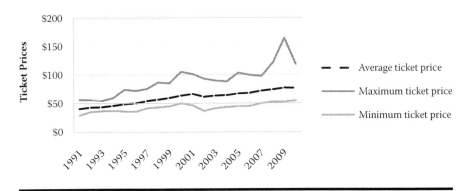

Figure 10.2   NFL ticket price changes, 1991–2009.

Figure 10.2 shows the maximum ticket price, average ticket price, and minimum ticket price for the NFL. Note that the maximum and minimum price are still averages, but for the team, not for the league. All teams have premium and less expensive seats, but the maximum ticket price represents the team with the highest average ticket price. Maximum average ticket prices spiked in 2009, a result of the pricing policies adopted by the Dallas Cowboys at their new stadium. Ticket prices (in real terms) have been increasing and the maximum average ticket price is roughly twice the minimum average ticket price.

The same changes for MLB appear in Figure 10.3. While ticket prices are lower when compared to the NFL, maximum average ticket prices skyrocketed across the past decade, but minimum prices did not increase at the same rate. One might be tempted to credit (or blame!) the New York Yankees for this; however, for the 20 years that data are available, the Yankees have had the highest ticket prices only four times. It is true that they had the highest ticket price in 2009 (the first year of their new stadium), but the other three years were all before 1998. The Boston Red Sox had

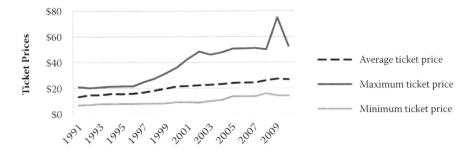

Figure 10.3   MLB ticket price changes, 1991–2009.

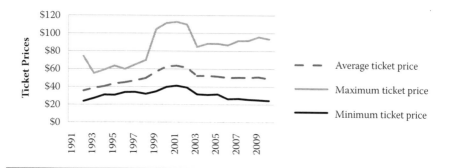

Figure 10.4 NBA ticket price changes, 1991–2009.

the highest average ticket price from 1998 to 2008 as a result of the relatively small capacity of Fenway Park.

In the NBA (Figure 10.4), ticket prices (especially for the teams able to charge the highest prices) dramatically increased beginning in the 1998–1999 season and then declined and actually approached the original levels in the 2002–2003 season. During this time, both the Los Angeles Lakers and the New York Knicks dramatically increased prices and that explains the peak of the maximum average tickets. This was not simply a phenomenon for the Lakers and Knicks. Even the teams on the low end (Golden State Warriors) increased prices in the late 1990s only to lower them a few years later.

Finally, for the NHL (Figure 10.5), for both high- and low-end teams, ticket prices seem to be flatter across the last couple of decades compared to other leagues. While there is some variation, ticket prices have not increased much once adjusted for inflation. What is particularly interesting is that ticket prices were low right before and after the 2004 lockout. Teams may have had to drop ticket prices the season before to lure fans who knew a work stoppage was eminent. They may have had lower ticket prices the year after to lure fans back to the league.

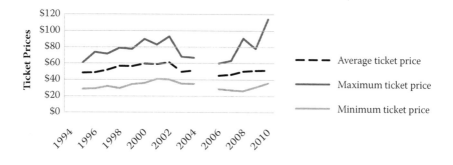

Figure 10.5 NHL ticket price changes, 1991–2009.

Are Ticket Prices Too High, Too Low, or Just Right?

The ticket prices teams charge have been somewhat of a puzzle to economists, not because prices are too *high*, but because they are too *low*. While a number of fans will claim that prices are clearly too high from their perspective, virtually all of the research shows that, on average, professional sports teams actually set their ticket prices too low, at least if they are trying to maximize ticket revenue. Some teams might have prices that are high and it is hard to argue otherwise with some of the previous examples. As a rule, however, teams set prices relatively low. That is, if teams increased their ticket prices, ticket revenue would increase. Even when the Yankees cut prices for their premium seats in half, they would have had to sell twice as many just to stay revenue neutral. While they may have sold more than twice as many, there were likely other reasons for the price decrease. For those that doubt this observation, a quick check of any online ticket reselling service will illustrate that, for most teams and for most games, there is a vibrant market where tickets are sold for prices that exceed what the teams charge.

Basic economics suggests that raising ticket prices can have three effects on profits. The first is that an increase in price increases the cash inflow for each ticket sold. The second is that a team will sell fewer tickets, which decreases cash inflow. The third is that higher prices will decrease costs because there are fewer fans. When there are large crowds, teams might spend more in the form of extra security or for janitorial services and maintenance.

Regardless, the cost to the team of one extra fan attending a game is not large, so marginal costs are negligible. Basically, teams weigh the per ticket gain from the price increase with the feared decrease in the number of tickets sold. Most businesses will raise prices until the benefit of increasing prices equals the cost of raising prices. In the absence of variable (marginal) costs, this means maximizing revenue. If teams are maximizing revenue from tickets, their ticket prices should be such that a 1-percent increase in prices leads to a 1-percent decrease in the number of tickets sold. At this point, it is impossible to get more revenue from ticket sales. If prices are more than this point, not enough people are buying tickets. If prices are under this point, the team is not getting enough revenue from each sale.* The statistical analysis done to date argues that ticket prices are too low to be maximizing ticket revenue.

Figure 10.6 shows the difference between a profit maximizing and revenue maximizing price.

Although firms will always want to maximize profit instead of revenues, in sports these two things are almost the same. Because, as previously stated, the marginal cost of an extra fan is small, there is little difference between profit maximization and revenue maximization in sports.

---

* The mathematics of the profit/revenue maximization problem are shown in Appendix 1.

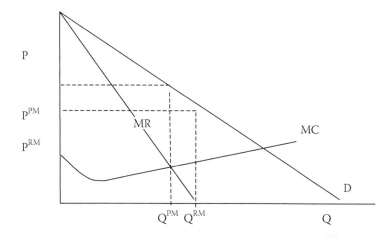

Figure 10.6   Profit maximizing versus revenue maximizing.

Statistical analysis shows that when teams do raise ticket prices, it has very little effect on attendance. In the NFL, for example, almost every game is sold out. As a result, an increase in ticket prices has virtually no effect on how many people attend the game. This, in and of itself, is evidence that ticket prices are too low. Certainly, if most NFL teams increased ticket prices by $1, they would still sell out. The only change is that the team's profit would increase at the expense of fans. In other sports, where sellouts are less common, raising ticket prices still doesn't change attendance levels very much. For example, in 2007 the Los Angeles Dodgers raised ticket prices by 26.9 percent. Their attendance actually increased by more than 1,200 fans per game even though they won six fewer games. There is example after example of this in professional team sports. While few people would argue that raising ticket prices is the cause of an increase in attendance, it *does not* seem to have a large negative effect.

There also is other anecdotal evidence that ticket prices are too low. For instance, at many sporting events, ticket resellers offer tickets for much higher than face value. While teams do not like this practice, teams know that these resellers often enjoy robust profits, providing evidence that prices are too low. Every year Super Bowl tickets are sold for many times their face value. The question that emerges, then, is why doesn't the NFL sell the tickets at that value in the first place? Also, there are many sporting events that fans know will sell out. There are clearly sold-out games where a marginal increase in ticket prices will not affect the size of the crowd in any way.

When prices are too low, that is to say that a price increase will have a relatively small effect on quantity sold, the pricing is labeled *inelastic*. When prices are too high, a price increase will have a large effect on quantity sold, and that is an example of *elastic* pricing. If the price is such that a 1-percent increase causes a 1-percent decrease in quantity, the phenomenon is labeled *unit elastic*. This is the price that

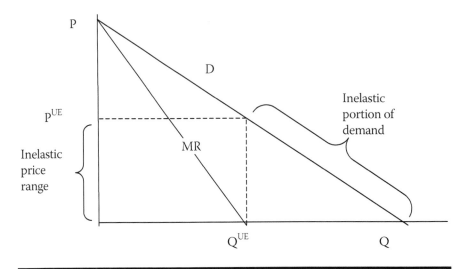

Figure 10.7   Inelastic pricing.

maximizes revenue. If additional fans increase a team's cost, then the team should actually have elastic ticket prices to maximize profits. As previously argued, the price for most sports tickets are actually low, so it is in the inelastic portion of demand. Figure 10.7 illustrates inelastic pricing.

As the figure shows, with inelastic pricing, not only are prices lower than the unit elastic price level (revenue maximizing prices are equal to the unit elastic price), the number of tickets sold is higher than the optimal level. Geometrically, a sports manager should think about the total revenue being the price multiplied by the quantity. As a result, revenue can be represented by the rectangle shown in Figure 10.7. The rectangle is the largest when the price and quantity are at the unit elastic levels.

Why Are Ticket Prices Inelastic?

There are many potential explanations for inelastic pricing (Fort, 2004).

More Fans at the Game Mean Increased Concession Sales

While low ticket prices do not maximize ticket revenue, it does get more fans to the game. This would imply that teams have an incentive to get fans into their facility, even if it means decreasing ticket revenue. As noted, teams sell a variety of products. When more fans come to the game, this could help other sources of revenue. The most obvious source of revenue that a high attendance helps is parking and concessions (Zimbalist, 1992; Krautmann and Berri, 2007; Coates and Humphreys, 2007). When there are more fans at the game, there are more consumers buying parking or concessions, both of which are often important sources of revenue for the team.

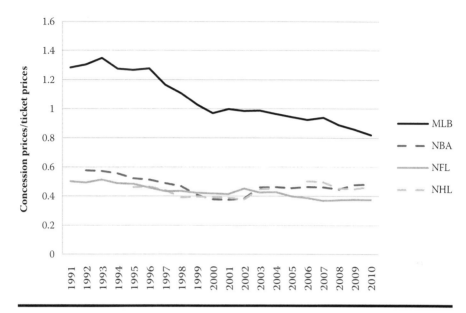

Figure 10.8   Ratio of concession to ticket prices for the four major sports leagues.

Figure 10.8 illustrates the ratio of concession prices and ticket prices. Of course, fans do not always buy the same concessions, but the graph gives us a sense of how important concessions are for each league. Concessions used in this graph are one-fourth of the Fan Cost Index with an average ticket price subtracted.* While the Fan Cost Index certainly overestimates what the average fan spends at a game, this does show us how leagues vary with each other and over time.

One clear conclusion from the graph is that MLB earns a higher percentage of its revenue from concessions compared to other leagues. This may be due to the fact that MLB has the lowest average ticket prices. Appendix 2 shows an economic model where the benefit of fans at the game is more than just ticket revenue.

More Fans at the Game Increase Advertising and Sponsorship Sales

Again, a low ticket price means more fans will attend the game. When more fans are at the game, it also is easier to find sponsors or advertisers that are willing to pay for ad space in the facility. If there are more fans at the game, there are more people looking at the advertisements. Therefore, demand for advertising increases

---

* The Fan Cost Index is available at www.teammarketingreport.com and represents the cost of four people attending a game. Included in the Fan Cost Index is the price of two adult average-price tickets, two child average-price tickets, two small draft beers, four small soft drinks, four regular-size hot dogs, parking for one car, two game programs, and two least expensive, adult-size adjustable caps.

and teams can charge a higher price for advertising space or sponsorship, which can be a very important source of revenue.

More Fans at the Game Lead to a Larger Fan Base

Bigger crowds also mean more potential fans. Moderate fans enticed by lower ticket prices may be more likely to return to a game or become an extreme fan of the team (Ahn and Lee, 2007; Lee and Smith, 2008). As friends and family of sports fans know, rooting for a team can be addictive. Therefore, getting fans to the game with low ticket prices might provide increased revenue in the future. Sometimes getting somebody to the game can make them a fan for life. Not only does this mean a higher attendance in the future, it also means higher television ratings and more merchandise sales in the future.

More Fans at the Game Increase Television Audiences

There is some evidence that attendance and television ratings are actually compliments and not substitutes. This means that, if attendance is higher, the television audience is more robust, too. It is certainly true that games with high demand have a high attendance and a large television audience. The effect is more than that. Even after trying to control the demand for the game, it seems as though attendance drives viewership. For a given game, more fans will watch the game on television if there are more people in the stands. Most fans like watching games on television when there are a lot of fans in the stadium or arena. It seems to give a more exciting feel to the game. Thus, if a lower ticket price leads to a larger crowd, this might help television ratings.

There are examples of football teams making fans sit on one side of the football field for televised games. Usually, if there are empty seats, television cameras try to hide it. In 2009, when the New York Yankees had very expensive seats behind home plate, there was no way to hide this from the cameras. Therefore, it was considered an embarrassment to the organization that so many seats were not sold in the first year of its stadium.

While the effect of attendance on television is probably positive, the effect of television on attendance is less clear. Many team owners in the past have been concerned that televising games will reduce the number of people that are willing to go to the game. Many universities were worried that too many televised games would lead to lower attendance. European football leagues have claimed that televising a game leads to a smaller crowd. Also, televising baseball games was once thought to have caused the dramatic decrease in minor league baseball teams in the 1950s. The data cannot sustain the fears of lower attendance. While attendance at televised European football matches is slightly lower, leagues that embrace television seem to do very well in the long run. While some fans might stay home and watch the game, more people become fans and might go to the game in the future.

Lower Prices Help a Team's Image and Reputation

The first four explanations all involve getting more fans to the stadium. There seems to be some other explanation needed with regard to the decision to raise prices because some teams sell out all of the time. For example, the Green Bay Packers have a season ticket waiting list of more than 80,000 people. Their games have been sold out since 1960. The Washington Redskins supposedly have a waiting list for season tickets of more than 150,000 people. Certainly, these teams could sell the same amount of tickets if they increased the price a little bit. In other words, a change in price would have absolutely no impact on attendance. There is some value to having these waiting lists or to having a remarkable number of consecutive sellouts. Sellouts and waiting lists help marketing.

Teams that sell out their games or have long waiting lists tend to advertise this fact. Even if the team does not advertise these things, other fans will. Most sports fans want to know if a team's games typically sell out. It gives the fan two signals. One is that the team's ticket is a "hot item" and they should want to go, the other is that they should get their ticket early. This type of marketing can be worth a lot to a team.

Lower Prices Produce Goodwill

Another explanation unrelated to getting more fans to a facility is that low-ticket prices may give the team some goodwill with fans. If the fans believe they are being gouged, they are less sympathetic toward things like the public sector's investment in facility (Fort, 2004b). If facilities have already been built with public money, it may be a disservice to the community to have high ticket prices. Regardless of public money, because sports teams are very public businesses, managers certainly want the team thought of in a positive way. It is clearly important for sports teams to have a strong, positive public image.

Teams Actually Are Pricing in the Elastic Part of Demand

Why does statistical analysis show that ticket prices are too low? One final possible explanation is that the statistical analyses are incorrect. Economists try to understand the demand for tickets. They control for things such as the quality of the team, types of players, the quality of a stadium, local population, average income, recent work stoppages, other sports teams in the area, day of the week, time of the game, quality of the opponent, and many other things that affect how badly fans want to watch the game live. It is possible, however, that they are not doing a good enough job. For example, the New York Yankees have a higher ticket price and higher attendance than the Pittsburgh Pirates. In fact, teams with higher ticket prices tend to have a higher attendance. Does this mean that higher ticket prices causes higher attendance? No. This means that other factors, such as market size, team quality, or team brand cause demand to be different for different teams. If demand is high for a team, prices and attendance also should both be high. This means that the challenge for researchers is to completely control for these other factors. If managers understand the dynamics of their markets, then researchers might mistakenly find that teams are pricing their tickets too low. For example, if the Dodgers made some improvements to Dodger Stadium in 2007 (when prices and attendance increased) or if there was something about the team that drew fans to the game, this can cause the researcher to err.

While it is possible that statistical analysis does not perfectly estimate the effect of ticket prices on attendance, in all likelihood, the analysis is correct in showing that ticket prices are low. While most researchers are diligent in their attempt to find the correct estimates, there is other evidence that ticket prices are too low. Remember, if ticket prices were optimizing ticket revenue, we would not see as much reselling, nor as many sellouts.

Price Discrimination

Price discrimination is when firms charge different customers different prices for identical goods. There are many types and degrees of price discrimination, and sports teams use most of them. For example, many sports teams will sell identical seats at different prices, depending on who buys them. Although this might be less common with major professional sports teams, many teams might give a senior citizen or child discount just like the zoo or the movies. This is because senior citizens and children (or rather families with children) typically have a lower demand than other fans. Because their demand is smaller, teams can generate more revenue by charging a lower price. Remember, even though children might love to go to games, a reasonable substitute might be the zoo or the movies. If the price for admission to those activities is less, their parents' willingness to pay higher prices for their tickets to a game will be understandably lower. From a financial standpoint, the more teams can dissect the demand curve, the more revenue they can generate. In other words, if a team can better guess a customer's willingness to pay by some characteristic, then they can more efficiently charge prices. Figure 10.9 shows this graphically. It is assumed that some groups (we will call them "fanatics") have a very high demand for sports. We will call the people that have a lower demand for sports "casual fans." The team will get more revenue if it can charge fanatics and casual fans different prices.

One common example of price discrimination in sports is student discounts. Often university students pay less for tickets than the general public. There are a few reasons for this, especially if students are paying for tickets at their own university. Because students are already paying for tuition, it may not seem fair to charge them the same price as other people. Also, the university might have an interest in getting students to the game so they develop a deep allegiance. Another reason is that they have less disposable income, so they might have a lower demand than

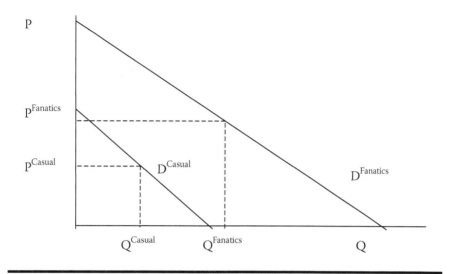

Figure 10.9 An illustration of price discrimination.

others. Therefore, they are charged a lower price. There are other ways in which sports fans differentiate themselves. For example, fans differ in the type of seats they buy, when and how they buy the tickets, or what types of games they attend. While these differences are related to price discrimination, there are other explanations as well that are discussed later in the chapter.

Luxury Seats and the Grandstand (Or Deck)

Up until this point, pricing has been discussed as if there was a single charge for every ticket to each game. Nothing could be farther from the truth. As any sports fans knows, better seats are more expensive than the "cheap seats" far from the action. While a luxury suite and a "nosebleed" seat are far from being identical goods, this has some similar characteristics to price discrimination. This is a way to separate fans on the high end of the demand curve with fans on the low end. It is important to note that corporations and businesses are more likely to buy suites or luxury boxes compared to individual fans. In regions with numerous firms and with large corporate payrolls, a far more aggressive pricing strategy could be followed with regard to high-quality seats. In turn, those regions with fewer large firms and lower corporate payrolls may need to have a different set of pricing targets.

Bulk and Group Discounts

The price of a ticket also could change if tickets are bought for multiple games. Many teams offer multiple-game packages at a slightly cheaper rate. All major sports teams offer season ticket packages as well as other multigame packages. Again, bulk and group discounts are related to price discrimination. It might be the case that some fans get diminishing returns from attending games. That is, they would really like to go to one game, but after that they become less interested. Therefore, demand decreases for multiple games. Many teams offer a discount if fans attend multiple games. In addition, large groups of fans might be able to get a discount for a particular game. Financially, this is similar to multiple-game packages. Many fans in a group may have a relatively low demand for attending a game and they may be more likely to attend if the tickets are cheaper. Of course, some of those fans also may be more likely to attend if they can go to the game with other members of their group.

Product Bundling

As with many service industries, sports teams often bundle goods with ticket prices. Product bundling is simply offering multiple goods and selling them as one. The idea is similar to selling in bulk, but instead of selling a multiple number of one good at a time, it is selling multiple goods at one time. Usually sellers are willing to sell at a discount if the buyers commit to buying multiple items. Sports seem to offer an ideal situation for bundling. Because an empty seat is a perishable good (it is worthless after the game is over), the goal for many teams is to simply get the fans to the game. Even though the cost is often very high to produce a big-time sporting event, it costs virtually nothing to have additional fans at the game. Therefore, if teams can offer other things to entice some fans, it can be very worthwhile.

Items that are commonly bundled with sports tickets are parking or maybe some concessions.* Often luxury seating comes with many complimentary items, such as food, beverages, or souvenirs (e.g., game-day programs, midgame statistics reports). Furthermore, sometimes teams can offer items to fans that no one else can. For example, only the franchise can offer some unique experience with the team (e.g., standing along the runway where players enter the field). Some teams offer season ticket holders special events with players or a former player. While these items or events are free with the purchase of the ticket, in reality, the tickets are priced higher because of these additional amenities.

Product bundling has strong marketing advantages. For example, product give-aways are simply bundling items together. Hats, bats, bobbleheads, and posters are common examples. One of the more famous examples is the all-you-can-eat section

---

* Ticket resellers also have used bundling with sports tickets, but for a different reason. While there may be a legal limit on resale price of a ticket, clever entrepreneurs circumvent these restrictions by bundling services into the tickets. These services (or extra goods) have included simple things like a pencil or coffee cup, or delivery services. Frequently there are no limits on the resale price of a ticket if it is attached to other goods and services provided by a reseller.

at Dodger Stadium in Los Angeles in the Right Field Pavilion (alcoholic beverages are not included). The obvious question is whether or not it is wise to offer an all-you-can-eat section. Most people's first thought is of the potentially unlimited cost of food that some fans might eat. But, how much could a large number of Dodger Dogs cost to produce? As with many of these pricing strategies, the real question is: What would these fans have spent if there was no all-you-can-eat section? The Dodgers hope that most of these fans would not have come to the game if it were not for these seats. In this case, each fan represents an additional $30 ($32 on the weekend) and maybe they will buy a beer or some souvenirs. Furthermore, if new fans have a good time and come back again, revenues increase, and if they return to another game, they might become lifelong Dodger fans. The Dodgers' fear is that an unusually large number of Dodger fans, who would have attended the game without the all-you-can-eat offer, self-select themselves and purchase seats in the Right Field Pavilion. Maybe these fans were already spending $50 on a ticket and food before the promotion. If that is the case, then the Dodgers would gain few benefits from the promotion. Given that a number of sports teams are now offering all-you-can-eat seats, it seems likely that a large number of the people attending are new fans generating additional revenue for the team.

Universities sometimes bundle tickets of different sports. For example, it is not uncommon for fans to be unable to buy season tickets for just one sport; they must purchase season tickets to multiple sports. This might be the most advantageous when one sport is not as popular at a university. Often teams bundle other goods with tickets, but only if certain things happen during the game. It is becoming more common to have "giveaways" tied to game statistics. The example of the 2010 Seattle Seahawks is illustrative. When the Seahawks defeated the San Diego Chargers, fans received a free 7-Eleven slurpee and an Oberto beef jerky (because the team scored a touchdown in the red zone), six free toppings on a Papa John's pizza (they scored three touchdowns and won), a small stack of buttermilk pancakes at the International House of Pancakes (they scored 21 points), Jack in the Box Jumbo Jack burger (more than three sacks of the opposing quarterback), and Top Pot doughnuts (more than 100 yards passing). As if those inducements were not sufficient, 50 fans received a yearly Xbox subscription because there were two kickoff returns for touchdowns, and one fan won tickets from Seattle to Hawaii as the Seahawks scored with less than two minutes remaining in the half. If only the Seahawks would have scored a defensive touchdown, fans would have received a free haircut from Great Clips (Rovell, 2010).

Variable Ticket Pricing

More and more teams are charging different prices for different games. It has long been the case that playoff tickets were generally more expensive than regular season games. Some teams are now changing their regular season ticket pricing based on the opponent, which is known as *variable ticket pricing*. As discussed in Chapter 9, demand changes based on the opponent. Therefore, teams can maximize profit by charging different prices based on the opponent. Teams like the San Francisco Giants will charge a lower price if the visiting team is not a team that typically draws well. In MLB, having the Yankees as an opponent typically increases attendance between 20 and 30 percent compared with some other teams. Teams know this and now many of them are charging a higher ticket price when the Yankees visit. This practice is becoming more common in European soccer. For example, Fulham FC increased ticket prices by 80 percent when they played Manchester United. There has been some fan resistance in the United States where this is a relatively new phenomenon. While it might make economic sense to charge different prices for "premium games," if the practice aggravates fans, the additional revenue might generate other costs that lead to an overall decline in revenue levels.

Day of Game Pricing

When consumers buy a ticket to an event the day of the event, sometimes the ticket is less expensive and sometimes it is more expensive. It is not always clear which strategy is appropriate for the sellers. Ultimately, it depends on the price elasticity of consumers who buy tickets early compared with consumers who buy tickets late. It might be the case that fans who buy sports tickets early are the most dedicated and do not want to take a chance on missing the game. If this is the case, then demand is very *inelastic* and quantity will not change much from a change in price. Fans who buy tickets at the last minute might be more passive and more likely to forego the game if prices were higher (more *elastic*). If this is the case, then a discount for fans who buy tickets the day of the game would be appropriate.

Alternatively, it might be the case that fans are not worried about ticket availability, but rather they are worried about their own availability or desire to go to the game. There is a value to being able to wait to decide to attend a game. Fans might end up not wanting to go to a game because something else came up or maybe the team's performance has declined. If a fan can get the same ticket on game day as months earlier, one would think they would wait to make their purchase. In this case, demand for tickets could be higher or more *inelastic* on game day and prices should be slightly higher.

Also, if it is easier for teams logistically to have the tickets sold earlier, then there should be an additional charge on game day. In 2010, the Baltimore Orioles began charging slightly more for tickets on the day of the game. Apparently they believed that fans were not as concerned about ticket availability as they were with being able to wait to buy their tickets. Or, it was better for them to have fans buy tickets early. Either way, charging fans more when they procrastinate and giving "early" fans a break could increase their revenue.

Dynamic Pricing

Teams like the Cleveland Indians have started to use dynamic pricing. This means that prices change depending on shifts in demand. If sales are high for a particular game and there are few seats left, prices for that game will increase. If sales are lagging, prices will decrease. Not only does this method respond to changes in the demand fans have to attend a particular game, it also adjusts if demand was not estimated properly. For example, if a team starts to perform well, demand will increase, and in a dynamic pricing system, the cost for tickets will rise. Also, if demand is higher than previously thought at the beginning of the season, then dynamic pricing will increase and adjust to reflect demand. This is similar to the way the airlines price tickets. Frequent fliers know very well that often the price paid depends on when the ticket was purchased. There is one drawback that is similar to variable ticket pricing. Some sports fans resent the fact that others paid less for their ticket. This can be a common issue for sports teams when they issue discounts for certain seats or games.

Personal Seat Licenses

Another important trend in sports ticket pricing is personal seat licenses (PSLs). Although this mechanism can vary, fans buying a PSL have the right to buy tickets to future games (frequently season tickets). Sometimes fans who buy a PSL receive a discount price for each future ticket purchased. Those who do not buy a PSL pay a higher price. PSLs are often sold before a new facility is built so the team (or public sector if there is a shared financing plan) has more "up-front" money and, therefore, needs to borrow less to pay for the cost of construction. NFL teams have most often sold PSLs. The Utah Jazz, the Toronto Raptors and Maple Leafs (for the Air Canada Centre), and the Charlotte Bobcats also sold PSLs to help offset the cost of the arenas in which they play. Table 10.1 illustrates the use of PSLs by NFL teams.

The Carolina Panthers were able to raise $100 million in after-tax revenue from their sale of PSLs (Ostfield, 1995). Combined, the New York Giants and the New York Jets raised more than $500 million for their new stadium. Many things, including team quality and market size affect the price of the PSLs (Salaga and Winfree, 2010). Typically PSLs cost from a few hundred dollars to tens of thousands of dollars.

First, the scale of the investment has led to the creation of secondary markets as fans look at their PSLs as investments and assets that could be sold if they wanted to liquidate their investment. Of course, the value of their investment rises and falls with the quality of play. In some markets, however, where there are very long waiting lists to buy tickets, the value of a PSL could increase.

Table 10.1 Timeline on the use of PSLs in the NFL

Year Venue Opened	Team	Name of Program
1995	St. Louis Rams	Personal Seat License
1996	Carolina Panthers	Personal Seat License
1998	Baltimore Ravens	Personal Seat License
1999	Cleveland Browns	Personal Seat License
1999	Tennessee Titans	Personal Seat License
2001	Pittsburgh Steelers	Seat License
2002	Houston Texans	Personal Seat License
2002	Seattle Seahawks	Charter Seat License
2003	Chicago Bears	Personal Seat License
2003	Green Bay Packers	Personal Seat License
2003	Philadelphia Eagles	Stadium Builder License
2004	Cincinnati Bengals	Charter Ownership Agreement
2009	Dallas Cowboys	Seat License
2010	New York Giants	Personal Seat License
2010	New York Jets	Personal Seat License

Second, the income generated by PSLs is nothing more than the present value of a per ticket surcharge. In other words, fans purchasing PSLs simply impute or add that value to the price of the ticket. The team could dispense with PSLs and charge higher ticket prices, or it could charge a PSL and a lower ticket price. The market that exists for the PSL and the ticket is the same. For the team or a city, the PSL generates more up-front cash. In the long run, however, the total cash (higher ticket prices versus PSL plus slightly lower ticket prices) is the same. The present value of the PSL does improve a team's cash flow and, therefore, is more beneficial. The risk or drawback is that asking, in advance, for money as opposed to a payment each year, can alienate some fans.

Colleges and universities have also started issuing PSLs, although sometimes they are identified as "contributions." Often colleges will require fans to make an annual contribution that is a de facto PSL. Even when colleges do not have this system, those individuals who make large donations receive the opportunity to purchase the best seats for games. Thus, the donation becomes a sort of PSL. Regardless of whether it is part of an official PSL program or not, a portion of these annual prepayment "contributions" is treated as a tax deduction (contribution to a nonprofit organization) under the existing U.S. Internal Revenue Code.

One question that arises is: Why do teams have PSLs? In other words, why don't teams just simply raise ticket prices instead of making fans pay for a PSL and then pay for tickets? There are a couple of possible explanations for this. One reason is that revenue generated from PSLs is often treated differently than other revenue. For example, in the NFL, revenue from PSLs is not shared with other clubs and the players. Ticket revenue, however, is included in the revenue sharing plan. Teams can only issue a PSL when they are building or renovating a stadium. Therefore, PSLs are a way for the NFL to give teams an incentive to build a new stadium which helps the league.

Another possible explanation for the increase in PSLs is two-part pricing also called a two-part tariff. Two-part pricing also is used by businesses, such as Sam's Club or Costco. Customers pay a membership fee and then get a discount on products. In sports, this happens at places like golf courses. Golfers can pay per round of golf, or they can typically pay a yearly membership. Why would a store, golf course, or sports team do this? Because it can increase the quantity sold and the revenue that the firm or team receives. If there is no PSL, fans will pay for tickets until their willingness to pay is at least as great as the ticket price. With a PSL, however, teams can capture the entire willingness to pay for the entire season.

Suppose a team prices tickets at the optimal price and a typical fan buys three tickets, but the fan will buy eight tickets at a discounted price. Clearly the fan is happier when the tickets are discounted. To buy tickets at the discounted price, however, the team can charge for a PSL. The price of this PSL would be equal to the sum of the differences of willingness to pay and the discounted price. Therefore, the team receives more revenue with a PSL and lower ticket prices than with higher ticket prices. Appendix 3 gives an example of this. Because most NFL games are sold out, the two-part pricing explanation seems unsatisfactory. Because the NFL does not really need to sell more tickets, the revenue-sharing explanation may be more appropriate.

Teams have tried different ways to initiate PSLs. One informative example involves the New York Jets/Giants stadium. Even though the Jets and Giants share the same stadium, they sold their PSLs in different ways. Like a vast majority of teams with PSLs, the Giants set prices for their PSLs and some fans were not happy. Understandably, fans can get angry when they must pay just for the right to buy a ticket. While Jets fans may not have been happy about the PSLs, their club handled things differently. For some of the best seats, the Jets sold the PSLs using an auction. Because demand for the PSLs was not entirely known, an auction gets fans to offer a bid at least close to their willingness to pay. Therefore, the Jets generated more revenue for some of the premium seats. Also, fans seemed less dissatisfied because the Jets let the market set the price. In summary, PSLs should be thought of as a futures market for tickets. The PSL is itself an option. The fan buys the PSL or pays an option that means they secure seats for the future at a price that is lower than it would be if the PSL did not exist. If the team plays well and demand increases, the fan can sell the ticket or the PSL for a higher price and make a profit. If demand drops, the fan could own a PSL or tickets worth less than the face value of the investment.

Condominium Seats

For some arenas in Europe, "condominium seats" have been sold in an effort to raise more revenue to reduce construction loans. One American university also sold condominium seats to pay for the cost of a facility's renovation. The price charged, usually several hundred thousand dollars, ensures the buyer that he or she can occupy a seat for every game or event that is held at the facility for a fixed period of time (usually 10 or 20 years). The condominium seat buyer does not have to pay for any ticket to any game or event during their period of tenure. In other words, just like a condominium in a building, the purchaser owns the seat for every day and can watch every event. Managers have to carefully price their "condominium seats" because it commits them to provide the owner with tickets to every single event at the facility. In the case of a university, loyalty to the institution might be a real inducement, but the purchase could make the buyer less likely to make other philanthropic gifts to the alma mater.

Futures Options

Another pricing strategy that has become more popular is selling futures options. This happens in the case of playoff tickets, which can often be hard to secure. In a manner similar to PSLs, teams and leagues have started to sell the right to buy playoff tickets for a particular team. The main difference from PSLs (or condominium seats) is that a team may or may not actually appear in the playoffs. If the team does not appear, then the buyer holding the futures ticket loses the value of his/her investment. If, however, the team does appear, then the buyer is guaranteed a seat at the future price paid, not the actual face value of the ticket. This has been done somewhat informally for Super Bowl tickets. Many fans would only like to purchase Super Bowl tickets if their favorite team is going to play. Once the Super Bowl teams are known, tickets often become very expensive. While the NFL sells the tickets at face value, secondary markets typically charge much more. Therefore, if one does not wish to purchase the tickets on the secondary market, it is possible to buy a futures option. That is, you can buy the right to purchase the ticket if your favorite team is playing in the Super Bowl or some other playoff game.

MLB has officially started selling futures options on playoff tickets.* The main difference is that MLB sanctions the selling of the futures, instead of involving

---

* http://mlb.mlb.com/mlb/tickets/ticket_reservations.jsp

a third party. MLB calls this a "postseason ticket reservation." For the 2010 season, fans were able to buy these reservations for either a division series for $10, a league championship series for $15, or the World Series for $20. Given that each household is supposed to be limited to one game, two tickets per series, this led to a maximum price of $90 for postseason reservations. Given what we know about demand, one would think that the optimal price would be different for different teams. For example, one would suspect that the value of such an option would be higher for the New York Yankees than the Pittsburgh Pirates. Not only are there more fans in New York to buy tickets, but the probability of the Yankees appearing in the playoffs is typically higher compared to the chance of the Pirates making it to postseason play. Regardless, this difference in demand will clearly change the quantity demanded given that prices are constant and, in 2010, the Yankees sold out all of their "postseason ticket reservations." Of course, MLB on their website tries to leverage small-market fan loyalty by asking: "How optimistic *are* you?" This is a clever marketing ploy designed to enhance revenues.

Ticket futures are a form of insurance. There is a certain probability that an event will happen, like your favorite team making the playoffs. If this happens, you want to be prepared. Therefore, if you buy this option, you will not be gouged by high ticket prices in secondary markets or even worse, be without a ticket. On the supply side of the market, the sellers can sometimes make more money than just selling the ticket after the playoffs are known if they sell options to fans of different teams. As with many of these strategies, however, there could be a balance of short-term revenue weighed against customer dissatisfaction. With sports, though, as in many other industries, paying higher prices for things that were not charged for in the past, customer anger might be noticeable. The question is if the anger shows up on the balance sheets.

Pay What You Want

Another interesting phenomenon is letting fans or customers pay whatever they want. This may seem odd, but this is becoming a more attractive pricing strategy for some businesses. While some fans may take advantage of this pricing strategy and not pay much, many fans will actually pay more. If fans actually paid what they were willing to pay (probably not many fans would), this would be a form of price discrimination. Typically this type of pricing has been limited to things related to fundraising or nonprofit activities, such as car washes or museum entrance fees. This has become more common, and some restaurants are letting customers pay what they want.

This happened in sports with the British soccer team Mansfield Town. For one game, the team allowed fans to pay what they wanted. Apparently prices varied from "as little as three pence to as much as £50" (Etoe, 2010). The usual ticket price was £16. It is not clear whether the price per person was up or down, but the team did enjoy a large crowd for that game. There could be many effects of a pricing strategy such as this. On the negative side, fans might not pay much. Furthermore, even though the crowd was large, there may be a substitution between fans who would go to some other game with fixed prices, but instead went to the game with no set prices. On the positive side, many fans went to the game. This will increase concession sales, it might create more long-term fans, and it might also create some goodwill with fans.

In a similar fashion, the Florida Panthers have started selling season tickets by allowing fans to make an offer, which may or may not be accepted (Talalay, 2010). This is similar to the more known *Priceline* strategy. While this is different from Mansfield Town's strategy in that not all offers are accepted, they are selling tickets at a discount that fans chose. Again, even if this is a bad strategy in terms of maximizing ticket revenue, it may help concession revenue and advertising revenue. One downside is that it could anger season ticket holders who have already paid full price for tickets.

Media Prices

As already discussed, revenues from media outlets are becoming more and more important for teams. Pricing broadcasting rights and other media contracts is very different from ticket prices. In fact, typically teams do not price media contracts. Instead, teams sell rights to the highest bidder. Broadcasting fees are sold to the highest bidder through the team, league, or conference. This is generally done by using a sealed bid auction. This means that media providers will submit their bids for the broadcasting rights, and then the team, league, or conference will accept the highest bid.

Although radio and the Internet is a source of revenue for most major teams, the money from television contracts accounts for the vast majority of media revenue. Teams sell television broadcasting rights in two ways: nationally and locally. When thinking about major professional sports, most leagues have a national contract. Teams do not have to worry about negotiating these contracts because they are done by the league. National contracts are an important source of revenue for virtually all major sports leagues including professional golf and tennis. Local contracts also can be important for leagues like MLB, the NBA, and the NHL. The local contracts are negotiated by the team.

It is similar for college sports. A vast majority of college sports teams negotiate media contracts through their conference. A select few teams do not belong to a conference and they negotiate their own contracts. For example, Notre Dame football does not belong to a conference and has its own national contract with NBC for its football games. On the other hand, it can be difficult for independent teams without the cachet of Notre Dame to negotiate a national contract. What makes pricing media contracts so different from pricing tickets is that there are very few parties involved. For example, if a media company wants to show professional football games, the NFL has a virtual monopoly. Media companies must go through the NFL. Even if media companies are not picky about which professional sport they want, there are still only a few prominent professional sports leagues. Even when teams sell broadcasting rights individually, they still might have a local monopoly on their sport. College sports are also in the mix, but clearly there are not that many ways for media companies to get the sports programming that they want.

There are more media outlets, but it is still not a perfectly competitive market. Most major sporting events in the United States are seen on FOX, NBC, ABC, CBS, or one of their subsidiaries. The number of buyers and sellers is always important in any market. Buyers always want fewer buyers, and sellers always want fewer sellers. If there is only one buyer (monopsony), the price will be low. If there is only one seller (monopoly), the price will be high. This helps us understand why teams often prefer to sell rights collectively through the league as opposed to each team selling its rights individually.

Selling rights collectively can have two effects. First, if teams sell rights collectively, there is an incentive to sell rights to fewer games. This is because if fewer games are televised, the price per game is higher. Essentially the market is moving up the demand curve. Selling collectively is essentially creating a monopoly, which means that teams can earn higher profits by restricting the number of game sold. Second, if the league is selling rights, they can charge whatever media companies are willing to pay. If teams are selling rights, media companies can buy rights from the team with the best deal.

On average, teams are better off if they can collectively sell broadcasting rights. It gives the teams and league more market power. In the United States, the Sports Broadcasting Rights Act of 1961 allows leagues to collectively sell their broadcasting rights. As discussed, college sports were not afforded this same right until the University of Oklahoma and the University of Georgia sued the NCAA. For events like the NCAA Men's basketball tournament, broadcasting rights are collectively sold. In 2010, the NCAA sold broadcasting rights to the tournament for both television and Internet to CBS and Turner Broadcasting for $10.8 billion, a 14-year contract paying $740 million per year to the association.

There are also many differences in the way European football teams sell their media rights. Some leagues sell their rights through individual teams (La Liga, Serie A), while some rights are collectively sold. The English Premier League sells media rights collectively, but there are differences with the North American leagues that collectively sell rights. For example, for many years the English Premier League sold exclusive rights to BSkyB, a European network. The European Commission forced the league to sell rights to more than one network starting in 2007. Also, the league does not share the rights equally. The large-market teams (more specifically teams that are on television more often and/or teams that win more often) receive a larger share of the revenue. With the contract starting in 2010, the English Premier League receives £594 million (about $912 million) per year.

The only teams that might be worse off with collectively sold media rights are the large-market teams. Typically, collectively sold broadcasting fees are divided evenly among teams (the English Premier League is an exception). Even though fees will be higher on average, large-market teams might be able to individually negotiate more money than they would get through the league. Sometimes a large slice of a small pie is bigger than an equal slice of a bigger pie.

Merchandise Pricing

Creating optimal prices for merchandise has elements of ticket and media pricing. Merchandise is no different from tickets in that there is a demand for merchandise and there is an optimal price that balances increasing prices with selling more of the product. In theory, the elasticity of merchandise is similar to the elasticity of ticket sales. The number of buyers and sellers in the market also is important. Teams have a monopoly with regard to selling merchandise for their team. To the extent that fans choose between buying merchandise from different teams in the same league, they gain more market power if they collectively sell merchandise. For example, there is a demand for LeBron James's jersey. There is also a demand for Kobe Bryant's jersey. If teams are individually selling merchandise, the Miami Heat would be competing with the Los Angeles Lakers to sell jerseys. If the NBA is selling jerseys, they will raise the price of both jerseys and increase revenue for the teams.

What constitutes sports merchandise has actually changed over time. Today, even tickets could be considered merchandise. For example, on May 19, 2010, Roy Halladay of the Philadelphia Phillies threw a perfect game against the Florida Marlins. A perfect game is very rare and this was only the 20th in MLB history. What is interesting about this, from a financial standpoint, is what the Marlins did with the tickets. Because tickets to this event became a collector's item, they sold tickets even after the event had happened. They were able to sell tickets to the game, after the game, at the original prices. One drawback from this is that it may not be good publicity to sell tickets to an event that has already happened, especially when it is marketing a performance of a visiting player. During the same season, Matt Garza threw a no-hitter for the Tampa Bay Rays. The Rays did something similar by offering fans tickets to the game, after the game had been played, but only to fans who attended a charity event.

References

Ahn, S. and Lee, Y. H. 2007. Life-cycle demand for Major League Baseball. *International Journal of Sport Finance*, (2) 25–35.

Coates, D. and Humphreys, B. R. 2007. Ticket prices, concessions, and attendance at professional sporting events. *International Journal of Sport Finance*, 2 (3) 161–170.

Etoe, C. 2010. Attendance doubles as Mansfield fans pay what they want. BBC, February 6, on-line edition, http://news.bbc.co.uk/sport2/hi/football/teams/m/mansfield_town/8502204.stm (accessed April 10, 2011).

Fort, R. 2004a. Inelastic sports pricing. *Managerial and Decision Economics*, 25 (2) 87–94.

Fort, R. 2004b. Subsidies as incentive mechanisms in sports. *Managerial and Decision Economics*, 25 (2) 95–102.

Krautmann, A. and Berri, D. 1997. Can we find it at the concessions? Understanding price elasticity in professional sports. *Journal of Sports Economics*, 8 (2) 183–191.

Lee, Y. H. and Smith, T. 2008. Why are Americans addicted to baseball? An empirical analysis of fandom in Korea and the U.S. *Contemporary Economic Policy*, 26 (1) 32–48.

Ostfield, A. 1995. Seat license revenue in the National Football League: Shareable or not?. *Seton Hall Journal of Sport Law*, (5) 599–610.

Rovell, D. 2010. The Seattle "Freehawks" show teams future of sports marketing. CNBC, September 28, on-line edition, http://www.cnbc.com/id/39398351/The_Seattle_Freehawks_Show_Teams_Future_Of_Sports_Marketing (accessed April 10, 2011).

Salaga, S. and Winfree, J. 2010. Secondary market demand for National Football League personal seat licenses and season ticket rights (working paper). University of Michigan.

Talalay, S. 2010. Florida Panthers: Name your own price for tickets. Retrieved from http://blogs.trb.com/sports/custom/business/blog/2010/08/florida_panthers_name_your_own.html

Zimbalist, A. 1992. *Baseball and billions: A probing look inside the big business of our national pastime*. New York, NY: Basic Books.

Appendix 1

In this section we illustrate pricing that maximizes revenue. In general, firms maximize the following profit function:

$$\pi = QP(Q) - C(Q)$$

where π is the profit, Q is the quantity sold, P is the price of the product, which is a function of the quantity sold and C is the cost function, which is also a function of the quantity sold. $QP(Q)$ represents the total revenue and $C(Q)$ represents the total cost. Using calculus, we can find that firm's maximize profit when marginal revenues equal marginal cost:

$$MR = QP'(Q) + P(Q) = C'(Q)$$

where $P'(Q)$ is the change in price when quantity increases, or the slope of the demand curve, and $C'(Q)$ is the change in the cost from additional quantity.

For sports a simplifying assumption is possible. When more fans arrive at a game, the costs are not that much more. It is true that more fans may mean higher custodial or maintenance costs, but usually these additional costs are minimal. Therefore, it can be assumed that $C'(Q) = 0$ and teams only need to worry about maximizing revenue. If marginal costs are not minimal, this would lead to higher optimal prices and lower optimal quantities.

Therefore, it is optimal for teams to set prices where marginal revenue equals zero, or when $QP'(Q) + P(Q) = 0$. This shows that there are two effects of changing quantity (or price) on revenue. If the number of fans who show up increases by one person, then the team will get additional revenue equal to the price of the ticket, but they also will lose money on all of the fans they already had because they had to decrease prices to get that additional fan.

An analogous way to think about this would be using the price elasticity. Rearranging the equation in the previous paragraph produces:

$$\frac{-P(Q)}{QP(Q)} = 1.$$

The left half of the equation is known as the price elasticity. The elasticity shows what percent of consumers or fans will not come if prices are increased 1 percent. Revenues are maximized when the elasticity equals 1. In other words, revenues are maximized if you are at the point where a 1 percent increase in price will lead to a 1 percent decrease in quantity. If elasticity is equal to more than 1, it is said to be elastic. This means consumers are sensitive to price and prices should be decreased to maximize revenue. If elasticity is less than 1, it is inelastic. In this case, consumers are not sensitive to price and prices should increase to maximize revenue.

In this case, an example can be very useful. Suppose that demand for some sporting event is given by:

$$P = 80 - 4Q$$

and the cost is given by:

$$C = 20$$

Note that the cost does not change depending on how many people show up to the game. In this case profit is given by:

$$\pi = 80Q - 4Q^2 - 20$$

which is just price multiplied by quantity minus the cost. Using calculus, we can show that the marginal revenue is equal to:

$$MR = 80 - 8Q$$

(if demand is linear so that it is in the form of $P = a - bQ$, then marginal revenue can be written as $P = a - 2bQ$). If marginal revenue is set equal to zero, then the optimal quantity is 10. To find the optimal price, the optimal quantity of 10 in the demand curve is used to show that $P^* = 80 - 4(10) = 40$. Therefore, the optimal price is \$40, which will bring in 10 people. Plugging this back into the profit function yields:

$$\pi = 80(10) - 4(10)^2 - 20 = 380$$

At most, the team can earn \$380 profit.

An analyst can also can use the elasticity. In this example, elasticity equals:

$$\frac{-(80 - 4Q)}{QP(Q)}$$

Using calculus $P'(Q) = -4$. Even without calculus, one can still think about its interpretation. What this is saying is that when quantity increases by 1, price goes down by 4 (if demand is linear so that it is in the form of $P = a - bQ$, then $P'(Q)$ is equal to $-b$). Therefore, the elasticity becomes:

$$\frac{-(80 - 4Q)}{-4Q}$$

which can be reduced to:

$$\frac{(20 - Q)}{Q}$$

If the elasticity is set equal to one, the optimal quantity is 10, which means that the optimal price is $40. If the price is set at $41, the price is elastic. If price is set at $39, the price is inelastic.

Appendix 2

This section analyzes pricing with multiple revenue streams. Assume, as in Appendix 1, that demand for tickets is given by:

$$P = 80 - 4Q$$

and the cost is given by:

$$C = 20$$

However, now assume that each fan at the game is worth an average of $16 because they might buy concessions or park a car. In this case, profit is given by:

$$\pi = 80Q - 4Q^2 - 20 + 16Q$$

which is price multiplied by quantity minus the cost plus ancillary benefits from extra fans. Using calculus, it can be seen that the marginal revenue is equal to:

$$MR = 96 - 8Q$$

This time, if marginal revenue is zero, then the optimal quantity is 12. To find the optimal price, we use the optimal quantity of 12 in the demand curve to show that:

$$P^* = 80 - 4(12) = 32$$

Therefore, the optimal price is $32, which will bring in 12 people. In this case, if ticket prices are $40, then 10 people go to the game and the team earns $540, but if ticket prices are $32, the 12 people go to the game and the team earns $566.

The price elasticity is the same as in the last example:

$$\frac{(20 - Q)}{Q}$$

If quantity is 12, then elasticity equals .667, which means that the prices are in the inelastic range.

Appendix 3

This section examines two-part pricing. Again, as in Appendix 1, it is assumed that demand for tickets is given by:

$$P = 80 - 4Q$$

and the cost is given by:

$$C = 20$$

In this case, though, it is assumed this is the demand for one individual and that individual may buy multiple tickets. Now, suppose the team could charge the fan the exact price the fan would be willing to pay for each ticket. If the team could do this, they would charge the fan $800 for a bundle of 20 tickets. The value $800 can be found by finding the area under the demand curve or by integrating the demand function. However, it is not likely that the team will be able to charge the fan a price equal to their willingness to pay. They could, however, charge a PSL fee of $800 and then give the tickets to the fan for free. Clearly teams are not likely to give tickets away, but this happens in this model because no marginal costs are assumed. What is key in this example is that the team has generated $800 in revenue. Because of costs, profits are $780. Furthermore, the team sold a total of 20 tickets.

Chapter 11

Capital Budgeting and Team Investments

Introduction

This chapter focuses on capital budgeting techniques and the benefits and costs of different types of financial investments that teams make. Capital budgeting is the process of evaluating and selecting long-term investments that are consistent with a firm's goal. Almost every firm's goals, at least in a financial sense, include the generation of profits. Capital budgeting typically refers to long-term investments. Although there are myriad financial decisions that teams constantly make, the focus in this chapter is on the longer term commitments that include the (1) purchase of the franchise, (2) the building of a facility, and (3) investments in players. Managers have to understand critical and fundamental financial concepts and apply them to these investments. There are a few financial concepts that are unique to the sports business, and these also are addressed in this chapter. At the heart of this book is the observation that the sports business has become dominated by large-scale investments in real estate, the media, and entertainment. When this happens, teams become part of a larger conglomerate. These other investments must be considered when analyzing the financial returns of team. In a sense, the team is at the center of the conglomerate, but some of the other activities could actually account for more of the profits produced by the overall set of businesses linked to each other because of the existence of the team. In addition, when a team is involved with the building of a new facility, ownership must estimate the new revenue streams that will be created. These revenue streams have to increase profits to the point where the investment in the facility makes financial sense. If a facility costs too much, a team's financial position could, in theory, be stronger in an older facility. In a similar manner, it is important to keep in mind when investing in players the additional revenue that could be raised, and these funds have to exceed the cost of acquiring a new player. A team's owner and management staff must consider as well the effect a "star" has on the other players on the team. If the star is seen as taking too much of the team's revenues, jealousies can arise leading to discontent. In terms of owning a team, building a new facility, or signing players, it is essential to assess each investment as it affects an owner's complete portfolio. At the end of the chapter, is an analysis of the cost of some of these investments using a cost of capital approach.

Team Investments

Chapter 8 discussed franchise valuation. In that chapter, historical and current values were analyzed using different financial models. Profits taken out of the team's operations were largely ignored in the valuation process. In contrast, in this chapter, the different investments are compared in terms of their rate of return and risk level. Correlations also are assessed to understand how various assets are related and what might be a particular team's optimal strategy for producing profits. In sports, as with any industry, it is important to understand that the value of investments relative to profit levels can change depending on what else an investor owns.

Like any investment, team owners and their managers need to focus on expected profits and the level of risk assumed when they buy a team or make any other long-term commitment related to the franchise. One way to assess that return is through an estimate of value, but typically it makes more sense to assess rates of return and some quantitative measures of risk. To do this, it is imperative to know what is meant by rate of return (and a manager needs to understand his/her owner's expected rate of return). While "return" can mean the amount of profit earned across a certain period of time, "rate of return" compares the profit with the initial investment. The rate of return is then expressed as a percentage of the investment made. Calculating a rate of return for an asset can be slightly more complex as it is necessary to account for both an increase in the value of an asset as well as any cash flow that was received from the asset. The rate of return across a given year can be calculated by:

$$k_t = \frac{C_t + V_t - V_{t-1}}{V_{t-1}}$$

where k_t is the rate of return in period t, C_t represents any cash flows in period t, and V_t represents the value of an asset in period t. V_{t-1} is the value of the asset in the previous period (a period is almost always a year so that an annual rate of return is presented). If the asset is a publicly traded stock, the value would simply be the price of the stock. In the case of sports teams, it is the price or value of the franchise. Cash flow is a general term that could represent dividend or profits. In the context of buying sports teams, the rate of return of the team would be any profits that owners received plus the increase in value, all divided by the value of the team in the preceding year.

Calculating a return is usually straightforward if reliable data are available. The difficult part is estimating expected future returns. Finding the expected return can be very difficult and it always helps to have some institutional knowledge. For example, is the league going to receive a big media contract in the future? If so, one would expect profits to increase. Also, trends are very important. As noted in Chapter 8, the value of all major professional sports teams in North America has increased over the past several decades. If one thinks that the economy will enter into a prolonged contraction, then future returns will not be as robust. For the purposes of this chapter, the focus is on averages of past results. While this might be a somewhat crude measure, it is a convenient starting point. Expected return of an investment as the average of past results is given by the formula:

$$\bar{k} = \frac{\displaystyle\sum_{j=1}^{n} k_j}{n}$$

where $\bar{k}$ represents the expected return, k_j is the return in year j, across the last n years.*

Past rates of return are not always the best measures of future rates of return. If a team won the championship, one would expect profit levels to increase not only for that year, but probably the year after. But, because most teams do not win the championship every year, it could be expected that returns could decrease in future years. If, on the other hand, the team experienced some bad luck in the past, returns might be expected to increase. Good financial analysts show some foresight into the revenues and costs of the firm. It is not uncommon to offer projections based on different scenarios and to offer a range of expected outcomes.

---

* If we had more information about the chances of different outcomes, a weighted average could be found. For example, if there were some prior knowledge about the probabilities of certain outcomes, or if we wanted to put more weight on more recent outcomes, we could then use those probabilities to find a better expectation about future returns. The weighted average is calculated by:

$$\bar{k} = k_j p_j$$

where k_j is the return for outcome j and p_j is the probability of outcome j.

Risk

Once future returns are estimated, the next factor to be considered is risk. One definition of financial risk is the variability of returns of an asset. If the expected returns are for the most part known with little variability, then there is little risk. On the other hand, if future returns are very unclear and dependent upon numerous factors, then there is a high level of risk (or uncertainty). Nearly all investors are risk averse and try to minimize it. Some financial managers are willing to assume larger levels of risk when there is an expectation of far more substantial returns. When there is greater risk, there is usually the opportunity for far more earnings and profits. Historically, investments with low risk (bonds, U.S. Treasury Bills) have had low average returns over the long run. Investments with high risk (small companies) have had high average returns, although the journey to a long-run average can involve numerous peaks and valleys (a bumpy ride). In terms of sports teams, it is not necessarily clear what constitutes a risky investment. In a major sports league, most teams have relatively similar risks, especially when revenue is shared. An expansion team might be considered risky because it is often hard to estimate demand in a market until a team is in the region. Maybe a team in a new startup league would be considered risky; one can imagine situations where future returns on sports teams were somewhat easy to calculate and situations where future returns were difficult to project.

Risk can come from a variety of sources. Because the biggest investments for sports teams are players and the facilities used, that is where assessments must be initially made. Probably the most common type of risk for sports teams is the risk of player performance. Often player or team performance is highly variable across time. Furthermore, team revenue changes drastically depending on how players perform. There is also some risk associated with the team's facility. If a facility is not popular or does not work in terms of enhancing the fan "experience," money is lost.

There are also many general types of risk that can be associated with most industries. A general type of risk is *business risk* or the need for a firm to support its operating costs. *Financial risk* deals with satisfying *all* financial obligations. All firms face *market risk*, which comes of the uncertainty in consumer preferences and needs, which are dynamic. When thinking about market conditions and changes, it also must be remembered that some businesses actually thrive in a poor economy (and enjoy less risk). How is this possible? Many consider localized entertainment to be countercyclical, for example, meaning they have high returns in a bad economy. While most sports teams and businesses prefer a good economy (anticipating less risk and higher prices when the economy is robust), some minor sports teams might be somewhat indifferent.

Market risk also involves political or social events that could change demand. *Event risk* is another common type of risk. While many events could take place to adversely affect sports teams, a common worry among owners (and fans) is a work stoppage. As sports fans know, leagues can have problems between the players' union and the owners. A lockout or strike will lead to a sharp decline in short-term revenues. *Tax risk* is the risk that tax laws could change. While analysts can often foresee tax law changes into the near future, long-term decisions can be dramatically changed by changes in tax law (see Chapter 12). Some leagues (e.g., the NHL and NBA) encounter *exchange rate risk* when teams in the same league play in more than one country. Because some teams earn revenue in the United States and some teams earn revenue in Canada, a quick change in the exchange rate can elevate or depress the purchasing power of teams. As noted in Chapter 8, interest rates are critical in calculating team values, so teams face *interest rate risk*. Furthermore, when the interest rate increases, the value of investments decrease. *Liquidity risk* is the risk that firms will not have enough liquid assets to meet their obligations and *purchasing power risk* is the risk of inflation. These are just a few types of risk.

Risk and Uncertainty

People often use *risk* and *uncertainty* interchangeably and, in some ways, there is no problem with that. Be aware, however, they do not measure exactly the same phenomenon. Financially, risk can be defined as the variability of financial returns associated with a given asset. Uncertainty is a concept that deals more with *unknown* chances. In other words, risk is randomness with known probabilities and uncertainty is randomness with unknown probabilities (Knight, 1921). If the chances of various outcomes are known, then an accurate measure of risk exists. If the chances of various outcomes are unknown, there is great uncertainty. It is possible for an investment to be risky, but not uncertain. It also is possible for an investment to not be risky, but very uncertain.

For example, the NBA uses a lottery system for their player draft. They use what is called a weighted lottery system, meaning that poor performing teams have better chances at getting a higher draft pick than better performing teams. People can and do calculate the probabilities of various teams getting the first overall pick. In other words, the risks regarding which team will get which draft pick can be calculated. There is no uncertainty about those risks. There can be great uncertainty regarding the drafted players. Some Number 1 draft picks have met expectations but others have not. While people can still estimate performance measures for drafted players, it is not an exact science. There may be things about the player that the team does not know and, as a result, there is some uncertainty (and risk) regarding the drafted players.

Again, a financial analyst *might* use previous returns to estimate the risk of the investment. It is possible that better information is available than historical returns.

To keep consistent with the calculation of expected value, it can be assumed that past returns are the best measure for expected returns. One measure of risk is the standard deviation of the returns. The standard deviation of the returns is given by:

$$\sigma_k = \sqrt{\frac{\sum_{j=1}^{n}\left(k_j - \bar{k}\right)^2}{n-1}}$$

The standard deviation represents a measure of dispersion or, in the case of investments, risk.* On average, the return will be one standard deviation away from the average return. The standard deviation is most useful when different investments are considered.

Because investors almost always want less risk, they would rather buy an investment with a small standard deviation of returns. A financial analyst's job is sometimes straightforward. If two investments have the same expected rate of return, but one has a smaller standard deviation, then the preferred choice is obvious. The investment with the smaller standard deviation is clearly better. Conversely, if two investments have the same standard deviation and one has the higher expected return, then it is the better investment. The problem comes when one investment has a higher expected return and a higher standard deviation.

In most markets, there is a tradeoff between risk and reward. If investments have a high risk, there should be a high average reward. How does an analyst compare an investment with high risk and high reward with another investment that offers lower risks and returns? One way is by using the coefficient of variation. While the coefficient of variation is quite crude, it does provide some critical or valuable insight. The coefficient of variation is given by:

$$cv_k = \frac{\sigma_k}{\bar{k}}$$

In other words, the coefficient of variation is the standard deviation divided by the average return. Because a good investment has low risk and high reward, a low coefficient of variation is ideal. Just because an investment has a low coefficient of variation, however, does not mean it is a good investment. There may be other

---

* If we know the probability of every outcome, the standard deviation is calculated by:

$$\sigma_k = \sqrt{\sum_{j=1}^{n}(k_j - \bar{k})^2 p_j}$$

Most programs, such as Excel, have a default setting that calculates a standard deviation assuming all probabilities are equal.

Table 11.1   Packers' operating profit, 1997–2003

Year/Measure	Operating Profit/Measurement ($)
1997	7,099,031
1998	8,047,411
1999	6,993,945
2000	–419,517
2001	2,769,928
2002	3,268,025
2003	23,198,367
Average	8,983,847
Standard Deviation	8,643,856
Coefficient of Variation	0.962

metrics that are useful as well, or there could be circumstances that make that investment unwise. If an investor is not very risk averse, he/she will care more about the expected return than the standard deviation. Conversely, if he/she is very risk averse, he/she will care more about the standard deviation.

The Green Bay Packers' financial statements provide some context for the analysis of returns. Table 11.1 illustrates the Packers' operating profit (profit level before interest payments, dividends, and taxes) from 1997 to 2003.

Table 11.1 shows that on average, the Packer's made slightly less than $9 million in operating profit for the seven years reported. The standard deviation was also almost $9 million, making the coefficient of variation just under 1. The rule of thumb is that most of the time values will fall inside two standard deviations of the average.* So, while it depends on distributional properties, a rough confidence interval would be from a loss of $8.3 million (the mean minus two times the standard deviation) to a gain of $27.3 million (the mean plus two times the standard deviation). To analyze it a different way, if the coefficient of variation is more than about .5, then there is certainly a possibility of a loss.

The best use of these data would be in predicting the 2004 operating profit. The data can be used to determine if profits increased. While a more sophisticated approach involving a regression or time-series analysis might be ideal, a casual assessment indicates that there is no obvious growth, up or down. While 2003 was

---

* If the data follows a normal distribution, then values will fall within two standard deviations of the average 95.4 percent of the time. There is, however, no reason to assume that raw data will follow a normal distribution.

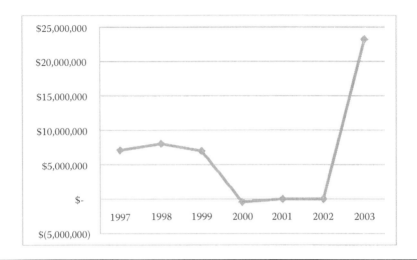

Figure 11.1   Graph showing the Green Bay Packers' operating profit.

a more robust year financially, the three years prior to that were not. The graph in Figure 11.1 also shows no clear trend.

While this graph may show that profits might be growing (a trend line does have a positive slope), it is hard to make a firm statement with one data point that is high. The Milwaukee *Journal Sentinel* did report that the Packers had a profit, *after taxes*, of $18 million in 2005 and $22 million in 2006. So, an analysis showing that profits were increasing would have been prescient. *Forbes* estimated that the value of the Packers' more than doubled from 2001 to 2005, which illustrates what can happen when profits dramatically increase.

Diversification and Correlation

Many financial analysts preach diversification, or having unrelated assets. If a portfolio* has investments that are completely unrelated and, thus, is quite diversified, then risk will normally not be as high as a portfolio dominated by correlated assets. Diversification in sports could mean owning a basketball team and a NASCAR team. Diversification is often more difficult that it would appear. Even in the case of a basketball team and a NASCAR team, there could be things that affect both in the same way. For example, maybe both are dependent upon the national economy. One strategy to diversify would be to invest internationally. Occasionally, major sports owners do own teams on different continents. In any case, it is usually safer to make investments that diversify a portfolio.

Diversification must be balanced against having too many unrelated business investments. It is common for investors to own firms that are related to each

---

* A portfolio is simply a group of investments.

other. In fact, as financial experts know, correlated investments can be managed to decrease risk. Owning two risky investments that are negatively correlated can be very effective in decreasing risk. For instance, there could be sports teams that are countercyclical, that is, they thrive in a weak economy. In a recession, many fans might go to minor league sporting events. Therefore, owning minor league teams might be a hedge against a bad economy that reduces demand for major league events.

Owning multiple teams in the same region could be another way to decrease risk by having negatively correlated assets. Using an extreme example, suppose that a fixed number of fans will attend games during the basketball/hockey season in Detroit. In other words, fans will go to exactly one game and they will decide between a Detroit Pistons or Detroit Red Wings game. If this is the case, there would be some risk and uncertainty with owning either the Pistons or Red Wings. If jointly owned, that risk is eliminated.

On the other hand, there might be factors that will affect both the Pistons and Red Wings in the same way, which will create some positive correlation between the two. If the Detroit regional economy declines, there might be fewer fans for both the Pistons and Red Wings. If this is the major effect, then owning both the Pistons and Red Wings would be very risky. Of course, this is ultimately an empirical question to be answered with data. Some teams might be positively correlated while others are negatively correlated.

The extent to which the Red Wings and Pistons are substitutes (negatively correlated) or complements (positively correlated) can be measured. Ideally, an analyst would look at profits of the two teams, but as a proxy, what is assessed here are attendance levels across 10 years (Table 11.2). Other things, such as media contracts, are clearly important for profits and many things affect attendance. As a result, looking only at attendance is not sufficient, but some important insights are possible.

On average, the Pistons have a slightly higher attendance and a much higher standard deviation. With the exception of the lockout year, the Red Wings had the same attendance from 2003–2004 to 2006–2007. This almost certainly represents sellouts. Because the Pistons average only a slightly higher attendance, but have much more risk, their coefficient of variation is quite a bit higher than that of the Red Wings. Some might say that the Red Wings are the better investment, but it all depends on one's level of risk aversion. If the investor really does not like risk, then the Red Wings are the better investment. If the investor does not care too much about risk, then the Pistons and their higher attendance are the better investment.

The correlation is most important. Across the recession and the escalating unemployment levels in Southeast Michigan, attendance has declined. Also, when the teams won more games, attendance rose. The correlation is mildly negative, meaning that when the Pistons are doing well, typically the Red Wings are not, and vice versa. This shows that there is a risk aversion reason to owning both teams, but

Table 11.2 Detroit Pistons and Detroit Red Wings attendance

Season	Pistons Attendance	Red Wings Attendance	Total
2000–2001	607,323	819,785	1,427,108
2001–2002	760,807	822,373	1,583,180
2002–2003	839,278	822,378	1,661,656
2003–2004	872,902	822,706	1,695,608
2004–2005	905,119	lockout	905,199
2005–2006	883,040	822,706	1,705,746
2006–2007	905,116	822,706	1,727,822
2007–2008	905,116	775,394	1,680,510
2008–2009	896,971	814,474	1,711,445
2009–2010	768,826	781,847	1,550,673
Average	834,450	811,597	1,646,046
Standard Deviation	96,649	18,953	99,274
Coefficient of Variation	0.116	0.023	0.060
Correlation of Pistons and Red Wings (excluding 2004–2005)			−0.085

that fans will continue to support both teams and not simply attend the games of the one that wins the most games.

Suppose the owner of the Pistons is considering buying the Red Wings. The standard deviation of fans for the Pistons is 96,649. If the Pistons' owner also bought the Red Wings, the standard deviation would only increase to 99,274. So, this would be a way to increase the investment with very little risk. There are other reasons to own multiple sports teams in the same city (which the NFL does not allow). For example, because teams are seasonal, owning multiple teams might cut costs. An NBA team's marketing department might be very busy in the fall, but an MLB team's marketing department might be busy in the spring. So, it might make sense to have one marketing department for both teams. There also could be institutional knowledge that is useful for both teams. Teams also could advertise to sports fans more easily by using other teams in the market. Teams could increase as well their market power by owning multiple teams in a market. Another reason for owning two teams could be that sports teams are negatively correlated and this decreases the risk of the owner.

Facility Investments

Financial analysts have to focus on the *net present value* (NPV) and the *internal rate of return* (IRR) from a new facility. As illustrated in Chapter 9, a new facility will increase attendance *ceteris paribus* (with all other factors remaining the same).* A successful new facility should produce financial benefits that exceed the costs. The benefits, as well as the costs, are not always straightforward and easy to calculate. First, what is the counterfactual to a new facility? In other words, what would happen if a new facility were not built? Maybe the old facility would continue to be used and attendance would remain unchanged; attendance could also decrease if fans were disappointed with the experience produced during their visits. Perhaps a new facility should be compared to an alternative new facility. Furthermore, a new facility can affect more than just attendance. It is not always clear what exactly the benefit of a new facility will be. The cost side can be complicated as well. Often there is a mix of private and public funding, so the private cost is not always the total cost.

Even though benefits and costs of a new facility are not always obvious, the NPV of Oriole Park at Camden Yards can be estimated. Finding the NPV of an investment is similar to finding the value of a team. The discounted value of all cash flows has to be found. The NPV of an investment can be given by:

$$NPV = CF_0 + \frac{CF_1}{(1+r)^1} + \frac{CF_2}{(1+r)^2} + \ldots + \frac{CF_3}{(1+r)^N} = \sum_{t=0}^{N} \frac{CF_t}{(1+r)^t}$$

where CF_t is the cash flow in year t, r is the discount rate, and the investment lasts for N years. Note that, in other similar equations in the book, the first value is discounted. In this NPV formula, the first value is not discounted. Often when an NPV is calculated for an investment, there is one large outflow that is relatively immediate and should not be discounted. After the initial investment is made, often future cash flows are inflows.

One difficulty with estimating NPV is finding the appropriate discount rate, which was discussed in Chapter 8. Often some type of interest rate can be used, but the amount of risk involved with the cash flows also should be taken into account. One way to do this would be to use the Capital Asset Pricing Model discussed in Chapter 8. Another difficulty with estimating NPV beforehand is that cash flows are not always easy to predict. The number of additional fans a new facility generates is not always easy to calculate even after the facility is built, let alone before it opens. Another difficulty is that the depreciation rate is not always known, but if the cost of capital is known (cost of capital is discussed at the end of the chapter), it might be a reasonable depreciation or discount rate.

---

* Certainly it is possible for attendance to decrease with a new stadium if the team performs poorly, but almost certainly attendance will increase if all other factors are the same.

Another common technique is to calculate the IRR. The internal rate of return is simply the depreciation rate that gives the investment a net present value of zero. A high internal rate of return means profits as a percentage of the investment. The formula for IRR is given by:

$$NPV = \sum_{t=0}^{N} \frac{CF_t}{(1 + r)^t} = 0$$

This equation implies that there is some rate, r, that makes the NPV of an investment zero. That rate is the IRR.

Table 11.3 provides some data pertaining to Oriole Park at Camden Yards. The first seven columns (Season, Finish, Wins, Losses, Attendance, Average Ticket Price, and Ticket Revenue) can all be found in Chapter 1. Given these data, the first thing for a financial analyst to do is adjust for inflation and put the financial values into real or constant terms. The eighth column provides a measure of inflation (the Consumer Price Index) and the ninth column adjusts ticket revenue so that it is in real 2010 dollars.*

The tenth column then finds the increase in real ticket revenue compared to the ticket revenue in 1991, the last year the Orioles played in Memorial Stadium. This brings up the question as to whether the ticket revenue from Camden Yards should be compared to the last season in Memorial Stadium. This is difficult to say. In Chapter 9, previous academic research was used to estimate the average effect of a new stadium. In this case, because the focus is on one specific team, it might be better to analyze the Orioles' attendance pre- and postplay at Oriole Park at Camden Yards. Even though the team did perform poorly with a record of 67 wins and 95 losses in the last year of Memorial Stadium, the team enjoyed a record year relative to attendance. This may be due to the fact that there is often a jump in attendance during the last year of an old facility because fans want an opportunity to enjoy the nostalgia and memories. This tells us that, if anything, the impact of Oriole Park at Camden Yards could be underestimated because attendance and ticket revenue at Memorial Stadium may have been lower than what took place in its last year. With so many factors influencing attendance, a single year offers little insight as many things change each year.

The eleventh column in Table 11.3 discounts the change in real ticket revenue by 10 percent each year. In other words, this figure is the NPV of Camden Yards. If the discounted cash flows from Oriole Park are added together from 1992 to 2010, the resulting figure is $264.7 million. This figure is much larger than the estimated increase in ticket revenues noted in Chapter 9. Not only was this analysis done differently, but Oriole Park is considered one of the most successful ballparks

---

* To put ticket revenue into 2010 dollars, the nominal ticket revenue data was multiplied by 216.7 (the 2010 value of the Consumer Price Index) and divided by the Consumer Price Index value of that year.

Table 11.3 Impact of Oriole Park at Camden Yards on attendance

Season	Finish	Wins	Losses	Attendance	Average Ticket Price ($)	Ticket Revenue ($)	Consumer Price Index	Real Ticket Revenue ($)	Change in Real Ticket Revenue ($)	Discounted Change in Real Ticket Revenue ($)	
										(r = 10%)	(r = 18.43%)
1991	6th AL East	67	95	2,552,753	8.04	20,524,134	134.6	33,040,959			
1992[1]	3rd AL East	89	73	3,567,819	9.55	34,072,671	138.1	53,462,020	20,421,061	18,564,601	17,243,673
1993	3rd AL East	85	77	3,644,965	11.12	40,532,011	142.6	61,590,181	28,549,222	23,594,398	20,356,224
1994	2nd AL East	63	49	2,535,359	11.17	28,319,960	146.2	41,973,784	8,932,825	6,711,363	5,378,277
1995	3rd AL East	71	73	3,098,475	13.14	40,713,962	150.3	58,697,180	25,656,221	17,523,544	13,043,633
1996	2nd AL East	88	74	3,646,950	13.14	47,920,923	154.4	67,252,856	34,211,898	21,242,896	14,687,048
1997	1st AL East	98	64	3,612,764	17.02	61,489,243	159.1	83,745,567	50,704,608	28,621,429	18,380,455
1998	4th AL East	79	83	3,684,650	19.77	72,845,531	161.6	97,677,472	64,636,513	33,168,751	19,785,099
1999	4th AL East	78	84	3,432,099	19.82	68,024,202	164.3	89,713,696	56,672,738	26,438,250	14,648,257
2000	4th AL East	74	88	3,295,128	19.78	65,177,632	168.8	83,667,924	50,626,965	21,470,775	11,049,564
2001	4th AL East	63	98	3,094,841	18.23	56,418,951	175.1	69,818,694	36,777,735	14,179,409	6,777,971

(continued)

Table 11.3 (continued) Impact of Oriole Park at Camden Yards on attendance

Season	Finish	Wins	Losses	Attendance	Average Ticket Price ($)	Ticket Revenue ($)	Consumer Price Index	Real Ticket Revenue ($)	Change in Real Ticket Revenue ($)	Discounted Change in Real Ticket Revenue ($)	
										(r = 10%)	(r = 18.43%)
2002	4th AL East	67	95	2,655,559	18.23	48,410,841	177.1	59,232,071	26,191,112	9,179,825	4,075,868
2003	4th AL East	71	91	2,454,523	20.15	49,458,638	181.7	58,982,080	25,941,122	8,265,640	3,408,838
2004	3rd AL East	78	84	2,744,018	22.53	61,822,726	185.2	72,333,590	39,292,632	11,381,675	4,359,937
2005³	4th AL East	74	88	2,624,740	22.53	59,135,392	190.7	67,193,869	34,152,910	8,993,528	3,199,987
2006	4th AL East	70	92	2,153,250	22.53	48,512,723	198.3	53,010,975	19,970,016	4,780,663	1,579,976
2007	4th AL East	69	93	2,164,822	22.45	48,600,254	202.4	52,026,733	18,985,774	4,131,857	1,268,387
2008⁴	5th AL East	68	93	1,950,075	23.85	46,509,289	211.1	47,744,733	14,703,774	2,909,063	829,476
2009	5th AL East	64	98	1,907,163	23.42	44,665,757	211.1	45,838,550	12,797,591	2,301,759	609,613
2010	6th AL East	66	96	1,733,018	23.42	40,587,282	216.7	40,587,282	7,546,323	1,233,884	303,538
Camden Yards Average		74.5	83.84	2,842,117	18.52	50,695,684		63,397,329			
Total								1,204,549,257	576,771,040	264,693,318	160,985,827

¹ First season that the team played in Oriole Park at Camden Yards.

ever built. Now, let's introduce the cost of the ballpark. It has been reported that in 1991, Camden Yards cost $100 million to build, which is $160,985,884 in 2010 dollars. If the cost is subtracted from the estimated benefit, the NPV of the investment is $103.7 million. This is a remarkably positive net value, and the value produced in 2011 and in future years is not considered. Future ticket revenue will show that the NPV of this stadium will be even higher.

What is the IRR for Oriole Park? If the cash flows were constant, then a calculator could be used. As described in Chapter 5, financial calculators have five keys: "PV" is the present value, "PMT" is a constant payment made every period, "N" is the number of periods, "I/Y" is the depreciation rate, and "FV" is the future value. An analyst would simply solve for I/Y, which in this case represents the IRR, by imputing the other four values. Because the change in ticket revenues varies over time, a financial calculator cannot find the IRR.* Using other programs, the actual IRR is 18.4 percent (again a remarkable return). This also is a real rate of return (adjusted for inflation). Certainly any investment with a real IRR of 18.4 percent should be considered a success. Without adjusting for inflation, the IRR is more than 24 percent. Notice that in the last column, when the values are discounted at 18.4 percent, the sum of the values equals the cost of the stadium with some rounding error. This indicates that if the discount rate was 18.4 percent across time, the NPV would be zero. Clearly, Oriole Park has been a success. This analysis does not even consider changes in concession, parking, and advertising revenues, or other benefits. The high NPV and IRR values illustrate why other MLB teams often copy Oriole Park.

Player Investments

The most important investment for teams is their players. As we saw in Chapter 3, for most professional sports franchises, player salaries are the highest cost. Clearly the value of the players is high as well. While some sports fans cannot fathom why some players make as much as they do, there is some basic economics behind player contracts. Players make as much as they do for the most part because that is how much value they bring to the team. While the same measures of expected value and risk pertain to the investment in players, we will examine some other basic financial concepts and how they are related to players.

Value of a Player

To understand the value of a player, financial managers must understand the *marginal revenue product* (MRP) of each athlete (Scully, 1974). MRP is an economic idea

---

* A program, such as Excel, can be used to find the IRR in this case. It can, however, still be relatively difficult. Using formulas in Excel, one can try various rates to see if the NPV is positive or negative and adjust accordingly. This will eventually give an accurate IRR. There are other programs that can more easily give the IRR on a given investment.

that is not always straightforward, but can be applied to any worker. To understand MRP, two other terms have to be defined, *marginal product* and *marginal revenue*. A worker's marginal product is the additional units of output they create. For example, if a company is making footballs, then a worker's marginal product would be the additional number of footballs that are made because of that individual. Although probably no individual actually makes footballs from start to finish anymore, everyone at the football company helps create some number of footballs. The number of footballs made because of a specific worker is the marginal product of that specific worker. The goal of athletes is to win games. Therefore, a player's marginal product is the number of games that player helped the team win. While a player's marginal product is not exactly known, especially before the season starts, teams must make their best guess. If the St. Louis Cardinals win 100 games, but would have won only 85 games without Albert Pujols (but with a replacement player that would play for a much smaller salary), then Albert Pujols' marginal product is 15 games. For baseball, a player's marginal product is similar to their *wins above replacement* (WAR) statistic. In basketball, it is similar to the term *wins produced* (for a mathematical explanation of wins produced, see Berri (2008)). In sports like football, where players are so dependent on each other, the marginal product is much harder to estimate.

Marginal revenue also is critical to understanding any particular player's value. If the team wins more games, the franchise earns more revenue. A team's marginal revenue is the additional funds earned from one more win. Remember, this is not just revenue from ticket sales, but revenue from all of the revenue streams that were discussed in Chapter 3. For example, if the St. Louis Cardinals receive $3 million in additional revenue for each game they win, then that is their marginal revenue. A player's marginal revenue product is then simply his/her marginal product multiplied by the marginal revenue. With these assumptions, Albert Pujols' marginal revenue product is $45 million (15 × $3 million). Remember that a player's marginal product might depend on how good the team is without that individual, and a team's marginal product also might depend on how many games the team wins.* Players also might bring in more value than through their marginal product. For example, basketball icon Michael Jordan brought fans to the games late in his career when he was not helping the team win that many games. In 1998, Mark McGwire and Sammy Sosa increased demand for their teams as a result of their home run race.

Marginal Value of Wins

The marginal value of winning games is a function of many things. For example, because teams are becoming integral components of

---

* In baseball, there are different estimates of WAR. For example, fWAR and rWAR are estimates of marginal product. If two players had identical playing statistics, their fWAR would be the same, but their rWAR is dependent upon the team on which they played. For more information, see http://www.tangotiger.net/wiki/index.php?title=WAR

entertainment companies, the marginal revenue from winning is increasing. Today if a team wins, it does not just increase ticket sales, but also sales from concessions, parking, and souvenirs. A team's media revenue might depend on winning as well. Furthermore, if the team owner also has interests in restaurants, hotels, or casinos surrounding the facility, it will increase the marginal revenue of players even further. Not only does this ownership integration increase profits, it also increases the value of players. Therefore, all of these things have increased player salaries across the past decade or two.

People often do not make the connection between revenues and player salaries. Player salaries exploded during the 1990s, but this is because revenues soared as well. For example, when owners receive large media contracts, a share of this goes to the players. Also, if teams start receiving sponsorship dollars, a share goes to the players. A much larger share of these revenues go to the players if the revenues depend on how the team performs. For example, the NFL receives most of its revenue from national media contracts that are always shared. So, although financially the NFL might prefer if large-market teams win, whoever wins does not affect the bottom line that much. On the other hand, if a league receives most of its income from gate revenue, then the franchise is very dependent on winning and the players become more important.

Correlation of Players

Just like the financial performance of teams might be correlated, the performance of players could be correlated as well. Players can be complements or substitutes just like other investments. For example, in some sports when one position player plays well, this can affect the performance of other team members. If a quarterback has a good game, it is likely that the wide receivers also have a good game. If a goalie has a good game, it might be due to the defensemen. Assume for a moment that when the quarterback has a good game, the running back tends to have a poor game. Teams should be thinking about how their players play together. If a football team has a good quarterback, is it better to invest in wide receivers or running backs? If a team's management believes it is in their best interest to focus on a passing game, then they should invest in wide receivers. This would be a more risky move. If the team wants to be balanced, they should invest in a running back. This would cause the team to have more average games and would be a more conservative strategy. It is hard to say which strategy is best, but team owners and managers should clearly be aware of how their investments are related to each other.

Option Value for Players

In finance, an option is something that gives an investment some flexibility. There are many types of options. For example, a *call* is the option to *buy* an investment at a specified price at a certain time in the future. A *put* is an option to *sell* an investment at a specified price at a certain time in the future. A call or a put does not force the investor to buy or sell the investment, but allows the sale or purchase if it becomes a good business decision to do so. There are other types of options as well.

Many players have a type of option. In fact, nearly all players give teams some options. Because of the uncertain nature of sports, teams always like to have options. For example, suppose that a hockey team has an injury-prone starting goalie with a 30 percent chance of getting hurt during the season. Suppose that the same team has a defenseman who can play goalie if necessary. The uncertainty of the starting goalie's health can create an option value for the defenseman. Now, consider three possible outcomes. The first outcome is that the starting goalie remains healthy and gives up an average of one goal per game. The second outcome is that the starting goalie gets hurt and the defenseman must play goalie. With this outcome, the team gives up an average of two goals per game. That results from the loss of the starting goalie and the requirement to replace the defenseman. The third outcome is that the goalie gets hurt and nobody else on the team can play goalie very well. If the team is not able to find a reasonable replacement, this will hurt the team drastically and they will give up three goals per game. Table 11.4 shows the possible outcomes.

If the hockey team can use the defenseman as the backup goalie, then on average the team will yield 1.3 goals per game. If they have no reasonable replacement for goalie, they will yield 1.6 goals per game.* Therefore, the option value of a defenseman's ability to play goalie is the difference of the two averages or .3 goals per game.

If this is the case, it should be part of a player's marginal product. If we assume that the defenseman is worth .5 goals per game when he is playing as a defenseman, then his total benefit also should include the .3 goal option value, for a total value

Table 11.4   Option value of a player

		Backup Goalie	
Goals Given Up Per Game		Defenseman	None
Goalie's health	No injury (70 percent chance)	1	1
	Injury (30 percent chance)	2	3
Expected value of goals yielded per game		1.3	1.6

---

* With the defenseman replacement, the expected value is equal to .7(1) + .3(2) = 1.3. Without the defenseman, the expected value is equal to .7(1) + .3(3) = 1.6.

of .8 goals.* That value is worth a certain amount of wins. If .8 goals produces 10 additional wins across the season, then the player's marginal product is 10 games. Most owners, managers, and fans have an intuitive understanding of option values. Certain "utility" players often are valuable just in case they are needed. Having options is always a benefit; if a team is hiring a player, it is helpful to be able to quantify these options.

Why Do Teams Take Risks with Players?

In finance, risk is always a crucial factor when dealing with investments. Typically when an investment has a high risk, fewer investors will want to buy that investment, lowering the price. In other words, if there are two investments that have the same expected return, the riskier investment is typically cheaper because a majority of investors are risk averse and prefer not to gamble and to secure positive returns with the least possible risk.

Ironically, in sports, it has been shown that teams often prefer riskier players (Bollinger and Hotchkiss, 2003; Hendricks, DeBrock, and Koenker, 2003). What are "risky" players? One example is baseball teams drafting high school players instead of college players who are older and have played more games. Another example of a risky player is one that is injury prone. Yet, another example is just a player that has a performance that varies greatly. Research has shown that given the same expected return, teams actually prefer riskier players. That is, if two players have the same expected performance but different variances of performance, the player with more variance (more risk) would get paid more.

So why do teams prefer risky players? Are sports teams less risk averse than other types of businesses? One possible explanation is that teams hire risky players because the team can bench them if they do not perform (Lazear, 1998). If players are very risky, meaning that they might perform very well or very poorly, teams can typically bench players as soon as their performance declines. Financially speaking, players have an option value. Teams have the option of not using that investment if the investment or player does not perform well. A slightly different example than the previous option value example can prove illustrative. Suppose a team has 20 roster positions, but can only play 10 players at a time. Further suppose that a team can either hire 20 players that they are certain will perform at an average level or 20 players that will perform very well half of the time and very poorly half of the time. If the team hires the 20 "risky" players, then, on average, 10 of them will perform well and those are the players that will get most of the playing time. Certainly this option value for players has something to do with teams hiring or drafting riskier players.

There is another possible explanation for teams hiring risky players. It is possible that sports teams face a unique revenue structure. Typically, when a firm produces

---

* Note that the defenseman is worth .5 goals per game when the regular goalie is healthy and the defenseman is worth 1.5 goals per game when the regular goalie is injured.

more goods, the additional revenue from producing the goods decreases, and there are diminishing marginal returns. If teams are producing wins, then this might not be the case. A traditional business would rather produce a certain amount of goods every year than produce a high amount one year and a small amount the next year. Again, sports teams might be different. Let's think of these alternatives for sports teams. Would a team rather have a .500 record every year, or finish in last place half of the time and win a championship half of the time. Given how fans respond to team quality and the additional revenue from playoffs, their revenues might be higher if their win/loss record varied from year to year. Obviously teams want to win every year, but given their constraints, they might be better with a 50-percent chance of winning and a 50-percent chance of losing, than a 100-percent chance of winning just half their games. To say it another way, there is a big difference between a first place team and an average team compared to the difference between an average team and a bad team. This implies that teams might have an increasing marginal revenue curve. While economists typically do not like the idea of an increasing marginal revenue curve, there are reasons to think why this could be the case (Fort and Winfree, 2009). If teams do have an increasing marginal revenue curve, it might explain why teams have an incentive to hire risky players. This might be especially true for small-market teams. One can imagine that the only way small-market teams with small payrolls can win is by taking chances on players who might or might not pan out.

Player Contracts

What is the cost of hiring or signing a player? Different sports have different nuances concerning player contracts, but there are some common and basic aspects. Most contracts in professional sports are multiyear. Therefore, what is critical is the contract's present value. To find the present value of a player's contract, future payments must be discounted:

$$Present\ Value = \frac{salary_1}{(1+r)^1} + \frac{salary_2}{(1+r)^2} + \ldots + \frac{salary_3}{(1+r)^N} = \sum_{t=1}^{N} \frac{Salary}{(1+r)^t}$$

where *salary_t* is the player's salary in year *t*, *r* is the discount rate, and the contract is for *N* years. If the salary is the same for each year, then the present value can be calculated using a financial calculator.*

---

* In this case, the financial key "N" would be equal to the number of years of the contract, "I/Y" would be the discount rate, "PMT" would be the amount of the salary, and "FV" would be equal to zero assuming there is no payment at the end of the contract. "PV" would then be solved for to find the present value of the contract. If there is a signing bonus that the player gets as soon as the contract is signed, that would be added to the present value of the contract because no discounting is necessary for the signing bonus.

In 2000, many wondered how the Texas Rangers could sign Alex Rodriguez to a 10-year, $252 million contract. While this was certainly a large contract, it was not really a $252 million dollar contract in present value terms. If the contract was for $25.2 million each year for 10 years, and a 10-percent discount rate is applied, the contract was "only" worth $154.8 million dollars (if the payment was at the end of the year). Because one dollar is worth less in the future than it is today, owners would prefer to delay payments to players. That is, they would rather pay players farther into the future. Conversely, players would prefer to be paid as early as possible or to have their contracts "front loaded." A lower discount rate would increase the present value of the contract.

Owners, in contrast, like to "back load" contracts. In other words, sometimes players are paid more at the end of their contracts and sometimes they are paid more at the beginning of their contracts. For example, suppose Alex Rodriquez's contract was back loaded so that he received $10.2 million a year for the first five years and $40.2 million for the next five years. The net present value of this contract is $133.3 million (at a 10-percent discount rate). On the other hand, if the contract was front-loaded so that he received $40.2 million a year for the first five years and $10.2 million for the next five years, then the net present value is $176.4 million. While these are all "$252 million contracts," clearly Alex Rodriquez would prefer a front-loaded contract and the Rangers would prefer a back-loaded contract. In reality, both sides know and understand the net present value of the contract. So, if for some reason, the team would prefer not to make large payments early, they would have to compensate the player by increasing the "back" end of the contract so that the net present value is the agreed amount. In other words, Alex Rodriquez and the Rangers agreed to a net present value of approximately $154.8 million for 10 years, but there are many different payment schemes that will give a net present value of $154.8 million. Remember, the value of a long-term contract is never what is reported in the news.

Back loading or front loading might be done for various reasons. For example, in the NFL or NHL, where there is a salary cap, teams might not be able to pay players more than a certain amount in certain years. Therefore, their contracts are adjusted in years that the team has more "cap space." So, while there might be some issues with things like guaranteed versus nonguaranteed money, or maybe a player needs the money early, in principle, it is the net present value of a contract that is important, not the actual amount of money paid.

Incentives in Contracts

Another common occurrence in sports contracts is incentive clauses. Of course, putting incentives in contracts is not unique to sports. Virtually every industry deals with what is called the *principal–agent problem*. The principal–agent problem is when two entities, the principal and the agent, have different incentives. The classic example is when a worker does not work hard. In some cases, the employer and employee can have differences of opinion about what is expected. This is not the only case of a principal–agent problem. Some people have blamed financial analysts for the drastic drop in housing prices in 2008 and 2009. Many have said that because some investors were not risking their own money, they took too many risks. Because too many analysts were taking too many risks, the price of housing rose, not as a result of its inherent value, but because of the risk some were willing to accept that housing prices *would* increase. To try to fix this problem, workers often have incentive clauses in their contracts so that their goals are the same as the company's. One example is when employees receive a commission or a percentage of the profit they made for the company.

The story of Ken O'Brien gives insight into the challenges of these issues for sports teams and their managers (Brown, 1990). When Ken O'Brien was a quarterback for the New York Jets, he had an incentive in his contract linking his salary to his quarterback rating. This may sound like a good idea. A quarterback's rating is reduced by incomplete passes, but not by sacks. As all quarterbacks do, O'Brien had an option when all of his receivers were covered. He could throw the ball out of bounds for an incompletion or he could wait and get sacked. While under certain situations a sack might be helpful, more than likely the team would rather he throw the ball out of bounds. Because he lost money every time he threw the ball out of bounds, he might have decided to be sacked. Even former Jets quarterback Joe Namath noticed the flaws in his contract saying, "I'm amazed at [O'Brien's] accuracy, but I see him hold the ball more than he should. I always thought it was better to have second and 10 than second and 18. I don't like incentive contracts that pertain to numbers" (Anderson, 1988).

This shows that teams must be careful when giving incentives in contracts. It is not hard to think of other examples that might create problems. If an NBA player is paid based on how many points are scored, then that player is more likely to be selfish and shoot the ball all of the time. In other sports, such as baseball, the performances are more individual and not dependent on teammates. This makes it easier to place mutually beneficial incentive clauses in contracts. For example, if a player gets a bonus for winning a Gold Glove Award, it is hard, but not impossible to see how that would hurt the team. The trick is that the team should give players incentives that are completely compatible with the team's goals. The team wants the players to win games. So, teams or leagues typically give a bonus if players reach the championship. If a player is paid based on how many games the team wins, much of that is out of the player's control. On the other hand, if the player is paid based on individual statistics, his/her selfish play could hurt the team.

Other incentive issues involve the length of a player contract. There are advantages and disadvantages to long-term contracts. While a longer term contract provides some security for the player and team, there is also some risk that the performance of the player will change as the player ages. Also, there is some evidence that players perform slightly better on average in the last year of their contract (Berri and Krautmann, 2006). Presumably this is because players do not have guaranteed money for the next year and their future earnings depend greatly on their current performance. One should remember, though, that athletes already have a large incentive to perform well. Therefore, any changes in effort through contract incentives will probably be somewhat small.

Opportunity Costs

In economics, an opportunity cost is the cost of the next best thing you could have done with your money. If there is a situation where one investment does not preclude other investments, then the opportunity cost can be thought of as the cost of borrowing money, the interest rate. The opportunity cost of an investment is the second best use of the funds. While opportunity costs might seem like a straightforward idea, it can be enlightening. For example, think about the draft choices made by the Oakland Athletics as described in the book *Moneyball* (Lewis, 2003). Lewis noted the Athletics drafted catcher Jeremy Brown in the first round. The point here is not whether Jeremy Brown should have been a first round draft pick or not, a point debated by general manager Billy Beane and his scouts. While Billy Beane argued that the player was highly undervalued, he seemed to agree that Brown would have been drafted much lower had they not drafted him. Therefore, even if Jeremy Brown, in fact, was good enough to be a first-round draft pick, the Athletics should not have drafted him in the first round assuming they could have gotten him in later rounds. By picking him in the first round, he had a relatively high opportunity cost. Presumably, the Athletics could have picked him in a later round and drafted a different player in the first round, one they may not have had the opportunity to draft otherwise. Every time an investment is made, the opportunity costs should be considered.

Sunk Costs

A sunk cost is a cash outlay that has already been made. In the middle of an investment, the sunk cost is money that has already been paid. The important point is that sunk costs should have *no bearing* on future decisions. Again, this concept seems straightforward, but apparently some sports teams do not have a full grasp of this concept. For example, once a player's contract has been signed, the amount owed to the player is a sunk cost for the team. The player will earn that money regardless of whether or not he plays. The player's salary should have no bearing on future team decisions. Most sports fans have heard teams or announcers say something to the effect of, "Well, he makes too much money to sit on the bench." If a player is not performing up to expectations, and there are other players who are playing better, it makes no sense to play the underperforming athlete. Teams should not compound mistakes by playing athletes simply because of their salary.

Players and Capital Budgeting

To discuss capital budgeting regarding players, managers must first understand *independent* and *mutually exclusive* investments. Independent investments are those that are completely unrelated and that do not eliminate alternatives. For example, the type of beer that Joe Lewis Arena sells has no effect on which goalie the Red Wings sign. Mutually exclusive investments are those that are completely related and cannot both be executed. For example, if an NFL team signed Tom Brady (in his prime) as their quarterback, it would be virtually impossible to also sign Peyton Manning (in his prime). With mutually exclusive investments, teams must choose one or the other, which may raise the opportunity cost of the investment. Some investments are related, but not necessarily mutually exclusive. Independent and mutually exclusive investments present the two extremes.

Independent investments are related to the idea of *unlimited funds*. If investments are independent, then choosing an investment has no bearing on other investments. The same might be true if an investor has unlimited funds. If an investor had unlimited funds, then a financial analyst should use an *accept–reject* method to judge investments. That is to say, if an investment meets a certain criterion, usually a certain rate of return, then the investment should be made. For example, if a team can borrow as much as they want from a bank, then each investment that will have a higher rate of return than the interest rate should be made.

In sports (as well as in many other industries), investors do not have unlimited funds and investments are not independent. In other words, if five different quarterbacks would help the team, the team cannot say, "Let's just sign all of them." The opposite of unlimited funds is *capital rationing*. With capital rationing, investors or firms must use a *ranking* method and only choose the best investments. That is to say, teams will choose the one quarterback that helps the team the most (financially).

There are many ways in which leagues impose a situation where capital rationing must be used. One example is roster limits. In most industries, firms hire workers as long as their MRP is higher than their salaries. In this situation, employees are judged based on the ratio of their MRP and wages. If employees of type A are only paid 50 percent of their MRP and employees of type B are paid 90 percent of their MRP, then firms will always prefer type A. Even if the productivity (MRP) of type A employees was only half of type B, the firm will simply hire twice as many type A employees.

Roster limits and limited playing time changes this. If an NBA team can only have 12 players, then they are now worried about the difference between MRP and wages, not the ratio. For example, suppose rookies have an MRP of $2 million, but are only paid $1 million. Suppose that superstars have an MRP of $10 million, but get paid $8 million. If there were no roster limits, the teams would sign as many rookies as possible because they are only paying 50 percent of MRP instead of 80 percent.* With roster limits, teams have a fixed number of slots, so this means the profit maximizing strategy is to sign as many superstars as possible. In this case, superstars make the team $2 million as opposed to $1 million for rookies.

Salary caps have a similar effect. When teams are constrained, they must rank players and choose the best ones. Many teams would like to invest more in player talent, but they are restrained by the salary cap. With the same MRPs and salaries of players in the previous paragraph, a salary cap might give an incentive to have more rookies as opposed to superstars. Every league with a salary cap also has roster limits, so the net effect is ambiguous. Regardless, teams are forced to use capital rationing.

With an understanding of how the sports industry is different than other industries with regard to capital rationing, different valuation techniques for players can be compared. The first is the payback period. The payback period is simply the time that an investment takes to recover the investment cost. Sometimes firms use the payback period as a capital budgeting technique because it can be easy to calculate and it does give some implicit consideration of the timing of cash flows. The clear problem, however, is that the payback period does not consider the net present value of the investment, any kind of rate of return, or the risk of the investment. For example, one investment may recover its costs very quickly. If an alternative investment recovers its costs more slowly and then gains big returns after that, it might be a much better investment. Although the payback period might be a reasonable first method to use, especially if there is a high level of uncertainty dealing with the investments, it is usually considered an inferior technique.

Another capital budgeting technique is simply using net present value (discussed earlier). Most financial analysts consider net present value to be a superior method to the payback period. This is a very common method and for good reason. By depreciating future values, it gives an accurate measure of the investment in current dollars. Players also can be evaluated in terms of the team's IRR. Although calculating the internal rate of return can be useful, one disadvantage is that investors are forced into calculating one rate. Net present value, for example, is flexible enough that analysts can change the depreciation rate. This problem can be especially egregious if it is comparing investments of different length. Changing depreciation rates can be difficult to foresee and the limit of using one rate is an advantage in the sense that it boils down the investment to one metric.

A technique not yet discussed is the *risk adjusted discount rate*. As the name implies, this is a rate of return that takes into account some risk level. One drawback of NPV and IRR is that risk is not considered. The tricky part of determining a risk-adjusted rate is that the investor must put some value on risk. For example, an owner could say, "I need $100,000 to assume the risk of that player." In this case, the risk-adjusted discount rate is calculated the same way as an internal rate of return, except that, instead of being zero, the net present value should be –$100,000.

---

* A team can realistically only play so many players. This would imply that after a while, MRPs would dwindle. The example is simplified for illustrative purposes.

Table 11.5   Various contracts for hypothetical players

Factor	Player A	Player B	Player C	Player D	Player E
Signing Bonus	$1 million	$3 million	$1.1 million	$1.5 million	$3.1 million
Yearly Salary	$3 million	$3 million	$1 million	$1 million	$3 million
Marginal Revenue Product	$3.5 million	$4.1 million	$1.5 million	$1.6 million	$4.1 million
Risk Adjustment[a]	$1 million	$1 million	$1 million	$0.2 million	$0.2 million
Length of Contract	4 years[b]	5 years	5 years	5 years	5 years

[a] This represents how much owners need to be compensated due to the risk of the player. Remember it was noted earlier in this chapter that it appears that teams prefer risk. So, this could be looked at as a liability of having not enough risk.

[b] Because Player A only has a four-year contract, that would allow the team to sign another player for the 5th year, but we will ignore that for the purposes of this example.

The final technique examined is the risk-adjusted net present value. This takes risk into account in the same way as the risk-adjusted discount rate and, therefore, has the same pluses and minuses. If one can easily value the risk of the investment, then the risk-adjusted net present value is a very attractive method. Table 11.5 presents five different players with varying signing bonuses, yearly salaries, marginal revenue products, and risk levels.

To sign player A, the team needs to offer a $1 million signing bonus and a yearly contract of $3 million. The player gives the team a marginal revenue product of $3.5 million. To remove any risk involved with the player, the team would be willing to pay $1 million and the length of the contract is four years. For each player, it is assumed that end of the year payments and a 10-percent depreciation value for the team owner. It is also assumed that the signing bonus is paid at the beginning of the first year. Therefore, using a financial calculator, the players have the values (in millions) shown in Table 11.6. Table 11.7 shows the results using the payback period, net present value, internal rate of return, risk adjusted discount rate, and a risk-adjusted net present value.

As Table 11.7 illustrates, there are five different investments and each one could be "best" depending on the capital budgeting technique. Thus, the obvious question is: Which investment is best? As noted earlier, the payback period is usually worse than finding the net present value or internal rate of return, so player A is not the best investment. If risk is factored into the decision making, then player B or C should be selected. If there is no capital rationing, then the investment with

Table 11.6   Financial values of players

Factor	Player A	Player B	Player C	Player D	Player E
N	4	5	5	5	5
I/Y	10%	10%	10%	10%	10%
PV[a]	–1/–2	–3/–4	–1.1/–2.1	–1.5/–1.7	–3.1/–3.3
PMT[b]	.5	1.1	.5	.6	1.1
FV	0	0	0	0	0

[a] The first value is the signing bonus and is subtracted from the present value to calculate the net present value. It also is used to calculate the internal rate of return. The second value is the signing bonus with the risk adjustment. This is used to find the risk adjusted discount rate and is subtracted from the present value to find the risk adjusted net present value.
[b] The yearly payment is the player's marginal revenue product minus his/her salary.

Table 11.7   Various assessment techniques

Technique	Player A	Player B	Player C	Player D	Player E
Payback Period[a]	2 years	3 years	3 years	3 years	3 years
Net Present Value	$.584	$1.170	$.795	$.774	$1.070
Internal Rate of Return	34.90%	24.32%	35.51%	28.65%	22.75%
Risk Adjusted Discount Rate	0%	11.65%	6.11%	22.50%	19.86%
Risk Adjusted Net Present Value	–$.416	$.170	-$.205	$.574	$.870

[a] If there are small constant payments throughout the year, the payback period can be calculated by dividing the present value (without any risk adjustment) by the yearly payment. However, since there are end of the year payments, the payback period represents the number of years needed to completely pay off the initial investment.

the highest risk-adjusted discount rate might be the best. If players were more like stocks, player D would be the best. That is because player D only costs approximately half the investment ($1.7 million versus $3.3 million) of player E. If these athletes were similar to traded stocks, investors would just buy two of player D. In sports, that is not an option as there are a fixed number of players and roster spots. In that case, the team would want to choose the player with the highest risk-adjusted net present value, player E. This shows the importance of understanding the investment environment. Because of the mutually exclusive nature of players, using net present value (or risk-adjusted net present value) is clearly the more appropriate technique.

Is the Market for Players Efficient?

Economists and financial analysts are always trying to see if different markets are efficient. *Efficiency* can have different definitions and many people argue whether financial markets are efficient. The *efficient market hypothesis* deals with financial markets and can have slightly different definitions. Many would say that the efficient market hypothesis holds if the price of assets accurately reflects all of the available information and immediately reacts to new information. Intelligent people can disagree on whether certain markets show "irrational exuberance" or whether they price investments with amazing precision. While the market for things like stocks can be very different than the market for players, there can be the same debate about whether player markets are efficient.

Professional sports teams and sports analysts are always trying to determine if the market for players is efficient. That is, do teams pay players the "correct" amount with regard to how much they help the team? For example, many have argued that statistics such as on base percentage are, or at least were, undervalued in MLB (Lewis, 2003). If that is the case, teams with a given payroll could win more games if they signed players with a high on base percentage as opposed to a high batting average. While there is evidence that the player market in MLB was inefficient in this regard, it is always easier to say that, after the fact. For example, after the ".com" bust of the 1990s, analysts were saying that the market was clearly overvalued. Some have argued that, at the time, the market was not overvalued, just unlucky. Or maybe it was simply difficult to foresee the .com bust before the fact. Maybe some of the companies, in fact, did have high potential, but that potential was never realized. It is easy to say the stock market was overvalued after everything has played out.

While people can dispute whether player markets can be inefficient, research shows that while this may have been the case, the market for talent in MLB has corrected this (Hakes and Sauer, 2006). Typically when there are inefficiencies in markets, they correct themselves. While some might argue that MLB owners and managers were slow to correct this inefficiency, once the inefficiency is known, sports player markets seem to quickly correct for any excessive payments. Because markets such as these are often efficient, this makes the risk and correlation of players very important.

It is important as well to remember that what can be perceived as an inefficiency may reveal something about fan or owner preferences. For example, some have argued that scoring points is overvalued in the NBA (Berri, Brook, and Schmidt, 2007). The argument is that players who do other things, such as get rebounds, make great passes, and play tough defense, help teams win more, but players are not paid enough for this. What if fans like to see fast-paced, high-scoring games? It is possible that the team's objective is not to maximize wins, but maximize fan satisfaction. This could mean that teams will pay certain types of players a premium for their type of play because this is what fans want to see. The old sports sayings, "Drive for show, putt for dough" and "Offense sells tickets, defense wins championships," come to mind.

Cost of Capital

Because any investment should give returns higher than the costs, the cost of capital is the rate of return that a firm must earn on the projects in which it invests to maintain its market value. The target capital structure is the desired optimal mix of debt and equity financing that most firms attempt to maintain. An example proves useful in understanding why there sometimes needs to be an optimal financing mix of debt and equity financing. Suppose that someone purchases a team for $500 million. The team has an expected internal rate of return of 8 percent and the cheapest financing for the owner is debt financing at 7 percent. Now suppose that, immediately after, a different team is for sale for $500 million, but the owner has used all available debt financing. The new team has an expected internal rate of return of 12 percent and the cheapest financing is now equity financing at 13 percent. The problem for the owner is that there are limits to how much debt financing can be supported. Even if the first team's expected return was higher than the cost of financing, it may not have been a good decision because there is also a cost to using all of one's debt financing to sustain the investment. In other words, there may be an opportunity cost when using debt financing. Many investors always use a mix of debt and equity financing. If the investors had used 50-percent debt financing and 50-percent equity financing, the cost of financing would have been 10 percent (.5*7%+.5*13% = 10%). If the investors had thought of the cost of capital as being 10 percent, they would have foregone the first team and bought the second team. Not only would they have expected to make 2 percent more than the costs as opposed to 1 percent, but they would have also had more debt financing available to them because they only debt financed $250 million instead of $500 million. The optimal mix of debt and equity financing may not be 50 percent of each, but usually using a mix of financing will help the firm use the best investments.

Before identifying the optimal mix of debt and equity financing, analysts need to be sure all costs have been included. There are often various costs associated with issuing and selling bonds and stocks called flotation costs. Flotation costs typically include administrative costs or underwriting costs. For example, suppose a team issues a 20-year bond with a $1,000 par value and a 5-percent coupon rate. Further, let us suppose that underwriting and administrative costs are 3 percent of the bond. Therefore, the net proceeds, or the money received from the sale of a security, is only $970, not $1,000. If we calculate the cost of capital after we include the flotation costs, we find that the cost of the bond is 5.25 percent (PV = 970, PMT = –50, FV = –1000, N = 20). The floatation costs increase the cost of capital in this case by one-quarter of a percent. It is important to note that for corporate bonds there are also taxes that need to be taken into account to find the cost of capital.

Calculating the cost of equity capital is different than the cost of debt capital, but the cost of issuing a preferred stock is somewhat similar. The cost of issuing preferred stock is simply the annual dividend divided by the net proceeds. For example, if a firm receives $100 from selling a share of preferred stock and the dividend is $4 per year, then the cost of obtaining the capital is 4 percent.

The cost of capital as it pertains to common stock is more unknown because it deals with the firm's future profits. Selling common stock to fund investments is somewhat more complicated because it deals with selling future dividends, which is unknown. Because companies can be valued by using the constant growth model, an analyst can use the same model to estimate the cost of capital for common stock. Rearranging the constant growth model indicates that the cost of capital for common stock is given by:

$$k = \frac{D}{P} + g$$

where k is the cost of capital, D is the dividend payment, P is the price of the stock, and g is the expected growth rate of the dividend. For example, if a firm sells a share of common stock for $100, the dividend is $4 per year, and it grows at 2 percent, then the cost of obtaining the capital is 6 percent.

What is the optimal mix for financing capital? In what some call a "perfect market," it does not really matter if firms use debt capital or equity capital, which is known as the *capital structure irrelevance principle* (Modigliani and Miller, 1958). This is because, if the market is efficient, the prices of stocks and bonds should adjust so that investors are indifferent between buying stocks or bonds and firms are indifferent between selling stocks or bonds. In this "perfect market" there are no taxes, no flotation costs, symmetrical information, and one interest rate. These are the things that might make debt or equity financing more attractive. One of the benefits of debt financing is that issuing bonds often includes tax breaks. Because interest payments from bonds can be deducted from taxes, this often makes debt financing attractive. Using debt financing increases the possibility of bankruptcy because interest payments must be made. There also can be agency costs with debt finance, which means that the lender needs to make sure the borrower is using the funds appropriately. There also can be issues associated with investors not having full information. Especially with small firms, it is possible that the owner knows more about the future profits of the firm than other outside investors.

In Chapter 8, we did not focus on the depreciation rate when valuing teams. If an analyst can calculate the weighted cost of capital for the firm, this is a reasonable choice to use for the depreciation rate. If there is a mix of debt and equity financing, then the weighted cost of capital is given by:

$$k_W = w_D k_D + w_E k_E$$

where k_W is the weighted cost of capital, w_D and w_E are the percentages of debt and equity finance used, and k_D and k_E are the costs of debt and equity capital. If preferred and common stock were both used, the weighted cost of capital should account for their differentiation as well.

It should be underscored that when facilities are built, an owner typically uses bonds or cash. If a facility is completely financed with a bond, then all of the cost of capital comes from that instrument of debt. If cash is used, then the cost of capital could be considered the return the owner would have received from the next best investment. In most instances, owners rely on a mix of equity (cash) and debt financing, and if other investors are involved (minority owners), then the principal owner creates equity partners by selling portions of the team.

There are various methods to find the optimal mix of debt and equity financing, such as the EBIT-EPS (earnings before interest and taxes–earnings per share) method. There are typically a few shortcomings with these methods. Finding the optimal mix depends on the risk of various financing tools as well as the opportunity cost of utilizing too much of one type. As noted earlier, reliance on debt financing reduces the ability to borrow for other investments and reliance on cash could leave the owner with too little liquidity. Finding the right mix relative to risk is an important management decision for an owner and the senior management of a firm.

References

Anderson, D. 1988. 'Super' Jets question today's Jets. *The New York Times*, August 7.

Berri, D. 2008. A simple measure of worker productivity in the National Basketball Association. In *The business of sport*, eds. B. Humphreys and D. Howard, 3 volumes, 1–40. Westport, CT: Praeger.

Berri, D., Brook, S., and Schmidt, M. 2007. Does one simply need to score to score? *International Journal of Sport Finance* 2 (4) 190–205.

Berri, D. and Krautmann, A. 2006. Shirking on the court: Testing for the incentive effects of guaranteed pay. *Economic Inquiry* 44 (3) 536–546.

Bollinger, C. and Hotchkiss, J. 2003. The upside potential of hiring risky workers: Evidence from the baseball industry. *Journal of Labor Economics* 21 (4) 923–944.

Brown, C. 1990. Firms' choice method of pay. *Industrial and Labor Relations Review* 43 (3) 165S–182S.

Fort, R. and Winfree, J. 2009. Sports really are different: The contest success function and the supply of talent. *Review of Industrial Organization* 34 69–80.

Hakes, J. K. and Sauer, R. D. 2006. An economic evaluation of the moneyball hypothesis. *Journal of Economic Perspectives* 20 (3) 173–185.

Hendricks, W., DeBrock, L., and Koenker, R. 2003. Uncertainty, hiring, and subsequent performance: the NFL draft. *Journal of Labor Economics* 21 (4) 857–886.

Knight, F. 1921. *Risk, uncertainty, and profit*. Boston: Hart, Schaffner, & Marx; Houghton Mifflin Co.

Lazear, E. P. 1998. Hiring risky workers. In *Internal labour market, incentives, and employment*, eds. I. Ohashi and T. Tachibanaki. New York: St. Martin's.

Lewis, M. 2003. *Moneyball: The art of winning an unfair game*. New York: W. W. Norton.

Modigliani, F. and Miller, M. H. 1958. The cost of capital, corporation finance, and the theory of investment. *American Economic Review* 68 (3) 261–297.

Scully, G. W. 1974. Pay and performance in Major League Baseball. *American Economic Review* 64 (6) 915–930.

Chapter 12

League Policies, Taxes, and Profits

Introduction

This chapter focuses on the ways in which league policies and taxes affect the profits of sports teams. Both professional and collegiate sports leagues are somewhat unique in that there are many (externally enforced and required) policies that dictate how teams receive money and how those funds can be spent. Most of these policies are in place to achieve some level of competitive balance, but fail to achieve any semblance of parity on the field. There are also many taxes unique to the sports industry that can have a large effect on a team's profits. Taxes or tax laws, such as player taxes or the roster depreciation allowance, certainly change the profit structure in sports.

League Policies

League policies, such as player drafts, revenue sharing, luxury taxes, and salary caps, can be of tremendous importance for a team's bottom line and for the salaries of the players. Players' unions are constantly negotiating policies or seeking new ones. Owners, too, debate new policies and practices, and each year there are subtle and sometimes profound changes that impact the athletic programs of NCAA-affiliated institutions. The conflicts between owners and players have led to work stoppages. For example, the 2004–2005 NHL season was cancelled because players and owners could not agree on the implementation of a salary cap. MLB lost one of its World Series when owners and players could not agree on policies. And, the NFL has not only lost games, but owners used replacement players for some of them. When the NFL decided to use replacement players, not every team agreed with this action, illustrating a level of disagreement on policies, tactics, and practices among the owners. At this writing, labor unrest threatened future seasons for the NFL, NBA, and the NHL.

Many sports league policies seem to be very misunderstood. This is because these policies are complicated and affect a lot of groups. For example, while on the face of it, revenue sharing might seem to hurt the profit of large-market teams, economic theory suggests that it could actually help them. Why? Revenue sharing leads to lower player salaries, but how or why is not obvious to the casual observer. This chapter attempts to look deeper into the effect of various league policies.

In many ways, sports leagues can be thought of as a contest between franchise owners to secure a championship. That championship, in turn, can boost profits if an owner can raise ticket prices and secure additional earnings from advertising and the sale of food and beverages. Of course, the level of new profits is a function of demand from fans and the cost of securing the players who make winning possible. Owners make investments to improve their chances of winning, and the more they win, the higher the payoff. From a financial standpoint, sports leagues are not a winner-take-all contest. In other words, the team that wins the championship does not receive all of the league revenue. The more a team wins, however, the more revenue its owner should receive. Therefore, teams have an incentive to invest so they can win more often. Like most contests, there are two basic ways of manipulating this system. A league can try to change how teams invest in winning or they can change the payoff structure. League policies, such as salary caps, luxury taxes, and player drafts, are aimed at lowering the investment that each team makes. If a policy can lower player investment, then the costs for teams should decrease. On the other hand, a policy, such as revenue sharing, changes the payoff structure. Revenue sharing creates a financial situation that is more even between winning and losing teams. This also decreases the incentive to invest in winning because losing teams are assured of receiving money from those franchises that earn more money even when they lose games and fail to qualify for the playoffs. The support from large-market teams for revenue sharing is based on the expectation that lower player salaries might yield benefits for them even if they have to share some of their revenue. Of course, players do not want the incentive to invest in players decreased. That is why they should in actuality oppose revenue sharing plans.

Before focusing on these policies, a few essential concepts need to be understood. First, teams will invest in players and a facility to the point where the marginal return of that investment equals the marginal cost. In other words, if teams are profit maximizing, total revenues do not dictate how much they will invest. Owners and financial analysts always concentrate on marginal analyses. No matter how profitable a team is, when signing a new player, the issue of concern is whether or not that player has the potential to produce more money than he will cost. Some league policies can change either the marginal revenue or marginal costs of an investment in talent (luxury taxes, etc.). This can change the competitive balance of a league* and/or player salaries.

Second, complete competitive balance (where all teams are of equal quality) is probably not an optimal financial outcome for a league. While fans and pundits typically want more balance,† there can be too much balance from a profit-maximizing perspective. Some fans prefer to watch games with favorites and underdogs. The NCAA's men's basketball tournament, March Madness, flourishes, in part, because there are underdogs who periodically upset favored teams. Casual fans who only follow the tournament and might not know who is an underdog are easily informed by the seeding process. In that way, almost everyone knows who is "supposed" to win the game. In this instance, then, a lack of competitive balance has helped create a sports phenomenon now worth hundreds of millions of dollars to the NCAA. Similarly, one can have a reasonable argument whether Michael Jordan was good for the NBA or if Tiger Woods is good for the PGA, but both for a period of time reduced the competitive balance in their sports. Although great athletes and teams distort competitive balance, they often create new fans for a league that might not have been there otherwise. Their presence also elevates the value of upsets, which, if and when they occur, generally attract a great deal of media attention (even after the game or match). Some fans even like to root for continual underdogs (Chicago Cubs). Furthermore, there are more fans in bigger markets. For example, if the Royals started winning as much as the Yankees year after year, this would be bad financially for MLB because a small fan base in Kansas City cannot generate as much revenue as the larger one in New York. As pundits often point out, leagues prefer to have big market teams in the championship series because it typically helps television ratings (and elevates earnings for the league).

Player Drafts

Player drafts have a long history in professional sports. The first draft appears to have taken place in 1915 when the Australian Football League instituted a metropolitan zoning program to stop owners from signing players from across the country. What their plan entailed was limiting teams to the players in their home or

---

* Competitive balance can mean the variation of team quality within a season, across seasons, or variation of who wins championships. The standard deviation of winning percentages is a common metric of within season balance. The standard deviation of a team's winning percentage over time could be one measure of balance across seasons. A Herfindahl index or Gini coefficient are sometimes used to measure balance in terms of championships.

† For example, much of MLB's Blue Ribbon Panel Report was aimed at helping the leagues balance.

geographic region. The NFL also had a type of geographical selection process when it became the first major North American league to formalize a draft in 1936. The professional team located in the area in which the athletes played their collegiate ball had the right to draft those players. This was done to capitalize on the stronger popularity of college football at the time and transfer some of that excitement into the fledgling NFL. The first player drafted, Jay Berwanger (University of Chicago), by the Chicago Bears, decided not to play professional football. The NBA followed with a draft for the 1949–1950 season; the NHL initiated its draft in 1963 and MLB followed suit in 1965. While a few domestic and many foreign players do not enter the professional ranks through a draft, a vast majority of athletes enter their professional careers through a selection process overseen by the leagues.

Player drafts are a good way to understand the actual effects of policies. Many believe that by allowing teams with the least wins to draft first will somehow improve those teams' future on-the-field performance because they will then get the best new talent. The problem with this logic is that profit maximizing teams should invest in talent to the point where marginal returns from that talent equals marginal costs. The player draft does not really change this relationship. If a smaller-market team acquired a player with substantial talent, the amount that an owner could earn from employing that athlete could be far less than the owner of a larger-market team could earn. Should that player receive less in compensation because of the differentials in income related to market size? In the end, the team in the smaller market will trade the rights to that player to a larger-market team and receive some of the excess profits earned in the larger market. This is seen throughout Europe when teams receive transfer payments to allow athletes to move to larger markets.

With this observation in mind, what effect does a player draft have on competitive balance? Not much. Certainly, there are exceptions. For example, LeBron James changed the fortunes of the Cleveland Cavaliers, but they and he never won a championship, and James eventually decided to relocate to a larger market. Another reason drafts do not change balance much is that, even if a team does draft a good player, that may simply "crowd out" an opportunity for another athlete. This means that the team may have signed a different player if they had not drafted a particular player.

To be sure, some drafted players do end up helping a team, but the effects for the most part are short term and small. People like to point to the NFL where the draft has changed the fortunes of teams (e.g., the Indianapolis Colts and Peyton Manning). In the NFL where the largest revenue source is equally divided by all teams eliminating the reality of the existence of a small market, the impact is the exception that will not be consistently present for the other leagues. Analysis seems to indicate that balance before a player draft is really no different than the balance after the draft. So, what is the point of the draft? Are leagues simply going through a meaningless process? Drafts do have one important component regarding team finances. Player drafts are very effective at restricting player pay. Drafts create a complete monopsony situation where there is only one team with which the player can negotiate. This means that the players have no bargaining power. Therefore, team profits will increase with a player draft and the players will be paid less, as their true value is never rewarded.

If players' salaries decrease with a draft, one might wonder why each players' union have agreed to it. Player unions and owners agree to many policies and practices, but it is important to note that younger players do not have as strong a voice in the players' union compared to veterans. One reason players might be willing to keep a draft is because it does not affect veteran players and their representatives. Further, pushing economic sacrifice onto rookie players to secure rewards for veteran players appeals to the largest proportion of a union's members. A player draft might seem particularly appealing to veteran players when an alternative could be a salary cap.

Revenue Sharing

As with player drafts, many fans believe that revenue sharing is designed to increase competitive balance. After all, if a large-market team shares some of its revenue with a small-market team, total revenues should even out. A report from MLB's Blue Ribbon Panel convened in 1999 and 2000 to assess the state of the business of baseball-endorsed expanded revenue sharing arguing that smaller-market teams would have the resources to attract and retain better players. With those better players, it was argued that these franchises would be able to more effectively compete for championships.* It is true that revenue sharing evens out the funds available to different franchises (as it does in the NFL). That, however, does not imply that small-market teams will invest more in talent. What owners do with the money they control is still subject to the return generated when it is spent or invested.

Total revenue, in fact, should be irrelevant to any investment made in players. If the team is profit maximizing, it is *marginal* revenue that is important. Teams should invest in talent until marginal cost equals marginal revenue. Sports leagues could force the teams to use the money on player salaries, but this is not easy. First, a team could replace whatever they are spending on player salaries or investment with the payment from a revenue sharing program. For example, if a team's payroll is $60 million and the team receives $40 million from shared revenue streams, are they using the shared revenue on payroll? One could argue they need to pay players $100 million, but the team could argue that they would pay players only $20 million without revenue sharing funds from the league. Second, investing in talent includes more than player salaries. For example, sometimes there are substantial player development costs.

---

* The Committee's members were Richard C. Levin (former president of Yale University), George J. Mitchell (former U.S. Senator), Paul A. Volcker (former chairman of the U.S. Federal Reserve Bank), and George F. Will (ABC News).

Again, an obvious question is: Why do leagues have revenue sharing if small-market teams may not use the funds to invest in player talent? One reason might be because some revenue is generated by the league, not individual teams, and, therefore, must be shared. Most of the NFL's revenue comes from national television contracts and, as noted, is shared equally among teams. These revenues can give some teams the financing needed to make some desired investments. What is sometimes forgotten is that the Colts, in their negotiations with the public sector for a new stadium, underscored that it was only possible to afford players such as Peyton Manning if the franchise could secure an effective return on that investment. The public sector then decided to pay more than 80 percent of the cost for a new stadium, permitting the Colts to secure a favorable return on their investment in Manning. In this example, then, revenue sharing alone did not make it possible for the Colts' to attract and retain a star quarterback. It was revenue sharing *plus* a financial investment by the public sector that exceeded the investments in facilities used by larger-market teams in New York or Philadelphia.*

Also, payments from large markets to small markets might be to appease small markets because they typically are not allowed to move into large markets. When the Dallas Cowboys franchise was created, the population of the Dallas/Fort Worth region was less than one-half of its current size (2.5 million people in 1970 and 6.7 million in 2010). The value of the Cowboys in this market—and without the creation of a second franchise—creates substantial windfall profits for the team's owner. Smaller-market owners could organize to force the creation of another team or threaten to relocate to enjoy the benefits of that growth. In exchange for not relocating and not creating a second franchise in the Dallas/Fort Worth area (for which a franchise fee would create income for the other team owners), revenues are shared providing other owners with a benefit from the extra profits earned by the Cowboys.

A third reason is that just like player drafts, revenue sharing decreases player salaries. How? Revenue sharing decreases player salaries because teams only receive a percentage of any one player's marginal revenue product. All owners share the value of an Eli Manning or a Tony Romo in a larger market as a result of the NFL's revenue-shaping policies. This means neither the Giants nor the Cowboys will pay these players their true market value since their owners cannot realize the full return on their performance in the New York metropolitan area or in the Dallas/Fort Worth region. This makes the players less valuable to any single owner and because players only negotiate with one owner, their ultimate salary is lower even if they produce more profits for the entire league. As a result, revenue sharing decreases salaries and this helps all owners, not just those with

---

* As this is being written, two proposals for a new stadium in Los Angeles to attract a team or new franchise for the region have surfaced. Both proposals would have very little investment by the public sector, underscoring again the very favorable arrangement in Indianapolis that permits the Colts to secure a return on the investment of their shared revenues in star players.

franchises in small markets. Small-market teams benefit from revenue sharing because they get a transfer of money and they pay less in talent. Large-market teams gain from the decrease in player costs, but must make a monetary transfer to small-market teams. Larger-market teams also enjoy monopoly rents from the artificial scarcity of another team in their region.

This does not mean that revenue sharing has no effect on competitive balance. The effect is quite complicated and depends on exactly how talent investment affects team revenues. The interesting thing about this is that research actually shows that if revenue has any effect, it will probably hurt balance and not improve it. (Appendix 1 shows the mathematics behind this intuition.)

Another issue that owners grapple with regarding revenue sharing is what revenue should be shared. As noted, sharing decreases the incentive to invest in assets that create revenue. Owners do not mind this change with regard to player talent because it reduces their costs and, if it binds all teams, there is no change in outcomes. Because it is unlikely that the overall talent level in a league will change with a decrease in player pay, the only net result is a decrease in player pay. This is not the case with investments in new facilities. While winning is a zero sum game for the league, the amount of revenue from new facilities is not fixed. While revenue sharing can decrease player pay, it might not make building new facilities worthwhile. If an owner knows that some amount of new revenues generated by his or her investment in a new facility must be shared with other owners who did not agree to pay for this particular facility, the rational response is to invest less and build a less desirable facility. That, in the end, leads to lower league revenues and a far less satisfying fan experience. For that reason, one might argue that revenues from new facilities should not be shared with noninvestors.

Luxury Taxes

A luxury tax is different from revenue sharing in that only large-market teams pay it. Technically, a luxury tax is usually a tax on a *percentage* of a team's payroll that exceeds a certain threshold. But, if larger payrolls lead to more revenue, then the luxury tax becomes the equivalent of a tax on high revenue (usually large-market) teams and is nothing more than a revenue sharing program under another name. Because only large-market teams pay the tax, however, it is much more effective at increasing competitive balance. While some luxury taxes might not be large enough to make a big difference in balance, only having large-market teams contributing to shared revenue programs is certainly more effective than having every team give some of its earnings in a revenue sharing pool.

MLB has a relatively straightforward luxury tax. Every year, MLB has a threshold and if payrolls exceed that amount they are taxed. MLB's tax has almost become known as the Yankee tax because they have paid $174 million in luxury taxes since

2003. All other teams combined have paid $16 million.* Although the payroll of the Yankees dwarfs the MLB average every year, this luxury tax should give them some incentive to lower their expenditures. If that occurs, the players receive less money (including players of smaller-market teams) implying owners would keep a higher percentage of revenues. Because a luxury tax should indeed help competitive balance and promote parity, it is reasonable to wonder if the luxury tax actually helps the Yankees. This idea is similar to the "Yankee paradox." The paradox is that if fans care about balance, the Yankees could be better off if they lost more often just to generate some uncertainty. Taken to the extreme, would fans want to watch a sporting contest if the outcome is known? Apparently fans would watch such a contest, at least in certain situations. Fans come to watch the Harlem Globetrotters, and they have an incredibly long winning streak. To be fair, that might be more of an entertainment experience and less a classical sporting event. The empirical evidence, however, seems to suggest that competitive balance has a relatively small effect on fan demand. At the very least, it would be incredibly difficult to argue that it would be in the Yankees' financial interest (or any other team's financial interest) to lose more. Although the long-term effect of competitive balance on a league is difficult to test,† it seems hard to imagine a team being "too" successful.

The NBA has a luxury tax as well, but it seems to be a bit more inclusive in that many teams pay the tax. Some analysts label the NBA policy a soft salary cap. The difference between a soft salary cap and a luxury tax might simply be semantics. After all, what is the difference between being charged a penalty for spending more than is permitted or being taxed after a certain threshold? The NBA's tax is very steep and teams must pay a 100 percent tax on every dollar that exceeds the established threshold.

Salary Caps

The NFL, NHL, NBA, and MLS all have some form of a salary cap, and most in these leagues seem to be financially stable and profitable.‡ While all of these leagues do have a cap, teams can circumvent the established ceiling or level. Sometimes certain types of players do not count against the cap. Also, even if player payroll is capped, teams still might pay more for player development or coaches.

---

* http://www.cbssports.com/mlb/story/12691992/yankees-only-team-hit-with-luxury-tax-must-pay-257-million

† The problem with testing long-term effects on leagues is that many factors are always going on at the same time. Furthermore, parity is not a simple thing to measure and it typically does not dramatically change quickly. So, although some leagues see increases or decreases in overall demand, it is difficult to know the long-term effect of competitive balance.

‡ As this was written, some NHL teams are indeed encountering financial problems. As noted in earlier chapters, the sheer number of teams and other entertainment options in those markets, not player salaries, are at the root of the financial challenges for the Phoenix Coyotes, the Atlanta Thrashers, the Columbus Blue Jackets, and at least one or two other teams.

The intuition or logic behind a salary cap is fairly straightforward. The cap ensures that all teams will have the same payrolls. This, in the long run, should equalize the chance of winning and successful teams will be a function of the management skills of owners, their general managers, and their field managers. An effective salary cap can take market size and fan base out of the equation. A salary cap is the most effective way to increase competitive balance. A salary cap for players does not mean that differences in team payrolls will not exist. One team might decide to pay more for their coaches. In practice, though, salary caps seem to be the most effective policy tool for equalizing teams.

The question that remains, however, is: Is a cap good for the league? Even though a cap clearly restricts player pay, it is not entirely clear if it increases profits. The NFL would clearly prefer that the Dallas Cowboys, New York Giants, and Chicago Bears win more games than the St. Louis Rams, Kansas City Chiefs, or Carolina Panthers. Why? Larger markets have more fans and higher incomes meaning people in these markets will be more likely to pay more for tickets to see games. If they do pay more, then revenues will be higher. So, even though a league will clearly save on costs with a salary cap, a salary cap also might mean less revenue.

There are other management issues with a salary cap. For one thing, players do not like caps. Very few workers in any industry like the idea of having a limit on what can be earned. As a result, if players agree to a salary cap, owners might have to make other concessions to establish a collective bargaining agreement. Another problem is that, as with any type of restriction, there might be ways to circumvent it. For example, teams might give other things to players besides salary. It might be possible for large-market teams to entice players with such things as state-of–the-art facilities or other amenities. (Some teams have given players access to the team's airplane for their personal use.) This can certainly happen in professional sports, but it is commonplace in college athletics. After all, if you cannot pay a player, the next best thing would be to have things on campus that players will enjoy. Also, teams might be able to back load or front load contracts to try to manipulate salary caps. Leagues try the best they can to police such things, but it is hard to limit or restrict everything teams can give players.

The NHL has a salary floor requiring all teams to pay a minimum amount for their players. Furthermore, if a league institutes a floor with a cap, this may assuage the players union. The effect of various league policies on different teams is summarized in Table 12.1.

Promotion and Relegation

Another league policy that seems to contribute to competitive balance is promotion and relegation. Promotion and relegation is the practice of having various levels of leagues and promoting some teams into better leagues and relegating others to lower divisions or leagues. This increases balance as lower quality teams are demoted and

Table 12.1   Short-term effects of league policies

Team Type	Player Draft	Revenue Sharing	Luxury Tax	Salary Cap
Large-Market Team's Profit	Increases	Ambiguous	Decreases	Ambiguous
Small-Market Team's Profit	Increases	Increases	Increases	Increases
Player Salaries	Decreases	Decreases	Decreases	Decreases
Large-Market Team's Win Percentage	No effect	Possible small increase	Decreases	Decreases
Small-Market Team's Win Percentage	No effect	Possible small decrease	Increases	Increases
Competitive Balance	No effect	Might decrease	Increases	Increases

teams that are improving can be elevated from a lower league. Without promotion and relegation, last place teams will still compete in the same league the next year (as occurs in the United States). If a team is threatened with relegation, an owner might invest more in talent.

While this policy might help competitive balance, it certainly does not help team profits. Anytime the incentive for player investment increases, salaries rise (good for players) and costs increase (bad for owners). Generally team owners are in favor of policies that increase balance by decreasing marginal revenues for large-market teams. Although large-market owners might not like this, at least player salaries are decreasing (as noted earlier) for the larger-market team as well. In the case of promotion and relegation, competitive balance is improved as a result of increasing the marginal revenue earned by smaller-market teams. But, this also means that while competitive balance is improved, player salaries will increase.

"Closed" and "Open" Leagues

There are some interesting differences between North American and European sports leagues. Economists often describe North American sports leagues as "closed" as there are no competing leagues in other countries offering similar salaries. This means the absolute talent level does not depend on salaries. In other words, if players' pay doubled for the NFL, it is likely that the teams would still have the same personnel. Therefore, if policies like player drafts, salary caps, luxury taxes, or revenue sharing decrease salaries, it will not decrease the overall talent level as there is nowhere else for the players to go. Some policies might change the distribution of talent, but not the overall level of talent. There might be slight exceptions to this rule, but, for the most part, the talent level is fixed.

This is certainly not the case for European leagues. European leagues are described as "open." The most popular European soccer leagues compete with each other for players. Great Britain, Germany, Italy, and Spain all have separate leagues, and it is not always clear which league is best. The best players in the world are distributed across many leagues. A salary cap might indeed restrict costs, but it also could have a severe effect on the overall talent level of the league. The best players will simply leave for leagues where there is no salary cap and the policy will have a detrimental effect on the league.

Collective Bargaining

Why do leagues implement policies as opposed to allowing each team to function independently as they see fit? Each league does consider itself a sort of "loosely coupled partnership" and actions are needed to advance the collective self-interest even if pursuing that goal interferes with some of the individual interests of particular teams and owners. Some of the policies are the result of the strength of the players union. Labor and ownership (management) in every industry wrestles for a division of the profits produced by their collection action. When labor gains strength through organized efforts, a logical response for owners is to do the same. The NFL players' association is considered by some to be relatively weak compared to those representing players in the other leagues. While some of this may be a historical anomaly, some of it might be because NFL players do not typically have long careers and most players are members of the union for but a brief period of time. Furthermore, the NFL is not considered a "superstar league" where one or two players can dominate to the point that they change the success level of a team. A star quarterback requires a great line, but a Michael Jordan or LeBron James can more easily change the fortunes of a team by themselves. That is why the NBA is considered a "star league" to a far greater extent than the NFL. In MLB, no matter how great one player is, he bats only four times per game or pitches every fifth game. Stars in those leagues need a far more extensively developed supporting cast of players to win a championship. As a result, if the NBA's top five superstars wanted a policy, they might be able to get it because of the demand for those players. In the NFL, the role of supporting players and the short playing career of the athletes has led to a relatively weak union. What is the result of a relatively weak union? The answer is a salary cap. In the NBA, the cap evolved through the efforts of the commissioner to guarantee each of the small number of players on a team a relatively high salary *if* the union agreed to cap what a superstar earned. In that instance, appealing to the union's middle class allowed the owners to circumvent the power of the league's star athletes.

The story of the NHL cap is illustrative. Prior to the 2004–2005 lockout, wages were increasing in the NHL while revenues were stagnant. The NHL owners demanded a salary cap. While the players union agreed to a salary cap, the amount they asked for was much higher than the owners would accept. When negotiations stalled, the owners cancelled the 2004–2005 season. A lost season is always far more difficult for labor then it is for an owner. While some of the players joined other leagues, where salaries were usually far lower, some of the owners also owned minor league hockey teams, junior league hockey teams, NBA teams, and MLB teams, some of which enjoyed revenue growth during the lockout. In addition the team owners were able to place other events in the arenas they owned or managed, and these produced some income as well. After a year, the players agreed to a salary cap that was actually less than the owners originally offered. While the power of any players union depends on many factors, whatever strength it can manifest rests on the ability of its membership to forego a season of play.

League Specifics

NFL

The NFL might be the most egalitarian of all the leagues. Since 1994, they have had a hard salary cap, which is structured so that players receive approximately 60 percent of defined total revenues (game-related excluding luxury seating and after a $1 billion deduction for total expenses). Currently, however, the owners believe this produces too little return for them and, during this writing, the owners and players are engaged in a contentious round of negotiations. Most teams spend the total amount of money specified as the cap. There is also a salary floor that mandates that teams spend at least 84 percent of the salary cap. Because revenues in the NFL have been increasing, the salary cap also has been increasing each year, meaning there is more money for player salaries. Table 12.2 shows the growth of the cap from 1999 to 2009.

The NFL shares all national media revenues that account for most of their revenue. Furthermore, the visiting team receives 34 percent of gate revenue. Therefore, the amount of revenue shared among all teams is very high. The salary cap, combined with a high level of revenue sharing, creates a situation where teams are relatively equal both on the field and financially. Students are reminded that the labor agreement that is reached for the 2011 season (or those that follow) will be different from the arrangements noted here.

MLB

MLB is somewhat unique compared to the other leagues in that it has no salary cap, but does have, as noted, a luxury tax. If the payroll of a MLB team exceeds a certain

Table 12.2 NFL salary cap

Year	Salary Cap
1999	$58.3 million
2000	$62.2 million
2001	$67.5 million
2002	$71 million
2003	$75 million
2004	$80.5 million
2005	$85.5 million
2006	$102 million
2007	$109 million
2008	$116 million
2009	$129 million

* Some sources claim slightly different numbers.

threshold, then teams must pay a tax on the amount above that threshold. Over time, these thresholds have increased ($148 million in 2007, $155 million in 2008, $162 million in 2009, $170 million in 2010, $178 million in 2011) and the tax percentage changes depending on how many times the team has exceeded the threshold (22.5 percent for the first instance of overspending, 30 percent for the second time, and 40 percent for the third time and all subsequent times). If a team had a payroll of $198 million in 2011 and it was the second time a luxury tax was required, the amount of the tax would be $6 million (.3 × ($198 million − $178 million) = $6 million). MLB also shares their entire national television contract, 31 percent of local media revenues, and all revenues from MLB Advanced Media. Compared to the NFL, the variance in terms of revenues is very high. In MLB, the ratio of top revenue-generating teams to the lowest revenue-generating teams is about 3:1.

NBA

The NBA has a salary cap, a luxury tax, and a modest level of revenue sharing. This can make revenue structures very complicated, but the NBA seems to be in between the NFL and MLB in terms of financial equality. The New York Knicks and Los Angeles Lakers typically earn the most revenue and, of late, this has exceeded $200 million (each). Small-market teams, such as the Memphis Grizzlies and Milwaukee Bucks, generate a little less than half of that (approximately $90 million each).

Table 12.3   NHL salary cap and floor

Year	Salary Cap ($millions)	Salary Floor ($millions)
2005–2006	39.0	21.5
2006–2007	44.0	28.0
2007–2008	50.3	43.9
2008–2009	56.7	40.7
2009–2010	56.8	40.8

While the financial nature of the NBA is probably more similar to MLB (many games and local television contracts), salary caps and the abundance of revenue sharing make the teams slightly more equal financially.

NHL

Ever since the lockout of the 2004–2005 season, league policies have dramatically changed in the NHL. Before the lockout, costs were increasing and revenues were essentially flat. This led to the owners successfully negotiating a salary cap with a salary floor. Table 12.3 shows the cap figures since the lockout. As Table 12.3 illustrates, in percentage terms, NHL payrolls have increased quite a bit since the lockout. NHL payrolls are still far below that of the other major leagues.

Competitive Balance

The oft-stated goal of revenue-sharing programs is to enhance competitive balance; it is now time, then, to look at the effect these policies have had on competitive balance. Competitive balance itself is a difficult concept to define. As a result, attention is focused initially on *within* season competitive balance. In other words, how even are teams in a particular season? One popular metric of within season competitive balance is the standard deviation of winning percentages at the end of the season. Figure 12.1 shows the standard deviation of winning percentages for the four main leagues across the past five decades. What is interesting is that it appears that the NFL has the highest standard deviation (least balanced) followed by the NBA, the NHL, and MLB (most competitive balance), although there are exceptions. Over the past five decades, these leagues have seen many changes in league policies, but it might be hard to argue, using this graph, that these policies have changed balance at all. There might be slight differences when the NFL or NHL instituted salary caps, but these differences are small. This graph shows that the biggest determinants in season balance are things that are inherent in the sport or league. For example, things like the number of games played or the very nature

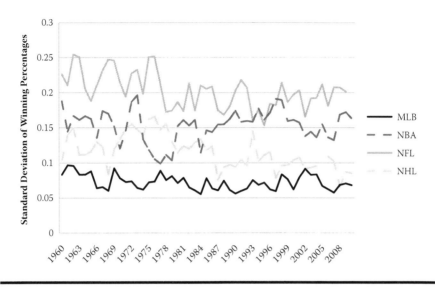

Figure 12.1   Within season competitive balance.

of the game seem to determine how closely teams will be at the end of the season in terms of winning percentage.

What should the measure of competitive balance be across seasons? If a league is balanced across seasons, then poorly performing teams have a better chance of improving the next season compared to an unbalanced league. A basic metric that identifies this type of balance is the correlation of winning percentages from one season to the next. If the correlation is high, that means the league is unbalanced

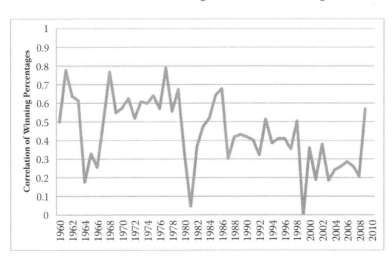

Figure 12.2   Across season competitive balance for the NFL.

and the same teams tend to win year after year. Figure 12.2 shows the correlations of winning percentages for the NFL. It appears that the league has gotten slightly more competitive over time, but the trend is not entirely obvious. On average, this correlation is lower during the salary cap years, but not by that much.

Figure 12.3 shows this metric for MLB. As with the NFL, there is no obvious trend. The correlation seemed to be relatively low in the 1990s, but then increased again. While MLB has had varying revenue-sharing and luxury tax policies, they have not had the dramatic shifts in policies of some other leagues. Still, it would be difficult to see a clear shift in balance due to policies.

Figure 12.4 shows the correlation of winning percentages across seasons for the NBA. Again, there seems to be no trends or shifts. There was a period of relatively high turnover of quality teams in the late 1970s, but it was short-lived.

Figure 12.5 shows across season balances for the NHL. While it is still too early to tell, the correlation does appear to be lower after the lockout. But again, this could simply be a statistical anomaly. Perhaps in a few years, the data will be more obvious about the effect of the salary cap.

Competitive balance also can be defined by championships. Figure 12.6 shows the number of different champions for each decade from the 1970s to the 2000s. From Figure 12.6, it is difficult to see any evidence of which league is the most balanced. It is interesting to see that many more NHL teams are winning championships across the last couple of decades compared to the 1970s and 1980s. The NBA, on the other hand, has seen an opposite trend. It should be remembered that this type of competitive balance depends on many variables including the number of teams and playoff structure, which could change over time. The NHL and NBA

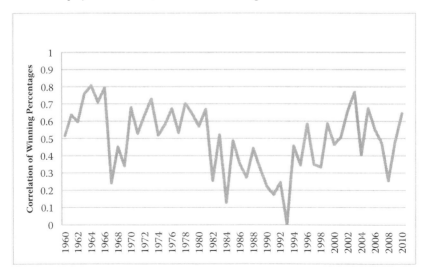

Figure 12.3   Across season competitive balance for MLB.

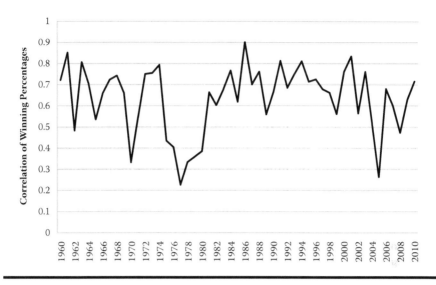

Figure 12.4   Across season competitive balance for the NBA.

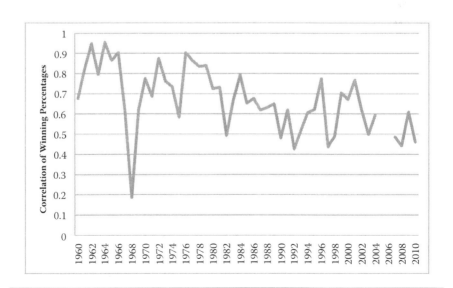

Figure 12.5   Across season competitive balance for the NHL.

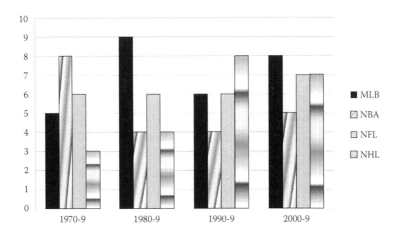

Figure 12.6   The number of different champions per decade.

are somewhat similar in these variables; the differences between the two leagues are somewhat puzzling.

Taxes

Taxes impact expenditure decisions and profitability. Managers must remember that an assessment of the effect of taxes focuses on the marginal rate, not the average. Just as with an investment in talent, managers want to consider marginal benefits and marginal costs. The average tax rate is equal to the total amount of taxes divided by taxable income, while the marginal tax rate is defined as the percent of taxes paid on one extra dollar of income. The United States, as well as most countries, has a progressive tax system (Table 12.4). This means that firms or teams that have a higher taxable income are taxed at a higher rate. Furthermore, personal tax rates are different from corporate tax rates (the United States is one of the few countries where the corporate tax rate is higher than the personal tax rates). As a result, businesses have various average tax rates and marginal tax rates.

The reason managers use the marginal tax rate for most decisions is because most financial decisions will have a small effect on income. For example, suppose a team is considering investing in talent to increase revenue. If the team calculates that this increase in investment will increase profits by $1 million, then the increase in taxes depends on their current marginal tax rate (unless the increase in income changes their tax bracket). Suppose the team currently has a 35 percent tax rate. Then the increase in the after tax profits is only $650,000 ($1,000,000 × (1 −.35)). While after tax profits still increase, it can alter investment strategies. Many times whatever costs are incurred also will be included before taxes, so the financial analyst can simply look at benefits and costs before taxes. It is possible

Table 12.4 2010 United States corporate tax rates

Over	But Not Over	The Tax Is	Of the Amount Over
$0	$50,000	$0 + 15%	$0
$50,000	$75,000	$7,500 + 25%	$50,000
$75,000	$100,000	$13,750 + 34%	$75,000
$100,000	$335,000	$22,250 + 39%	$100,000
$335,000	$10,000,000	$113,900 + 34%	$335,000
$10,000,000	$15,000,000	$3,400,000 + 35%	$10,000,000
$15,000,000	$18,333,333	$5,150,000 + 38%	$15,000,000
$18,333,333	And over	$6,416,667 + 35%	$18,333,333

that this investment excludes the possibility of other investments in a different time period that might have increased after tax profits even more. In the example above, if the extra $1 million generated $650,000 after taxes, it is possible that the same investment would generate $800,000 before taxes the next year. If for some reason the marginal rate was lower the next year, possibly due to certain tax breaks or a decrease in profits, it might make sense to delay the investment. Because tax rates are generally progressive, there is usually an incentive to smooth out profits over time instead of earning massive profits during one year.

Also, because many teams are often in complicated ownership structures, it is sometimes easy to move profits so that they are taxed at the lowest possible rate. Just as multinational corporations try to move profits to the country with the lowest tax rates, sports teams try to move profits where the lowest tax rates exist. Given the prominence of multifaceted corporations in contemporary sports, teams often have the opportunity to easily move funds. The differences in tax rates could be between different countries, personal and corporate taxes, or other tax discrepancies.

Here is a simplified example to illustrate the point. Let us suppose that an owner of a hockey team also owns a beer corporation. Let us further suppose that the beer corporation "sells" one million cans of beer to the team for $5 each. If the profits of the hockey team are reported on the owner's personal taxes, consider the outcomes if the personal tax rate is 25 percent. Furthermore, 16 percent of all hockey revenue is shared. This means that the owner gets to keep 63 percent ($(1 - .25) \times (1 - .16)$) of all hockey revenue as the after tax profit. In other words, 37 percent of revenue is either shared or taxed. If the beer company is a U.S. corporation and their taxable income is between $10 and $15 million, then according to Table 12.4, their marginal tax rate is 35 percent. In this case, the owner keeps more revenue from beer than hockey. Therefore, the owner might consider selling the beer for a higher price. If the price of the beer was an extra dollar, it would result in an extra $20,000 ($1,000,000 × (.37 − .35)) in after tax profits. On the other hand, if the beer corporation had a taxable income between $15 and $18.3 million, it would actually want to sell the beer to the hockey team for less. While this is a simplified example, it illustrates that, with complicated ownership structures, it is possible to move profits to the lowest marginal tax rate.

There are also many other common financial tax laws that all businesses should plan for. For example, when corporations receive dividends from other firms, there are special tax laws. Dividends are usually 70 percent excluded from taxes. This means that only 30 percent of dividends are added to taxable income. Even a smaller percentage might be added to taxable income if the company owns a large percentage of the firm giving dividends. The reason that a majority of dividends are excluded from taxable income is because dividends have already been taxed.

Another major tax issue is capital depreciation. Depreciation occurs when capital loses value because it ages. Therefore, firms add the loss of the value of capital to their costs. The IRS allows firms to depreciate capital because it is a real cost of doing business even though it does not affect short-term cash flow. The *depreciable value* includes the total cost of an asset, including any installation costs. Depending on the type of capital, there are many ways of depreciating assets. The length of time an asset is depreciated (the depreciable life) and the rate of depreciation varies. For instance, things like buildings depreciate very slowly and have a long depreciable life while items like computers typically depreciate very quickly and have a short depreciable life. Also, straight-line depreciation means that the asset depreciates the same amount each year. However, because most assets depreciate more rapidly when they are new, sometimes double-declining, straight-line depreciation is used.*

Roster Depreciation Allowance

Many industries receive special tax exemptions and the sports industry is certainly no different. In fact, one could argue that the sports industry has mastered tax loopholes. One of the more remarkable tax laws dealing with professional sports is the roster depreciation allowance. After he bought the Cleveland Indians in 1946, Bill Veeck convinced the U.S. Congress to allow baseball teams to depreciate their roster. There are several odd things about this. First of all, depreciation usually pertains to capital. So, things like buildings, automobiles, or even cattle are generally depreciated for tax purposes. Players are clearly labor and not capital. Second, because players are labor, they should get paid according to their productivity. This means that teams should be paying players whatever they are worth and, if the

---

* Double declining and straight-line depreciation are examples of depreciation rates. Many methods of depreciating capital entail front-loading value to enhance the present value of the taxes saved.

players do lose value over time, their contract should reflect this. Third, depreciation implies that an asset's value decreases across time. As any sports fan knows, often players get better before their productivity declines. Fourth, player costs are already considered when finding profit. Because the owners do not literally own the players, the cost of players is counted against profit and depreciated. Nonetheless, the "Veeck loophole" began when Veeck sold the Indians in 1949 and this meant teams could then pay less in taxes by depreciating their roster.

While Veeck began the roster depreciation allowance, the Milwaukee Braves may have perfected it in 1964 (Leeds and Von Allmen, 2008). Bill Veeck may have depreciated the value of his roster, but the Braves claimed that more than 99 percent of the purchase price of the team was represented by the value of the players. As a result, they used the entire value of the team as the amount that should be depreciated. The Braves also depreciated their players using straight-line depreciation across a 10-year span. This means that they deducted 10 percent of the depreciable value from their taxable income for 10 years. In 1964, corporate tax rates went from 52 percent to 48 percent, so the team was able to save about half of the value of the team in taxes (approximately 5 percent of the team value for 10 years).

One of the more remarkable features of the roster depreciation allowance is that once the team is sold to new owners, the roster depreciation allowance starts all over again. Typically, when a firm depreciates capital, it can do it only once. For one thing, normally capital actually is depreciating in value. So, if a building depreciates to zero, it cannot be depreciated a second time. Furthermore, if capital is sold at a value higher than its legal depreciable value, then the firm must pay taxes on the difference. This does not seem to be the case for sports teams. Teams are allowed to depreciate the team value again once the team is sold. Across the years, the specifics of the roster depreciation have changed. In 1976, the U.S. Congress declared that owners could depreciate 50 percent of the team over five years, which came about after Bud Selig successfully depreciated 94 percent of the Seattle Pilots in 1970 before he moved the team to Milwaukee. In 2004, the Internal Revenue Code was changed to allow owners to depreciate 100 percent of the value of the team over 15 years (Coulson and Fort, 2010). Although the depreciable value increased, the depreciable life decreased, which has an offsetting impact.

This special tax allowance not only increases profits, but it also increases the value of the team. Because future after-tax profits are higher, the value of the team is also higher. Today when people buy teams, the roster depreciation allowance is built into the price. When the roster depreciation allowance started initially, it would have increased profits as well as the value of a team.

Again an example is illustrative. Assume an owner depreciates 100 percent of the sale price of a team over 15 years, just as Congress changed the law in 2004. Suppose a team is purchased for $1 billion and makes $100 million a year in profit. Suppose also that the tax rate is 30 percent. Then each year, for 15 years, after-tax profits are increased by $20 million ($1 billion × .3/15). Over the 15 years, this is a total of $300 million. Assuming a 5 percent depreciation rate, the present value is

$207.6 million.* While we know that the value of money changes over time, the nominal value of this tax loophole is equal to the value of the team multiplied by the tax rate. Even assuming a 5 percent depreciation rate, the value is still more than two-thirds of the tax rate times the value of the team. It should be remembered that in our example the team's profits would have to be at least $66.7 million per year in order to take full advantage of this depreciation. Table 12.5 illustrates the change in cash flows from the roster depreciation allowance.

While Table 12.5 is somewhat redundant in that the only column that changes is the net present value of the savings, other methods of depreciation, such as double-declining and straight-line depreciation changes the amount depreciated from year to year. It also must be noted that teams are becoming large entertainment complexes that can easily move profits. Therefore, teams can typically earn enough profit to fully take advantage of this depreciation. Furthermore, because a future owner can renew the roster depreciation, the current owner should be able to increase the sale value.

Player Taxes

Another fiscal issue that is somewhat unique to sports is player taxes, otherwise known as jock taxes or the "Michael Jordan tax." While specific "jock taxes" are clearly unique to sports, the same basic idea does pertain to other industries. These are taxes imposed on visiting players. The idea is that because the players are earning their income in various states, they must pay various state taxes on that income. In fact, most states have passed laws requiring visiting players to pay taxes on their income earned in that state. (Technically, this is referred to as an earnings tax. An earnings tax is an income tax paid based on where one works, not where one lives.) While these taxes are usually relatively low, given the salaries of players, they can generate substantial amounts. One problem with these jock taxes is that they are not always enforced. Everyone making income in a different locality is subject to that state and local government's income taxes. If an earnings tax structure is used, the government where one works should be the recipient of the tax dollars. High profile athletes constitute one of the few groups likely to actually pay these taxes. In the United States, only Tennessee, Florida, Texas, and Washington D.C. have no jock tax, although Tennessee has a jock fee. Illinois has a jock tax, but does not impose the tax on athletes that play for teams in areas with no jock taxes; however, Illinois is the only state that does not let athletes credit jock taxes paid against

---

* If the policy before 2004 is used, 50 percent of the team could be depreciated over five years, and the net present value is $129.9 million. Although this value is less, the team could be sold and the new owner could renew the roster depreciation allowance more quickly, so the best policy for the owners is ambiguous.

Table 12.5 Example of roster depreciation allowance

Year	Depreciable Value ($)	Depreciation Rate	Amount Depreciated ($)	Tax Rate	Tax Savings ($)	Net Present Value of Tax Savings ($ millions) (5% monetary depreciation)
1	1 billion	6.67%	66.7 million	30%	20 million	19.05
2	1 billion	6.67%	66.7 million	30%	20 million	18.14
3	1 billion	6.67%	66.7 million	30%	20 million	17.28
4	1 billion	6.67%	66.7 million	30%	20 million	16.45
5	1 billion	6.67%	66.7 million	30%	20 million	15.67
6	1 billion	6.67%	66.7 million	30%	20 million	14.92
7	1 billion	6.67%	66.7 million	30%	20 million	14.21
8	1 billion	6.67%	66.7 million	30%	20 million	13.54
9	1 billion	6.67%	66.7 million	30%	20 million	12.89
10	1 billion	6.67%	66.7 million	30%	20 million	12.28
11	1 billion	6.67%	66.7 million	30%	20 million	11.69
12	1 billion	6.67%	66.7 million	30%	20 million	11.14
13	1 billion	6.67%	66.7 million	30%	20 million	10.61
14	1 billion	6.67%	66.7 million	30%	20 million	10.10
15	1 billion	6.67%	66.7 million	30%	20 million	9.62
Total			1 billion		300 million	207.59

their Illinois state income tax.* Ohio has enabled local governments to institute an earnings tax on commuters, and athletes playing games in the state are treated no differently from any other commuter.

Tax Incentives and Disincentives

Tax incentives affect athletes just like any other workers. For example, sprinter Usain Bolt skipped a race in the United Kingdom because of their tax laws. Organizers of the race were willing to pay Bolt an appearance fee, but according to the U.K.'s tax laws, the sprinters in the race would have to pay "a 50-percent tax on their appearance fee as well as a proportion of their total worldwide earnings."† Because there would actually be a tax on Bolt's worldwide income, he could have actually lost money from running the race. One might wonder how the United Kingdom can tax "worldwide" income. Essentially, the U.K. taxes pro-rated endorsements from athletes. If an athlete has 20 percent of his/her events in the United Kingdom, then the country will tax 20 percent of his/her endorsements. These taxes also have prevented golfers from playing in the United Kingdom and stopped soccer games from being played there as well. The country gave an exemption (tax incentive) to enable the London Olympic bid to go forward. The incentive offsets the disincentive applied to Bolt.

In 2010, former MLB commissioner Fay Vincent wondered why star players were not taking advantage of tax laws (Vincent, 2010). Vincent argued that players with large contracts could save millions of dollars in taxes if they negotiated for a percentage of ownership in the team. This way, the player's income would be in the form of capital gains, which is taxed at a lower rate than ordinary income. As Vincent points out, there have been player/owners in the past, such as Mario Lemieux with the Pittsburgh Penguins. The NBA currently prohibits people from being both a player and an owner, while MLB does not. While there are certainly some issues with having players being part owners, Vincent is correct that there are certainly possible tax savings for the players, and it may become more common in the future.

State Taxes

There is certainly nothing unique to the sports industry with regard to state taxes; all but seven states have some form of an income tax. This can affect the bottom

---

* For more information, see http://www.taxfoundation.org/research/show/26503.html
† http://news.bbc.co.uk/sport2/hi/athletics/8812123.stm

line for certain teams. One of the more recent examples involved LeBron James and Cliff Lee. When James left the Cleveland Cavaliers for the Miami Heat, he left for less money. The magnitude of the difference in salary might not be as large as one might first think. As some have pointed out, the highest state income tax is 5.9 percent in Ohio, while Florida has no state income tax (Windhorst, 2010). Furthermore, Cleveland has a 2-percent earnings tax yielding a state and local tax rate of approximately 8 percent.* Players for the Miami Heat might have to pay taxes on the income they earned during their away games because of jock or earnings taxes, but they do not have to pay taxes on the income they earn from home games. To offset the higher tax rates involved with living and working in New York City, the Yankees' offer to free agent Cliff Lee included a commitment to enhance the salary offered by his net tax obligations to New York State and New York City. The Texas Rangers in their proposals highlighted the tax advantages of playing in a state without any tax on income.

While these taxes directly affect players, this also gives teams from states with no or low state income taxes a slight advantage to sign players. Suppose LeBron James's goal is to maximize his after tax salary and that he can make $20 million per year in Cleveland. In Cleveland, he must pay roughly 8 percent of his income as a tax with offsetting credits from those states and cities that tax his income from his away game appearances. If the net tax obligation was just 4 percent, his $20-million income shrinks to $19.2 million (before calculation of his federal tax obligations). This implies that a team like the Miami Heat, with no state income tax, only has to offer James slightly more than $19.2 million.

Ticket Taxes

Local governments in numerous states are authorized to levy ticket taxes. In 2007, some legislators in the state of Michigan proposed adding a 6 percent state sales tax on tickets sold to sporting events, concerts, and movies. The Detroit Tigers issued a press release, part of which is reproduced here.

They Already Tax Our Work, Don't Let Them Tax Our Play

In the next few days, the [Michigan] legislature is expected to introduce a new "Luxury Tax" of 6 percent on all tickets to attend professional sporting events, concerts, shows, and movies in Michigan. It is estimated that this new tax will increase ticket prices by over $100 million per year:

■ $24 million per year tax on sports tickets for Tigers, Red Wings, Pistons, Lions, Michigan International Speedway, minor league baseball, and hockey.

---

* In New York City, state and city income taxes total 12.62 percent for high earners.

- $48 million per year tax on shows and performances like those at the Fox Theater, Palace, DTE, Meadow Brook, Purple Rose Theater, and DeVos arena for shows like *Sesame Street Live, Lion King, White Christmas,* and performances by the American Idols.
- $32 million per year tax on movie tickets to every movie in every movie theater in the state:
  - A family of four with season tickets to the Tigers would be forced to pay new taxes ranging from $230 to more than $1,200 per year.
  - A family of four with season tickets to the Red Wings would be forced to pay new taxes from $597 to more than $1,900 per year.

We Must Stop the Ticket Tax

The Ticket Tax Targets Families, Kids, and Teenagers.

Taking your family to a ball game, a show, or a movie is one of the most cherished traditions in Michigan. It's not a luxury. It's the way we spend our hard earned money after all the taxes are taken out of our paychecks and all the bills are paid. It's how teenagers spend their babysitting money and kids spend their allowances.

The Ticket Tax Targets Working Families:

Most of the tickets to attend sporting events, shows, and movies are not purchased by corporations and the wealthy. Michigan's working families purchase them. Families that are struggling today to survive today's difficult economic conditions in our state. Families that already pay income taxes and sales taxes, and $3.20 for a gallon of gasoline.

If Lansing Is Going to Tax Our Work . . . Don't Touch Our Play:

The Legislature is already looking to raise the income tax across the board on working families and retirees. Why add an additional burden on Michigan's working families?

The Highest Ticket Tax in the Region:

The Ticket Tax would give Michigan the highest sports and entertainment ticket tax in the region. Illinois, Indiana, Ohio, and Pennsylvania have a "0" tax on family fun.

$3.20 Per Gallon, a Tough Economy, and
a Ticket Tax Don't Add Up:

The high price of gas and a tough economy are forcing Michigan families to seek entertainment venues closer to home. Adding the burden of a ticket tax might just put the cost of a family night out for a concert or a ball game out of reach.

The Legislature May Take Action on The
Ticket Tax without a Public Hearing:

The state Legislature may take this tax up without a public committee hearing, which would give fans across Michigan an opportunity to tell them how ticked off they are about this ticket tax. That's why people need to act today to contact their legislators. This may be the only chance to tell your lawmakers what you think about this ticket tax idea.

It is clear that a tax on sporting events is not good for sports teams or fans. Part of the burden of the tax will fall on teams as the tax is added to the price of a ticket. If the price increases 3 percent because of the tax, the net revenue declines since the tax is 6 percent. Fans will also have to pay higher ticket prices. To be sure, the magnitude of tax incidence will be adjusted depending on the slopes of the demand and supply curves. Also, a few fans will be deterred from attending any sporting event because of the tax. What is somewhat strange is that the public sector subsidized many of the sports facilities in Michigan when they were built. Government officials can reasonably disagree on whether having sporting events is a good thing or a bad thing, but either way it is inefficient to subsidize a facility and then place a tax on the events held in the structure. This tax also could have created some animosity between teams that play in facilities where the public sector made an investment and those that play in facilities paid for by the team.

Tax Exempt Status for Universities

Colleges and universities enjoy tax-exempt status, which means they do not have to pay taxes on revenue generated by sports. This also means that university donors can write their donations off of their taxes, even though they often receive things for their donations, such as better seats at football games. This has come under scrutiny in recent years. In 2009, the Congressional Budget Office examined the tax exemption that college athletics receives.* The report concluded that 60 to 80 percent of

---

* The full report can be found at http://www.cbo.gov/ftpdocs/100xx/doc10055/05-19-Colle-giateSports.pdf

revenues in college athletics come from commercial activities. Of course, colleges and universities receive revenue from commercial activities outside of sports as well. The difference is that the magnitude is much larger for athletics compared to the rest of the university. So, while many would like to change the tax laws regarding collegiate athletics, the report from the Congressional Budget Office seemed to indicate that changing these tax laws would be difficult.

Profits

As noted earlier, knowing what the actual profits are for sports teams can be difficult. Given the current ownership structures some teams have and the lack of public data, it is not always clear how much was earned. Data are available for a few teams, (e.g., Green Bay Packers), but, for the most part, analysts only have access to estimates of revenues and costs. There is an incentive to try to avoid statements that would illustrate that substantial profits were earned. Teams might move revenues depending on the marginal tax rates for their various related companies, but there are other considerations as well. Because of the public nature of sports teams, owners are usually better off if they can claim they are losing money. This is because owners often negotiate with local governments for subsidies to build new facilities and with the players' unions for salary caps. In 2004, just before the 2004–2005 NHL lockout, the owners hired an accounting firm to perform a financial analysis of every NHL team. The report concluded that the NHL owners lost a combined $273 million during the 2002–2003 season. This certainly strengthened the owners' argument for a salary cap. The report recognized the difficulties of finding profits for all hockey teams. As page 4 of Arthur Levitt's (former chairman of the SEC and presently a senior adviser to The Carlyle Group) report stated,[*]

> The 30 teams represent 30 different businesses with different histories and unique business arrangements. For example, the teams have different owners and ownership structures, different financing arrangements, different contract terms with the municipalities and facilities in which they play, and different sponsorship and media arrangements. It should be noted that all teams play in venues used also for nonhockey events, including college basketball (e.g., Carolina Hurricanes and North Carolina State Wolfpack), professional basketball (e.g., Los Angeles Kings and the Los Angeles Lakers and Los Angeles Clippers), rodeos (e.g., Calgary Flames and the Calgary Stampede), and concerts. The relative significance of hockey to nonhockey events varies widely from arena to arena. In some instances, such as in Columbus, the facility is owned by an independent unrelated third party. In other instances, a

---

[*] http://www.nhl.com/nhlhq/cba/archive/levitt/levittreport.pdf

municipality may own the facility, while in still other instances, the team owner may own either a controlling interest or a minority interest in the facility. Because of the economic and business circumstances unique to each of the teams, the UROs* and URO instructions are designed to include all hockey-related revenues and expenses of each team, regardless of how that team is legally structured, operates or the ownership of the facility it plays in. The goals of the URO are to provide instructions to the teams so they report their business activities on a comprehensive basis using standard instructions and enable the compilation and presentation of a full and accurate statement of the League's combined financial results based upon a comprehensive picture of the entire business of hockey, including all revenues and expenses related to operating an NHL franchise.

While the owners certainly did nothing illegal, it is impossible to know if $273 million represented the total losses of NHL owners.

Leverage

It is often useful to know how sensitive profits are to a change in revenues. The amount of leverage that a firm has represents how much of their revenues or assets are tied up in costs or liabilities. Analysts need to think of a firm's leverage in terms of how narrow its profit margin is over the course of a year or how much net wealth a firm has compared to its liabilities and to understand how leverage and revenues generate into profits. This can be broken down further into operating leverage and financial leverage. The degree of operating leverage is defined as the percentage change in operating income (earnings before interest and taxes)[†] divided by the percent change in sales. If sales increase by 1 percent, then operating income will increase by the degree of operating leverage multiplied by 1 percent. The degree of operating leverage is calculated by:

$$Degree\ of\ Operating\ Leverage = \frac{Revenue - Total\ Variable\ Cost}{Revenue - Total\ Variable\ Cost - Fixed\ Cost}$$

The reason that variable costs are included in the numerator is because, if revenues or sales increase, variable costs must increase as well. Revenue could be considered quantity times price and the total variable cost is quantity times variable costs per unit. If more units are sold and quantity goes up, both revenues and total variable costs will go up. The denominator is simply operating income.

---

* A URO is a unified report of operations.
† Operating income is the same as earnings before interest and taxes as long as there is no non-operating income.

An example is illustrative. Suppose revenue is $200, total variable costs are $100, and fixed costs are $50. In this example, the operating leverage is 2. Another way of looking at it is if revenue increases 1 percent (so that revenue is $202 and total variable cost is $101), then the operating income increases 2 percent (operating income goes from $50 to $51). For this firm, whatever gain it sees in sales, it will be twice the increase, in percentage terms, for operating income.

The degree of financial leverage is defined as the percentage change in earnings (after taxes and financial payments) divided by the percent change in operating income. If operating income increases by 1 percent, then earnings will increase by the degree of financial leverage multiplied by 1 percent. The degree of financial leverage is calculated by:

$$Degree\ of\ Financial\ Leverage = \frac{Revenue - Total\ Variable\ Cost - Fixed\ Cost}{Revenue - Total\ Variable\ Cost - Fixed\ Cost - Interest\ Payments - \dfrac{Preferred\ Stock\ Dividends}{1 - Tax\ Rate}}$$

In the case of financial leverage, operating income is in the numerator and net income is in the denominator.

Continuing with this example, if a company has operating income of $50, interest payments of $10, pays $14 in preferred stock dividends, and is subject to a tax rate of 30 percent, net income is $20. Because the operating income is $50 and the net income is $20, the firm's financial leverage is 2.5. Again, going back to the definition, if operating income increases 1 percent (from $50 to $50.5), then earnings will increase 2.5 percent (from $20 to $20.5).

Using both operating leverage and financial leverage, a manager can find the firm's degree of total leverage, which is defined as the percentage increase in earnings divided by the percentage increase in sales. The degree of total leverage is given by:

$$Degree\ of\ Total\ Leverage = \frac{Revenue - Total\ Variable\ Cost}{Revenue - Total\ Variable\ Cost - Fixed\ Cost - Interest\ Payments - \dfrac{Preferred\ Stock\ Dividends}{1 - Tax\ Rate}}$$

Notice the degree of total leverage is simply degree of operating leverage times financial leverage. In this example, if the firm's sales increased 1 percent (revenue minus total variable cost would go from $100 to $101), then the firm's earnings would increase 5 percent (from $20 to $21). Another way of looking at it is if operating leverage is 2 and financial leverage is 2.5, then total leverage is 5. This means that whatever the percentage increase in sales, it will increase earnings by 5 times as much. Alternatively, if sales decrease, then earnings decrease by fivefold in percentage terms. It is easy to see how highly leveraged firms are risky because they are sensitive to changes in sales. Firms or teams that have high leverage are riskier because they are sensitive to sales. Breaking the leverage down into operating leverage and financial leverage allows a firm or team to see what part of the business creates the risk.

As noted, leverage also could be examined in terms of assets and liabilities, which is known as *accounting leverage*. The formula for accounting leverage is relatively straightforward:

$$Accounting\ Leverage = \frac{Total\ Assets}{Total\ Assets - Total\ Liabilities}$$

This shows, in terms of the firm's wealth, how sensitive stockholder equity or the firm's net worth is to a change in assets. If a firm has a high degree of accounting leverage, then a small change in assets can have a big impact on the firm's net worth.

Like most industries, the degree of leverage can vary depending on the sports organization. For operating leverage, it depends on the profitability of the team. Because a new stadium is expensive and would probably be considered a fixed cost, this can increase the operating leverage for many teams. For example, the return on a new stadium depends very much on attendance levels. The profitability can be very sensitive to any changes in attendance.

The degree of financial leverage might be team dependent, but typically there is no reason why sports teams should be borrowing inordinate amounts of money relative to other industries. In fact, the NFL restricts owners from borrowing more than $150 million by using the team as collateral. This means that interest payments are essentially capped for NFL teams. While teams in other leagues might have fewer restrictions, it simply depends on the particular team owner.

Accounting leverage is also team dependent. Some teams have assets far greater than liabilities. This means there is little chance of insolvency or bankruptcy. Other teams might have a very small net worth and any change in assets, without changing liabilities, would greatly impact the team.

The Importance of Leverage

During the recent financial crisis, the importance of leverage became apparent. After all, leverage is one of the key differences in the severity between falling housing prices around 2007 and 2008 and the "dot.com" bubble that burst from 2000 to 2002. Total stock market losses from the beginning of 2000 to the end of 2002 were about $7.5 trillion. While the "dot.com" crash was substantial, it seemed to have a relatively minor effect on the greater economy. In other words, the financial system seemed to absorb these losses fairly well. Falling housing prices tell a different story. From their peak in 2006, home prices fell roughly 35 percent, which meant total losses of $7.7 trillion. While this loss mostly burdened homeowners, some have estimated that roughly 20 percent was imposed by the financial sector. Needless to say, the financial sector did not handle these losses well.

One main reason the financial sector could not easily handle these losses is leverage. Liabilities of financial firms were nearly as much as their assets. Stockholder equity was small compared to assets. For example, Morgan Stanley, Bear Stearns, and Merrill Lynch all had a leverage ratio of over 30:1 at the end of 2007. This meant that total liabilities were around 97 percent of total assets. In this instance, financial firms did not have a lot of capital, but instead investments were all intertwined between different financial investments. This degree of leverage typically works well in a good economy, but clearly does not during a poor economy. When the financial sector had to absorb losses, their absolute magnitude might have been more than the company's net worth. Furthermore, any bankruptcies of financial firms might put pressure on the other interconnected financial firms. Because financial firms had little capital and were all highly leveraged, a crisis for the industry resulted.

References

Coulson, N. E, and Fort, R. 2010. Tax revisions of 2004 and pro sports team ownership. *Contemporary Economic Policy* 28 (4) 464–473.

Leeds, M. A. and von Allmen, P. 2008. *The economics of sports*, 3rd ed. Boston: Pearson Publishing.

Vincent, F. 2010. Albert Pujols's capital opportunity. *Wall Street Journal*, November 29, online edition. http://online.wsj.com/article/SB100014240527487044627045755906 00879687646.html (accessed May 14, 2011).

Windhorst, B. 2010. LeGone: LeBron James announces he's leaving Cleveland Cavaliers for Miami Heat. *The Plain Dealer* online edition, July 8, http://www.cleveland.com/cavs/index.ssf/2010/07/legone_lebron_james_confirms_h.html (accessed May 14, 2011)

Further Reading on League Policies

El Hodiri, M. and Quirk, J. 1971. An economic model of a professional sports league. *Journal of Political Economy* 70 1302–1319.

Fort, R. and Quirk, J. 1995. Cross-subsidization, incentives and outcomes in professional team sports leagues. *Journal of Economic Literature* 33 1265–1299.

Rottenberg, S. 1956. The baseball players' labor market. *Journal of Political Economy* 64 242–258.

Szymanski, S. 2003. The economic design of sporting contests. *Journal of Economic Literature* 41 1137–1187.

Szymanski, S. 2004. Professional team sports are only a game: The Walrasian fixed-supply conjecture model, contest-nash equilibrium, and the invariance principle. *Journal of Sports Economics* 5 111–126.

Szymanski, S. and Kesenne, S.. 2004. Competitive balance and revenue sharing in team sports. *Journal of Industrial Economics* 52 165–177.

Vrooman, J. 2009. Theory of the perfect game: Competitive balance in monopoly sports leagues. *Review of Industrial Organization* 34 5–44.

Winfree, J. and Fort, R. Forthcoming. Nash conjectures and talent supply in sports league modeling: A comment on current modeling disagreements. *Journal of Sports Economics*.

Appendix 1

In this appendix, the math behind league policies and how they affect profits, player salaries, and competitive balance is presented. For simplicity, a model for a two-team league is used. Obviously, virtually all sports leagues have more than two teams, but it helps to make some generalizations about policies. First, an investment in talent leads to winning. This relationship is known as the contest success function and mathematically is represented by $w_i(z_i, z_j)$. That is, team i's winning percentage, w_i, is a function of the talent investment by team i, z_i, and j, z_j.* Thankfully, leagues do not simply calculate the investment in talent for each team and then calculate winning percentages. In other words, more goes into winning than just a team's investment. Nonetheless, when teams invest more, they win more,

$$\frac{\partial w_i}{\partial z_i} > 0 \,,$$

and when the other team invests more, the winning percentage goes down,

$$\frac{\partial w_i}{\partial z_j} < 0 \,.$$

Additionally, the two winning percentages have to add up to one, $w_i(z_i, z_j) + w_j(z_j, z_i) = 1$, which also means

$$\frac{\partial w_i}{\partial z_i} = -\frac{\partial w_j}{\partial z_i} \,. ^\dagger$$

The reason that teams invest in talent is because if they win more, they will get more revenue. Team i's revenue function, denoted by R_i, is given by $R_i\big(w_i(z_i, z_j)\big)$, where

$$\frac{dR_i}{dw_i} > 0 \,.$$

It is important to note that the revenue function is different than the contest success function in that it differs depending on the market size of the team. For example,

---

* As noted, there is a difference here between "open" and "closed" leagues. In "open" European leagues, teams can invest in talent and not affect the talent level of other teams. In "closed" North American leagues, teams must increase their talent by decreasing the talent level of some other team. Nonetheless, in either type of league, teams invest in talent, which determines the winning percentage.

† One common contest success function that is often used is

$$w_i = \frac{z_i}{z_i + z_j} \,.$$

if both teams won half of their games, the large-market team would have a higher revenue than the small-market team. The profit function of team i is given by:

$$\pi_i = R_i\left(w_i(z_i, z_j)\right) - z_i$$

Taking the derivative of that function means the team will invest in talent until the marginal benefit of investing equals the marginal cost of talent,

$$\frac{dR_i}{dw_i} \frac{\partial w_i}{\partial z_i} = 1,$$

which holds for both teams. This implies that:

$$\frac{dR_i}{dw_i} \frac{\partial w_i}{\partial z_i} = \frac{dR_j}{dw_j} \frac{\partial w_j}{\partial z_j}.$$

We assume that for any given winning percentage,

$$\frac{dR_l}{dw} > \frac{dR_s}{dw}$$

where l denotes the large-market team, s denotes the small-market team, then if the further common assumption is made that talent investment has positive but decreasing returns,

$$\frac{\partial^2 R}{\partial z^2} < 0,$$

and because the contest success function is the same for both teams, the large-market teams will invest more in talent, $z_l > z_s$, and will have a higher winning percentage, $w_l > w_s$.

Salary Cap

The simplest policy to consider is a salary cap. Talent investment and team payroll or salary are not completely the same thing, but for our purposes it is assumed that a league is limiting all talent investment. It is assumed that the cap is restrictive on both teams. In this case, $z_i = z_j$ and $w_i = w_j$. Therefore, the model says that both teams should be of equal strength, implying that competitive balance is maximized. Furthermore, player salaries are lower than in the absence of a policy. The effect on profits is ambiguous at least for the large-market team. If the decrease in costs (talent investment) outweighs the decrease in revenues from a lower winning percentage, then large-market teams will enjoy increased profits with a salary cap. For the small-market team, talent investment decreases and winning increases, and therefore, profits increase.

Revenue Sharing

Thus far it has been assumed that teams keep all of their revenue, but in the case of revenue sharing, a team's profit is given by:

$$\pi_i = (1 - \alpha)R_i\left(w_i(z_i, z_j)\right) + \alpha R_j\left(w_j(z_i, z_j)\right) - z_i$$

where α is the proportion of revenue that is shared.* Again, taking the derivative so that teams invest until the marginal benefit equals marginal cost indicate that the following equation will hold:

$$(1 - \alpha)\frac{dR_i}{dw_i}\frac{\partial w_i}{\partial z_i} + \alpha\frac{dR_j}{dw_j}\frac{\partial w_j}{\partial z_i} = 1.$$

And, again, because this is true for both teams, that means that:

$$(1 - \alpha)\frac{dR_i}{dw_i}\frac{\partial w_i}{\partial z_i} + \alpha\frac{dR_j}{dw_j}\frac{\partial w_j}{\partial z_i} = (1 - \alpha)\frac{dR_j}{dw_j}\frac{\partial w_j}{\partial z_j} + \alpha\frac{dR_i}{dw_i}\frac{\partial w_i}{\partial z_j}$$

and because

$$\frac{\partial w_i}{\partial z_i} = -\frac{\partial w_j}{\partial z_i},$$

this implies that in equilibrium:

$$\frac{dR_i}{dw_i}\left[(1 - \alpha)\frac{\partial w_i}{\partial z_i} + \alpha\frac{\partial w_j}{\partial z_j}\right] = \frac{dR_j}{dw_j}\left[(1 - \alpha)\frac{\partial w_j}{\partial z_j} + \alpha\frac{\partial w_i}{\partial z_i}\right].$$

If this equation is invariant of α, then revenue sharing has no effect on competitive balance. This would be the case if winning is a linear function of talent investment. In other words, if talent investment has a constant effect on winning, then revenue sharing has no effect on competitive balance. If, however, talent investment has a decreasing return to winning,

$$\frac{\partial^2 w}{\partial z^2} < 0,$$

---

* Here it is assumed that a percentage of revenue simply goes to the other team. Sometimes leagues split pool sharing, where revenues go into a pool and then the revenue is shared. If the revenue in the pool was split evenly between the two teams, then teams would be sharing exactly half of the revenue in the pool.

then revenue sharing actually decreases competitive balance. If i is the large-market team and

$$\frac{\partial^2 w}{\partial z^2} < 0,$$

then the bracketed term on the left-hand side will increase and the bracketed term on the right-hand side will decrease as α gets larger. In equilibrium,

$$\frac{dR_i}{dw_i}$$

must decrease and

$$\frac{dR_j}{dw_j}$$

must increase to maintain equilibrium. If it is assumed that winning increases revenues at a decreasing rate,

$$\frac{\partial^2 R}{\partial w^2} < 0,$$

then the winning percentage of the large-market team must increase and the winning percentage of the small-market team must decrease.

Revenue Sharing and Player Salaries

From this point forward another simplifying assumption is made. The marginal benefit of talent investment on revenue is unaffected by the other team's talent investment,

$$\frac{d^2 R_i}{dz_i dz_j} = 0.$$

Although this cross derivative is probably not equal to exactly zero, it is not unreasonable to assume that it is sufficiently small. Also, just to simplify the math, w is suppressed such that revenue is a function of the two teams' investment, $R_i(z_i, z_j)$, analyzing the effect of revenue sharing on player salaries. Implicitly differentiating the equilibrium condition with respect to α yields:

$$\frac{dz_i}{d\alpha} = \frac{\dfrac{dR_i}{dz_i} - \dfrac{dR_j}{dz_i}}{(1-\alpha)\dfrac{d^2 R_i}{dz_i^2} + \alpha\dfrac{d^2 R_j}{dz_i^2}} < 0$$

so that overall expenditure on talent by the league is given by:

$$\frac{d(z_i + z_j)}{d\alpha} = \frac{\dfrac{dR_i}{dz_i} - \dfrac{dR_j}{dz_i}}{(1-\alpha)\dfrac{d^2 R_i}{dz_i^2} + \alpha \dfrac{d^2 R_j}{dz_i^2}} + \frac{\dfrac{dR_j}{dz_j} - \dfrac{dR_i}{dz_j}}{(1-\alpha)\dfrac{d^2 R_j}{dz_j^2} + \alpha \dfrac{d^2 R_i}{dz_j^2}} < 0$$

Therefore, revenue sharing will unambiguously decrease player salaries.

Revenue Sharing and Profits

In this section, the effect of revenue sharing on profit for the large-market team and the small-market team is analyzed. Most analysts assume that revenue sharing is bad for the large-market team's profits. Certainly, one effect is that the large-market team is sharing more revenue than the small-market team. Earlier, it was argued that revenue sharing decreases spending for players. Furthermore, if anything competitive balance will worsen, which means more revenue for the large-market team.

For the small-market team, their profit will increase from the direct effect of sharing less revenue than the large-market team. Similarly, the small-market team enjoys increased profit from the decrease in players' salaries. The worsening in balance, however, hurts the profit of the small-market team. Mathematically, the effect of revenue sharing on profits at the equilibrium is given by:

$$\frac{d\pi_i}{d\alpha} = -R_i + R_j - \frac{dz_i}{d\alpha} + (1+\alpha)\frac{dR_i}{dz_i}\frac{dz_i}{d\alpha} + \frac{dR_i}{dz_j}\frac{dz_j}{d\alpha} + \alpha\frac{dR_j}{dz_j}\frac{dz_j}{d\alpha} + \frac{dR_j}{dz_i}\frac{dz_i}{d\alpha}$$

where $- R_i + R_j$ is the direct effect of sharing the revenue,

$$-\frac{dz_i}{d\alpha}$$

is the effect on profits of decreasing player salaries, and the rest of the equation represents the change in profits from the change in competitive balance. While the effects of revenue sharing on profits are ambiguous, if revenue sharing does not greatly change the winning percentages of the teams, then it will have a positive effect on small-market teams. The effect on large-market teams would still depend on the magnitude of the differences in the revenue of the two teams and the decrease in the investments made in talent.

The Effects of a Luxury Tax

In this section, the effect of a luxury tax is analyzed. There is an important distinction between this model and the model dealing only with revenue sharing. The team is being taxed on investment in players and typically luxury taxes are placed on a team's payroll. Therefore, this model is not quite as general. Note that it still assumes

$$\frac{d^2 R_i}{dz_i dz_j} = 0$$

and revenue is only a function of the two teams' investment, $R_i(z_i, z_j)$. If team i is the large-market team, and there is no revenue sharing, then the profit functions for the large and small market are

$$\pi_i = R_i\left(w_i(z_i, z_j)\right) - \overline{z} - (1 + \tau)(z_i - \overline{z})$$

$$\pi_j = R_j\left(w_j(z_j, z_i)\right) - z_j$$

where $\overline{z}$ is the limit of investment that is not taxed and τ is the tax rate. Note that it is assumed that the large-market team is taxed and the small-market team is not. Therefore, the first order conditions are

$$\frac{d\pi_i}{dz_i} = \frac{dR_i}{dw_i} \frac{\partial w_i}{\partial z_i} - 1 - \tau = 0$$

$$\frac{d\pi_j}{dz_j} = \frac{dR_j}{dw_j} \frac{\partial w_j}{\partial z_j} - 1 = 0$$

Luxury Tax, Player Salaries, and Competitive Balance

Here the effect of a luxury tax on player salaries is analyzed. Implicitly differentiating those equations with respect to τ gives us:

$$\frac{dz_i}{d\tau} = \frac{1}{\dfrac{d^2 R_i}{dz_i^2}} < 0$$

$$\frac{dz_j}{d\tau} = 0$$

Thus, the overall expenditure on talent by the league is negative; therefore, player salaries decrease. Because the large-market team is the only team that is taxed and only the large-market team will change payroll by decreasing talent investment, competitive balance will be improved.

The Luxury Tax and Team Profits

Again using implicit differentiation, the following effect of a luxury tax on profit is identified:

$$\frac{d\pi_i}{dt} = \frac{dR_i}{dz_i}\frac{dz_i}{dt} - (z_i - \bar{z}) < 0$$

$$\frac{d\pi_j}{dt} = \frac{dR_j}{dz_i}\frac{dz_i}{dt} > 0$$

Therefore, under reasonable assumptions, the luxury tax will decrease profits for the taxed teams and increase profits for the small-market team.

References

Ahn, S. and Lee, Y. H. 2007. Life-cycle demand for Major League Baseball. *International Journal of Sport Finance*, (2) 25–35.

Alexander, D. and Kern, W. 2004. The economic determinants of professional sports franchise values. *Journal of Sports Economics*, (5) 51–66.

Allan, G. and Roy, G. 2008. Does television crowd out spectators? New evidence from the Scottish Premier League. *Journal of Sports Economics*, 9 (6) 592–605.

Allan, S. 2004. Satellite television and football attendance: The not so super effect. *Applied Economics Letter*, 11 (2) 123–125.

Anderson, D. 1988. 'Super' Jets question today's Jets. *The New York Times*, August 7.

Badenhausen, K., Ozanian, M. K., and Settimi, C. 2009. Recession tackles NFL team values. *Forbes*, September 2, On-line edition, http://www.forbes.com/2009/09/02/nfl-profootball-business-sportsmoney-football-values-09-values.html (accessed on May 13, 2011).

Baimbridge, M., Cameron, S., and Dawson, P. 1995. Satellite broadcasting and match attendance: The case of rugby league. *Applied Economics Letters* 2 (10) 343–346.

Baimbridge, M., Cameron, S., and Dawson, P. 1996. Satellite television and the demand for football: A whole new ball game. *Scottish Journal of Political Economy*, 43 (3) 317–333.

Beckstead, D., Brown, M. W., and Gellatly, G. 2008. The left brain of North American cities: Scientists and engineers and urban growth. *International Regional Science Review*, 31 (3) 304–338.

Berri, D. 2008. A simple measure of worker productivity in the National Basketball Association. In *The business of sport*, Eds. B. Humphreys and D. Howard, 3 volumes, 1–40. Westport, CT: Praeger.

Berri, D., Brook, S., and Schmidt, M. 2007. Does one simply need to score to score? *International Journal of Sport Finance*, 2 (4) 190–205.

Berri, D. and Krautmann, A. 2006. Shirking on the court: Testing for the incentive effects of guaranteed pay. *Economic Inquiry*, 44 (3) 536–546.

Berri, D. and Schmidt, M. B. 2006. On the road with the National Basketball Association's superstar externality, *Journal of Sports Economics*, 7 (4) 347.

Bollinger, C. and Hotchkiss, J. 2003. The upside potential of hiring risky workers: evidence from the baseball industry. *Journal of Labor Economics*, 21 (4) 923–944.

Brown, C. 1990. Firms' choice method of pay. *Industrial and Labor Relations Review*, 43 (3) 165S–182S.

Brown, E., Spiro, R., and Keenan, D. 1991. Wage and nonwage discrimination in professional basketball: Do fans affect it? *American Journal of Economics and Sociology*, 50 (3) 333–345.

Brown, M. 2009. Understanding the real value of MLBAM and MLB network. The Biz of Baseball, January 19, http://bizofbaseball.com/index.php?option=com_content&view =article&id=2878:understanding-the-real-value-of-mlbam-and-mlb-network&catid= 26:editorials&Itemid=39 (accessed January 19, 2011).

Buraimo, B. 2008. Stadium attendance and television audience demand in English League football. *Managerial and Decision Economics*, 29 (6) 513.

Buraimo, B., Forrest, D. and Simmons, R. 2006. Robust estimates of the impact of broadcasting on match attendance in football (working paper). Retrieved from Lancaster University Management School, England website: http://www.lums.lancs.ac.uk/publications/viewpdf/003093/business ofbaseball: #1 New York Yankees, The 2010 Forbes April 7, on-line edition, http://www.forbes.com/lists/2010/33/baseball-valuations-10_ New-York-Yankees_334613.html (accessed April 7, 2011).

Cagan, J. and deMause, N. 1998. *Field of schemes: How the great stadium swindle turns public money into private profit.* Monroe, ME: Common Courage.

Carbot, C. B. 2009. The odd couple: Stadium naming rights mitigating the public-private stadium debate. *Florida International University Law Review*, (4) 515–542.

Carmichael, F., Millington, J., and Simmons, R. 1999. Elasticity of demand for rugby league attendance and the impact of BSkyB. *Applied Economics Letters*, 6 (12) 797–800.

Chapin, T. 2002. Beyond the entrepreneurial city: Municipal capitalism in San Diego. *Journal of Urban Affairs*, 24 (5) 565–581.

Chapin, T. 2004. Sports facilities as urban redevelopment catalysts: Baltimore's Camden Yards and Cleveland's Gateway. *Journal of the American Planning Association*, 70 (2) 193–209.

Clapp, C. M. and Hakes, J. K. 2005. How long a honeymoon? The effect of new stadiums on attendance in Major League Baseball. *Journal of Sports Economics*, 6 (3) 237–263.

Coates, D. and Humphreys, B. R. 2005. Novelty effects of new facilities on attendance at professional sporting events. *Contemporary Economic Policy*, 23 (3) 436–455.

Coates, D. and Humphreys, B. R. 2007. Ticket prices, concessions, and attendance at professional sporting events. *International Journal of Sport Finance*, 2 (3) 161–170.

Coulson, E. N. and Fort, R. 2010. Tax revisions of 2004 and pro sports team ownership. *Contemporary Economic Policy*, 28 (4) 464–473.

Davis, M. C. 2009. Analyzing the relationship between team success and MLB attendance with GARCH effects. *Journal of Sports Economics*, 10 (1) 44–58.

Erie, S. P., Kogan, V., and MacKenzie, S. A. 2010. Redevelopment, San Diego style: The limits of public-private partnerships. *Urban Affairs Review*, 45 (5) 644–678.

Etoe, C. 2010. Attendance doubles as Mansfield fans pay what they want. BBC, February 6, On-line edition, http://news.bbc.co.uk/sport2/hi/football/teams/m/mansfield_ town/8502204.stm (accessed April 10, 2011).

Fama, E. F. and French, K. R. 1992. The cross-section of expected stock returns. *Journal of Finance*, (47) 427–465.

Farrell, M. 2009. New York Times puts NESN on block. Multichannel News, http://www. multichannel.com/article/162920-New_York_Times_Puts_NESN_Stake_On_Block. php (accessed January 3, 2011).

Fizel, J. and Bennett, R. 1989. The impact of college football telecast on college football attendance. *Social Science Quarterly*, 70 (4) 980–988.

Forrest, D., Simmons, R., and Szymanksi, S. 2004. Broadcasting, attendance and the inefficiency of cartel. *Review of Industrial Organization*, 24 (3) 243–265.

Fort, R. 2004a. Inelastic sports pricing. *Managerial and Decision Economics*, 25 (2) 87–94.

Fort, R. 2004b. Subsidies as incentive mechanisms in sports. *Managerial and Decision Economics*, 25 (2) 95–102.

Fort, R. 2006. The value of Major League Baseball ownership. *International Journal of Sport Finance*, 1 (1) 3–8.

Fort, R. and Winfree, J. 2009. Sports really are different: The contest success function and the supply of talent. *Review of Industrial Organization*, 34 (1) 69–80.

Gabler, N. 2007. *Walt Disney: The triumph of the American imagination.* 2nd ed. New York: Alfred A. Knopf.

Gitman, L. J. 2003. *Principals of managerial finance.* New York: Addison Wesley.

Gitter, S. and Rhoads, T. 2008. If you win they will come: Fans care about winning in minor league baseball (Working paper). Retrieved from Towson University website: http://pages. towson.edu/trhoads/Gitter%20and%20Rhoads%20WEA08.pdf (accessed April 11, 2011).

Gottdiener, M. 2001. *The theming of America: American dreams, media fantasies, and themed environments*, 2nd ed. Boulder, CO: Westview Press.

Hakes, J. K. and Sauer, R. D. 2006. An economic evaluation of the moneyball hypothesis. *Journal of Economic Perspectives*, 20 (3) 173–185.

Hannigan, J. 1998. *Fantasy city: Pleasure and profit in the postmodern metropolis.* New York: Routledge Press.

Haupert, M. J. 2010. *The economic history of Major League Baseball.* E.H.net, February 1, http://eh.net/encyclopedia/article/haupert.mlb (accessed December 20, 2010).

Hausman, J. A. and Leonard, G. K. 1997. Superstars in the National Basketball Association: Economic value and policy. *Journal of Labor Economics*, 15 (4) 586–624.

Hendricks, W., DeBrock, L., and Koenker, R. 2003. Uncertainty, hiring, and subsequent performance: The NFL draft. *Journal of Labor Economics*, 21 (4) 857–886.

Hitchcock, M. Undated. Welcome to PETCO Park: Home of your Enron-by-the-sea Padres. Berkeley Law: University of California Boalt Hall, http://www.law.berkeley.edu/sugarman/PETCO_Park_and_the_Padres_____Mark_Hitchcock.pdf (accessed December 18, 2010).

Hochberg, P. R. 1973. Second and goal to go: The legislative attack in the 92nd Congress on sports broadcasting practices. *New York Law Forum*, (18) 841–896.

Hyland, T. 2009. The big ten network: It's here to stay. About.com Guide to College Football, March 12, online edition, http://collegefootball.about.com/b/2009/03/12/the-bigten-network-its-here-to-stay.htm (accessed September 23, 2009).

Judd, D. R. and Fainstein, S. S. 1999, eds. *The tourist city.* New Haven, CT: Yale University Press.

Kaempfer, W. and Pacey, P. 1986. Televising college football: the complementarity of attendance and viewing. *Social Science Quarterly*, 67 (1) 176–185.

Kahane, L. and Shmanske, S. 1997. Team roster turnover and attendance in Major League Baseball. *Applied Economics*, (29) 425–431.

Kahn, L. M. and Sherer, P. 1988. Racial differences in professional basketball players' compensation. *Journal of Labor Economics*, 6 (1) 40–61.

Kanazawa, M. T. and Funk, J. P. 2001. Racial discrimination in professional basketball: Evidence from Nielsen ratings. *Economic Inquiry*, 39 (4) 599–608.

Knight, F. H. 1921. *Risk, uncertainty, and profit.* Boston, MA: Hart, Schaffner & Marx; Houghton Mifflin Co.

Krautmann, A. and Berri, D. 1997. Can we find it at the concessions? Understanding price elasticity in professional sports. *Journal of Sports Economics,* 8 (2) 183–191.

Lazear, E. P. 1998. Hiring risky workers. In *Internal Labour Market, Incentives, and Employment,* eds. I. Ohashi and T. Tachibanaki. New York: St. Martin's.

Leadley, J. C. and Zygmont, Z. X. 2005. When is the honeymoon over? National Basketball Association attendance 1971–2000. *Journal of Sports Economics,* 6 (2) 203–221.

Leadley, J. C. and Zygmont, Z. X. 2006. When is the honeymoon over? National Hockey League attendance 1970–2003. *Canadian Public Policy/Analyse de Politiques,* 32 (2) 213–232.

Lee, Y. H. and Smith, T. 2008. Why are Americans addicted to baseball? An empirical analysis of fandom in Korea and the U.S. *Contemporary Economic Policy,* 26 (1) 32–48.

Leeds, M. A. and von Allmen, P. 2008. *The economics of sports,* 3rd ed. Boston: Pearson Publishing.

Levine, M. V. 2000. A third world city in the first world: Social exclusion, racial inequality, and sustainable development in Baltimore, Maryland. In *The social sustainability of cities: Diversity and the management of change,* eds. M. Polese and R. Stren, 123–156. Toronto: University of Toronto Press.

Levitt, Jr., A. 2004. Independent review of the combined financial results of the National Hockey League 2002–2003 season, February 5, http://www.nhl.com/nhlhq/cba/archive/levitt/levittreport.pdf (accessed April 10, 2011).

Lewis, M. 2003. *Moneyball: The art of winning an unfair game.* New York, NY: W. W. Norton.

Long, J.G. 2002. Full count: The real cost of pubic funding for major league sports facilities and why some cities pay more to play. Ph.D. dissertation, Harvard University.

Longley, N. 1995. Salary discrimination in the National Hockey League: the effects of team location. *Canadian Public Policy,* 21 (4) 413–422.

Longley, N. 2006. Racial discrimination. In *Handbook on the economics of sport,* Ed. W. Andreff and S. Szymanski, 757–765. Northampton, MA.

Mandelbaum, M. 2004. *The meaning of sports: Why Americans watch baseball, football, and basketball and what they see when they do.* Cambridge, MA: Perseus Books Group Public Affairs.

Mason, D. and Rosentraub, M. S. 2010. Financing a new arena in downtown Edmonton. Unpublished report, City of Edmonton: University of Alberta, Department of Physical Education and Recreation.

Matheson, V. A. 2006. The effects of labour strikes on consumer demand in professional sports: revisited. *Applied Economics,* 38 (10) 1173–1179.

McIntosh, M. 1971. Changes in the organization of thieving. In *Images of deviance,* ed. S. Cohen. Harmondsworth, UK: Penguin.

Mikesell, J. 2009. *Fiscal administration: Analysis and applications for the public sector,* Boston: Wadsworth Publishing.

Miller, J. E. 1990. *The baseball business: Pursuing pennants and profits in Baltimore.* Chapel Hill: North Carolina University Press, 1990.

Miller, P. 2007. Private financing and sports franchise values: The case of major league baseball. *Journal of Sports Economics,* (8) 449–467.

Miller, P. 2008. Major league duopolists: When baseball clubs play in two-team cities, (working paper). Retrieved from Minnesota State University, Mankato website: http://krypton.mnsu.edu/~millep1/papers/Major%20League%20Duopolists%20-%20May%202006.pdf (accessed December 30, 2010).

Miller, P. 2010. Big ten network: Big man on campus. *Minneapolis Star Tribune*, May 5, online edition, http://www.startribune.com/sports/gophers/92558764.html (accessed January 18, 2011).

Mills, E. S. and Hamilton, B. W. (1997). *Urban economics*, 5th ed. Addison Wesley.

Modigliani, F. and Miller, M. H. 1958. The cost of capital, corporation finance, and the theory of investment. *American Economic Review*, 68 (3) 261–297.

Morse, A. L., Shapiro, S. L., McEvoy, C. D., and Rascher, D. A. 2008. The effects of roster turnover on demand in the National Basketball Association. *International Journal of Sport Finance*, (3) 8–18.

Munson, L. 2010. NFL's lockout-likelihood plot thickens. *Courtside Seat*, http://sports.espn.go.com/espn/commentary/news/story?page=munson/100617 (accessed January 17, 2011).

NCAA 2011–2014 Championship Host City Bid Specifications. 2010. Retrieved from http://www.ncaa.org/wps/portal/ncaahome?WCM_GLOBAL_CONTEXT=/ncaa/ncaa/sports+and+championship/general+information/championships+administration/general+bid+template+(oct+2010) (accessed January 18, 2011).

Newman, M. 2006. The neighborhood that the ballpark built. *The New York Times*, April 26, online edition, http://www.nytimes.com/2006/04/26/business/26ballpark.html (accessed December 18, 2010).

Ostfield, A. 1995. Seat license revenue in the National Football League: Shareable or not? *Seton Hall Journal of Sport Law*, (5) 599–610.

Pine, B. J. and Gilmore, J. H. 1999. *The experience economy: Work is theater & every business a stage*. Harvard Business School Press.

Putnam, R. D. 2000. *Bowling alone: The collapse and revival of American community*. New York, NY: Simon & Schuster.

Putsis, W. and Subrata, S. 2000. Should NFL blackouts be banned?. *Applied Economics*, 32 (12) 1495–1507.

Quirk, J. P., and Fort, R. D. 1992. *Pay dirt: The business of professional team sports*. Princeton, NJ: Princeton University Press.

Riess, S. A. 1980. Sport and the American dream: A review essay. *Journal of Social History*, 14, 295–303.

Riess, S. A. 1999. *Touching base: Professional baseball and American culture in the progressive era*. Chicago: University of Illinois Press.

Rosentraub, M. S. 1999. *Major league losers: the real cost of sports and who's paying for it*. New York: Basic Books.

Rosentraub, M. S. 2010. *Major league winners: Using sports and cultural centers as tools for economic development*. Boca Raton, FL: CRC Press/Taylor and Francis.

Rosentraub, M. S. and Joo, M. 2009. Tourism and economic development: Which investments produce gains for regions? *Tourism Management*, 30 (5) 759–770.

Rosentraub, M. S. and Swindell, D. 2009. Doing better: Sports, economic impact analysis, and schools of public policy and administration. *Journal of Public Affairs Education*,15 (2) 219–242.

Rosentraub, M. S., Swindell, D., and Tsvetkova, S. 2009. Justifying public investments in sports: Measuring the intangibles. *Journal of Tourism*, 9 (2) 133–159.

Rovell, D. 2010. The Seattle "Freehawks" show teams future of sports marketing. CNBC, September 28, online edition, http://www.cnbc.com/id/39398351/The_Seattle_Freehawks_Show_Teams_Future_Of_Sports_Marketing (accessed April 10, 2011).

Salaga, S. and Winfree, J. 2010. Secondary market demand for National Football League personal seat licenses and season ticket rights (working paper). University of Michigan.

Sandomir, R. 2007. Yankees' YES network stake not for sale. *The New York Times*, August 3, online edition, http://www.nytimes.com/2007/08/03/sports/baseball/03yes.html?_r=2 (accessed April 7, 2011).

Sandomir, R. 2011. University of Texas will create its own sports network with ESPN. *The New York Times College Sports Blog*, January 19, ttp://thequad.blogs.nytimes.com/2011/01/19/university-of-texas-will-create-its-own-sports-network-with-espn/?ref=sports (accessed January 20, 2011).

Schmidt, M. B. and Berri, D. J. 2002. The impact of the 1981 and 1994–1995 strikes on Major League Baseball attendance: A time-series analysis. *Applied Economics*, 34 (4) 471–478.

Schmidt, M. B. and Berri, D. J. 2004. The impact of labor strikes on consumer demand: An application to professional sports. *American Economic Review*, 94 (1) 344–357.

Scully, G. W. 1974a. Discrimination: The case of baseball. In *Government and the Sports Business*, Ed. R. Noll, 221–273. Washington D.C.: The Brookings Institution.

Scully, G. W. 1974b. Pay and performance in Major League Baseball. *American Economic Review*, 64 (6) 915–930.

Scully, G. 1995. *The Market Structure of Sports*. Chicago: University of Chicago Press.

Shaikin, B. 2011. Fox advances Frank McCourt money to help cover Dodgers' operating expenses. *Los Angeles Times*, January 15, online edition, http://www.latimes.com/sports/la-sp-0115-mccourt-dodgers-20110115,0,7861995.story (accessed January 17, 2011).

Shelley, B. 2006. No more Vero Dodgers? Not entirely! Message posted November 4 to http://dodgers.scout.com/2/586774.html (accessed May 10, 2011).

Shiller, R. 2005. *Irrational exuberance*. New York: Random House.

Siegfried, J. and Hinshaw, C. E. 1979. The effect of lifting television blackouts on professional football no-shows. *Journal of Economics and Business*, (32) 1–13.

Sloane, P. J. 1976. Restrictions on competition in professional team sports. *Bulletin of Economic Research*, 28 (1) 3–22.

Smith, C. 2001. *Storied stadiums: Baseball's history through its ballparks*. New York: Carroll and Graf.

Smith, E. 2011a. Texas, ESPN reach $300 million deal to air longhorn network," *USA Today*, January 19, On-line edition, http://content.usatoday.com/communities/campusrivalry/post/2011/01/texas-espn-agreement-longhorn-network/1 (accessed January 19, 2011).

Smith, E. 2011b. Report: ESPN will pay Texas $12 million per year to distribute the longhorn network. *USA Today.Com*, January 19, On-line edition, http://content.usatoday.com/communities/campusrivalry/post/2010/11/report-espn-will-pay-texas-12-million-peryear-to-distribute-the-longhorn-network/1 (accessed January 19, 2011).

Souhan, J. 2010. Earl Santee: He built it. *Minneapolis Star Tribune*, December 26, online edition, http://www.startribune.com/sports/twins/112415774.html (accessed December 29, 2010).

Swindell, D. and Rosentraub, M. S. 2009. Doing better: Sports economic impact analysis, and schools of public policy and administration, *Journal of Public Administration Education*, 15 (2) 219–242.

Szymanski, S. 2003. The economic design of sporting contests. *Journal of Economic Literature*, 41 (4) 1137–1187.

Tainsky, S. Undated. Derived demand in the National Football League, *Journal of Sports Economics* (forthcoming).

Tainsky, S. and Winfree, J. 2010. Discrimination and demand: The effect of international players on attendance in Major League Baseball. *Social Science Quarterly*, 91 (1) 117–128.

Talalay, S. 2010. Florida Panthers: Name your own price for tickets. Retrieved from http://blogs.trb.com/sports/custom/business/blog/2010/08/florida_panthers_name_your_own.html (accessed January 18, 2011).

Thompson, E. P. 1981. *Protest and survive*. London: Monthly Review Press.

Usain Bolt snubs London meeting over tax laws. 2010. BBC, July 12, online edition, http://news.bbc.co.uk/sport2/hi/athletics/8812123.htm (accessed April 10, 2011).

U.S. Bureau of the Census estimates for 2009, http://www.census.gov/popest/metro/CBSAest2009-annual.html (accessed January 27, 2011).

Vernellis, B. 2010. Michigan athletic department projects revenues to top $100 million in 2010–11. *Ann Arbor.Com*, June 17, http://www.annarbor.com/sports/athletic-department-projects-revenues-to-top-100-million-in-2010-11/ (accessed January 19, 2011).

Vincent, F. 2010. Albert Pujols's capital opportunity. *Wall Street Journal*, November 29, online edition, http://online.wsj.com/article/SB10001424052748704462704575590600879687646.html (accessed May 14, 2011).

Walker, D. 2009. The big ten network is alive and well. *Milwaukee Journal Sentinel*, September 23, online edition, http://www.jsonline.com/blogs/sports/40560627.html (accessed September 23, 2009).

Walter, T. 2010. Green Bay Packers have big plans for real estate surrounding Lambeau Field. *Green Bay Press Gazette*, July 25, online edition, http://www.greenbaypressgazette.com/article/20100725/GPG0101/100722122/Green-Bay-Packers-have-big-plans-for-realestate-surrounding-Lambeau-Field (accessed January 23, 2011).

Windhorst, B. 2010. LeGone: LeBron James announces he's leaving Cleveland Cavaliers for Miami Heat. *The Plain Dealer*, July 8, online edition, http://www.cleveland.com/cavs/index.ssf/2010/07/legone_lebron_james_confirms_h.html (accessed April 10, 2011).

Winfree, J. and Fort, R. 2008. Fan substitution and the 2004–05 NHL lock out. *Journal of Sports Economics*, 9 (4) 425–434.

Winfree, J., McCluskey, J., Mittelhammer, R., and Fort, R. 2004. Location and attendance in Major League Baseball, *Applied Economics*, (36) 2117–2124.

Yankees only team hit with luxury tax, must pay $25.7 million. 2009. CBSSports, December 21, online edition, http://www.cbssports.com/mlb/story/12691992/yankees-onlyteam-hit-with-luxury-tax-must-pay-257-million (accessed April 10, 2011).

Zimbalist, A. 1992. *Baseball and billions: A probing look inside the big business of our national pastime*. New York, NY: Basic Books.

Zimbalist, A. and Long, J. G. 2006. Facility finance: Measurement, trends and analysis. *International Journal of Sport Finance*, (4) 201–211.

Zuber, R. and Gandar, J. 1988. Lifting the TV blackout on no-shows at football games. *Atlantic Economic Journal*, 16 (2) 63–73.

Index